Travels
In
Scotland
(1842)

By
J. G. Kohl

Translated with Introduction and Notes
by
Ursula Cairns Smith and J.M.Y. Simpson

Part One (Chapters I – XII)

The Thames flows proudly to the sea,
Where royal cities stately stand;
But sweeter flows the Forth to me,
Where Bruce once had high command.

Part Two (Chapters XIII – XXIV)

Farewell to the mountains high cover'd with snow,
Farewell to the straths and green valleys below;
Farewell to the forests and wild hanging woods,
Farewell to the torrents and loudpouring floods!

Dresden und Leipzig

Arnoldische Buchhandlung

1844

TRAVELS IN SCOTLAND (1842) BY J.G. KOHL
Published 2012 by J.M.Y. Simpson at www.lulu.com

ISBN 978-1-4716-4858-8

The quatrain on the title-page appended to Part I is based on the opening of Burns's poem 'The Banks of Nith'. However, the third and fourth lines of this are *But sweeter flows the Nith to me, / Where Cummins ance had high command*, 'Cummins' being the immensely powerful Comyn family. The quatrain appended to Part II is the second stanza of Burns's 'My Heart's in the Highlands'.

The cover image is *On the Road to Loch Turret* by Sidney Percy (1868).

Johann Georg Kohl

Acknowledgements

It is impossible to exaggerate the extent to which we are indebted to many kind friends for elucidating references in the text. Such help ranged from the explanation of a technical term to time spent in researching in libraries or archives. All were essential to casting light on J.G. Kohl's text, and to every one of the following the translators express their profound gratitude: Alan Alexander, Ronnie Black, Alison Bowers, Philip Bowers, Peter Broadhurst, John Burnett, Michel Byrne, Fiorna Cairns Smith, John Lawrence Cairns-Smith-Barth, Sondra Miley Cooney, George Davidson, Sandy Fenton, Con Gillen, Gregor Hutcheson, John Laver, Caroline Macafee, Claire MacGregor, Duncan Macmillan, Murdo MacDonald, Tom McCallum, Jane Mallinson, Rob Maxtone-Graham, John Sawyer, Farquhar Macintosh, Catherine Schwarz, Peter Schwarz, Maurice Shepherd, Bill Slee, Simon Taylor, Wamberto Vasconcelos, and Gerald Warner. The staffs of the National Library of Scotland, Edinburgh City Library, Perth City Library, Innerpeffrey Library, the Mitchell Library, Glasgow, and the Centre for Research Collections of Edinburgh University Library, were outstandingly efficient, friendly, and helpful. However, especial thanks are due above all to Catherine McFarlane: her untiring and enthusiastic researches in various places along J.G. Kohl's route have enriched the present translation and notes far above our initial expectations. Caroline Macafee, Catherine McFarlane, and Wamberto Vasconcelos also provided invaluable assistance in the process of publication.

Ursula Cairns Smith
J.M.Y. Simpson

Publications Consulted

Banfield, Edwin 1991 *Barometer Makers and Retailers 1660 – 1900* Baros Books, Trowbridge

Banfield, Edwin 1993 *The Italian Influence on English Barometers* Baros Books, Trowbridge

Cameron, Ronald, Henderson, Christine, and Robertson Charles 1997 *Changing Life in Scotland and Britain 1830 – 1930* Pulse Publications, Fenwick, Ayrshire.

Chalmers, John 2003 *Audubon in Edinburgh* National Museums of Scotland Publishing, Edinburgh.

Clabburn, Pamela (ed.) 1976 *The Needlework Dictionary* Macmillan, London

Coutts, James 1909 *A History of the University of Glasgow from its Foundation in 1451 to 1909* James Maclehose, Glasgow

Cowan, Edward J. and Finlay, Richard 2000 *Scotland since 1688: Struggle for a Nation* Cima Books, London

Courier and Advertiser (Dundee), 16 August 1991, p. 9, article on the Empress of Morocco

Cunliffe, Barry et al. (eds) 2001 *The Penguin Atlas of British and Irish History* Penguin Books, London

Daiches, David 1969, revised 1976 *Scotch Whisky: its Past and Present* Fontana/Collins

Davies, Norman 1999 *The Isles: a History* Macmillan, London

Devine, T.M. 1999 *The Scottish Nation 1700-2000* Allen Lane The Penguin Press, London

Fenton, Alexander 1993 'The Highland Lowland Boundary in Scotland' in Cox, H.L. (ed.) *Kulturgrenzen und Nationale Identität* Ferd. Dümmlers Verlag, Bonn

Fenton, Alexander 1999 'The Nineteenth Century Scottish Landscape through the eyes of a German Traveller' in Grieshofer, Franz and Schindler, Margot (eds) *Netzwerk Volkskunde: Ideen und Wege* Verein für Volkskunde, Vienna

Ferguson, William 1968 *Scotland: 1689 to the Present* (The Edinburgh History of Scotland Volume 4) Mercat Press, Edinburgh

Fothergill, Rhoda (undated) *The Inches of Perth: a Short Account* Munro and Scott Ltd., Perth

Henderson, Jan-Andrew 2000 *The Emperor's New Kilt: the Two Secret Histories of Scotland* Mainstream Publishing, Edinburgh and London

Acknowledgements

Herman, Arthur 2001 *The Scottish Enlightenment: The Scots' Invention of the Modern World* Fourth Estate, London

Houston, R.A. and Knox, W.W.J. (eds) 2001 *The New Penguin History of Scotland: from the Earliest Times to the Present Day* The Penguin Press in Association with the National Museums of Scotland, London

Hunter, Thos. 1883 *Woods, Forests and Estates of Perthshire* Henderson, Robertson and Hunter, Perth

Keay, John and Keay, Julia (eds) 1994 *Collins Encyclopaedia of Scotland* HarperCollins, London

Killeen, Richard 2001 *A Short History of Scotland* Gill and Macmillan, Dublin

Lauder, Thomas Dick 1843 *Memorial of the Royal Progress in Scotland* Adam and Charles Black, Booksellers to the Queen

Lawson, Peter and Son 1836 *The Agriculturalist's Manual: Being a Familiar Description of the Agricultural Plants Cultivated in Europe: Including Practical Observations Respecting those Suited to the Climate of Great Britain and Forming a Report of Lawson's Agricultural Museum in Edinburgh* Blackwood, Edinburgh

Lynch, Michael 1991, rev. edn 1992 *Scotland: a New History* Pimlico, London

Lynch, Michael 2001 *The Oxford Companion to Scottish History* Oxford University Press, Oxford

McGovern, Una (ed.) 2002 *Chambers Biographical Dictionary* 7th edn, Chambers Harrap, Edinburgh

McKerrachar, Archie 1988 *Perthshire in History and Legend* John Donald, Edinburgh

Mackie, J.D. 1964 *A History of Scotland* Penguin Books, Harmondsworth

Magnusson, Magnus (ed.) 1990 *Chambers Biographical Dictionary* 5th edn, Chambers, Edinburgh

Maxtone Graham, E. 1935 *The Maxtones of Cultoquhey* Moray Press

National Record of the Visit of Queen Victoria to Scotland in 1842 1843, The Perth Printing Co.

O'Brien, Patrick K. et al. (eds) 2000 *Philip's World History Encyclopedia* George Philip Ltd, London

Parissien, Steven 2001 *George IV: The Grand Entertainment* John Murray, London

Perth Museum and Art Gallery 2001 *Perth Silver: a Guide to Perth Silver and Silversmiths*

Plumb, J.H. 1956 *The First Four Georges* Batsford, repr. 1966 Fontana

Prebble, John 1963 *The Highland Clearances*, Penguin Books, London

Raftery, Barry (ed.) 2001 *Philip's Atlas of the Celts* George Philip Ltd, London

Richards, Eric 2002 *The Highland Clearances* Birlinn, Edinburgh

Ross, David 1998, updated edn 2002 *Scotland: History of a Nation* Lomond Books, New Lanark

Scott, Hew 1923 *Fasti Ecclesiae Scoticanae: Succession of Ministers in the Church of Scotland from the Reformation* Oliver and Boyd, Edinburgh

Scrope, William 1839 *The Art of Deer-Stalking; Illustrated by a Narrative of a Few Days' Sport in the Forest of Atholl, and with some Account of the Nature and Habits of Red Deer, and a Short Description of the Scotch Forests* John Murray, London

Shearer, John Jnr. 1883 *Antiquities of Strathearn* D. Philips, Strathearn Herald Office

Statistical Account of Perthshire by the Ministers of the Respective Parishes 1844 Blackwood, Edinburgh

Steel, Tom 1984 *Scotland's Story* HarperCollins, London

Stewart, George 1881 *Curiosities of Glasgow Citizenship: As Exhibited Chiefly in the Business Career of its Old Commercial Aristocracy* James Maclehose, Glasgow

Swift, Gay (ed.) 1984 *Batsford Encyclopaedia of Embroidery Techniques* Batsford, London

Thomson, Derick S. (ed.) 1983, 1994 *The Companion to Gaelic Scotland* Gairm, Glasgow

Tytler, Patrick Fraser 1842 *History of Scotland* William Tait, Edinburgh

Whitfield, Clovis and Martineau, Jane (eds) 1982 *Painting in Naples 1606 – 1702: from Caravaggio to Giordano* Royal Academy of Arts and Weidenfeld and Nicolson, London

Zaczek, Iain and Phillips, Charles 2004 *The Complete Book of Tartan* Hermes House, London

* * * * *

Contents

J.G. Kohl's List of Contents

Part One

Contents

doctor – Medicines for particular **'diseases'** -- A **'box-bed'** – Village libraries – **Doune-Castle –
Doune-Lodge – Black cattle** – **'Lady Victoria'** – Triumphal arch in Bridge of Allan – The busy bee of
Bridge of Allan

* * * * * * *

A Note on the Translation

The original German text frequently contains names, words or phrases in occasionally idiosyncratic English or other languages, printed in a distinctive roman type-face that stands out against the usual 'black letter' of the bulk of the text, including the detailed list of contents. Presumably the author wishes to add local colour to the account of his journey. In our translation we reproduce these unchanged **in this type-face**. Usually these are enclosed in quotation marks, but sometimes not; this varying usage is retained as is the author's (or printer's) apparently haphazard use of capital letters, hyphens, italics and word-separation. Any accompanying translation into German by the author is omitted here if it is simply a repetition.

Names of persons or places mentioned in the rest of the text are given in their modern spelling in this translation. Where the original German text uses a different spelling, this is reproduced in *an italicised foot-note* without comment. The translators felt that to retain in the text the author's unusual, and on occasion baffling, spellings would be too distracting, but at the same time they did not want to deprive the interested reader of the opportunity of seeing the author's versions: some of these were current in 1842, others are clearly mistakes.

Foot-notes inserted by the translators are enclosed in [square brackets]. All other foot-notes are those of the original text and, to make this absolutely clear, are here marked by the author's initials *JGK*.

The author very often writes *England* or *English* when referring to the United Kingdom of Great Britain and Ireland (as it was then) or even to Scotland, and *British* where only *English* would be accurate; this random usage has been retained everywhere without comment.

In all cases where the reader might question the accuracy of reproduction or translation, we append [sic].

The author's original text is sometimes flowery and characterised by long intricate sentences, as was typical of German of that period; occasionally, however, it is stylistically undistinguished, even clumsy. In the main, the translation reflects such variation, though the more indigestible sentences have been divided and the more inelegant repetitions varied or eliminated. Lengthy paragraphs have been split. Certain features of the author's style, such as the frequent omission of the word *and* before the last item in a list, are retained, as are occasional non-sentences and at least one startlingly mixed metaphor.

* * * * * * *

Translators' Introduction: J.G. Kohl and Scotland in 1842

The Author

Johann Georg Kohl was born in Bremen on 28 April 1808. From 1828 onwards he studied at the Universities of Göttingen, Heidelberg and Munich, attending lectures on law, ethnography, 'technology', and mathematics. On the death of his father he abandoned his studies, going in 1830 as tutor to aristocratic families in Courland (a duchy in the west of Latvia, at that time ruled by Russia) and six years later to a similar position in St Petersburg. During this period he travelled extensively in the Baltic regions and in Russia.

In 1838 he returned to Germany, to Dresden, working as a journalist but also publishing accounts of his travels, notably *Die deutsch-russischen Ostseeprovinzen* [*The German-Russian Baltic Provinces*], published in 1841 in two volumes, and *Reisen im Inneren von Rußland und Polen* [*Travels in the Interior of Russia and Poland*], published in the same year in three volumes. These were so successful that for the next twelve years Kohl journeyed throughout Europe, assiduously publishing successive accounts, sometimes in as many as three volumes, of his travels in Austria, Hungary, Ireland, Scotland, England, Wales, France, Denmark, Schleswig, Holstein, the Alps, the Low Countries, Istria, Dalmatia, Montenegro, and the lands bordering the Rhine and the Danube. Numerous as they are, these early books illustrate only one area of his wide interests.

In December 1853, encouraged by the great explorer and naturalist Alexander von Humboldt, Kohl began a series of visits to libraries in Berlin, Paris, Oxford and London to study and to copy historical maps that documented the discovery and exploration of the Americas, and in October 1854 he took the collection of the resulting facsimiles, his so-called *Codex Americanus Geographicus*, to the United States. These drawings were the most comprehensive collection of cartographic reproductions in America at that time and in 1856 Congress commissioned Kohl to duplicate them for a proposed catalogue of early maps of America. They now form part of the Johann Georg Kohl Collection in the Geography and Map Division of the Library of Congress (*see* http://www.loc.gov/spcoll/136.html).

This Kohl Collection also includes his massive twenty-nine-part manuscript study of the early history and exploration of the west, south and east coastlines of the United States, commissioned by the U.S. Coast Survey and undertaken between 1855 and 1857. Describing, among other things, the geography of the West Coast, the hydrography of the Gulf of Mexico, the harbours of the Atlantic Coast, and the Gulf Stream, it consists of written and hydrographic descriptions, route charts, narrative accounts of expeditions, catalogues of maps, bibliographies of historical source material, facsimiles of maps, and relevant manuscripts. (In Chapter XXIII of the present work Kohl outlines an utterly impractical proposal for vast national historical and cultural collections. Perhaps in assembling this American collection he was to some extent trying to realise such a scheme.)

These American projects were the material for a new series of books by Kohl, published then and later, on the history of the discovery of the New World and the growth in knowledge of its geography, such as *Geschichte des Golfstroms* [*History of the Gulf Stream*] (1868) and (in English) *History of the Discovery of the East Coast of North America, particularly the Coast of Maine* (1869). His interest in Native American culture is reflected in *Kitschi-Gami* (1859), translated into English in 1860 and published as *Kitchi Gami: Life among the Lake Superior Ojibway* – a collection of essays about the Ojibwa Indians of Lake Superior in which incidentally he adumbrates ideas that later found fuller expression in Franz Boas's Introduction to the *Handbook of American Indian Languages* (1911) – and in his popular *Geschichte der Entdeckung Amerika's* [*History of the*

Discovery of America] (1861). Perhaps unexpectedly, given its period of composition, but not unexpectedly in view of its author, this latter is neither romanticised nor Europe-centred and it points out the negative impact on Native Americans of the coming of Europeans.

What was perhaps the last of his accounts of his own travelling was his *Reisen in Canada und durch die Staaten von New-York und Pennsylvanien* [*Travels in Canada and through the States of New York and Pennsylvania*] (1856) which is still relevant for the study of the history of Pennsylvania Dutch (a North American dialect of German, in spite of its name). During his time in the United States, Kohl became friendly with several American scholars and men of letters, including Longfellow, Washington Irving and Emerson.

In 1858 Kohl returned to his birthplace, Bremen, where he finally settled after an absence of thirty years, and in October 1863 was appointed Director of the City Library. This was the stimulus for yet more books, this time cultural-historical studies of Bremen, for example *Denkmale der Geschichte und Kunst der Stadt Bremen* [*Monuments of the History and Art of the City of Bremen*] (1863) and *Der Bremer Rathskeller* [*The Bremen City Hall Beer Cellar*] (1866). He also contributed prolifically to the foremost German newspapers and periodicals of the time.

One final major area of Kohl's output must be mentioned, his pioneering contribution to theoretical geography, in particular the study of human contact, migration and settlement. Such geographical studies include his early *Der Verkehr und die Ansiedelung der Menschen in ihrer Abhängigkeit von der Gestalt der Erdoberfläche* [*Human Movement, the Establishing of Settlements, and their Dependence on the Shape of the Earth's Surface*] (1841, 2nd ed. 1850) and his late *Die geographische Lage der Hauptstädte Europas* [*The Geographical Location of the Capital Cities of Europe*] (1874). In these seminal works he stressed the constraints imposed by natural surroundings on human settlements and networks of travel, produced a mathematically formulated theory of the spherical development of cities, and forecast the appearance of high-rise buildings and underground shopping malls. (His observation on p. 19 of the present work on the upward growth of the Old Town of Edinburgh is relevant to this theory.)

Kohl was Honorary Member or Corresponding Member of numerous learned societies and in 1869 received two honorary doctorates, from the University of Königsberg in Prussia and from Bowdoin College in Maine, USA. His last major work, published in 1877 long after he had left America, was *Geschichte der Entdeckungsreisen und Schiffahrten zur Magellan's-Straße und zu den ihr benachbarten Ländern und Meeren* [*History of Journeys of Discovery and Voyages to the Strait of Magellan and to the Neighbouring Countries and Seas*]. He died in Bremen on 28 October 1878.

Kohl was no narrow specialist. As he himself wrote: 'My ears had early apprehended the word *polymath* and with delight I heard of men who had tried to acquire for themselves the entire range of human knowledge. Although I soon perceived that in our time this was no longer possible, nevertheless I did not cease to pursue the vision that floated before me. For I have never been able to devote myself to a single Muse so completely that I would have considered anything that did not belong to her domain as merely trivial.'

Such admirably all-encompassing interest is one of the attractions of this extraordinary man's account of his visit to Scotland, for in his *Reisen in Schottland* [*Travels in Scotland*], published in 1844, he presents a series of pictures of a country in the process of undergoing all kinds of changes, some of them common to other countries in and beyond Europe, others peculiar to Scotland itself. Not only does Kohl give a narrative of his route, of the many scenes and incidents that he observes, and of the adventures that befall him, but he also reflects on aspects of urban and rural life, notes advances in industry and agriculture, instructs his readers in details of Scottish history, geography and geology, indulges in philological speculations, describes typical games, comments on political and ecclesiastical life, discusses literature, and gives samples of the Scots and Gaelic tongues – all this informed by warm humanity and a quiet sense of humour.

Europe in 1842

In the autumn of 1842, when Kohl made his journey, Europe and other parts of the world were undergoing momentous transformations in almost every area of life. Kohl was well aware of this and in various places in the present work optimistically describes these changes as 'progress'. For example, in an extravagant reference to Diana of Ephesus he speaks of *our present era – this goddess with a hundred breasts, this nurse with a thousand skills* (p. 86); he observes that *The world is in the grip of such tremendous progress that to observe this progress and describe it becomes almost impossible* (p. 39); and triumphantly, if repetitively, points out that *it is glorious that our tremendous era is truly advancing with tremendous steps to such a tremendous fulfilment* (p. 161). What were these changes and why was Kohl so optimistic? Several overlapping and intertwining contributory factors can be discerned, and each, as we shall see, was relevant to Scotland.

In the first place, the so-called Age of Enlightenment (see p. 70) of the eighteenth century had had an irreversible and continuing effect. This philosophical movement, embodied in the work of French writers such as Voltaire and Montesquieu, had spread to other countries in Europe and America, one of its underlying principles being a belief in the power of human reason and in human progress. Inevitably, this resulted in a constant questioning of authority and of traditional beliefs; 'authority' included ecclesiastical and political structures while the beliefs included those of political systems, social hierarchies, science, and established religion. The importance of rational human behaviour came to underpin the work of eighteenth and early nineteenth century economists, philosophers and political thinkers, such as Benjamin Franklin, David Hume, Adam Smith, Immanuel Kant, Thomas Paine, Thomas Jefferson and Jeremy Bentham.

This intellectual development was mirrored by events in politics in the late eighteenth and early nineteenth centuries. New systems of government had come into being, and new countries. At the time of Kohl's travels in Scotland the independence of the United States of America lay only sixty-six years in the past, the French Revolution fifty-three, and the creation of Belgium only twelve. The end of the Napoleonic Wars, which had irrevocably changed the political face of Europe, had taken place within the lifespan of anyone over the age of twenty-seven. Other political changes were still in the making. For example, the 'Germany' to which Kohl frequently alludes was not a political entity but still only a linguistic concept covering the mosaic of innumerable kingdoms, principalities, archduchies, electorates and other territories in which German was the official language; it would be another thirty years before the creation of Bismarck's German Empire. The Kingdom of Great Britain (created in 1707) had become the United Kingdom of Great Britain and Ireland as recently as 1801 and in it the lengthy progress towards universal suffrage had begun only in 1832: the Great Reform Act that Kohl mentions (p. 10) gave the vote to middle-class male property owners and created parliamentary seats for previously unrepresented large industrial cities. And in 1842 the United States of America totalled only twenty-six, of which the youngest, Michigan, had been admitted to the Union six years previously.

At the same time, vast technological changes were taking place, summed up in the words *Industrial Revolution*. The phrase had already appeared in French in 1837 in Adolphe Blanqui's *Histoire de l'économie politique en Europe depuis les anciens jusqu'à nos jours* and the intended comparison with the French Revolution is evidence of an awareness that the metamorphosis taking place was enormous. It was the transformation of an ancient economy largely based on agriculture to one dominated by manufacturing industry and the key to it was the application of power-driven machinery to such manufacture. This revolution began in Britain about 1760, though its roots go back to the seventeenth and even the sixteenth centuries, and by the end of the eighteenth century it was spreading to the United States and to the rest of Europe.

New, more powerful, machines for the production of textiles had been invented and this had led to the construction of buildings to house them; people thus gradually ceased to spin thread and weave cloth in their homes (so-called 'cottage industry') but instead worked in factories. At first these factories were powered mainly by water-wheels. However, a steam engine had been invented by Thomas Newcomen in 1705 and James Watt's improvement of it in 1769 (see p. 12) came to replace water-wheels as the main source of power for driving machines in the factories and mills of the emerging Industrial Revolution. As a result, factories no longer had to be built near rivers; towns now rapidly grew up near coalfields instead. Increasing numbers of country-dwellers moved into these towns in search of employment and in the course of the nineteenth century the proportion of populations living in the towns and cities of industrial nations rose sharply. Factories came to produce not only textiles but an enormous variety of other artefacts including pottery, cast iron, components of warships, guns, bricks, chemicals, agricultural implements, and heavy machinery. This mass production of goods required an expanding network of transport, at first roads and canals, then, after about 1830, railways. These last, relying on steam-power, truly revolutionised travel in making it possible for individuals to move over longer distances and in a far shorter space of time than had ever been imagined.

Accompanying this burgeoning industrialisation, partly responding to its needs, partly stimulating it to yet further development, were massive increases in scientific discoveries and inventions. Like the political changes and the Industrial Revolution itself, these had their beginnings in the eighteenth century or even earlier, but the speed of innovations was now accelerating at a dizzying pace in such diverse fields as chemistry, geology, ballooning, submarine navigation, steam-powered traction, electricity, the physics of light, mathematics, astronomy, photography and medicine. In the ten years preceding 1842 the numerous latest practical advances had included the use of ether as an anaesthetic, the vulcanisation of rubber, the invention of the electric telegraph, the crossing of the Atlantic Ocean by steamship, the first electric generator, and the first German railway. *Progress* and *science* had become the catchwords of the period.

Moreover, practical innovations were not confined to industrialisation and factories. Contemporary with the first part of the Industrial Revolution in Great Britain, from roughly 1760 to 1830, a series of changes in farming practice had taken place, later to be termed the *Agricultural* or *Agrarian Revolution*. The changes were of diverse types. Common land was fenced in to form compact private farms and enclosed fields. New schemes of cultivation were introduced: potatoes, turnips, and clover came to be planted regularly, and the alternate planting of cereal and nitrogen-fixing crops ('the rotation of crops') did away with the necessity of leaving land fallow. New agricultural implements and machinery were invented and introduced, for example threshing machines, horse-drawn reapers, and devices for planting seed beneath the surface of the soil so that it was not at the mercy of birds or wind. Animals were now systematically bred for the quality of their meat as well as for their strength or the quality of their wool. Arable land was reclaimed from moors and marshland. In short, agriculture, too, became scientific and the result was a dramatic increase in the production of food.

And there was yet another strand, this time an aesthetic or cultural movement, namely Romanticism. This was a complex mixture of different ideas and attitudes that arose at the end of the eighteenth and the beginning of the nineteenth centuries and swept across Western Europe and Russia. It concerned the arts in general and literature in particular. From a growing interest in folklore in Germany the belief had arisen that products of the uncultivated popular imagination, 'spontaneous' outpourings of the unlettered common people, could equal or even surpass those of educated poets and writers; as a result, ballads and folk-tales became immensely popular. Romantic writers, musicians and painters came to value individual human experience, feeling and imagination rather than the concrete orderly world of Classical artists and so they sought to embody individual ideals and passions in their work. Their creations were an expression of their inner feelings and imagination as much as of their technique, the emphasis being on creativity, spontaneity, and sentiment. In keeping with the popularity of folk-culture, Romantic artists were disposed towards a tradition of 'romance', of myth, and of the mediaeval. Further elements in the Romantic movement were a love of the exotic and a love of nature: the 'exotic' meant anything pertaining to a country other than that in which the artist resided, provided that it was picturesque, while 'nature' was the great outdoors, now seen as something to be enjoyed and marvelled at, not as something to be feared or avoided as being 'uncivilised' (see for example Coleridge's poem *Frost at Midnight*, William Turner's landscape paintings, or Beethoven's 6th Symphony, the 'Pastoral'). Furthermore, the natural consequence of dwelling on creative folk genius was an outpouring of nationalistic expression, whether that of a free nation, as in the patriotic paintings of the Frenchman Delacroix, or that of a subjugated one, as in the music of the Pole Chopin. Thus Romantic artists tended to be champions of liberal and progressive causes, so for example Wordsworth applauded the French Revolution, Beethoven inveighed against tyranny in his opera *Fidelio*, and Byron fought heroically for Greek independence. In consequence, artistic life, too, was imbued with the idea of change or even revolution.

Scotland shared in those European movements[1], sometimes in a distinctively Scottish way, and in Kohl's observations of Scottish life we see all aspects of this participation.

Scotland and Early Nineteenth Century European Developments

The eighteenth and early nineteenth centuries were a period of quite astonishing achievement in intellectual and artistic circles in Scotland, formidable advances being made in a wide variety of areas. As well as the towering figures of the philosopher David Hume (1711 – 76) and the philosopher and economist Adam Smith (1723 – 90), the country had in the same period nurtured such great scholars as the moral philosopher Francis Hutcheson (1694 – 1746) (Adam Smith's teacher), the mathematician Robert Simson (1687 - 1768), the chemists William Cullen (1710 – 90) and Joseph Black (1728 – 99), the physiologist Robert Whytt (1714 – 66), the 'father of geology' James Hutton (1726 – 97), the 'father of sociology' Adam Ferguson (1723 – 1816), and a host of other outstanding pioneers. No doubt it is to such men that Kohl alludes in his Foreword when he speaks of the 'lucid thinkers' of Scotland. This period, when Scotland became one of the most important centres of intellectual culture in the western world, is often referred to as the 'Scottish Enlightenment' and, as the term suggests, it was by no means solely an importation from the Enlightenment of the European mainland but had its own characteristics and its own roots in Scottish history.

Associated with the Scottish Enlightenment was Edinburgh's extraordinary literary eminence in the eighteenth and nineteenth centuries. Kohl encountered evidence of this in his visits to the Advocates' Library and to the publishing house of William and Robert Chambers. Although the inauguration of the library of the Faculty of Advocates took place just slightly earlier than the period conventionally assigned to the Enlightenment, the library played a full part in that intellectual phenomenon, especially in the latter part of the eighteenth century, and David Hume himself was at one time Librarian. In the eighteenth century, too, Edinburgh developed as a centre

---

[1] [See, for example, what the author has to say about progress in Scotland on p. 90.]

for intellectual publishing, the three-volume first edition of the *Encyclopaedia Britannica* appearing between 1768 and 1771 (and indeed the next eight editions were produced there). The work of the brothers Chambers and other publishers added in full measure to such distinguished endeavour.

For Kohl, the most striking visible evidence of the Scottish Enlightenment was its architectural result, namely the magnificent New Town of Edinburgh, conceived in 1752 'to enlarge and beautify the town' and laid out from the middle of the eighteenth century onwards; it is the largest Georgian city development in the world and has been well described as a 'symphony in stone'. The New Town that Kohl saw and admired was of almost the same extent as that which still exists in the twenty-first century, apart from a portion at the West End which was not finally completed until 1860. Princes Street Gardens, another object of his admiration, had been laid out between 1816 and 1830 for the owners of properties in Princes Street and were somewhat more extensive than at the present day since they included an eastern portion, soon, however, to be given over to the new Joint Station of the expanding railway system. The construction of the New Town had been undertaken in order to allow the prosperous citizens of Edinburgh to escape the horrors of the Old Town that lay to the east of the Castle. Kohl not only gives us (p. 22) a graphic account of the unbelievable squalor that existed in the Old Town in 1842 but also (p. 23) castigates the inhabitants of the New Town for neglecting to attempt to improve the lot of the unfortunates who lived in the Old. Since in general Kohl allows his emotions to show only when they are favourable to what he describes, his anger on this occasion is all the more telling.

In contrast to the elegance of Edinburgh's Enlightenment New Town, Kohl's first glimpse of a Scottish city had been a quite different witness to the times in which he lived. As his ship approached Glasgow, the sun had become a mere sombre red patch in a black polluted sky, evidence of that city's position as a principal centre of the Industrial Revolution in Scotland. Later he explored one of the sources of this pollution, Tennant's chemical works at St Rollox, and marvelled at the height of its smoke-stack (although, given the blackness of the sky, he seems to have overestimated its efficacy in recommending it as an ideal installation that entire cities ought to copy). Nevertheless, the human consequences of the Industrial Revolution were not lost on Kohl. On the one hand, he paints a poignant picture of the unemployed in Glasgow, thronging the streets near Glasgow Cross on a Saturday night: he had in fact – in the very first paragraph of the book as he recounts his sea passage to Scotland – already drawn attention to the influx of the Irish destitute in search of work. On the other hand, he documents the obverse of this coin, namely the growing affluence of the well-to-do in Glasgow, in his account of the handsome new buildings in course of construction in the city, and he points a striking contrast between rich and poor in his description of the difference between the streets on a Saturday night and on a Sunday morning.

Indeed before reaching Glasgow, Kohl had already encountered another aspect of the Industrial Revolution in the form of improved transport facilities. He notes the number of lighthouses round the Scottish coasts, the numerous steamships on the Clyde, and the dredging of that river so that ships could sail into Glasgow. In later chapters he gives an account of the Caledonian Canal, the network of steamer connections between Scottish ports and the islands, and the triple link of road, canal and railway across the central belt of the country. He himself travelled from Glasgow to Edinburgh on the Edinburgh and Glasgow Railway, opened earlier in that same year, and must have alighted at Haymarket since the Joint Station (later renamed Waverley) was built only some three years later. In view of the strict Sabbatarian principles fashionable at the time (and alluded to elsewhere by Kohl, for example on p. 123 and p. 131), it is perhaps unexpected that he was able to travel on a Sunday as he did. Railway construction, the first phase of 'railway mania', was about to begin on a large scale in Scotland, but by 1842 only a few lines were in existence. Consequently he had to travel to Stirling by boat up the River Forth and from there continued his journey by public transport in stagecoaches, by privately hired gig, or on foot.

What excited Kohl's particular admiration in Scotland, however, was not so much the effects of the Industrial Revolution as Scottish contributions to the Agricultural Revolution. He devotes sizeable portions of his text to laudatory descriptions of such things as drainage and to detailed reports of the inventions and implements on show at agricultural museums and exhibitions in Stirling and Edinburgh. From being one of the most backward systems of farming in Europe, Scotland had, as Kohl points out, become a leader. He remarks that the German-speaking lands could benefit from the advances being made in Scotland. Among the subjects that attract his attention are the various types of fences available (see p. 161) and the reclamation of fertile land by clearing it of peat, one of the methods used for disposing of this being to float it into rivers (see p. 165). (That in fact was the reason for the disappearance of the great oyster beds of the Forth mentioned on p. 36, since the peat muddied the water: oysters require clear water for their growth.) The progress being made in dairy-farming and horticulture was evident from his visits to the dairy at Taymouth Castle and the garden at Drummond Castle. Indeed horticulture had had a long tradition in Scotland and it was advances in the management of Scottish gardens that had stimulated the extraordinary improvements in Scottish farming.

As for the Romantic movement, Scotland had had a close connection with it since its very beginning; indeed it can be suggested that Scotland was the Romantic country *par excellence*. This connection is the theme of the fourth paragraph of Kohl's Foreword where, among other things, he mentions 'Ossianic heroes'. This is a reference to James Macpherson's *The Poems of Ossian*, first published in 1762 and then again 'greatly improved' in 1773, a collection of alleged translations from the Gaelic of the poet Ossian (Oisin) relating the exploits of his father, Fingal (Fionn mac Cumhaill), and of other heroic warriors of the third century. It would appear that Macpherson (1736 – 96) did use some authentic material, generously adapting and expanding it. The result was apparently quintessential ancient folk-poetry and so, whether authentic or not, the poems enjoyed an astounding success, becoming a literary sensation in Great Britain and on the European mainland. They were immediately translated into at least seven other European languages, and later into some twenty more, and proved to be one of the original stimuli for the entire Romantic movement. (It is striking that although Fingal had lived in Ireland (if he existed), ballads recounting his exploits had been brought to Scotland by the Gaelic-speaking Scots and so – many centuries later – he was still a familiar figure to at least one of Kohl's Highland guides, see p. 128.)

In the present work Kohl quotes approvingly several times from two great Scottish writers, Robert Burns (1759 – 96) and Walter Scott (1771 – 1832), both outstanding and innovative figures in European literature, vividly exhibiting the characteristic traits of Romanticism mentioned above. As is evident from Kohl's quotations, they wrote verse celebrating the countryside of their native land. In addition, both drew on ancient oral traditions, Scott publishing old ballads and Burns reworking folk-songs. Furthermore, Scott, drawing on Scotland's past, virtually invented the historical novel, while Burns, in addition to much of remarkable lyrical beauty, wrote verse, in the spirit of the French revolution, extolling the brotherhood of man,.

However, it is not only in his quotations from Burns and Scott that Kohl demonstrates the link between Scotland and Romanticism and his own enthusiasm for both. His visits to Edinburgh Castle, Holyrood Palace, Stirling Castle and Rob Roy's grave, his allusions to Mary, Queen of Scots, and to Bruce, reveal a fascination with the Romantic past, while his contemplation of an intriguing waterfall or his admiration of the beauty of Eskdale as he leaves Scotland reflect the Romantic attraction to Nature. From the point of view of a traveller from mainland Europe, such phenomena as Highland dress, snuff mulls, golf and curling, which Kohl investigates with fascination, must have appeared romantically exotic. Indeed he devotes an entire chapter to a detailed description of a painting by an eminent English Romantic painter, Edwin Landseer (1802 – 73). Landseer had first visited Scotland at the age of twenty-one and subsequently (though he was also an English court painter) produced scenes of the Scottish Highlands that are a kind of pictorial equivalent of Walter Scott's writings; reproductions of them became remarkably popular and promulgated a Romantic interpretation of the country that is consistent with that to be discussed below.

Developments Peculiar to Scotland

Not only did Scotland share in such transformations taking place in Europe and elsewhere, the country showed developments of its own, in its political, cultural, and religious life. Three of these are noteworthy in connection with Kohl's account of his travels: they are concerned firstly with reactions to the Union with England; secondly with Jacobitism, the Highlands, and a related new visualisation of Scotland; and thirdly with the impending 'Disruption'.

In the first place, less than one hundred and forty years had passed since the Union of the Parliaments of Scotland and England and the formation of the Kingdom of Great Britain in 1707. It is interesting that Kohl feels it necessary to mention this Union several times and on p. 163 he emphasises the fact that it was not an incorporating union (that is, one in which one country would become part of the other), adding perceptively that in spite of that Scotland had had to make certain concessions as the years passed. When the Union took place it had not been generally welcomed in Scotland: on the contrary, violent rioting against it had occurred; it appears to be a fact that the Act of Union was passed (in 1706) by the Parliament of Scotland only because sufficient noblemen had been bribed by England to vote for it (see the poem by Burns quoted on p. 78). Nevertheless, in the succeeding years, Scots had had to come to terms with their lack of political independence and this they did in various ways, whether consciously or not.

One way was to assert an intellectual independence, as witness the Scottish Enlightenment mentioned above. It would make no sense to claim that this flowering was a conscious reaction to the Union and in any case the seeds had been sown before 1707. But Scotland, and Edinburgh in particular, gained a renown throughout Europe, as indicated by Kohl in his Foreword, that was independent of the recently established Kingdom of Great Britain.

Another way was to participate energetically in the rapidly expanding British Empire, as it came to be called, and to owe allegiance to that rather than to the Kingdom of Great Britain. In the course of the late eighteenth century and in the nineteenth, Scottish soldiers, engineers, teachers, administrators and missionaries were to play a prominent part in the conquest, government and day-to-day running of overseas territories. *Her influence in the English* [sic] *colonies is great*, as Kohl writes in his Foreword, and in the course of his journey through Scotland he finds evidence of this connection. He mentions (p. 68) Sir David Baird, the general who had commanded the final assault on Srirangapatnam in the Fourth Mysore War and was celebrated as the leader of 'the heroes of "Seringapatnam" [sic]'. Bob, his Black guide in Perth, 'the poor dusky Red Indians' and 'the black children from the Sahara Desert' that he saw in the streets, may well have found their way to Scotland as a result of some association with this Empire. In fact, the connection can be traced beneath the surface of the text, as it were, whether or not Kohl realised the fact. In the Foreword he mentions 'Ossianic heroes' and on p. 117 he tells us that the island of Ulva is inhabited only by people with the surname Macquarry. The associations with the British Empire of these two passing references are as follows: firstly, a first cousin of the above-mentioned James 'Ossian' Macpherson was Sir John Macpherson (1745 – 1821), Governor-General of India, and secondly, Lachlan Macquarie (1762 – 1824), who served as a soldier in many parts of the Empire and became the enlightened Governor of New South Wales (later described as 'the father of Australia'), had been born in Ulva. Furthermore, though Kohl does not seem to have known, the 'General Malcolm' in whose honour the obelisk had been erected that he saw outside Langholm (p. 185) was Sir John Malcolm (1769 – 1833) who had been Governor of Bombay and one of the founders of the British Raj.

In the second place, a novel and romantically distorted perception of Scotland and of its history, particularly as regards the Highlands, had recently been created. To understand this change, it is helpful to recall the geological division of the country from south-west to north-east indicated by Kohl in his first chapter. This natural division, into Highlands and Lowlands, had been accompanied for centuries by a linguistic and cultural distinction. The Highlanders were speakers of Scottish Gaelic (a later form of the Old Irish tongue first brought by invaders from Ireland in the 4th century, though it had then spread far beyond the Highlands) while the Lowlanders were speakers of Scots (a later form of the Anglian tongue brought in the 7th century by invaders from England, though it had come originally from mainland Europe). This linguistic difference was accompanied by major differences in customs, dress and social organisation, due in part to later Norman influence in the Lowlands. Such differences inevitably resulted in intense mutual suspicion, if not downright hostility. The eighteenth century introduced a catalyst into this situation in the form of the Jacobite uprisings against the government, in London, of the Kingdom of Great Britain.

These Jacobite uprisings of 1715 and 1745 had been primarily dynastic affairs, the quarrel being between supporters of the Hanoverian royal line (imported to the Kingdom of Great Britain in the person of George I, the Elector of Hanover) and supporters of the previous Stewart (or 'Stuart' in the later French-style spelling) dynasty, the last monarch of whom had been Queen Anne. She had died in 1714 without leaving an immediate heir. Her most obvious Stewart successor was James Edward, who (in his absence) was proclaimed King James VIII at Aberdeen in the uprising of 1715, the Latin form of his name, Jacobus, accounting for the designation of his supporters. But James Edward Stuart was a Catholic and an unspecified Protestant descendant of the Electress Sophia of Hanover had already been chosen as Queen Anne's heir by the English Parliament in 1701 (long before her death and without reference to the Scottish Parliament); in fact fifty-seven candidates with a greater claim to the English and Scottish thrones were passed over because they were Catholics. As a result, the Elector of Hanover had duly become King George I in 1714. There was thus a strong religious dimension to the Jacobite uprisings. Nevertheless, they cannot be regarded as a struggle between Catholics and Protestants, since some Protestants, especially Episcopalians in the north-east of Scotland, supported the Stuart cause.

Both uprisings had started in the Highlands of Scotland, but they cannot be seen as an exclusively Highland movement either: for example, the most powerful Hanoverian supporter in Scotland was the Duke of Argyll, a Highlander whose clansmen fought on the side of the victorious government forces at the final battle of Culloden in 1746. It is equally wrong to see the uprisings as a confrontation between Scotland and England: Glasgow and the western Lowlands were violently hostile to the Stuart cause while in England there was a certain measure of support for the Jacobites, particularly in the uprising of 1715.

Nevertheless, following the total defeat of the Jacobites at Culloden in 1746, it was the Highlands that suffered catastrophically and irrevocably. A barbaric punishment was inflicted, a revenge that has justly been described as 'ethnic cleansing': known Jacobite individuals were sought out and given no quarter, Jacobite districts were harried and villages bombarded from the sea, cattle and crops were destroyed, government military bases were established, estates were forfeited and heritable jurisdictions[2] were abolished. These atrocities were carried out on the orders of William Augustus (1721 – 65), Duke of Cumberland and son of George II, who had commanded the

---

[2] [See p. 117.]

Travels in Scotland (1840) by J.G. Kohl

government troops at Culloden; his brutality attracted to himself the nickname 'Butcher'. The terrible consequence was that the traditional cultural fabric of the Highlands was destroyed forever.

Famously, but much less importantly, the wearing of Highland dress (alluded to by Kohl on p. 95), the carrying of arms, and the playing of bagpipes were forbidden by the Act of Proscription of 1747. However, Scotland had had a long history as a soldiering nation in the sense that it sent mercenaries abroad to fight on behalf of foreign powers; overwhelmingly, this was due to poverty at home. After Culloden, the government of Great Britain, in spite of its persecution of Jacobites, continued this tradition by raising Highland regiments to fight abroad, but this time for Great Britain. These soldiers not only bore arms but, perhaps surprisingly, were permitted to play bagpipes and wear distinctive kilted uniforms. By the time of Kohl's visit to Scotland, these soldiers, some of whom he encountered in Stirling (p. 49) had seen service in the Seven Years War (1756 – 63), the American Revolution (1776 – 83), and the Napoleonic Wars (1800 – 1815), to say nothing of their role in providing fighting forces and garrisons in the expanding British Empire. Eventually, in 1782, the wearing of Highland dress in Scotland was permitted again and in 1820 the Celtic Society of Edinburgh was founded under the chairmanship of Walter Scott: its primary aim was to encourage the wearing of Highland dress. Since Highland dress had not been worn by Lowlanders, this was a new development and a step in the direction of a novel view of Scotland and its history – the incorporation of Highland customs and history into a Romantic view of Scotland as a whole.

In 1806 the immediate male Stuart line died out and so the threat posed to the Hanoverian dynasty vanished. Stuarts could never again be monarchs of Great Britain. However, somewhat earlier, anachronistic Jacobite songs – written by, among others, Robert Burns and Carolina, Lady Nairne (1766 – 1845) – had begun to appear, expressions of longing for what might have been. Thus the Jacobite uprisings were fast becoming a distorted memory and Prince Charles Edward Stuart, son of James Edward, began to be regarded as an archetypal Romantic hero under the name 'Bonnie Prince Charlie' (as mentioned by Kohl on p. 69). He had commanded the 1745 uprising and after the massacre at Culloden in April 1746 lived as a fugitive in the Highlands until in September he escaped to the Continent. In spite of appalling sufferings on his behalf, he was not betrayed by the Highlanders, whether out of loyalty to him or because of their hatred of the government troops or both. The Highlanders' loyalty was not reciprocated by the Prince, yet spurious legends of his feelings of attachment to them began to proliferate in the nineteenth century. The dynastic and religious dimensions of the uprisings were forgotten and finally they came to be regarded, quite wrongly, as struggles for Scottish independence, as is seen, for example, in what Kohl has to say on p. 77 about Prince Charles Edward. However, it was the *British* throne that was at stake, not a Scottish one.

In 1820 George IV became king. Oddly for a Hanoverian, he had for long had a fascination with the Jacobites and now saw himself as the heir to both the Jacobite and Hanoverian dynasties. In 1822 he visited Scotland, the first monarch of the Kingdom of Great Britain to do so. The occasion was stage-managed by Walter Scott and he took the opportunity to publicise the growing Romantic view of Scotland and its history. The Regalia of Scotland (see p. 24) were transferred for the occasion to the Palace of Holyroodhouse; Scott wrote (anonymously) a pamphlet advising people how to behave and dress during the Royal visit; and a Grand Ball was organised in which the corpulent king appeared wearing flesh-coloured tights and a kilt. Since Highland dress was *de rigueur* for the Ball, weaving firms that already supplied tartan for the army were called upon to mass-produce appropriate cloth and in one week, it is said, three hundred unemployed tailors were pressed into service to make up the required garments. The visit was (in hindsight) richly comic but it was a triumph for the new vision of Scotland. Scott's Celtic Society was overwhelmed by enquiries about the niceties of Highland dress while the business of weaving tartan increased dramatically in the succeeding years. The king himself appears to be wearing a kilt in the statue of him that Kohl (p. 19) saw in George Street (though the street itself was named after George III).

One result of this new Lowland visualisation of Scottish history, which had now absorbed Ossian, Robert Bruce, Rob Roy, Mary Queen of Scots, Bonnie Prince Charlie, bagpipes, tartan and the kilt into one undifferentiated mix, was that the emblems (bagpipes, tartan, and kilt) of a defeated Highland people were taken over by their erstwhile opponents, surely the best way of neutralising the power of inconvenient symbols. Scotland now appeared to be a 'nation of Highlanders', as a critic complained. Kohl shared in this view of Scottish history, as is obvious from many places in his text, and it is consistent with this that he chose a stanza of the poem 'My Heart's in the Highlands', by Robert Burns, a Lowlander, as the motto for the second part of his account, which includes his own departure from Scotland.

But, as it happened, two of those symbols of the Highlands were somewhat spurious, for both the kilt and clan tartans were comparatively recent inventions. From the end of the sixteenth century, the usual Highland dress seems to have been the big plaid or *féileadh mòr*, a version of which is described by Kohl on p. 64 as being worn in conjunction with 'French clothing'. At the beginning of the eighteenth century, an English iron-works manager at Lochaber, Thomas Rawlinson, devised a much more suitable garment for his workers, a small plaid or *féileadh beag*; it was really just the bottom part of the big plaid. Pre-pleated, this was what became known as the 'kilt'. It was so convenient that it was adopted by the Highland regiments; it quickly became regarded as 'traditional Highland dress' and was accepted as such after the lifting of the Act of Proscription in 1782. The provenance of tartans is disputed, but it seems that the idea of using tartans as a means of identification is due to the army's use of regimental tartans and only in the first decades of the nineteenth century did the notion of clan tartans gain popularity. Thereafter the invention of tartans proliferated, tartans being designed and supplied to all who wanted them, and lists of tartans were drawn up by self-appointed bodies or individuals. One such list was encountered by Kohl (p. 102), the work of the 'Sobieski Stewart' brothers. These two, allegedly 'John Sobieski Stolberg Stuart' and 'Charles Edward Stuart' who claimed to be grandsons of Prince Charles Edward, were in fact John and Charles Allan, sons of an English naval officer; their *Vestiarium Scoticum* (which is presumably what Kohl saw) was presented as a collection of ancient tartans but it is completely imaginary. Nevertheless, tartan now became regarded as native to Scotland as a whole, rather than to the Highlands alone, and countless patterns were enthusiastically invented, named and classified, as Kohl himself tells us on p. 7. Indeed Queen Victoria and Prince Albert are said to have designed tartans ('Stewart Victoria' and 'Balmoral' respectively, see Chapter III, fn. xii) and the furnishings of Balmoral Castle became ornately decorated with tartan.

Though to some extent a Romantic fiction, this view of Scotland provided, for both Highlanders and Lowlanders, a convenient (and on appropriate occasions, visible) expression of their shared difference from England within the United Kingdom of Great Britain and Ireland.

Unfortunately, however, the sombre reality behind the symbols of the Highlands could not be romanticised and neutralised in the same way. One aspect of this reality was the dreadful suffering of the people themselves, another was their language, Scottish Gaelic. Both of these are mentioned by Kohl.

Before Culloden, land had been regarded in the Highlands as a communal resource held in trust by the chief for his people. Such a system was recognised neither in the Lowlands nor in England. After Culloden and the consequent destruction of the Highland social pattern, the chiefs came to be regarded as landowners in their own right, by the law and by themselves. The Agricultural Revolution put emphasis on the efficient use of land and in this view land was certainly not regarded as a communal inheritance but, on the contrary, as something to be exploited for gain. The most profitable use of Highland land was now held to be sheep farming and this required the displacement of the human population by those who now legally owned the land. Between 1785 and the end of the nineteenth century tens of thousands of Highlanders were forcibly driven from their homes to make way for sheep – to marginal land on the Highland coastline, or to the Lowlands, or to overseas colonies of the growing British Empire. Such evictions were known as the Clearances, carried out in some cases with extreme brutality and consequent unbelievably appalling misery. Kohl alludes to these on p. 55, using the English word *cleared*. While he concedes that this took place 'often with force', he appears to regard the introduction of sheep-farming as an unalloyed sign of progress: he may not have known the degree of suffering involved. But the situation was complex and indeed these evictions could be seen simply as a solution to the problem of maintaining a population on infertile land, on occasion carried out with the best of intentions. Nevertheless, the memory of the Clearances remains bitter, even in the twenty-first century.

As has been mentioned, Scottish Gaelic had been the language of the Highlands. Indeed it had been the language of large tracts of Scotland far beyond the Highlands until the introduction and spread of Anglian. It was not, however, the language of the Scottish Parliament and in 1616 the Privy Council passed an act designed to establish a school in every parish. One aim was to implant *the vulgar Inglishe toung* (i.e. Scots[3]) as the vernacular, so that *the Irische language* (i.e. Scottish Gaelic), which was described as a 'cause of barbarity' might be extirpated (*abolishit and removeit* in the words of the act). Nevertheless, Gaelic held its ground within the Highlands, though gradually dying out elsewhere, and in 1769 there were around 300,000 speakers of the language, almost a quarter of the population of Scotland. Attempts to eradicate the language continued, however, and their success can be seen in Kohl's descriptions of its decline, as he learned of it *in situ*, on p. 55 and p. 97. In spite of his awareness of progress in Gaelic lexicography and the writing of grammars (p. 98) and his own enterprise in eliciting Gaelic words from his guides (see for example p. 89-90), his attitude to the language is contained in the extraordinary pronouncement that good education can progress only through the medium of English, 'the Norman-Saxon tongue' (p. 54). In expressing this, he was only repeating a belief commonly, though not universally, held in the Lowlands.

The third distinctively Scottish development, involving the Church of Scotland and its pending Disruption, is well documented by Kohl (though he was distinctly unimpressed by what he witnessed by way of Scottish religious practice, see p. 11, p. 23, p. 41, p. 44, and pp. 79 – 80). The Reformed tradition in Scotland had been characterised throughout its history by a pronounced tendency to fissiparity, visible from the beginning in the formation of Episcopal versus Presbyterian factions. (It should incidentally be noted that though it became conveniently fashionable for the Presbyterians to call the Episcopal tradition 'the English church' – something which Kohl seems to have believed (see p. 9) – the Episcopal tradition was thoroughly Scottish, though admittedly Charles I later muddied the waters with the attempted wholesale imposition of bishops and an English prayer-book.) Most of the many splits within the various Presbyterian traditions were due to points of disagreement that now seem arcane and of minimal importance. However, the particular dispute that Kohl describes still appears, more than a century and a half later, to embody a

---

[3] [The Anglian language, as it had developed in Scotland, was first known as *Inglis* ('English'), the word still used in the document quoted above. But by the early 16th century the name *Scottis* had come into use instead, to distinguish it from the separate development of Anglo-Saxon in England; its modern form, *Scots*, is still employed with this meaning. Unfortunately, *Scottis* had originally been used to denote the Celtic language introduced from Ireland by the Scots, but this was replaced by *Erse* or *Irisch* when *Scottis* was given its modern meaning; *Erse* subsequently came to be regarded as pejorative or ambiguous, as possibly referring to the Gaelic of Ireland, and the word was replaced by the term *Scottish Gaelic*. The King James Bible of 1611 made the development of Anglo-Saxon, i.e. the English – as the word is understood nowadays – language, in its written form widely familiar in Scotland and after the Union in 1707 it displaced Scots in the educational system as the standard written variety, spoken Scots remaining in informal use.]

significant moral principle: it involved the question of patronage, namely whether an individual or body has the right to impose clerics on a congregation irrespective of the wishes of that congregation. (Kohl lays stress on the independence of the Church of Scotland from secular authorities; indeed such a situation, involving an officially established church, was highly unusual, if not unique, in Europe.) Kohl writes about the question of patronage on two occasions (pp. 40-44 and p. 58), taking the trouble to translate lengthy quotations from the Claim of Rights, and his phrase 'the ferment that is seething in the land' illustrates the vehemence of argument that he encountered.

As he mentions in a footnote (p. 40), shortly after his visit the dispute ended dramatically. Over a third of the clergy left the Church of Scotland in 1843 to form the Free Church of Scotland and to uphold the right of congregations to choose their own clergy. That event, the Disruption, was cataclysmic. Almost every parish in Scotland had to establish a duplicate church building where previously one had sufficed, with consequent immense financial burdens, to say nothing of the schisms caused within communities by the splitting of congregations. (Not until 1929 was this breach healed.)

Johann Georg Kohl as a Travel Writer

Kohl was of course not the first distinguished traveller to the Scottish Highlands, nor the first to leave an account of his journey. An early example of the latter is *A Description of the Western Islands of Scotland* by M. [Martin] Martin, Gent. of 1703. Following the publication of *Ossian* in 1762 and the 'discovery' of Fingal's Cave in 1772, there had been an increasing succession of visitors. Famously, in 1773 Samuel Johnson and James Boswell undertook an ambitious journey, much more extensive than that made by Kohl, taking in Edinburgh, Aberdeen, Inverness, Skye, Coll, Mull, and Glasgow, but thus missing Perthshire and the Trossachs, the area of the Highlands visited by Kohl. They published accounts of their travels, Johnson in 1775 in his *A Journey to the Western Islands of Scotland* and Boswell in 1785 in his *The Journal of a Tour to the Hebrides with Samuel Johnson*. Other works followed: Thomas Pennant's *A Tour in Scotland* in 1789 and *A Companion and Useful Guide to the Beauties of Scotland* by Sarah Murray in 1799. A two-volume guide to the Highlands was published in 1792 by William Gilpin, an English clergyman and in 1824 John MacCulloch published *The Highlands and Western Isles of Scotland*, a four-volume guidebook in the form of letters addressed to Walter Scott. Other nineteenth-century visitors included William Turner, Dorothy and William Wordsworth, Samuel Taylor Coleridge, John Keats, Felix Mendelssohn, Frédéric Chopin, and Nathaniel Hawthorne. Scotland was becoming a favourite destination for tourists and accounts of their travels were written by John James Audubon[4], Theodor Fontane, Jules Verne, and Queen Victoria herself, this last being an enthusiastic devotee of the Romantic view of Scotland encouraged by Walter Scott and held by Kohl.

Kohl, however, differed from these other writers in being, at this time of his life, what could only be described as a professional travel writer and his visit to Scotland was but one of many similar journeys he had undertaken previously in other lands. He is writing as a communicator rather than simply as a chronicler and thus always selects those things that will excite the interest of his German readers. It is precisely those things that captivate his non-German readers more than a century and a half later. The variety of facets of Scottish life that he chooses to write about is fascinating, as a glance at his detailed list of contents reveals. The mixture of straightforward facts interspersed with descriptions of places visited, together with anecdotes about the people he meets, is the work of a highly skilled journalist and *raconteur* as well as of a scholar; among many others, his accounts of attempting to play golf in a Perth drawing-room and of the charlatan Dr MacNab's

---

[4] [See Chapter 4, fn. 34. In his *Ornithological Biography* Edinburgh 1831-39, vol. V, pp. xii-xxii.]

lecture in Doune are masterpieces of amused and amusing observation. Kohl is worthy of great admiration for his enterprise throughout his journey. Obviously a man with a good command of English, he plainly was adept at easily making acquaintances and good-naturedly eliciting all kinds of information from them. Moreover he was remarkably daring, if not downright foolhardy, in his travelling alone through treacherous mountainous territory with a guide who turned out to be totally incompetent – his physical stamina on that long and difficult day is astonishing. His enthusiasm for Scotland is patent and heart-warming. An additional charm is imparted by Kohl's occasional phrases in endearingly odd English, by his several rudimentary line drawings, by his inaccurate quotations of poetry (from memory, one assumes – another cause for admiration), by attributions to the wrong authors, and by his (or his printers') failure to read his handwritten notes correctly (which is presumably the reason for such spellings as *Sconehaven*). Not only is the picture he has drawn us of the Scotland of 1842 extremely valuable, it is also highly entertaining.

Addendum -- A Note on Kohl's Samples of English, Scots[5], and Gaelic

Clearly J.G. Kohl must have known English well. He finds his way around Scotland without apparently encountering any difficulties arising from language; he is acquainted with works of English literature in the original, as his quotations show; and his translation into German in Chapter V of the legalistic convolutions of the Claim of Rights indicates a very high degree of competence in complex language.

His samples of the English he heard are fascinating and for the most part, though by no means always, they ring true as far as grammar and idiom are concerned. However, occasionally he seems to be back-translating from notes he made in German and once or twice he misunderstands, as when he translates *dun bull* into German as 'bull from the dunes' or thinks that *standard* as applied to roses means 'principal' rather than referring to the shape of the bushes. It may be that difficulties with pronunciation are responsible for some confusions; he seems to confuse *broth* and *brose* and, apropos curling, *rink* and *ring*. One might suspect that other misapprehensions are due to the English of his Gaelic-speaking guides, for example *mount* for *mound* and perhaps *bottom* for *bosom*.

Kohl makes almost no observations about the pronunciation of English (as distinct from what he says about Scots 'dialect'), though we do learn, on p. 81 and p. 93 that in 1842 Cockneys dropped their aitches and that they pronounced *fellow* like *fellor*, although unfortunately it is not clear what exactly he means by this transcription. His comment on p. 44, concerning a minister, that *fighting* sounds like *fechting* shows that Scots, or a mixture of Scots and English, was in use among some educated people in Scotland at the time. However, it is not clear whether that minister and those who referred to the 'Coogate' (Chapter IV, fn. 30) thought they were speaking Scots or English at those moments or whether in fact they were wont to make such a distinction at all.

His indication of the pronunciation of *whistling* as 'chwistling' is evidence of a pronunciation of <wh> as a sequence of the final sound of *loch* followed by the initial sound of *whales*. (This had been described in the early 17th century by the authority on pronunciation and spelling, Alexander Hume. The earlier Scots spelling as <quh> corresponds to it.) Admittedly this was spoken by a Highlander, but it may be assumed that speakers of Gaelic tried to acquire a Lowland pronunciation when they spoke English and indeed they may well have spoken Scots, though there is no evidence for this in Kohl's narrative.

---

[5] [See p. xxii, fn. 3]

Kohl was acquainted with written forms of Scots, as found in Scott and Burns, decorated with needless apostrophes, as though Scots were an impoverished form of English. He follows this convention in his own transcription of the Scots he heard in Perth and elsewhere. These transcriptions appear to be trustworthy in the main, though there are reservations about one or two items; attention to these is drawn in the translators' footnotes. Some alleged examples of Scots may have been the result of mishearing, for example *kolbes* (was this actually *clubs* or *clubbies*?).

In his analogy of Scots with Austrian and Alemannic forms of German (in Chapter 9), he is obviously viewing Scots as a dialect of English, though elsewhere he does seem to be conscious that Scots was actually a development, separate from English, of the Germanic tongues introduced from the Continent. Though Kohl frequently uses the word *Saxon*, it should be pointed out that while both Saxon and Anglian (specifically the Mercian variety) can be held to be the ancestors of modern English, it was Anglian (specifically the Northumbrian variety), not Saxon, that was the ancestor of Scots, to which additions from Scandinavian, Dutch and French were later made.

Whereas German, English, and Scots are all Germanic tongues and relatively very similar, Scottish Gaelic must have presented great problems for Kohl, for Gaelic, though very distantly related to English, is a Celtic language and as unlike English as are Russian or Greek, indeed more so.

In the first place, the grammar is dissimilar: for example, word-order is very different and the initial sounds of words change according to the type of word that precedes them. Perhaps as a result of this, Kohl gives us no sentences in Gaelic but confines his examples to single words. Needless to say, the vocabulary is quite unlike that of the Germanic languages so that, apart from borrowings from Scots or English, none of the words would have appeared familiar to him.

To complicate matters further, the speech-sounds used in Gaelic are very different from those of English, German or Scots and, at the time Kohl was writing, phonetic theory in Western Europe was in its infancy so that there was no technique available to him to describe accurately what he heard; in consequence, he had to give an inadequate imitated pronunciation in German letters of the alphabet. Moreover, though Gaelic spelling is generally systematic, it operates by transcribing syllables (as does English, for example *hat* versus *hate*) rather than successions of individual sounds (as does German) and the values of the letters of the Gaelic alphabet differ markedly from those of German. Kohl therefore had difficulty in relating the spellings of words in Armstrong's Gaelic dictionary of 1825 to their pronunciations, see p. 90, especially fn. 13. (This was the first dictionary of Gaelic, though word-lists had been published previously, and, as Kohl himself tells us in Chapter XIII, it was the work of Robert, the brother of William Armstrong, the schoolmaster at Kenmore with whom Kohl had spent the evening. Since Kohl gives examples of its spelling in footnotes, he must have had access to it.) Kohl therefore deserves great praise not only for his assiduity in eliciting pronunciations in a language that must have appeared very exotic to him but also for his transcriptions which provide information for us about the pronunciation of Perthshire Gaelic almost two centuries ago. Three examples of these imitated pronunciations will suffice: 'allopa', 'puntaht', and 'suchkars'.

He hears not only that the word spelled *Alba* ('Scotland') is pronounced in three syllables ('allopa'), with a vowel inserted between the sounds represented by the letters <l> and the <b> (this is a systematic feature of Scottish Gaelic pronunciation though not indicated in spelling) but also that the <b> in fact is the spelling for a p-sound.

Elsewhere he notes that what Armstrong spells as *buntat* ('potatoes') is pronounced 'puntaht'. Here again he realises that the initial sound is 'p', even though spelled with <b>, and he hears that there is an h-sound before the 't'. Thus we learn that this latter phenomenon, known as *preaspiration*, was found in the Perthshire Gaelic of the nineteenth century. It is not found in all accents of Gaelic. Indeed Kohl's example of the pronunciation 'suchkars' ('sugar', spelled by Armstrong *sucar*) shows that this preaspiration was stronger before a k-sound than before a t-sound, Kohl's spelling <ch> indicating the final sound of *loch*. Again, the strength of preaspiration in such different phonetic environments varies according to accent area.

His transcription 'suchkars' also shows that the initial sound was the initial sound of the English word *soot*, not of *shoot* as in some other accents of Gaelic (indicated by the modern spelling *siùcar*) and as in modern English. (In both English and Scots of the 18th century, *sugar* was pronounced either with an initial s-sound or with an initial sh-sound.) The final <rs> of 'suchkars' probably indicates that the r-sound was pronounced with the tongue slightly retracted to produce an accompanying slight hiss (in technical terms a sulcalised voiceless postalveolar fricative), a fact of relevance to Gaelic phonology.

Finally, the pronunciation of 'puntaht' in two syllables is itself a characteristic of Perthshire Gaelic, for that accent tended to lose final syllables found in other accents. Thus though Armstrong (himself from Kenmore in Perthshire) used the spelling *buntat*, in the *Argyleshire Pronouncing Gaelic Dictionary* by Niel (sic) M'Alpine of 1832 it is notated as *buntata*, an obvious indication of three syllables in a different accent of Gaelic, and in modern spelling it is written *buntàta*.

* * * * * * *

Foreword

In our European conglomerate of regions and peoples there are several countries and nations which, though small, enjoy distinguished and far-reaching reputations.

Like Switzerland, like Holland, Scotland too belongs to this group of countries. This remarkable little land is scarcely more extensive than a province of Scandinavia or Russia and before the eighteenth century had at no time very many more than a million inhabitants[1]. At every period of history individual cities can be found that contained as many citizens within their walls.

Even now, when our contemporary world teems with people, the total number of the Scottish nation amounts to a not much greater tally than the population of **Grosvernorsquare**, **Fleetstreet**, **Smithfieldmarket** and the other streets and squares of London that one can behold from St Paul's Church in one vista. And this Scottish nation includes the good folk of all the Hebrides and the Orkney Islands, and all Highlanders and Lowlanders who live their lives in the valleys and on the mountains of the Highlands and in the plains and hundred towns of the Lowlands[2].

Nevertheless, how extensive is the fame and influence of this nation! How highly praised are the beauties of this land! How numerous are the great poets, the warriors, the kings, and the statesmen that Scotland has produced, from the times of the Ossianic heroes who set bounds to the Roman Empire to the times of Robert Bruce and to that of the beautiful Scottish queen celebrated by Schiller[3], and indeed right down to our own days!

For in our own days, too, Scotland continues to be worthy of admiration, attracting all eyes to herself. Since the Union with England she has dedicated herself with energy and enthusiasm to the paths of culture and world dominion opened up by that Union; and to her old rivals, with whom she had fought for centuries in bloody wars, she now offers her all in manifold varieties of peaceful enterprise. Her towns vie with the British in trade and industry. Her influence in the English colonies is great. A relatively very large proportion of the lucid thinkers and the literary talents of Great Britain comes from Scotland. Popular education in the country has raised itself to a higher level than in England. In agriculture and horticulture Scottish farmers stand just as much at the forefront as do Scottish schoolteachers. And the landscape of the country itself is daily adorned and embellished by the hands of its inhabitants who plant woods, bring barren stretches of land under cultivation, and fill empty valleys with gardens and grand houses.

A journey through a country so rich both in memories of the past and in evidence of a creative present can afford nothing other than interest replete with variety, even though it be as brief and fleeting a journey as was granted to me in the autumn of 1842. This journey I have attempted to depict for the German reader in the following pages, and herewith venture to present and commend.

Dresden, January 1844.

The Author.

---

[1] In 1707 it had 1,050,000 inhabitants. *JGK*
[2] London has almost 2 million inhabitants and Scotland around 2½ million. *JGK*
[3] [Mary, Queen of Scots, in Schiller's play *Maria Stuart* (1801).]

I
The Clyde

Several Scottish gentlemen from the linen business, several from the silk business, some **'Cottontwiners'**, **'Cottonweavers'** and **'Cottonbleachers'**, and one, who, when I asked him concerning his business, replied **'I am in the woolen** [sic] **line'** – 'I habitually encompass them all under the general name **'Cottonlords''** a priest of the Episcopal Church in Ireland had said to me – these were my companions on the top deck of a steamship being shaken by a violent storm as it crossed from Belfast in Ireland to Glasgow in Scotland towards the end of October[1]. Destitute Irishmen, in rags and enveloped in a bleak cloud of misery, occupied the second deck; they were emigrating to the manufacturing towns of Scotland in order to seek there what they could not find in their own native paradise, namely work and bread[2]. The remaining space on the ship was filled with farm animals dead and alive, with poultry, turkey cocks, chickens, pigs and cattle; we accounted them all fortunate, for they were tormented neither by poverty nor seasickness.

We were heading NNE, for this north-north-easterly or north-easterly direction is that in which, coming from the west, one approaches the entire central part of Scotland, whether one sails up the Firth[3] of Clyde to Greenock or Glasgow, whether up Loch Fyne[4] to Inverary, or up Loch Linnhe[5] to Fort William. The reason is that all these long sea-lochs extend from south-west to north-east while conversely all the inlets on the east coast – the Firth of Forth, the Firth of Tay, the Moray Firth[6] – cut into the land from north-east to north-west[7]. Scotland can be regarded as a landmass multifariously incised and stratified in the direction indicated. Like these sea-arms, so also do its peninsulas and likewise its mountain ranges, its valleys and the majority of its inland lakes, lie in the direction of north-east to south-west. Indeed one even finds, as a geologist investigating the interior structure of its land surface, that all the different deposits of which it is composed lie mainly in that direction – not parallel to the principal length of the country from south-east to north-west, but on the contrary at an angle to it in the aforementioned direction from south-west to north-east. This geological and geographical stratification of the country is clearly accompanied by one that is morally and politically parallel; the political divisions of Scotland, the ethnic groups, the areas of customs and language – all extend in their principal direction from south-west to north-east.

The friendly lighthouses near Copeland Island, on the Maidens Rocks, near Corsewall Point on the coast of Scotland, near the Mull of Kintyre[8], on Pladda Island and on the island of Little Cumbrae[9], which gleamed in the north, south, west and east, prevented us from losing our way. We would fain have beheld at closer hand by daylight that which the Pladda light illuminated, for that light is situated near to the coast of the larger Isle of Arran. This is said to be a veritable jewel, both for the painter and for the geologist since it exhibits the most remarkable and most diverse configurations in the world; it is that piece of Scotland in which can be found everything to interest a geologist, from the old and oldest formations down to the new and newest, side by side as though in a book.

---

[1] [Cotton twiners manufactured cotton thread. For the phrase *cotton lords* see p. 10. The economically important cotton industry in the West of Scotland used unskilled immigrants from, among other places, Ireland.]

[2] [The Irish immigrant workforce of the 1830s and 1840s was employed not only in factories and mines but also, on a temporary basis, in harvesting, though presumably not at the end of October.]

[3] *Frith*

[4] *Fine*

[5] *Linne*

[6] *Murray-Frith*

[7] [Obviously a slip for *south-west*.]

[8] *Cantire*

[9] *Little-Cambray*

Near the light of Pladda Island one reaches the calmer waters of the Firth of Clyde and then near the lighthouse of Cumbrae the inner and narrower part of this arm of the sea, which is also further lit by the lights of Innellan[10] and Greenock. In this one night we saw no fewer than nine lights on our way. It is questionable whether on so short a stretch of sea anywhere can be found a better and more ample system of lights. The whole of Scotland has now twenty-seven lighthouses; all without exception have been constructed since 1810, either, for the greater part, newly built or so rebuilt that their present utility can be dated only from the period following that year. In point of fact, most were constructed only after 1820. One cannot overcome one's surprise at the recentness of this institution on those coasts off which ships have sailed for so long. The most famous and most costly of these lighthouses are on the **Bellrok**[11] [sic] and on the **Isle of May**[12] off the Firth of Forth and the Firth of Tay[13]. The erection of these two exceptional constructions cost almost as much as that of all the others taken together, namely 132,000 pounds sterling, while all the rest together cost 150,000 pounds sterling. Even now the entire annual expenses of all the Scottish lighthouses together amount to under 15,000 pounds sterling. Since the value of the cargo of many seagoing vessels by far exceeds this sum, all those twenty-seven lighthouses need save every year only one or two ships from sinking in order to pay for themselves. It is, however, probable that their beneficent effectiveness is to be reckoned much higher; hence it remains incomprehensible why such well invested capital was not put into lighthouses with greater readiness a long time ago.

The next morning, when there began that splendid illumination of the coastline which all sailors still prefer to the light of every lighthouse (I mean that provided by the sun), we found ourselves right opposite the town of Greenock, and before us to right and left lay open the pages of a new country. Even the first lines which we read therein were wondrously beautiful and we were almost seized by regret that we, studying Ireland for so long, had not come earlier to read them.

To our left gleamed the snow-capped peaks of the Scottish Highlands, one above the other. To the right stretched the unchangingly green plains of that landscape from which when still in his cradle the little Prince of Wales had taken one of his imposing titles, namely the Barony of Renfrew[14]. Behind us against the water appeared islands that we had passed during the tempestuous night and before us, to the north and south-west, the waters separated into several arms, Loch Long, the Gare Loch[15] and the River Clyde. From Greenock onwards the salt water of the sea is left behind and the expanse of water acquires the name of a river instead of that of a firth. To begin with, this river still preserves the dimensions of a bay two to three miles wide but gradually narrows to one mile, then to half a mile, and finally not far from Glasgow becomes as narrow as the Seine in Paris, and even narrower.

The journey on this stretch of the river from Greenock to Glasgow is one of the most beautiful excursions imaginable and there is no doubt that it would be one of the most famous and patronised river trips, did it not lie in Scotland, a country that is so distant from the centre of European societies. It is a great pity that such an attractive country as Scotland was not endowed with a more favourable climate. A land of such a varied and interesting outer aspect, of such an enchanting manner of delimitation from the sea, has no equal on earth; it should have deserved a place on the latitude of the Isles of the Blessed. How gloriously then would have served for cooling and refreshment all those sea inlets that so deeply pierce the land!

---

[10] *Inoland*

[11] [Also in the original translated literally as *Glockenfels*.]

[12] [Also in the original translated literally as *Mai-Insel*.]

[13] [It is the Bell Rock lighthouse (built 1807 – 11) that lies off the Firth of Tay and the Isle of May lighthouse (built 1816) that lies off the Firth of Forth. Both were built by Robert Stevenson (1772 – 1850).]

[14] [Baron Renfrew was one of the titles held by the heir apparent to the throne of Scotland originally, then successively to that of the Kingdom of Great Britain and to that of the United Kingdom of Great Britain and Ireland.]

[15] *Loch Garo*

I. The Clyde

One of the most beautiful spots on the river is Dumbarton and its old castle on a high rock of impressive formation. It guards the egress of the waters of Loch Lomond which here flow into the Clyde. But Dumbarton is not the only old castle ruin the foundations of which are bathed by the waters of the wide river; Newark Castle and Dunglass[16] are likewise interesting. Monuments too can be espied on the rocks on the river bank, for example the extremely striking one to the famous engineer Henry Bell[17]. This Henry Bell was the first to put a steamship on the Clyde and the Clyde was the first river in the entire old hemisphere that carried a steamship. Indeed, as Scottish writers assure us, this river had been used by more than twelve steamships before the fish in the Thames were disturbed in their repose by even a single one. It is said that in 1835 no fewer than sixty-seven steamships had sailed the Clyde.

As has been said, art, nature, antiquity and the present unite here to beautify everything. The old castles lie on the northern Highland bank[18], most towns – Greenock, Port Glasgow, Erskine, Renfrew, Paisley – on the southern Lowland bank.

Truly admirable are the measures that have been taken in modern times to improve navigation on the river. Even twenty-five years ago ships that had a draught of more than four feet could travel upstream only as far as the vicinity of Glasgow at high tide. By means of '**Dredging machines**' (of which six very considerable ones are now active on the river), by means of river rectification, excavations, blasting (two diving-bells, in which work is occasionally carried out under water on the rocks, also belong to the equipment for clearing the river), by the construction of breakwaters and moles, the river has finally been made to allow even big ships with a draught of sixteen to seventeen feet to go upstream right into Glasgow, at least at relatively high water. Only one place was pointed out to me which had been irremediable up to now and where the river at times threw up unmanageable quantities of sand. The captain of our steamship told us that the river could be maintained in its present artificial state only by an annual expenditure of almost fifty thousand pounds sterling. In 1841 the river taxes raised from ships had amounted to forty-six thousand pounds sterling. Probably then this sum also covers the interest on the capital which had to be borrowed in the first place.

The shipping channel in the river is indicated by a line of so-called '**Buoys**'. These buoys in England are usually large hollow iron pyramids which are anchored and float on the water, peering out of the green waves with their red and black painted tips swaying to and fro. Besides these buoys, however, many other devices can be seen on the river: for example, numerous small mileposts erected on sandbanks and rocks to show the distance from Glasgow, just as on a military road, and in addition a succession of small huts, called '**Biggins**'[19], in which lights are lit during the night so that the ships cannot miss the way that is so very distinctly indicated to them. Instead of these impressive aids, '**in the times of old**' they had nothing but so-called '**Parches**'[20]. These were large heaps of stones on top of which had been placed a thick pole with a basket, a barrel or some other marker of that kind. These parches, which have now become unnecessary, can still be seen along the way. And those '**times of old**', as we have said, were scarcely a few decades ago. Since the advances and improvements in the navigability of the inshore waters everywhere here have been so recent and have been effective for only such a short time, we can conclude from this what a future, what progress and further development of travel by ship, still lie ahead of us even here. However, it is observable that one branch of navigation here, as elsewhere too in England, has already passed its

---

[16] *Dun-Glaß*

[17] [Henry Bell (1767 – 1830), a native of Linlithgow, submitted plans to the Admiralty in 1800 for a steam vessel. In 1812 he started operating Europe's first commercial steamboat *Comet* on the Clyde.]

[18] [Newark Castle, mentioned above, lies on the southern bank.]

[19] [A word meaning 'anything built'.]

[20] [Properly *perches* (= 'poles serving as navigation marks).]

zenith, namely that of *river* steamships. It was two or three years ago that the largest number of *river* steamships used the Clyde and this number has since declined somewhat since steam travel on land (namely by railway) has entered in competition and is triumphing. The railways on the banks of rivers everywhere are securing victory for Gaia[21] over the unchanging realm of Neptune.

The further we travelled inland, the foggier became the air and finally, when we reached Glasgow, nothing was left of the sun but a sombre blood-red patch in the sky. Probably there are countries on earth in which the opportunity to see the sun's disc in such a state never arises and for whose inhabitants therefore the spectacle of such a Scottish and northern sun must be a stupendous phenomenon.

The smoke of Glasgow is especially unpleasant and harmful due to the many chemical works. I was told that on its account the botanical garden[22] had had to be moved from the vicinity of the city. The astronomical observatory[23] too had once been transferred because of the smoke.

* * * * * * *

---

[21] [Greek goddess of the earth.]

[22] [Probably referring to the establishment of the Botanic Garden beside the River Kelvin in 1841; before that an earlier Botanic Garden had existed on Sauchiehall Street from 1817 and an even earlier 'Physic Garden' in the Old College from 1705.]

[23] [The Astronomical Observatory had been built in 1760 on College Green but because of the smoky atmosphere was erected in Garnethill in the early 1800s by the Glasgow Society for Promoting Astronomical Science. Funds ran out and it came to an end around 1821. It was rebuilt on Horselet Hill in 1841 and taken over by the University of Glasgow.]

II
Glasgow

The first object in Glasgow that met our eyes was a colossal smoke-stack that towered over the city and its fog, as the Minster towers over Strassburg and St Stephen's Cathedral over Vienna. This stack is said to be the highest in the British Empire and is a veritable masterpiece of its kind. They told me it was four hundred and fifty feet high. Since this seemed incredible to me, and since I wanted to discover more about it there and then, my first expedition in Glasgow was devoted to this **'Tennant's Stalk'**[1], as the populace of Glasgow call the stack. Tennant is the proprietor of one of the biggest chemical works in the city, and indeed in the whole of England. In it sulphuric acid, soda and numerous other products are manufactured. The many noxious fumes that emanate from this factory could not be discharged into the air at a sufficient height, and the proprietor therefore decided, in order to avoid altercations with his neighbours, to erect such a huge construction as has no equal upon earth.

Naturally, the whole of Mr Tennant's chemical establishment occupies quite a significant expanse of ground, and from each furnace in the various departments an underground channel leads to the smoke-stack. These numerous brick-built channels combine underground into fewer but larger ones; these in turn debouch into the stack itself which in this way can draw off the smoke from all the furnaces at once. The workers told me that when they went down into these channels for any repair, if the hatchways were not properly closed, they would encounter such a powerful draught that they would have extreme difficulty in not being swept away with it. They gave me there and then the height of the smoke-stack as four hundred and thirty-five feet. It is built more or less as follows: it is a huge, circular, hollow pillar that narrows towards its apex. At the foot, it is supported on a very broad foundation upon the ground. The walls of the inner cavity or hollow pillar are thick at the bottom and become increasingly thin as they rise; however, they are said to be still sixteen inches thick at the very top. In addition, they are supported at the bottom by a second wall, which surrounds them like a casing, and which, gradually tapering like a cone, tightly enwraps the pillar more or less halfway up its height. Both the casing and the hollow core are connected and supported in the inside by vaults.

No doubt here and there in England some manufacturers have co-operated in the joint building of similar enormous installations for drawing off smoke. How good it would be, if in the future it were possible to expand these installations and extend them to whole towns. The entire smoke of all the houses would then be channelled off through underground ducts from a few giant stacks which could be erected in the vicinity of the town. These vast buildings could easily be transformed into elegant, decorated architectural monuments. The countless disfiguring little chimneys would disappear from the city. Since the whole scheme would be placed under the strict supervision of the authorities, many opportunities for the outbreak of conflagrations would be avoided, as would innumerable incidents of discomfort which the smoke now causes in our towns.

Glasgow stands out from the other industrial towns of Great Britain by the size and number of its chemical works. However, many other manufactured goods are also produced here. In order to have an overall view of them, or at least the greatest part of them, at the selfsame time, I visited the city's

---

[1] [Also in the original translated literally as *Tennant's Stange*. Charles Macintosh (1766 – 1843), who devised the rubber waterproof material that gave his name to a type of raincoat (now written *mackintosh*), also invented a bleaching powder, chloride of lime. Charles Tennant (1768 – 1838) patented this and in 1798 founded the St Rollox Chemical Works, reputedly the largest in the world, to produce it. The chimney, 455 feet high (the author may have misheard the height as 435 feet), was built in 1841 at a cost of £12,000. It was demolished in 1922.]

biggest textile warehouse, that of the brothers Campbell[2], who give employment to no fewer than two hundred 'Clerks' in their firm. Their warehouse and its sales area are one of the most interesting things of this kind that are to be seen. (The largest stores in Paris can boast of only one hundred sales assistants.) No merchandise attracted me more than the Scottish **checked clothes** [sic] which in Scotland are called 'Tartans'.

Of course, everywhere in Germany we are familiar with these Scottish checked garments, the vivid and yet very simple combination of colours of which has, it seems, found extraordinarily widespread approval throughout the whole of Europe. However, at the same time we seldom think what significance these narrow little stripes of colour possessed, and to some extent still possess, for the Scots. It seems that formerly checked materials were common among all peoples of Gallic origin and that the combinations of colour varied according to the difference of tribe. At least there appears a passage in Caesar in which he speaks of a similar practice among the Gallic peoples[3]. Just as in general the entire system of distinction of tribes or clans has survived in Scotland longer than in other Celtic countries, so also have the tribal clothing materials survived. Every clan had, and has, its own tartan[4]; in this usually one or other background colour predominates, shot through with strips of other colours. Both the breadth and the arrangement of the stripes, as well as the depth and shade of their colouring, all unchangeable, date from time immemorial. And that is precisely the interesting thing about this material, that every thread is still placed exactly where it was centuries ago, and that without question the people ascribed a particular meaning to every colour, or at least through custom became so attached to it to the extent that this or that colour combination was interwoven with the whole existence of their clan and their loyalty to it. I have been told of examples of Scots being seized by profound homesickness at the mere sight of the tartan colours of their clan. And into what vision is not Burns transported at the sight of the brightly coloured checked dress of his 'bonie Jean' of whom he sings:

> 'Down flow'd her robe, a tartan sheen [etc]
> Her mantle large, of greenish hue
> My gazing wonder chiefly drew;
> Deep lights and shades, bold mingling, threw
>   A lustre grand:
> And seem'd, to my astonish'd view,
>   A well known land.'[5]

In the bright tartan of his beloved, the poet goes on to imagine a whole map of Scotland with its rivers, woods, valleys, sea-inlets, gardens and fields, and he depicts this image.

Formerly there existed only those tartans which were intended for the clans or tribes and which were worn by no one other than members of the tribe. Now, however, a number of other new **patterns** have been invented and added, and so people talk of 'Clan-Tartans' and 'Fancy-Tartans'. By the former the ancient historical immutable weaves are understood, by the latter are meant the new

---

[2] [The warehouse of 'J. and W. | = John and William| Campbell' was situated first in the Saltmarket and then in Candleriggs.]

[3] It may be noteworthy in this connection that in many valleys of the Tyrol too people still weave checked cloth which is very like the Scottish, although it is not used for garments in the same way. *JGK* [*Gallic* means 'Gaulish', referring to the Celtic people who inhabited what is present-day France. The Tyrol (in present-day Austrian and Italy) is situated in the ancient heartland of the Celts.]

[4] [See, however, Introduction p. xxi.]

[5] [In a footnote the author gives an accurate prose translation of these lines. They are not, however, from Burns's poem 'Bonie Jean', but are the first line of stanza 11 followed by the whole of stanza 12 of his 'The Vision' and they describe the poet's 'native Muse'. The confusion probably arose because, in the omitted lines of stanza 11, Burns compares his Muse's leg to that of his Jean.]

designs, invented by manufacturers and usually dedicated to some eminent person in whose honour they are named.

Some clan tartans are very simple, for example, that of Rob Roy[6], the clan made so famous by Walter Scott. This consists simply of the crossing of two equally broad stripes of colour (a black and a red) which regularly alternate with one another. Others are very complicated, for example that of the Clan Royal Stewart[7] in which, although crimson stripes predominate, nevertheless yellow, black, blue, white, green ones also criss-cross each other in a colourfully complex way, which is not so easy to describe. It is striking that the colour red appears in almost every tartan. Of those that were shown to me, only the tribe of the M'Neils [sic] had no trace of red. After red, green appeared to be the most frequent colour, and there are tartans that seem almost completely green, for example that of the Clan Argyle[8]. It is told of that Duke of Argyle who appears in Walter Scott's Edinburgh dungeon[9] that he once gazed on the green colour of his clan's tartan in London with especial love and longing for his native land. Many tartans are also almost completely white, for example that of the Clan Clunie M'Pherson [sic][10]. It is remarkable, however, that not one single tartan is ugly and that in every case it is easily comprehensible how the children of a clan could develop a deep affection for their particular combination of colours. Now of course these historical colour patterns no longer possess their full significance of yore.

Since there are no longer any actual clans, no clan has any further exclusive right to this or that pattern[11], and anyone can buy Murray tartan, Rob Roy tartan, or Stewart tartan without fear of calling down on himself thereby the wrath of some enraged native of the Highlands. However, just as there still remains a certain, not quite faded, shadow of the old clan system, so there are still districts in which the ancient tartans are worn by preference, and on festive occasions, of which there have been several in the Queen's presence, everyone will certainly wear the tartan that his forefathers wore.

Famous fancy tartans are for example, Prince Albert's tartan, Queen Victoria's tartan, Lady Napier's tartan, Lady Eglintor's [sic] tartan. The last two[12] belong to the very latest inventions of this kind.

Most of these tartans are made in the big Scottish factories. However, there are also districts in Scotland in which the people themselves still produce their colourful clothes on their own looms.

Apart from the tartans, the big pieces of embroidery in the Campbell establishment laid claim to my attention. Here many young girls are occupied with embroidering bonnets, baptismal robes and other garments. They call this embroidery **'Moravian point'**[13] and so have probably received this

---

[6] [Although there was no clan Rob Roy, there is a Rob Roy tartan; it is said to have been worn by Rob Roy MacGregor (1671 – 1734), the historical outlaw and fictional hero of Scott's *Rob Roy*.]

[7] [Royal Stewart is not a clan but the name of a tartan, considered, it is said, to be the personal tartan of the Royal House of Scotland.]

[8] [The Campbell tartan is meant, the Dukes of Argyll being Campbells. *Argyll* is the spelling used nowadays.]

[9] [In Scott's *The Heart of Midlothian* Jeanie Deans asks the Duke of Argyle for his help in gaining the release of her sister from prison.]

[10] [The Macphersons of Cluny. The chief of this clan is known as Cluny Macpherson.]

[11] [See Introduction p. xxi]

[12] [In the Scottish Register of Tartans three Prince Albert tartans are listed, though at least one was designed after 1842. There is no Queen Victoria tartan but there is a Stewart Victoria tartan, said to have been designed by the Queen herself. Napier tartan and Montgomerie/Montgomery of Eglinton tartan are listed, but neither Lady Napier's nor Lady Eglinton's; if they existed, they must have been ephemeral.]

[13] [The Moravian Church, founded 1457 in the present-day Czech Republic, encouraged its women in producing peasant crafts to satisfy commercial markets, including embroidery making great use of satin, chain and stem stitches. Members of this Church later settled in Pennsylvania, Ireland and England, taking their expertise with them.]

branch of industry from Germany. They have invented the printing of the embroidery pattern straight on to the muslin that is to be embroidered, and thus make their work extraordinarily easier. Every month, with scarcely one hundred and fifty girls, they manufacture in this way between one thousand five hundred and two thousand prettily embroidered little bonnets for children. A large batch of these, in addition to a significant quantity of baptismal robes, regularly goes from here to London, where humanity is even more avid in reproducing itself than people in Glasgow are in reproducing embroidery in the factories.

The proprietors of this remarkable firm, Messrs. Campbell, began with one hundred pounds capital and now belong to the richest people in Glasgow, and one of them is Lord Provost[14] of the city. Chambers[15] assures us in his account of Scotland that in 1834 alone the sales of this establishment amounted to 433,021 pounds sterling, which is about 3,031,147 thalers in our money, a turnover the size of which is quite unknown in the world for a retail business of this kind, for it approaches the turnover of the largest wholesalers on the continent.

These gentlemen may perhaps have had to struggle hard to earn their money, but, on the other hand, often not much is necessary to become rich in Glasgow, sometimes only a single lucky idea, a quick smile from Fortune. Given the briskness of changes in Great Britain, given the size of the markets that are open here, every invention immediately has such a huge impact and, if it is successful, bears such quick and ample fruits as is not possible in the countries of others where the business horizon is more limited. I was given the example of a man who manufactured handkerchiefs, the colour and pattern of which became so fashionable in England, and also received such extraordinary approbation among the one hundred million English colonists, that in a short time he became a wealthy man[16]. As is natural, many other manufacturers also strove to produce these much desired handkerchiefs, but this became possible for them only after some time and several unsuccessful experiments, and, when they finally achieved their aim, the inventor had already reaped his advantage. In a country such as this, what Goethe gives us to understand in *Faust* is literally true – that minted gold lies in readiness in great heaps, and only awaits skilful hands to gather it up and put it into their owner's pockets. Here one does not require all the wisdom of Solomon, for it needs only one single practical idea – if there are two, it is even better – to give you that success in abundance, in the pursuit of which thousands of people have squandered hundreds of thousands of good ideas in vain.

Perhaps – indeed without any doubt, there lie at my feet hundreds of similar good ideas that would be capable of making me a millionaire, if only I could find them here and now. Others will find them and for some time live happily from them, but then they will also tread the path that I then trod harbouring these thoughts, namely the path to the graveyard. However, on this occasion my own path led merely to the graveyard of Glasgow, which abounds in monuments and generally is one of the most beautiful churchyards that Europe can offer.

They call it the Necropolis. And it can certainly be put on a level with **Père la Chaise**[17] [sic], if not in respect of abundance of monuments, at least in respect of the grouping of the same, and in respect of its location as a whole. It is a picturesque hill, which is covered with trees, graves and pleasant

---

[14] [Sir James Campbell (1790 – 1876) was Lord Provost of Glasgow between 1840 and 1843.]

[15] [In his *Picture of Scotland*, see Chapter IV. In fact, this amount refers to the entire wholesale and retail business of the firm.]

[16] [This was Henry Monteith (1765 – 1848) who in 1802 took over his brother James's weaving factory at Blantyre for the production, among other things, of Turkey-red handkerchiefs and in 1805 took over a dye-works at Dalmarnock in Glasgow, see this chapter, fn. 30. His Turkey-red dyeing process earned him a great fortune; he later became Lord Provost of Glasgow and subsequently Member of Parliament.]

[17] [Père Lachaise Cemetery (Cimetière du Père-Lachaise) was the largest cemetery in Paris.]

pathways between them, as are the hollows and valleys that surround it. The top of the hill is crowned by a magnificent monument to Knox, the great reformer of Scotland, whose work had to withstand a twofold struggle, firstly with Catholicism and then with '**Episcopacy**', the English Episcopalian Church[18]. Even in the last century, episcopacy threatened to become and remain the principal church in Scotland until finally, by means of the two bloody Scottish national and ecclesiastical revolutions[19], Knox's reformed church, that of the Presbyterians, was recognised as **the established church**.

This Glasgow Necropolis is of comparatively recent origin; for only in 1831 was the ground given over to the reception of the dead. The intention, as I later learned, plainly was to emulate, with its parklands, the **Père la Chaise** in Paris. The big new churchyard in Liverpool is also of recent origin, and one can point to a large number of similar endeavours in England, all dating from modern times, to make even the dead more comfortable.

Beside the hill of the Necropolis is the cathedral of Glasgow, the oldest and most interesting building in this city. It is said to contain the most beautiful crypt in Great Britain. Unfortunately, however, I was not able to see it, since I was denied entrance on account of repairs to the church that were being carried out. Yet again, one of the hundreds and hundreds of Gothic churches in Europe that was in the process of being repaired and restored in 1842. In some ten years' time Gothic Europe will be with us again, as it was in the fourteenth and fifteenth centuries.

Without exception, in all Scotland, and in England, and in Belgium, and in all Germany, and in France, and in other countries I found this zeal for Gothic restoration to be burgeoning, not only zeal for Gothic restoration but also, I must add, zeal for imitation of the Greek. For in Glasgow too, as in other British cities, the large number of buildings erected in Greek style, and equipped with an incredible abundance of Corinthian, Ionic, Doric columns, gives rise to wonder and amazement. The Hunterian Museum, the Stock Exchange, the **Townhall** are all buildings in the Greek style. The Stock Exchange gives most occasion for astonishment because of its extraordinary abundance of columns. In this respect it is even more Greek than the Greek buildings themselves.

This imitation of Greek buildings is a phenomenon that is making headway through the whole of Europe, from the Exchange in Petersburg, the Museum in Berlin, the Glyptothek in Munich, to the Madeleine and the Bourse in Paris, and to these **Exchanges** in England and Scotland. It is really remarkable that we are so active in the Gothic and Hellenic styles, and that everywhere we turn to one or the other if something out of the ordinary is to be built. It will be remarked of us a hundred years hence that the eighteenth and nineteenth centuries were not capable of producing an impressive new architectural style. Should it really be quite impossible to dispense with Greek columns, Byzantine cupolas and Gothic towers and arches? And should our architects be condemned, from now to all eternity, always to continue to imitate the classical style? Should not completely different figures and forms, as yet unseen by human eye, emerge from the ground and the brains of men? If we cannot imagine such things at present, that is no indication that their appearance on earth would not be possible. The Greeks in their time too, could not form any conception of a Gothic tower and of the beauty of a Gothic cathedral. It is strange that not one of our architects will be found gifted with such a great imagination that he could be charged with the task of creating even one building in a fully novel, but nevertheless beautiful and classical, style.

---

[18] [One might justifiably cavil at the adjective *English* to describe Scottish Episcopalianism in Knox's time, or at any other time in Scottish history, see Introduction p. xxii.]

[19] [Presumably this refers to the Jacobite uprisings of 1715 and 1745; but these were dynastic rather than purely religious, see Introduction p. xix. In any case, the author was misinformed, for before these uprisings the Presbyterian faction had been confirmed as the established Church of Scotland by the Settlement of 1690.]

The Necropolis and the cathedral lie at the end of the longest street in Glasgow, the High Street, in the neighbourhood of which can be found still more vestiges of the ancient and earliest part of the city. However, there are but few of these old remains – quite otherwise than in Edinburgh, the High Street of which still runs through the middle of the large old part of the city, which still stands as it did centuries ago. For, in the course of a century, Glasgow has raised itself almost from complete nothingness to become one of the most important cities of Europe, and it ranks in this respect with Dublin, with Berlin, with Petersburg and other similar remarkable recent urban creations of northern Europe. At the time of the Union with England, not much more than one hundred years ago, Glasgow was an unknown name in Europe and boasted only twelve thousand citizens. In the short period since, the city has multiplied its population almost twenty-four times. According to Chambers, in 1837 the population amounted to 240,000 and it can now (1843) be estimated at 282,000, since the city increases by about 7000 souls annually.

The '**Virginia lords**' – as the merchants were called who in the course of last century carried on from here such an intensive tobacco trade with the American colonies, and especially with Virginia – were the first to bring money and people into the city. However, later it was the *cotton* lords in particular whose business, expanding to such an extraordinary extent, immensely further increased the population of the city during the present century (in 1800 they counted only 75,000 inhabitants). The city of Glasgow has never within its walls had lords of the *land*. For the latter, the old noble towns in the east of the country were always the principal places of residence, and first and foremost, naturally, Edinburgh. In respect of the constituent elements of their populations, therefore, the two towns present a great disparity which invites comparison. Edinburgh brings together all that is distinguished by education, upbringing and high rank in Scotland. Glasgow in contrast is brand-new from head to toe and has merchants and manufacturers within its walls; there are some of them who, on the occasion of the recently introduced '**Incometax**'[20], reported their annual income as between thirty thousand and forty thousand pounds sterling.

Edinburgh's municipal privileges are of the most ancient date and, before the Reform Bill, it was the only town in Scotland which sent one member of its own to Parliament. Until that Bill (1832), Glasgow shared that right with several other places. Glasgow has therefore naturally always been Whiggish and for reform and progress; Edinburgh, however, not always. Paisley is the seat of the Scottish radicals; the '**Highland-counties**' are the principal supporters of the Tories.

In 1834, of the 134 cotton factories that Scotland possessed, no fewer than 100 belonged to Glasgow, and there were as many as 15,000 **powerlooms**. The number of Irish people in the town is said to amount to no fewer than 30,000. I saw the greatest part of this Irish population in the streets on the evening that I went home through the High Street and the '**Cross**', through the Saltmarket and '**Trongate**' (Glasgow streets). For it was a Saturday, on which day in the Irish and British towns all the poverty-stricken of the population are always outside until midnight. The crowd was especially dense in the streets in the vicinity of the Cross. Here the people were standing in tight groups and went to and fro in great numbers. '**Every saturday** [sic] **they go here backwards and forwards**' said my companion. Most factories in Glasgow were working with only half their workforce at the time, and it was estimated that in Paisley and Glasgow together over 12,000 people were without work and sustenance. Among these great masses of people were whole families of beggars wandering up and down, bewailing their misfortune, and on every street corner people were standing, pleading for bread; the sight of them all made an infinitely depressing impression. Several young, strong, well dressed persons cut particularly distressed figures; they had positioned themselves, stiff and dumb like waxen dolls, in the gutters beside the pavements – the usual place of English beggars – and in silence held out their hats in front of them beseechingly. When we asked them why they were

---

[20] [It had originally been introduced in 1798 but in 1842 Peel had imposed a rate of 7 pence in the pound.]

begging, they answered 'We have clothes that no one wants to buy, Sir, but we have no work and no bread'.

There can be no greater contrast than that between the sight presented by the streets of Glasgow on Saturday evening and that presented on Sunday morning. On Saturday the rich remain at home and leave the field to the poor; on Sunday the rich fill the streets and one can look for the poor in vain. On the first, it is the people who crave work and bread; on the second, it is those who have bread and go to church, the **churchgoing people**. It is well known that in Scotland Sunday is even more strictly observed than in England; although Sunday in London already seems, to the person who comes from Paris and from the Continent generally, to have a very solemn appearance, yet in this respect one can look down from Glasgow and Edinburgh on to London as though on to a veritable Sodom and Gomorrah. During the entire Sunday in Glasgow nothing can be heard or seen save the footsteps of the gentlemen and ladies who walk in long lines from one church to another[21].

I too visited several churches on that day; however, I must confess that I was little uplifted by the discourses of the preachers, although several, one in particular, had been recommended to me as the best speakers in Glasgow. There is a certain apostolic vehemence, a certain exaggerated and oriental mode of expression, in the sermons of these Presbyterian preachers, which stands in great contradiction to the visual simplicity of their church services and their character generally. They all talk in the manner of our Krummacher from Elberfeld[22], whose writings therefore perhaps have a larger public in Scotland than in Germany[23]. Withal, however, their oratorical garlands and images have all something so hackneyed in them that the listener does not receive the impression and conviction that their words proceed fervently and vigorously from a heart radiant with enthusiasm. It is the same fanatical Calvinistic spirit that Knox transplanted to Scotland and instilled into his compatriots and which, to this very day, still continues to rant in the sermons of these speakers. In truth, Knox must have been an extraordinary man to have dinned his spirit and his character into an entire nation in this enduring way, and indeed to have done this to some extent against the will and against the inclination of the national spirit. For, by its very nature, the cool, rational, sensible northern disposition of the Scots appears suited for nothing so little as for religious fanaticism and credulity, something that one would think to be more associated with a fiery temperament such as Spaniards, Arabs and other nations possess.

The University of Glasgow does not enjoy as much renown in Germany as does the University of Edinburgh although it is even older, having been founded in the year 1450, whereas the University of Edinburgh dates back to the year 1582. Edinburgh, however, wherein resides all that is excellent and splendid in the country, is of course also attended much more frequently by people from abroad. Furthermore, Glasgow University frightens off the foreign student by some archaic regulations that do not exist in Edinburgh. Thus, for example, in Glasgow all students are required to wear a certain ancient uniform[24], whereas this is not a stipulation at Edinburgh, which is altogether more similar to our own seats of higher learning than is any other British university. The buildings of the University of Glasgow[25] have a mediaeval, venerable and almost grim external

---

[21] [The author would have found a different situation in the High Street and Trongate area on the Sunday afternoon, due to the opening of public houses.]

[22] [Gottfried Daniel Krummacher (1774 – 1837), a noted Revivalist preacher and pastor in Elberfeld from 1816 until his death.]

[23] [At least one of Krummacher's works had been translated into English, namely his *Israel's Wanderings in the Wilderness*, London 1837.]

[24] [This was a scarlet gown, the wearing of which goes back to the 17th century. Its use in Glasgow and its absence in Edinburgh had already been noted by Daniel Defoe in his *Tour thro' the Whole Island of Great Britain*, Vol.3 (Letter 12, Part 2) of 1727.]

[25] [The main one was a magnificent 17th century building in the High Street. Some 30 years later the University moved to its present site on Gilmorehill and the old buildings were demolished to make way for a railway.]

appearance, the like of which even our monasteries hardly present. Our beautiful Austrian monasteries on the Danube do indeed seem very worldly and grandiose in comparison with these English college buildings. They are built of a dark, grey stone and in a very plain style; moreover, they are separated from the rest of the world by walls and gateways, and they retreat into quiet, clean, inner courtyards. Only in the building which houses the Hunterian Museum has the modern Greek style crept into the confines of the college. It is a handsome natural history museum, set up by the famous anatomist Hunter and donated to the University, and thus enjoys a particular distinction because of its magnificent anatomical exhibits. It may be said in passing that all the other objects which pertain to natural history represent not only choice examples of their kind but are also displayed in the most meticulous order. After the British Museum and the collections in Edinburgh, which are foremost among the British natural history collections, the **Hunterian Museum**[26] surely stands next in order of excellence. It ranks alongside the Natural History Museum in Manchester and surpasses the York and Oxford collections both in its richness and its arrangements.

The whole University of Glasgow is still rightly aglow with the fame of its renowned engineer James Watt, and there is a statue of him in the Hunterian Museum. There is also his portrait in oils in the assembly hall of the University. Some small pieces of apparatus on which he worked are also preserved.

As is well known, the young Watt was initially an engineer in the employment of Glasgow University which thus has earned the distinction of having been the first to recognise and further his genius. Watt has to be acknowledged as the actual inventor of the steam engine, for although there were steam engines in existence before him, it only became possible through the improvement which he added (the condenser) to give the steam engine that applicability which later we in turn were able to utilise. Watt seems to have been born to be the inventor of the steam engine, and he appears to have brooded over this life-long idea almost from childhood. In his biography of Watt, Arago[27] reports that when he was still only a young boy, one of his aunts had remonstrated with him thus: 'James, you ought to be ashamed, always sitting about idling and dreaming. I believe you sometimes do not even know what you are doing. Do you realise that you have not done anything all this time but watch the steam of the tea-kettle? You have been lifting the lid and putting it back, time and again; you have been holding it into the clouds of steam, watching how the steam, transformed into water, drips off it. Listen to me! Do not get lost in your daydreaming, James, but occupy yourself with something respectable and useful!' Is it too fanciful to believe that even at that early stage the idea of the steam engine had been growing, like an undeveloped embryo, inside the young boy's head?[28]

Just as the burgomasters of the various English towns have different titles and are sometimes called 'mayor', sometimes 'lord mayor' (in London, Dublin, York etc.), sometimes 'provost' and 'lord provost' (in Glasgow, Aberdeen etc.), so the governors or pro-rectors of the British universities have very different titles. In Dublin, for instance, they are called 'provosts, and here in Glasgow they are called '**Principals**'. But apart from this Principal there is also a 'Lord Rector' who is generally some great personage of the realm. This Lord Rector is elected by all the professors and students together, and therefore he has to be a very popular figure.

---

[26] [Named after Dr William Hunter (1718-83), a graduate of the University, who bequeathed to it his collections of books, manuscripts, coins, pictures, anatomical and geological speciments, shells etc.]

[27] [Dominique François Jean Arago, author of *Historical Eloge of James Watt,* 1839.]

[28] [Although this story appears to be founded in fact, the idea of a separate condenser, his principal contribution to the development of the steam engine, came to Watt (1736 – 1819) as an adult while walking on Glasgow Green in 1765. See Introduction p. xiv.]

II. Glasgow

It is noteworthy that two years ago a Tory, namely Robert Peel, was elected Lord Rector of Glasgow University, but that this year they chose a staunch Whig, the Marquis of Breadalbane. The question arises whether there are any other British universities which have placed liberal and progressive men at their head. Opposition against the Tory government is quite considerable in the whole of Scotland, and the Tories have lost so much ground even in Edinburgh that at the last Parliamentary election they did not even dare put up a single candidate. The universities of Oxford, Cambridge, Dublin and others are, as is well known, always pure Tory, but the University of Glasgow is '**rather a changing body**', as the English are wont to put it. Perhaps this derives from the influence which the students there exercise in the elections.

It is curious that, whilst the number of students at the other universities of Great Britain has almost always increased considerably, the '**Universitas Glasguana**' or '**Glasguensis**' – there is an argument about how to write it – has been losing students steadily. Between 1820 and 1826 there were nearly 1600 students here, and now there are only 1000, amongst whom, just as at Edinburgh, there are also many from the British colonies. At the English universities of Oxford and Cambridge all students must belong to the High Church or at least join it, and for this reason fewer young people from the often dissenting colonies go there than to the Scottish universities. The medical faculty attracts the most foreign students, and for this reason the disciplinary code for students at this faculty is particularly mild. It has often been remarked upon that the young people of this freedom-loving English nation are subjected to so harsh a discipline the like of which our own young people would simply not tolerate. For instance, one would not dare introduce into our lecture halls the Censor who in Glasgow sits beside every professor. It is the task of this Censor to observe the behaviour of the students during the lecture and to make a note of every misdemeanour and unseemliness. For instance, a very typical misdemeanour which he must note is the passion, so widespread in all English schools, for considering the desks of the colleges suitable material for exercises in engraving and for carving out all manner of things. I found large notice-boards in the Glasgow colleges, threatening such desk-top artists with severe penalties. For the psychologist it is an interesting phenomenon that our own wild, boisterous students, who would never permit their exuberance to be curbed in such a manner, often become transformed eventually into such obedient citizens, whilst the young men in Britain often grow up into such strong and stubborn men, perpetually in opposition.

What is still understood here by '**Humanity**' is philology, which used to be the case with us, or rather – since philology is principally limited only to Latin and Greek – knowledge of Greek and Latin, and in fact especially of the latter, since Greek is less avidly pursued in England than in our own country. '**A professor of humanity**' is a teacher of Latin. In the Middle Ages, when Latin really was the herald of all the Muses, this appellation was quite meet and proper. Nowadays, however, such ancient nomenclature, by now meaningless, ought to be relinquished by scholars just as the old feudal titles were relinquished by the nobility.

The new light of humanity that has dawned among the peoples of Europe as a result of the avid and industrious study of nature has only slowly managed to penetrate the old Latin humanity. It is only in recent times that a Professor of Natural History was appointed here, and only since 1818 have they had a '**Professor of chymistry**' [sic]. Until then only a '**Lecturer**' was tolerated for this branch of learning which is so extremely important for Glasgow. There are several more recent professorial chairs. **The old chairs** still possess many privileges, for instance, among other things, free lodgings in the College itself. The new chairs, of which about nine have been created since 1806, are now locked in battle over this with the old ones, with whom they wish to be classed equal. They demand free lodgings in the College and a vote in its internal affairs, but so far they have not achieved this. It is probable that the new chairs will soon be ranked equal with the old ones.

Travels in Scotland (1840) by J.G. Kohl

As regards nationality, the old prejudices and restrictions are also being discarded. The Scots used to admit only Scots as teachers. Hudgisson [sic][29] was the first Irishman to be accepted, and at present there are again one or two from Ireland teaching at this University. This is worth noting, for I do not believe that we in Germany are aware of the great distinction the different subjects of the Kingdom of Great Britain were still in the habit of drawing among themselves. However, there have always been as many Irish students at Glasgow's University as there have been Irish workmen in its **'Dying** [sic] **and colouring works'**[30]. These Irish students used to be mainly Presbyterians from the northern part of Ireland; they went to Scotland for their education, just as the Irish Catholics used to go to France and Spain. The establishment of the Catholic College of Maynooth[31] in 1785 provided a home-based education for Irish Catholics; in the same way, the **'home education'** of the Irish Presbyterians was provided for in 1810 by the establishment of a Presbyterian college in Ireland itself, the **'Belfast academical Institution**[32]**'** or **'the Presbyterian college of Ireland'**. Indeed, already some Presbyterians from Scotland go over to Ireland in order to receive their education at this Presbyterian college.

The majority of the impressive new buildings in Glasgow – the Exchange, the Western Club (an excellent structure), several banks (including a new Joint Stock Bank, now in the process of being built), and countless others, indeed almost all the private houses – are built of a sandstone which is found in the vicinity of the city. This sandstone looks very handsome when it is new. However, it has several disadvantages. In the first place there are many veins and blemishes in it; these arise from a scattering of iron particles and they disintegrate more quickly when exposed to air. Secondly, it is weaker in some places and flakes off there. In Glasgow and Edinburgh many fine buildings can be found which have been thereby spoilt.

The most elegant private houses in Glasgow can be found in the western area of the city, **the Westend**, into which those who gained wealth, **the moneyed people**, retreat. The situation here is just as in London. In Edinburgh too, and in several other English towns, there is a fashionable West End; these are not so-called simply in imitation of London but are truly the western parts of these towns. I should gladly learn how this phenomenon is to be explained. Perhaps it is connected with smoke and the prevailing winds. Most winds in England blow from the west, so the west ends of English cities must be the brightest and least smoky; perhaps it is for that reason that the refined world prefers to reside in them.

---

[29] [This is in all probability Francis Hutcheson (1694 – 1746), born in Drumalig, County Down, Ireland; he was Professor of Moral Philosophy in the University from 1729 until his death. He became a profound influence on the Scottish Enlightenment (see Introduction p. xv) and was one of the originators of Utilitarianism.]

[30] [There is no record of a factory with exactly this name, though the author may intend the phrase to be taken as a plural and may only be referring to the large number of Irish workers employed generally in Glasgow's chemical works. However, judging by the author's comment on secrecy in Chapter III, it could be to be a reference to the Cudbear Manufactory, Ark Lane, Dennistoun established in 1777 by George Macintosh (1739 - 1807, father of Charles Macintosh, see this chapter, fn. 1) for the manufacture of cudbear, a dye extracted from lichen. To preserve the secret of its manufacture, the factory was surrounded by a ten-foot high wall and the workforce was composed of monoglot Gaelic-speakers from the Highlands who lived on the premises and were sworn to secrecy. It may be that the author was confusing Irishmen and Highlanders. The phrase could instead (or also) be a reference to the factory originally established by George Macintosh in what is now French St., Dalmarnock in 1785 as the Dalmarnock Turkey Red Works and taken over by Henry Monteith (see this chapter, fn. 16) in 1805 as the Barrowfield Dyeworks. The processes involved in producing such dyes were closely guarded, and extremely lucrative, secrets in Europe in the late 18th and early 19th centuries.]

[31] [St Patrick's College, Maynooth, the National Seminary of Ireland, actually established in 1795.]

[32] [Now the Royal Belfast Academical Insitution, founded in 1810 and formally opened in 1814.]

II. Glasgow

Not far from this West End of the city I visited further that part of Glasgow, called '**Port Dundas**', through which passes an arm of the great canal that joins the Clyde and the Forth[33]. One must climb up to this canal, for it extends along the high bank of the 'Clydesdale' ('valley of the Clyde'), and so one can see from the distance the ships and their masts looming over the houses of the suburbs like towers. It appears to be an upside-down world, so that high above is observed what elsewhere is observed only down below. Small boats ply on this canal, drawn by a horse and called '**swift boats**'. But then it is also used by small seagoing vessels of between 100 and 200 tons load. For at high water the canal is eight to nine feet deep throughout.

Owing to the fragmented nature of the land, the canal system of Scotland is different from the Irish. In Ireland all canals branch out from one place, Dublin, while in Scotland several canals, separate from each other, cut through the land in different places. Two of these are especially important: firstly, here between the Forth and the Clyde, and secondly, in the north, in the Great Glen of Scotland (**Glen-more-nan-Albin**[34]), where the lengthy Caledonian Canal[35] runs. This canal is 116 feet broad and 15 to 20 feet deep, so it is a gigantic achievement and a true link between two seas, for the largest ocean-going vessels can sail into it from the sea without any trouble, traverse the interior of the country, and put to sea again on the other side.

* * * * * * *

---

[33] [Over 56 kilometres long, stretching from Bowling on the Clyde to Grangemouth on the Forth and featuring 40 locks and a 122 metre aqueduct at a height of 21 metres, the Forth and Clyde Canal was opened in 1790. It had five branches and was the busiest in Scotland.]

[34] [Properly *Gleann Mòr na h-Albann*.]

[35] [Over 96 kilometres in length, the Caledonian Canal is Scotland's longest, though two-thirds of its length are on existing lochs. It runs from Clachnaharry, near Inverness, to Corpach, near Fort William and thus in effect connects the North Sea and the Atlantic Ocean. It was opened in 1822.]

III
From Glasgow to Edinburgh

The great '**Dying** [sic] **and colouring works**'[1], which belong to the most interesting things that a stranger can look at in Glasgow, are a great '**secret**' and I entertained no hope that one of these would be revealed to me. In addition, now came the Sunday that enveloped so much else in secrecy for me and made it inaccessible. I therefore decided to leave that city of secrets that very day and towards evening made my way to the railway that leads to Edinburgh[2]. Here on the railway also everything was wrapped in secrecy, for it was a pitch-black night except in the narrow comfortable compartment of our carriage. This was very brightly lit[3] according to the attractive and praiseworthy custom of the English railways with the result that we could study the area through which we were travelling, if not **in natura** at least as it was depicted on the map.

It is in fact the most fertile, level, populated and heavily built-up region of Scotland, the real Scottish central belt, the heart of the Scottish Lowlands. The counties here, which lie between the estuaries of the Clyde and the Forth – that is, the counties of Ayr, Renfrew, Lanark, Dumbarton, Stirling, Fife, Linlithgow, Edinburgh – are all either accommodated completely in this central plain or to the extent of one half of their area, in which case they rise at the other end to the northern mountainous Highlands or to the southern mountainous Borders. These fine counties have a population twenty or even thirty times greater than many uncultivated counties in the mountain ranges. Thus, for example, in the counties of Renfrew, Lanark, Edinburgh, Fife, Linlithgow, Stirling there is one person for between one and four **acres**, while in the counties of Argyle, Inverness, Ross, Selkirk there is one person for every twenty to thirty-four acres. In fact, in the most northerly county of Scotland, Sutherland, which is even more thinly populated than Orkney and the Hebrides, there is only one soul per forty-three acres.

Here on this inner small plain of Scotland, scarcely sixty German square miles[4] in size, is centred almost the entire history of the country. Here are situated close to each other the most famous places in the land, the ancient royal residences of Perth, Stirling, Edinburgh; here within a small area are the most important and largest towns of the kingdom even now: Glasgow, Edinburgh, Paisley, Dundee. Here just as close to each other can be seen the famous battlefields, those of Stirling, Falkirk, Bannockburn etc, on which Scotland's fate was so often decided. Here in this narrow parcel of land was played out everything that was crucial and decisive for Scotland. Here was developed the Anglo-Saxon language of Scotland that outstripped the Celtic speech of the Highlands. Here the Reformation first gained a firm foothold, while the Highlands and the rest of the country had to follow. Here after the union of the two British kingdoms the remarkable inventions of the English manufacturing industry were first introduced. And here in this central belt the foremost Scottish highways of water, iron and stone run from sea to sea: in pride of place the Forth and Clyde Canal[5], next an old broad military road between Edinburgh and Glasgow[6], and finally, lying between these

---

[1] [See Chapter II, fn. 30. Presumably the author had been denied access to any such factory; after all, interested strangers could well be industrial spies.]

[2] [An advertisement, dated 21st June 1842, in the Post-Office Glasgow Annual Directory for 1842-43 p. 165, states that a Sunday train would leave Glasgow for Edinburgh at 5.30 p.m. According to the timetable, the journey took 2½ hours. Sunday services were discontinued in November 1846 and not resumed for some years.]

[3] [Such lighting was originally by feeble oil lamps, so *very brightly* must be relative to unlit carriages.]

[4] [This would be about 620 square kilometres.]

[5] [See Chapter II, fn. 33.]

[6] [This was not a military road, all but one of which had been built, following the 1715 Jacobite rising, in the Highlands (see Chapter XV, fn. 6). There had long been a route between Glasgow and Edinburgh. A horse-drawn post between the two towns was introduced in 1715 and the first stage-coach service in 1749. In 1751 the Turnpike Road Act was passed and thereafter the building and improvement of roads throughout the Lowlands had proceeded very energetically, but there is no record of a specific scheme to construct a 'broad' Glasgow-Edinburgh road.]

two and increasingly rendering both superfluous, the great new railway that goes direct from Edinburgh to Glasgow[7] and from both cities radiates out into the country with various branch lines.

The inhabitants of Berlin, who as is well known possess a wealth of jokes, have painted a witty representation of their city as it appears at night when the lanterns and lights are not burning. This picture is of course nothing more than an area of pitch-black set in a rectangular frame. Unfortunately the whole country that we were traversing was the very image of that 'Berlin by Night'. For the weather outside was so bad and the darkness so complete that I could not distinguish the merest detail either of the portion of Dunbartonshire or of the extremity of Stirlingshire that we passed through, or of West Lothian that we bisected right in the middle, or of Midlothian into which we travelled on our way to Edinburgh. My travelling companion, a patriotic Scot, wanted to show me absolutely everything in his native land; he pointed now to the right at the fine, large, populous villages near Falkirk, now to the left at the old Castle of Linlithgow a few hundred steps from us (Mary Stuart had been born there), now again to the right at some attractive country seat of a Scottish gentleman. Yet however hard I peered in the direction of his pointing finger I invariably encountered the same object at its end, namely impenetrable coal-black darkness.

* * * * * * *

---

[7] [See Introduction p. xvi. Services on the Edinburgh and Glasgow Railway began on 21 February 1842. The line is remarkably straight and level, thanks to good engineering (which involved long viaducts and three tunnels), apart from a steep gradient into Glasgow Station (now Queen Street Station) which, in the author's time, required trains to be cable-hauled out of Glasgow. It is still (in 2012) the principal of the four railway lines linking Edinburgh and Glasgow.]

IV
Edinburgh

In Edinburgh it at last became bright again, indeed so brilliantly bright that it seemed to me as though I had flown through a dark region of the cosmos from one star to another. I find this description not one whit too exaggerated. For I truly believed I had reached the centre of a new star when the railway released me from its darkness and I drove off in a small minibus[1] through the brilliantly lit streets[2], garden valleys and Castle Rock of Edinburgh.

However much one may have read about Edinburgh, one is constantly surprised and enchanted by this city whose location and arrangement of dwellings are uniquely beautiful. I believe that Edinburgh would be declared to be the most picturesque and handsome city in the world, had not envious fate utterly denied it one great advantage, that of an expanse of water; of such a thing Edinburgh possesses not one trace. It is purely an inland territory, a purely hill and valley city; it possesses all the attractions that the varying subtleties of ground, hills, mountains, precipitous rocks, valleys, depressions, crevasses can bring to a human habitation, yet it totally lacks the lively element of water. For Edinburgh is situated at a distance of two miles from the Firth of Forth and the little brook Leith, which does not even lay claim to the name of a river but is designated only as **'Water of Leith'**, steals modestly and shyly past the big city to the north-west. Apart from Birmingham[3], I know no town that is so devoid of water as Edinburgh; for apart from a small canal basin there is not even a tiny lake, not even a mill pond, within the city walls. Not far from the city there are some small lakes and I imagine that the citizens of Edinburgh must frequently go out to those lakes in order to see a stretch of water once in a while.

Because of its splendid position Edinburgh has been compared to Athens and so it is also called the Athens of the North, also of course partly on account of the flourishing academic life here. In fact the similarity is extraordinarily striking. For Athens too is almost completely a town of hill and valley. Only perhaps its Illysos[4] is somewhat larger and also nearer the town than the Water of Leith. Athens too, like Edinburgh, lies inland and has its Piraeus by the sea as Edinburgh has its Port of Leith. Even the hills near Edinburgh resemble those near Athens. I even believe that Athens would gain unquestionably more honour by being compared to Edinburgh than Edinburgh has from being measured against Athens. For there is certainly no doubt that, as far as natural location is concerned, everything is much more magnificent and beautiful here in the northern Athens than it ever was in the southern.

Actually my intention had been to continue my travels again the very next day in order to make use of the still relatively clement time of year for a small expedition to the Highlands. However, the sight of Edinburgh so filled me with rapture that I could not but first devote a few more days to that splendid town and study its layout.

In order to form a clear conception of it, one's eyes should first look at the focal point of the location and arrangement of the buildings of Edinburgh, namely the Castle Rock. This Castle Rock, an eminence of basalt that falls away precipitously on three sides, is admirably suited as an ancient

---

[1] These 'minibuses' are strange little one-horse, two-wheeled carriages for four people which are in use in Edinburgh. I should like to know whence that unusual word for that unusual little vehicle originated. For the English, who easily find that anything is too long, the word is still too long and they usually abbreviate it simply to 'bus', leaving off the syllable 'mini', saying, for example, **'Will you go by the bus?'** In Glasgow they have a similar carriage, which they call **'noddy'**. *JGK*

[2] [The source of this illumination was coal gas lighting, which had first been introduced to Edinburgh streets in 1819.]

[3] [Contrary to what the author implies, Birmingham had a large number of urban canals by the end of the 18th century.]

[4] [A river of Attica that flows into the sea near the Piraeus.]

fortress by virtue of its height and shape and by the fact that it dominates the plain for far around. Without doubt it was that which first encouraged human settlement here. Its building goes back to unknown antiquity as does the building of the Acropolis in Athens. Now it is topped with modern and ancient fortifications.

On one side the rock is linked to the adjacent land and it levels out, very gradually descending into a valley that lies between two other hills, one low, the '**Caltonhill**', and one high, the '**Salisbury-Craggs**'[5] of which the highest point is called '**Arthur's Seat**'. In the valley between these two hills, where, as explained, the outcrops of the Castle Rock disappear and are lost, is the old palace of the kings of Scotland, '**Holyrood-palace**'. Nowadays between this palace in the valley and that castle on the hill, the principal thoroughfare of old Edinburgh, the '**Highstreet**'[6], rises up on the ridge of those outcrops of the Castle Rock, connecting palace and castle fortress together in a straight line.

To the right and to the left of the High Street, which as we said is a street on a hill-ridge, numerous extremely narrow little alleyways fall away, on one side to the south, on the other to the north. These alleyways are called '**Closes**'. Usually they are barely wide enough to allow two people to pass each other easily in them. Moreover they are formed by astonishingly high houses and further, as explained, they run downhill so that they mostly resemble nothing so much as narrow fissures in a large mass of rock.

The aforementioned High Street with all its countless closes on both sides and with its houses stacked up to seven or eight or even nine storeys[7], one house jutting out above the other, forms the main part of the Old Town of Edinburgh, lying between Holyrood House and the Castle as though between two cardinal points.

On both sides of the ridge just described, which terminates in the steep pinnacle of the Castle Rock, are depressions or valleys. From Holyrood House the street called '**North Back of Canongate**' runs in the northern of these valleys and '**South Back of Canongate**' in the southern. The former leads into the vicinity of the fish-market and gardens that cover the northern valley, while the latter connects with several other old streets (**Cowgate, Grassmarket**) that occupy the southern valley.

On the far sides of both these valleys begins modern Edinburgh; this has surrounded that old centre with a girdle of fine modern buildings, especially on the far side of the broader and more distinguished northern valley. On the far side of this latter lies the largest and most splendid part of new Edinburgh; it was built only following the Union of Scotland with England and indeed for the most part only since the reign of George III. If we take no account of the many new buildings, streets and squares to the south of the Old Town as being unnecessary for the purpose of comparison, and also disregard the southern valley alluded to as being very narrow, then we may say that Edinburgh falls into an Old Town and a New Town, separated from one another by a deep valley filled with gardens.

The New Town lies opposite the Old and its main street (**Georgestreet**) runs parallel to the ancient High Street, likewise on the ridge of an elongated elevation which, however, is by no means as high as that of the Old Town. This George Street is one of the most imposing avenues in Europe, adorned with superb buildings and elevated statues, for example, of Pitt, George IV and so on. From it also branch off various wide, splendid streets which form the most remarkable contrast in the

---

[5] '**Cragg**' is probably the same Celtic word that appears in Ireland as '**Carrick**', in Wales as '**Craig**', and means there, as here, simply 'rock'. *JGK* [The author's philological surmise is correct. Nowadays the Edinburgh rock formation in question is spelt *Salisbury Crags*.]

[6] The one portion of this street near **Holyrood-house** is actually called '**Canongate**' and the other near the fortified castle '**Lawnmarket**'. *JGK*

[7] [One or two buildings even reached a height of 13 storeys at that time.]

world to the closes in the Old Town. They run down to a slope filled with gardens on the northern edge where the town begins again. Several square, circular, elliptical, octagonal open spaces and gardens (**Squares**) embellish this new part of the city, as well as a host of the most beautiful houses.

Of the two hills which we mentioned above and between which lie the valley and the parks of Holyrood House, one, Calton Hill, is still within the city but the other, the Salisbury Crags, is, on account of its excessive steepness and height, given over completely to the spirits of the heath. These Salisbury Crags are precipitous foothills of basalt, like Benmore or Fair Head[8] in Ireland. Their incline is sheer, almost vertical, and their grass-covered summit is home to goatherds and shepherds with their flocks. The sight of this huge volcanic formation is so primitive that one would think the breakers of a raging ocean must hurl themselves at that rock, as in Ireland, but instead at their foot is found displayed the elegance of a peaceful residential city. The sombre outline of the Salisbury Crags, almost leaping into the middle of the city, is visible from nearly every house and every street.

The other, the Calton Hill, is as we have said still a part of the city since it was easier to provide it with walkways, parklands and buildings. The Scots have, it seems, chosen it as the site of memorials to their principal heroes and poets, for it is furnished with several magnificent monuments. Firstly there is a tall monument[9] to Nelson which is like a kind of lighthouse, then one for Playfair[10], another for Dugald Stewart[11], and at the foot of the hill a fourth for the poet Burns. The last would have rejoiced on his deathbed if he had possessed only a fraction of the sum that was spent on monuments for him after his death. Finally can be seen the beginnings of a huge monument[12] that was to crown this hill of monuments, as does the Parthenon the Acropolis in Athens. This remarkable landmark, '**the national monument**', was to be a temple in imitation of the Parthenon and be dedicated to the memory of the victors of Waterloo. However, either the initial enthusiasm for this idea was not sufficiently enduring or it was out of all proportion to the subsequent anxiety of spending too much money. In short, only ten or twelve pillars of this temple, each costing one thousand pounds sterling, were completed.

In the above rough fashion we have sketched an outline of Edinburgh, and the points indicated contain the essential features of the enchanting picture offered by this city. Let now the entirety be envisaged. Only gradually were we able to assemble this by describing scene after scene, each immediately presenting itself vividly to the eye, and exhibiting itself briefly in ever novel, rapidly changing groupings as we drove about in a small '**Bus**': these splendid imposing streets of the New Town, which, though right-angled and regular, yet, since they slope upwards and downwards, are not wearisome; these elegant squares and gardens that everywhere have been inserted between the mansions; these tall buildings in the narrow streets of the Old Town which, dirty and miserable though they may be, yet appear beautiful and picturesque since they rise up on a hill; these dry valleys and ravines filled with gardens or houses, arched by other streets or splendid, magnificent bridges (even if Edinburgh has not a drop of water, it nevertheless possesses a wealth of bridges); now the view from the hurly-burly of the street above on to the animation of the market below; in addition, everywhere the most beautiful, richest and most interesting, oldest and newest, Greek and half-Gothic buildings in the most opulent style, and finally among these buildings the monument-topped Calton Hill, the Castle Hill covered with fortifications, and Arthur's Seat transformed by the

---

[8] *Bengore, Fairhead*
[9] [Dedicated in 1807 to Viscount Horatio Nelson (1758 – 1805), victor of the Battle of Trafalgar.]
[10] [John Playfair (1748 – 1819), geologist and eminent figure of the Scottish Enlightenment.]
[11] [Dugald Stewart (1753 – 1828), the leading English-speaking philosopher of his day.]
[12] [The National Monument, intended to be a memorial to the Scots who had died in the Napoleonic Wars, was begun in 1822 at an estimated cost of £42,000. But only £16,000 was subscribed and the project was finally abandoned in 1830, after only 12 Doric columns had been completed. The unfinished memorial became unofficially known as 'Scotland's Pride and Poverty'.]

sun or clouds – all of which are everywhere visible between the buildings. I maintain that if all the foregoing be imagined vividly, then will be gained merely a faint conception of what remarkable scenic pleasures a drive among the streets of this city must afford. Walter Scott[13] calls Edinburgh **'Scotland's darling seat'**. It is also called **'the Auld Reeky'** by the people; in so doing they still remember times past and ignore the admirable new transformations.

Without exception only prosperous and rich families seem to dwell in the beautiful, salubrious, elegant, indeed magnificent New Town. These are the professors of the University, an astonishing number of lawyers (it is said that no fewer than eight thousand inhabitants, including women and children, belong to this class) and also a number of families of the nobility and gentry, more precisely those whose income is not substantial enough to bear the expense of a permanent residence in London. But above all there are numbers of those belonging to the cultivated classes; they betake themselves to Edinburgh from all over Scotland and even from part of England, since in Edinburgh all the delights of a social and refined life are available more comfortably and more cheaply than in London. With regard to the size of its cultivated society and to the resources which that requires, Edinburgh is the second city in the British Empire and in this respect forms a marked contrast to Dublin with its habitual absenteeism of the gentry, of which no trace is to be found here. Since Edinburgh is not a city of trade and industry but on the contrary a city of University, courts of law and aristocratic residences, many people come here to have their children educated. The Scots, who emigrate to all quarters of the globe to attain wealth, mostly also settle in the capital of their beloved native-land when their efforts have been crowned with success. With the university alone no fewer than four thousand persons are said to be connected, either as students or professors or as professors' children, and it may therefore be quite true what the Scots claim, namely that almost one-third of the 150,000 inhabitants of the city belong to the educated classes.

Edinburgh looks particularly beautiful in the evening and I believe there is no other town in Europe that is so ornamented by the lighting of street lamps or of house lights. This is especially true of the Old Town, the houses of which, towering one above the other, are seen opposite from the long and splendid Princes' Street, which runs along the edge of that rich valley, devoid of water but rich in flowers and trees, like a quay by a river. This Old Town shimmers with countless lights even on normal weekdays like a starry sky, and like other cities on high feast-days. Yet it is poverty which is responsible for this profusion of lights. For all these great high buildings are packed with poor people up to their roofs. Every single room is inhabited by a family, and since these people are busy until late at night, a little light gleams from every window, while in the houses of the rich long suites of rooms often lie unused and dark.

'You must go yourself into the narrow alleys of the Old Town and see in what misery, in what squalor, the poor live there' said a German compatriot to me in Edinburgh. 'For if you do not do so, then you will probably go back to Germany, like so many other foreigners, and praise the magnificence of these English cities, the hospitality of their inhabitants, the splendid dinners and I know not what else, and completely ignore the poor, as the English ignore them. I tell you, if you will come with me and squeeze your way through these houses, you will see shocking things, the like of which you have never seen. For there exist there human conditions, scenes of filthiness and misery, that certainly do not occur in a respectable land, and certainly ought not to occur at all.'

Indeed, if I had not seen the conditions of the poor in Polish towns and if I had not witnessed much wretchedness, squalor and distress linked to penury elsewhere in the world, I would have said that the misery and desolate condition of the poor in parts of the Old Town of Edinburgh are the most pitiful thing that can been seen on this earth. One can scarcely make distinctions among the totality of poverty and misery that exists in this earthly vale of tears, but this much is certain, that the way

---

[13] [It is Robert Burns who almost does so. The first line of his 'Address to Edinburgh' is 'Edina! Scotia's darling seat!']

of life of these Edinburgh poor has its own quite specific evil and it chiefly arises from the extraordinary type of housing in this part of the city as we have described above.

Those closes are in fact the narrowest little alleys that exist anywhere in the world. For in comparison not only the narrow lanes in Genoa but even those of oriental cities are broad highways. Some show a gap between the houses which is literally only one or one and a half yards wide. Formerly the houses on the sides of these closes were inhabited by the nobility and many to this day still bear the names of old families, so for example, one is called '**Morrison's Close**', another '**Grey's Close**', a third '**Stewart's Close**', a fourth '**Blyth's Close**'. These gentlemen purposely built themselves into such narrow spaces to be the safer when the occasion arose and to be able to barricade their street. Even the name *close* seems to indicate this purpose. In some closes the coats of arms of such old families can still be seen affixed to the doorways. And in Blyth's Close can still be seen the residence of Queen Mary of Guise, who was Regent of Scotland from 1554 to 1560. It now lies half in ruins and is, like all the other aristocratic houses, inhabited from top to bottom by poor people.

In another close, called '**the Bakehouse Close**', is the old house of the Earls of Gosford, formerly an imposing building, now also inhabited by the poorest of the poor. Near it is the residence of an even more famous family, the Earls of Moray, and not far from it that of the Dukes of Queensberry, today a house for beggars. Similar illustrious houses, now demeaned, are found everywhere.

I have never yet found anywhere that the poor are clean, for only prosperity imparts a love of tidiness and cleanliness. In England even a high degree of prosperity is necessary to give rise to this love of tidiness, to which I can add cleanliness and thrift. The English poor are only all too often spendthrifts, drunkards, and sunk in filth. I think this is even truer of the Scottish poor. All in all one can imagine what repulsiveness, what stench, what squalor are encountered in those closes. Since sun and wind never enter them, they are almost always damp. In some places I found dirt lying that seemed to have been accumulating for years. Weird staircases, that often are built on from outside like ladders, lead into the interiors and upper storeys of the houses, some of which contain a maze of passageways, stone steps, and miserable hovels. Every now and then from these wretched dwellings and hovels can be glimpsed, through the aforementioned gaps in the streets, the most splendid and striking vistas and panoramas of the New Town with its gardens and hills. For, as I have already remarked, most of these closes slope down the hill and hence in part are stairways, and so occasionally it is possible to gaze down at the elegance beneath.

Cholera was appallingly rife in these houses, which were often impenetrable for the doctor as much as for the police, or for the sun and other beneficial elements, and it is said that even now infectious diseases never completely die out here. There are also many Irish people among the inhabitants of these crumbling walls and, since they just cannot bear to be without pigs, they often take these, their favourite animals, high under the roofs with them and rear them there in the bedchamber of some nobleman or knight of James the Fifth or Sixth. In Edinburgh they tell how, when during the cholera outbreak the police forced an entry and endeavoured to promote orderliness and cleanliness, a number of pigs had to be lowered from the window of the fourth storey because they had inadvertently been allowed to become too plump and fat to pass through the narrow stone doorway of the room.

Most of the crime in Edinburgh is perpetrated in these closes; they afford the best opportunity for people to carry out robbery and theft, to conceal stolen goods, or to commit a murder. Since in places pedestrians cannot pass by each other without bodily contact, the murderer can always flatten his victim against the wall, immediately making breathing and shouting impossible, and then complete the task with a blow. I think that these narrow alleys inspired the infamous murderer

Burke[14] with the idea of his dreadful murders, and one of these closes, called the West Port, which leads up out of the Grassmarket[15], was indeed the scene of his misdeeds; here he waylaid the handsome Italian organ-grinder boys and overpowered them with a suffocating mask of pitch.

I have to say that I conceived a kind of fascinated interest in the extraordinary circumstances and households of this ancient Edinburgh, which nowhere have their like, and visited them several times by night and by day. The depressing thought which forced itself into my mind was that these conditions will long continue to drag on, for an unforeseeable period. Of course, as I was told and as I observed here and there for myself, much is being done by the Edinburgh authorities to clean these closes, to tidy them up, to widen them, and where possible to do away with them altogether. Sometimes these old decayed buildings are completely demolished and dwellings elsewhere are assigned to the poverty-stricken inhabitants. However, the city of Edinburgh has only 30,000 pounds sterling in revenue and what it can utilise out of this for the improvement of the Old Town is insignificant in relation to the vastness of the Augean Stables[16] that have to be cleansed here. As I have said, these old buildings are so solidly built and so big that to pull even one of them down incurs much expense, and so it is predictable that they will continue to exist for a long time to come.

Many another town has been freed of its ancient troublesome problems by the terrible intervention of conflagration and has thus achieved an improved new style of building. However, even if such an occurrence were desirable here, it cannot be hoped for, precisely again because the buildings for the most part are so solidly built of stone[17].

Human nature is so strangely contrived that it is usually never stimulated to enthusiasm and assiduity either by beauty near at hand or by suffering near at hand. Were it not so, one would marvel that while among the affluent inhabitants of Edinburgh in the New Town on the other side of the aforementioned valley there are indeed societies for the conversion of the Jews and the black races, not a single one exists that has set itself the goal of collecting funds to purchase gradually some of the old slums in the Old Town in order to have them demolished and thereby bring somewhat more air and light, health and morality, into that warren of dwelling-places. The needs of black people and Jews in distant places are quite unknown to those in the New Town. What their own poor lack, however, and how they could be helped, the rich could learn for themselves most easily, since they have them constantly before their eyes. However, just as everywhere on earth there is more joy over a new convert, so too in Edinburgh there is more jubilation over one single baptised black man than over a hundred poor persons whose life is opened up to education, respectability and Christianity. The Edinburgh Presbyterians with their zeal for mission can be compared to a shepherd who has a hundred ailing sheep in his flock and who, instead of spending money on doctors and medicine to heal them, uses it for the purchase of a rare and expensive ram, when he could increase his flock vastly more by the restoration to health of his hundred sheep. To sweeten the bitterness of the cup of life of the destitute souls in the High Street and its closes, to take the toddy[18] mugs from their hands and to press the chalice of salvation to their lips – these would be such worthy aims of a missionary that I cannot understand why long ago prophets have not arisen with this objective. But it is obvious that when a missionary returns from the black people of Africa or from the brown people of Australia or from the Jews in Wallachia, people shower him

---

[14] [William Burke (1792 – 1829) and William Hare (1790 – ca. 1860), both Ulstermen, are believed to have murdered at least sixteen people by suffocation to supply bodies to Edinburgh's medical school for anatomy demonstrations.]

[15] [Translated literally in the original as *Grasmarkt*.]

[16] [Augeas was a king in Greek mythology whose stables had never been cleaned. Hercules diverted a river through them and so cleaned them.]

[17] [Presumably unknown to the author, there had been a great fire in November 1824 which resulted in new building on the south side of the High Street near Castle Hill.]

[18] **'Toddy'** means 'whisky' in Scotland. *JGK*

with praise and laurel wreaths quite otherwise than they would a nobleman who would make the closes and the High Street the scene of his husbandry.

The most noteworthy point of interest that I noticed on my repeated walks in the alleyways of the Old Town of Edinburgh were the Irish. By no means did I find them among the most wretched here; as a rule these were always the Scots themselves. Usually the Irish here are small **Shopkeepers**. People told me that the Irish here were better off with little than the Scots with much. 'Yes, we would even be doing quite well', an Irishman said to me, 'if we only could only obtain the very same rights as the Scots. But it is difficult for us **to get in the laws**.[19]'

A stroll from the eminence of the Castle Rock down the High Street and Canongate as far as Holyrood House and its beautiful gardens in the valley belongs to the most interesting urban walks that one can take anywhere. It begins at the top of the Castle with a viewing of the Scottish regalia which are kept in a small room, high up, in a part of the castle that is said to have been built by Mary[20] of Scotland. These Scottish royal insignia have had fortunes as remarkable as almost no other in Europe, apart from the Hungarian crown. The fact is that they disappeared completely for over a hundred years and no one knew where they were. In 1707 at the time of the Union of Scotland with England, some Scottish patriots concealed them, packed in a chest, in the high portion of the castle where they are now shown, and there walled them up secretly, I believe from fear that the English would make off with them to London[21]. Afterwards where they were hidden was completely forgotten. Not until 1818 were they found again and, after the wall was broken through, brought to the light of day – or at least to candlelight, for the little low-ceilinged room in which they lie in an iron-barred cabinet under constantly burning whale oil candles is not open to the sun.

I was told that Walter Scott had received some information about their place of concealment and had helped much in their detection and recovery. This seems to be a truly remarkable circumstance; for it is almost passes belief that some people had not always known about the place where the royal regalia were hidden[22]. This would indicate that among the higher Scottish nobility there were still several who until very recently were somewhat distrustful of the present state of affairs, and who still nourished a small glimmer of hope that on an appropriate occasion a practical use could once again be made of those royal insignia. Since the Union these have been no more than interesting antiquities, because when the kings of England put on the Crown of Great Britain[23], which is kept in the Tower of London, they simultaneously assume that of Scotland. That the regalia were not disturbed in their gloomy place of refuge in the revolution of 1745 can be explained by the fact that the castle did not fall into the hands of the Pretender Charles[24] Stuart who besieged it in vain.

Incidentally, these insignia consist of a crown, a sceptre made for James V, a sword that Pope Julius II presented to James IV, and of several other pieces. The circlet or hoop of the crown is said to

[19] [This may refer to earlier anti-Catholic laws, though the Catholic Emancipation Act had been passed in 1829. Otherwise it is mysterious: in 1842 Scottish law made no distinctions on grounds of nationality.]
[20] *Marie* [The author may be confusing St Margaret's Chapel (built on the highest point of the Castle Rock in the12th century, and still standing) with St Mary's Kirk (built slightly lower down also in the 12th century, but now vanished).]
[21] [In fact, the regalia, the Honours of Scotland, were delivered to the Commissioners of the Treasury who locked them up in an oak chest in the Crown Room of Edinburgh Castle.]
[22] [While one cannot disprove the author's surmise, there is no proof of it. In 1817 Scott persuaded the Prince Regent to grant a warrant to himself and the Scottish Officers of State to open the Crown Room and search for the Honours. They forced open the chest and found them undamaged, except for being 'tarnished and soiled with dust'.]
[23] [This probably refers to the Crown of St Edward, the official coronation crown; it had not been used to crown monarchs since 1689 though it was carried in procession at later coronations. It was used again in 1911 to crown George V and at the coronations of George VI and Elizabeth II.]
[24] *Carl*

have been made for Robert Bruce[25] – whenever possible, everything in Scotland dates from Robert Bruce, just as in Germany it does from Charlemagne[26] or in Hungary from St Stephen[27], or in Russia from Monomach[28]. In these regalia, besides the pearls and jewels of foreign origin, a principal role is played by the famous Scottish crystals which are called '**Cairngorms**'. A handsome big cairngorm reposes on James V's sceptre, another on a sceptre that dates back to James III's time. These cairngorms are smoke-coloured quartzes that are found in the granite of the Cairngorm Mountains in Inverness-shire in the north of Scotland. They resemble the even more northerly Icelandic crystals. Scottish patriots enjoy decorating their daggers, hunting knives, snuff-boxes, walking-sticks and suchlike with these pretty native stones, and here I even found them on the sceptre of the Kings of Scotland. Beyond these in Edinburgh Castle and those that are kept in the Tower of London, Great Britain has no royal insignia. For Ireland, though it is called a kingdom, possesses nothing comparable, apart from some old royal insignia of the provincial kings of Munster and Leinster which, so I was told, are still in the hands of Irish private individuals.

In almost every relatively important English city there is a similar castle-hill with an old or new fortification and with an old or new residence of a king or governor. It is strange that they almost all resemble one another. They are all more or less like Windsor Castle. And I would immediately recognise an English town castle at first glance and be able to tell it apart it from other castles without being able to enumerate all its characteristics and distinguishing marks in brief.

Amid unvaryingly beautiful views on all sides, one can walk across the high Castle Esplanade where English redcoats, called '**Lobsters**' by the civilians, are drilled, to the Old Town itself. This is connected on the left by a broad **earthen mound**[29] to the New Town and on the right to the suburbs by a splendid bridge (**George IV Bridge**) under which there surges the river of the humble populace of the Cowgate, or rather, as the Saxon Scots pronounce the name of this street, of the Coogate[30].

Near this bridge stand the splendid buildings of the old Scottish parliament and the highest seats of justice (**the courts of law**) of the Scottish kingdom, which also contain the famous libraries of the Scottish **advocates** (this name, well known in Germany, is found again here but is not used in England). The largest chamber of this building, which was erected for sessions of the Parliament, serves now as a kind of place of congregation or promenade for the legal fraternity. On my own promenade here I happened to come into this room just as several hundred lawyers (or '**Gown-men**', as people also call all practioners of civil law) had gathered, a curious sight for a stranger unused to it. For all these stalwart young men wore long robes like dressing-gowns and white powdered wigs. They have their own robing-room ('**gown-room**' they call it) where they carry out their toilet before they appear in the large assembly hall. Here an immense number of legal wigs and robes are to be seen. But what struck me more than the wigs in this gathering was the extraordinary handsomeness of the men congregated here, exhibited not only in their strong, imposing, manly faces but also in their elegant and slim frames. Everywhere that one has the opportunity to see many members of the educated classes of England together, one is astonished by this phenomenon. I believe that there are

---

[25] [King Robert I of Scotland (1274 – 1329), known as Robert the Bruce, defeated an invading English army under King Edward II at Bannockburn in 1314 (see Chapter XXII), thus ensuring that Scotland continued as an independent kingdom until 1707.]

[26] [Charlemagne (ca. 742 – 814), king of the Franks from 768, was crowned Emperor of the West by Pope Leo II in 800. After his death he attained legendary status as a model Christian king.]

[27] [Stephen (977 – 1038) ruled Hungary as King Stephen I from 997 until his death. He was canonised in 1083.]

[28] [Vladimir Monomakh (1053 – 1125), Grand Prince of Kiev and ruler of Russia as Vladimir II, 'a popular, powerful, enlightened and peaceful sovereign'.]

[29] [Begun as an improvised causeway in the 1760s, the 'Earthen Mound' was finally completed as a roadway in 1835; it is now known simply as The Mound.]

[30] [Written *Kuhgate* in the author's German original.]

few countries where the physical appearance of the upper classes, of the men as well as of the women, is without exception as impressive and noble as in Great Britain.

The Advocates' Library[31] is one of the most superb and excellent in Great Britain. It is one of the few that have the right to call for a copy of every new publication. It contains no fewer than 150,000 volumes, and in addition also a large quantity of manuscripts important for Scottish history. I have always been gladdened to see our ancient German characters employed in those old English manuscripts. Even in the time of Cromwell people still wrote in the German script and printing to begin with was done everywhere in German characters, just as at that time old English books too were illustrated with wood-cuts produced by German artists.

I admit I was thereby gladdened by reason of a kind of German patriotism, and I enumerated in my mind all the countries in which in earlier times our scritchy-scratchy letters were widespread: Scotland, Ireland, England, Norway, Sweden, Denmark, the Netherlands, Germany and Scandinavia. The Netherlands and Great Britain have now almost completely lost our style of writing. The French or Italian alphabet is pervading Europe with increasing success, and even in Germany some people are already writing and printing not with German but with Latin characters. The French, the English and other nations wish with all their hearts that we might follow their example; for they say that our weird letters alone already constitute a great barrier to their learning our language. So therefore, in order to strengthen a little the unifying bonds that embrace the European nations, and then to pay homage to beauty and distinctness as well (for in truth there is no denying that the roman letters are much more beautiful than the German), we should renounce the patriotism which could for instance be associated with these stunted dots and jots of letters, and allow our twenty-five[32] little soldiers of the quill to enlist under the Italian or rather the European flag and put on European uniform. It is noteworthy here that the Russians too have recently made their letters more similar to the Italian.

The library rooms and the reading-areas of the Edinburgh advocates and the so-called '**writers to the signet**'[33] (more or less equivalent to our notaries public) are the most enticing, handsome and comfortable that can be seen of their kind and to be a bookworm here must confer true delight. Here can be enjoyed all the elegance and comfort of the London clubs as well as all the erudition and richness of a German library. I do not know whether anywhere on the Continent one can read books in such comfort as here. I could not resist temptation and had them bring me the wonderful masterpiece of Audubon's on American birds and their habits[34]; I revelled here in the double enjoyment of English comfort and the solitude of the American forest.

I saw the American mountain- and wood-pigeon (**Columba montana**) bill and coo among flowers in the calyces of which brilliant little humming-birds were concealed. I looked into the nest of the

---

[31] [Founded in 1682, it was conceived from the beginning as far more than a legal library and reflected the wide scholarly interests of the Scottish Enlightenment. From 1710 it enjoyed the privileges of the Copyright Acts, as the author points out. In 1925 the Faculty of Advocates donated all but their legal books (a gift of some 150,000 books and manuscripts) as the foundation of the newly established National Library of Scotland.]

[32] [In German printing and handwriting at this time the upper-case letters *I* and *J* were not differentiated.]

[33] [Members of an ancient society of Scottish solicitors who had the exclusive privilege of preparing crown writs.]

[34] [John James Audubon (1785 – 1851), ornithologist, artist and writer, was born in Haiti of French parents and later settled in USA. His *The Birds of America* was a huge, double elephant folio (100 cm. x 66 cm.) work in four volumes, published in Edinburgh and London between 1827 and 1838. Audubon had paid five lengthy visits to Edinburgh and his contacts there (including Walter Scott) were crucial to the eventual publishing of this unique and sumptuous work. It consists of 435 hand-coloured, life-size prints of nearly 500 bird species, several of which are now extinct; only about 200 copies of the complete work were produced. Among the subscribers to its publication were the University of Edinburgh and the Society of Writers to her Majesty's Signet. The copy belonging to the Writers to the Signet (which the author saw) was sold in London by Sotheby's for £13,000 in 1959 and that belonging to the University of Edinburgh was sold in New York by Christies for £2,300,000 in 1992.]

horrible and ugly young of the '**Common-Cormorant**' and could hear with astonishment the awful cry that they emit for the sake of a berry brought by the mother-bird, unsure as to which of the dear little monsters she should give it. American insects and beetles and butterflies seemed almost to flit around me, so well were they depicted, and from the picture the **Wood Duck** almost snapped flies out of one's hand. I pitied the horror in the face of a small frog that a **Night-heron** was in the process of devouring and I admired the adroitness and fury of two American eagles that were locked in battle with one another. Withal it was not necessary for me, as it had been for Mr Audubon, to expose myself to the cold tempests and the hot sun, the suffocating air of the swamp and the swarms of mosquitoes, or to become entangled with trees or rocks; on the contrary I sat the while on splendidly upholstered easy chairs, my feet rested on sumptuous rugs which cover the floors of the rooms and reading-areas of these libraries, and at times I simply looked around the splendid rooms to enjoy their furnishings and general appearance, or sometimes poked the fires burning here and there in the glowing fireplaces of the library. Whoever is a devotee of refined bookish pleasures must come to England; for only here will he find the books and the surroundings essential for literary indulgence.

Opposite the library of the '**Writers to the signet**', in the middle of the High Street, is a spot where all of us have stood together at one time, namely the place on which was situated that old prison of Walter Scott, **the old Tolbooth**[35], the dark walls and gates of which are so brilliantly illuminated in his novel '**the heart** [sic] **of Midlothian**'. In general, wherever one goes in Scotland, one is reminded of Walter Scott's romantic scenes; everywhere here one treads on a soil that offers the greatest historical interest and at the same time is enhanced with the magical light of the novel and of poetry. There exists perhaps no other instance of a land having been depicted – in all its circumstances, its nature, its inhabitants, its history, its earlier and present state – in a series of flawless sketches by one single individual.

Another remarkable Scottish literary celebrity is in this very High Street, established not far from the site of the old Tolbooth. I mean the firm of the brothers W. and R. Chambers[36], whose publications have recently achieved such an extraordinary circulation and fame in Great Britain. These gentlemen are **authors, printers, publishers, bookbinders** and **booksellers** at one and the same time.

I had the opportunity of visiting their fascinating establishment in which all the operations appropriate to those different pursuits are carried out simultaneously. We have, I think, nothing comparable to show since our 'dreamy and unpractical' writers usually lack completely the necessary grain of business enterprise, whereas in England it is not so rare to see the producer and the salesman combined in the same person. I think that these Messrs. Chambers began with very small operations. Now, however, they have expanded these very widely and at the present time they employ nearly one hundred people in their book-manufacturing firm; there they bring books to complete realisation, from their dark origins in the recesses of the brain to the moment when they are presented neatly bound in morocco or leather to the intending purchaser.

All the books, which they either produce themselves or cause to be produced under their management, are so well and usefully written and so splendidly calculated to the needs of the public that almost all their enterprises are successful. The principal writer of the two is Robert (I imagine the older brother)[37] who lives not far from Edinburgh in Fifeshire and the other W(illiam?) is the chief businessman. As outstanding and informed authorities on their native land, they have above

---

[35] [This building stood on the High Street in Parliament Square in front of St Giles' Cathedral and had served various administrative purposes as well as housing a jail. It was demolished in 1811 and 1817.]

[36] [The address was 333 High Street.]

[37] [In fact Robert (1802-71) was younger than William (1800-83).]

all dealt with Scotland and presented it in all possible respects. They have compiled and published a good history of the country, an elaborate description of Scotland (**Chambers'** [sic] **Caledonia**[38]), a shorter portrayal for travellers (**Picture of Scotland**[39]). In particular they have dealt with single episodes in Scottish history, such as the '**History of the Rebellion in Scotland in 1745 and 1746**'[40] and the '**Traditions of Edinburgh and Reekiana**'[41]. These works are so competent that they are widely regarded as valuable reference books for the history and statistics of Scotland and are available throughout the country in numerous editions.

I think the brothers first embarked on a literary and bookselling career with these and other original works that enjoyed great success. They then continued with much larger enterprises. The first was a journal that is also familiar to us, '**Chambers' Edinburgh Journal**'[42], in which for a very reasonable price they brought to people's attention a wealth of interesting news and well written descriptions, narratives and observations; then appeared their so-called '**People's Editions**' which they began in 1837[43]. In these they presented reprinted editions of especially good, generally established and generally popular works which could interest the public. The prices are extraordinarily cheap, especially when one considers that the books are printed very accurately and on good paper. For example, the works of the celebrated Bacon[44], with a biography of that great man, are available for eight pence, Locke's treatise on reason[45] for six pence, Graham's[46] poems for five pence. A comparison of these prices with those at which one would otherwise obtain these books will show that Messrs. Chambers have reduced many perhaps to a tenth, indeed to a twelfth and a twentieth.

Another of their enterprises is their encyclopaedia, **Chambers' Information for the people**[47], again a large work of which, as I was told in their establishment, they sold (or as the English say **they threw off**) no fewer than 70,000 copies. They sell roughly as many copies of their journals. And the majority of their other works that they have taken into their publishing house have such a massive sale that they are almost all stereotyped[48].

However, their most striking undertaking is their '**educational course**'[49] upon which they embarked several years ago and in which they present the principles, rudiments and elements of all sciences (**principles of elocution, rudiments of chemistry, elements of geometry etc.**) in small, elegant, recommendable and useful books. All these books can be immediately obtained in their shop in a number of bindings, either **sewed** [sic] or in **cloth boards** or **bound in marocco** [sic], as one wishes.

One can infer from all the foregoing the extraordinary influence the business affairs of these two brothers cannot but exert on the instruction and edification of people in Scotland, and also on

---

[38] [Actually written in 3 volumes (1807 – 24) by George Chalmers and printed by Cadell and Davies, London and Constable, Edinburgh.]

[39] [1827, 4th ed. 1840]

[40] [*History of the Rebellion in Scotland in 1745, 1746*, first published 1827.]

[41] '**Reekiana**' from the popular name of the city, already cited above, '**Old Reeky**'. *JGK* [These are actually two books, *Traditions of Edinburgh* (1824) by Robert Chambers and *Reekiana, or Minor Antiquities of Edinburgh* (1833), published anonymously but written by Robert Chambers. The name *Reekiana* had been proposed by Walter Scott and C.K. Sharpe for a similar publication by them, but in the event Sharpe gave their material to Robert Chambers.]

[42] [This first appeared in 1832, was renamed *Chambers' Journal of Popular Literature, Science and the Arts* in 1853, and survived for more than a century until 1956.]

[43] [Actually in 1838. By 1840 the number of cheap reprints numbered thirty-two titles.]

[44] [Francis Bacon, 1st Viscount St Albans, 1561 –1626, the English philosopher, scientist and essayist.]

[45] [*An Essay Concerning Human Understanding* (1690)]

[46] [James Graham, 5th Earl and 1st Marquess of Montrose, 1612- 1650, the Scottish soldier and poet.]

[47] [Begun in 1833, this was a series of broadsheets on various topics, later (1840) bound in two octavo volumes.]

[48] [i.e. transferred from set-up movable type to a mould and thence to a metal plate.]

[49] [Begun in 1835, this was a series of low-priced textbooks; over a hundred titles were finally published.]

literature in the whole of Great Britain generally[50]. All their undertakings are of the same genre as those enterprises that emanated from the Society for the Diffusion of Useful Knowledge[51]. This first made popular in England all the '**Penny editions**' and '**People's editions**', and this seed afterwards flourished with a prodigality like the potatoes in Ireland. A countless number of booksellers and writers followed in the footsteps of Lord Brougham and his colleagues, and out of this same cast of mind then emerged that which those industrious Edinburgh writer-publishers brought to fruition.

That reminds me of another noteworthy English book that belongs to this class of publication and bears the title '**A Million of facts**'[52].

This book is, I think, the most extraordinary example of the recent English passion for compilation and scientific culinary art; it can be compared with the finest extracts of oysters and meat-stock for soups and sauces, the finest essences of lemon and apricot for beverages and sherbet. For in one single volume it contains in short summaries the recognised facts and conclusions of all sciences on earth: a short chemistry, natural history, botany (with instructions for drying plants), zoology, physics etc., then a short geography of all the countries of the world, a history of Greece, a history of Rome, of the Middle Ages, of modern times, all in special sections, and not only these and the other usual areas of study, but in addition a short comparative conspectus of the measures, weights, coins of all European countries, and finally even a biographical lexicon, in which can be found a compendious description, containing the salient facts, of the lives of the most illustrious men in the world. The author of this book is called Philipps; he had previously been editor of the **Monthly Magazine**[53] for thirty years and so came to learn the requirements of the English reading public. If that Persian king from *A Thousand and One Nights*, who in vain commanded his magi to offer him his entire library in one single, short, easily assimilated book, had lived to our and Mr Philipps's times, then he would have seen his wish fulfilled.

In the Foreword to that book we read: 'Why should we read? – In order to assimilate facts. – What renders the educated man congenial in company? – The knowledge of facts. – What is better than everything else for his education? – An adequate number of facts. – What does Baco [sic] say? – Someone who thinks and works intellectually without possessing an adequate number of facts in the storehouse of his memory, is like a seaman who sets sail on an ocean without a compass. I therefore offer the public the best that one can be offered, facts – a million of facts! for twelve shillings! that means about nine thousand facts, nay nine thousand useful, interesting, pleasant and instructive facts for one penny. Nothing cheaper has ever been seen.'

Although admittedly this sounds somewhat blatantly self-promoting, nevertheless the book is without question (and I have read a large part of it with interest) very good in its way, brief, concise, clear, accurate and factual. I know of absolutely no country in the world in which such shameless self-promotion is the rule, yet with such great excellence of the proffered wares, as in England. This exceptional book has received a succession of editions and has also recently been translated into French.

With amazement I visited the various departments of Messrs. Chambers: the lower storeys, in which the high-speed rotary presses operate; an upper floor, in which was installed a select library of

---

[50] [See Introduction p. xv-xvi]
[51] [The Society for the Diffusion of Useful Knowledge, founded 1825, was a voluntary philanthropic organisation devoted to the advancement of education; for example, it pressed for the introduction of a science curriculum in schools and published maps of British towns. Lord Brougham (1778 – 1868) was one of the founders and an assiduous writer of educational works.]
[52] [Richard Phillips (1767 – 1840) *A Million of Facts, Connected with the Studies, Pursuits, and Interests of Mankind*, 4th ed., 1839, Collins, Keese, New York]
[53] [*Monthly Magazine and British Register* (1796 – 1842)]

historical, geographical and linguistic lexicons and in which several young men were working; another room, in which young girls were folding and stitching pages; then the stockroom in which, in different areas, all these productions of the intellect lay stored in an abundance of immaculate little volumes; and finally the sales department, where the current merchandise lay ready to hand in various pigeon-holes as in an apothecary's shop. In a word, I admired **en détail** this whole book-factory; it is without doubt one of the finest that can be seen. I cannot but repeat at least that all its products, as many of them that I saw, appeared excellent, useful, indeed outstanding of their kind.

I find walking in the main streets of a big city among the works of the hand of man equally as interesting as, or indeed even more interesting than, walking in the valley of a great mountain-range among the creations of nature. Whereas in the latter one beholds mountains and their strata, in the former one gazes on high ancient buildings and their storeys; in the one there flutter butterflies, song birds, owls and birds of prey, in the other are people old and young. In the one are pretty flowers and poisonous ones; in the other are comely figures and repulsive ones. If in the one are observed clouds and sunshine, in the other are scenes of quarrelling and peace of the most vivid kinds. If in the one the Titans and giants sleep their thousand year long sleep, in the other rest the dwarves and human beings in the churchyards – beside '**Canongate-church**' lie the poet Fergusson[54] and Adam Smith the national economist, and down beside the **Greyfriars-church**[55] Blair[56] and Robertson, the poet Ramsay and other famous people. By the Exchange, by the Tron Kirk where the South Bridge crosses over, and further down, where the High Street narrows to a cramped passage-way called the Netherbow, there is always a remarkable jostling crowd of people, both busy and idle.

In that selfsame narrow cleft in the street lies also, as at the corner of a foothill, the house of that famous Scottish preacher and reformer, *John Knox*, who in 1559 made his home and set up his pulpit here in the capital of the country, having previously inflamed the people in various other parts of the realm with his vehement and forceful oratory against '**Roman clergy and Popery**'. According to Robertson[57], the Earl of Morton said of him at his burial 'Here lies he who never feared the face of a man'. Knox bears to our own Luther a remarkable similarity that invites comparison between them, but Knox outdid the latter in roughness and fire, just as the Scots of that period outdid us in savagery and brutishness, and he also differs from Luther in many other ways. He died in that same little house that can still be seen today, and he is reputed to have often addressed the populace from its oriel-window. If the Earl of Morton did utter the above words at his grave, it is remarkable that Knox himself on his death-bed made a remark that in a way can be regarded as a complement to the Earl's pronouncement. He said in fact 'God knows, I never hated the persons of those men against whom I called up God's thunder and judgement'. There can still be seen a small portrait of Knox, I think carved in stone, at the corner of that house, and beside it the words '**θεος – deus – god**'. Astonishingly, this house is now a '**Gin-shop**'[58], and a very well-frequented one at that, and one evening when I went into it, I could scarcely make my way out again among the little divisions of the room, crammed full of people enjoying their '**Dram**' (a small glass of spirits). Indeed, if it were possible for Knox to appear once again in the Netherbow, he would now have to drive out of the Temple quite different people and things that are equally as pernicious as '**superstition and popery**'. If it is not in the power of the Edinburgh authorities to banish the gin shop and the scandalous trade in spirits from the Reformer's house, at least they

---

[54] [Robert Fergusson (1750-74); Adam Smith (1723-90).]
[55] [Also translated literally in the original as *Grauenbrüderkirche*.]
[56] [Hugh Blair (1718-1800) a popular preacher and critic who pronounced Macpherson's *Ossian* to be genuine; William Robertson (1721-93), author of *The History of Scotland* (1760); and Allan Ramsay (1684-1758).]
[57] [See this chapter, fn. 56.]
[58] [Also translated literally in the original as *Branntweinhaus*, i.e. 'shop that sells spirits'.]

should remove the portrait of the man as quickly as possibly from it and obliterate the aforementioned three words, which stand in too great a contradiction to the hustle and bustle below.

On several old houses in the adjacent closes I observed oyster-shells affixed to the walls in the chalk. The same can be seen in London in some portions of The Tower and on various other old buildings in England. I should gladly learn whether an ancient superstition is connected with this English habit of attaching oyster-shells to walls or whether they are intended to serve solely as purposeless decoration[59].

If one now descends the length of the Canongate, one finally arrives at Holyrood House, down in the valley, as I have said. Although this mansion is no longer inhabited by kings, it nevertheless continues to be regarded as a royal palace; it therefore still exercises all the ancient entitlements and benefactions of such a place, as, for example, the protection (remarkable at the present day) afforded to debtors who have taken refuge in its vicinity and who in a prescribed area round the palace may not be arrested. The poor people who live in the little houses in the neighbourhood of the palace, still occasionally have the opportunity to rent out their dwellings at a good price to high-ranking debtors. If a debtor succeeds in entering this area with his cash, timeously and in secret, then he is quite safe from his creditors. Thereafter he sends for his family. His wife and daughters can go freely in and out and visit parties and acquaintances in the city. He himself, however, may not be encountered outside the vicinity of Holyrood until he has managed to conclude a settlement with the creditors whom he eluded, a settlement which gives complete freedom to him and to them at least a little of their money.

In addition, there still exists here a complete royal Scottish household, the exalted offices of which are no less numerous than those of the Queen's English household and have the special feature that they are almost all hereditary; they are bound up with the enjoyment of certain ancient privileges and stipends for the families who possess them. So there is still a **Hereditary Carver**, a **Hereditary Grand Constable**, a **Hereditary Standard-Bearer**, a **Keeper of the great Seal** and several other such offices, which are held by the families of the Dukes of Argyll, the Earls of Lauderdale, Errol and so on. In Europe there still exist several such outdated frameworks of particular royal households where the king is absent, at least in actual bodily presence – Austria has the greatest number, France has none at all, England has this Scottish array of offices. To the Scottish household there even belongs a separate Scottish bodyguard, '**the royal company of archers**'[60], of which the Duke of Buccleuch[61] is the captain and the Duke of Montrose one of the standard-bearers. Ireland is known to have only a vice-regal household in which incidentally a bodyguard of the viceroy is to be found, '**His Excellency's Company of battle-axe guards**'. In England the armed royal bodyguard is more colourfully constituted. In that royal household there is a troop of armed gentlemen (**Band of Gentlemen at arms**), then life-guardsmen (**Yeomen of the guard**), and finally the splendid corps of the '**Horse guards**' (the bodyguard on horseback).

The Palace of Holyrood was formerly a monastery, founded by David I, and only from the sixteenth century was it inhabited by several Scottish kings. In point of fact only four kings lived here for the greater part of their lives, namely the last three Scottish Jameses and Mary of Scotland. Much older royal Scottish residences are the castles of Perth, Stirling, Linlithgow and Scone, which now lie mostly in ruins. It was Mary[62] or, as the Scots and English usually call her, '**Mary Queen of Scots**' –

---

[59] [One suggestion is that they are placed on walls to ward off the Devil. Allegedly, the Devil cannot cross water and these shells represent the sea.]
[60] [First organised in 1676, it received a Royal Charter in 1704.]
[61] *Buccleugh*
[62] [Mary Stuart (1542 – 1587) (Mary, Queen of Scots), the daughter of King James V (who died when she was six days old), was queen of Scotland from 1542 to 1567. Sent to France when five years old, she married the future Francis II and thus became queen consort of France until his early death in 1560. She returned to Scotland in 1561 to begin her

probably they always add this phrase in order to distinguish her from her mother, who was also called Mary[63], and from her cousin, Queen Mary Tudor[64] – whose short stay here actually gave this palace its great name. The extraordinary events in the reign of this beautiful queen have remained so faithfully in the memory of the Scottish people that the rooms in which she lived here in Holyrood are still in the same state as she left them in 1567. Moreover, these events are remembered so faithfully that, throughout the whole of Scotland generally, people still point out the different spots that have become famous on account of Mary, not only the place in which she was born but also the place in which she gave birth to James VI, and the place in which she remained in hiding, and the places where she slept, where she hunted, where she was imprisoned and so on.

'The German gentlemen in particular who come to Scotland always enquire conscientiously about our queen and look at everything most closely' said the old palace servant-woman who showed me Mary's rooms. 'I think they have a poem at home which tells of Mary and which is well known in Germany.' Indeed, Schiller[65] has instilled in us such a romantic affection for Mary of Scotland, the Maid of Orleans, Fiesco of Genoa, Don Carlos of Spain, the Bride of Messina and for other foreign names that, wherever we go in foreign lands, we look for traces and relics of them. Goethe has filled us with just such a love for the Court of Este, Clavigo's dwelling, Iphigenia, the Burghers and Counts of Brussels – a love that we might well devote to the heroes and great figures of our own German history and our own native-land.

Without doubt, of the rooms in Europe that are still exactly in the same condition as they were in the time of this or that person, those of the Queen of Scotland are not the most lacking in interest. For as little as these rooms were then respected by the conspirators who broke in to murder the queen's foreign favourite, Rizzio, as highly do they seem to have been revered by posterity for three hundred years. For in fact they still appear almost as if their occupant, the queen, had just left them and would soon return. It is rare, and it requires all kinds of exceptional circumstances, for the scenes of earlier, far-off events to be preserved for the history-lover down to the tiniest detail – to the draperies, footstool, table-cloth and other particulars – so that he seems to be much closer to these events and imagines himself, as it were, to be a witness of them. The exceptional circumstances that provided this pleasure for history-lovers here in Holyrood were probably the fact that after **Mary Queen of Scots** the palace was lived in by James VI for only a short time, and thereafter never again, so that everything here remained more or less in its original condition.

I have the impression, as I have indicated, that to some extent Mary also belongs to us Germans. I picture the joy Schiller would have had in seeing Mary's bedchamber here in Edinburgh and her little work-table (which of course was much rougher than similar pieces of craftsmanship of the same period that we have in Germany) and the candelabras that she brought with her from France (because she could not find anything of the kind in Scotland) and all the other things that are tangible testimonies of the actual physical existence of the Mary that dwelt in his imagination. I believe therefore that my German readers will not find it wearisome to hear something more about these rooms.

The principal room, namely the queen's bedchamber, is extraordinarily small and narrow. The Earl of Bedford, who wrote an extremely interesting letter on the twenty-seventh of March 1566 about the episode of Rizzio to the **Lords of the Council** in England, says that this room is only twelve feet

---

reign but, as a Catholic, met hostility from her Protestant nobles who finally rose in rebellion. She fled to England in 1567 but was imprisoned by Queen Elizabeth, who believed that she was plotting to gain the English throne, and finally beheaded.]

[63] [Mary of Guise (1515 – 1560), the consort of James V, was Regent of Scotland from 1554 to 1560 while her daughter was in France. See also Chapter V, fn. 6.]

[64] [Mary I (Mary Tudor) (1516 – 1558), the daughter of Henry VIII, was queen of England from 1553 to 1558.]

[65] [The references are to the plays of Schiller and Goethe that individually deal with the personages mentioned.]

square and that a bed and a table stood in it; furthermore a private staircase and a secret door led into it from the King's room and so these too are part of the scene at the present time.

On the ninth of March 1566, on a Saturday evening at eight o'clock Queen Mary, Lady Argyll, several other ladies and Rizzio were dining at this table. Rizzio was certainly her confidant but not her lover, as Robertson clearly maintains and the Queen's husband, Henry Darnley, falsely suspected. Suddenly the said secret door opened and the King[66] entered, followed by Lord Ruthven[67], who was armed, and George Douglas. These three had plotted against Rizzio – the barons, because they refused to tolerate the influence of a favoured foreigner, the King because he believed Rizzio to be loved by the Queen, and thought to perceive in him the only barrier that stood in his way to wield that power over the Queen's heart that he wanted to wield, and therefore also over the sceptre that she held in her hands. The palace had already been packed with troops by one of the conspirators, the Earl of Morton, and so the Queen and her confidant were powerless in face of the said persons entering through the secret door. Rizzio, who had his cap on his head, apprehended this at a glance and began to tremble as Lord Ruthven, whose naturally wild appearance had been made still more sunken-eyed and excitable by a severe illness from which he had scarcely recovered, ordered him to come forward, saying that there was no place for him here. Queen Mary, who was in the sixth month of pregnancy, took up the word against him and replied that it was her will that David (this was Rizzio's Christian name) should remain there. 'Nay, this dishonours you!' interrupted her consort Darnley, the King, who had insisted that they should seize him in no place other than in that bedchamber because he wished to accuse him in the Queen's presence. While the King was saying this to the Queen, the hollow-eyed Lord Ruthven, who was still so weak from his three-month-long illness, from which he had roused himself for murder, that he could scarcely walk and scarcely carry his weapons, approached Rizzio and took him by the arm, saying that he intended to teach him his duty better. At that David jumped up, overcome by fear, caught hold of the Queen's garments and hid behind her. She did her utmost to protect him. However, the King seized the Queen in his arms, tore Rizzio's hands away, and pushed him to the side. Ruthven and Douglas threw him through the Queen's bedchamber right out of the door into an anteroom where Lord Morton, Lord Lindsey and others of his enemies were assembled. Actually it was not their intention to murder him immediately but rather they intended to hang him the next day. However, as they saw him staggering out, pale and in the grip of fear, one of them, filled with contempt, pulled out his dagger and stabbed him on the body. Many others did the same, and so he fell to the ground with fifty-six wounds. At that moment the old palace servant-woman opened wide the door and made every possible effort to demonstrate to the visitors that a dark shadow on the floor was the bloodstain caused by Rizzio's murder.

The King and Lord Ruthven remained a long time with the Queen in her bedchamber. She implored her husband to cause no harm to Rizzio and at the same time berated him for being the author of such a treacherous and heinous deed. It is said that he answered that Rizzio had maintained more intimacy, and deeper intimacy, with her than he, the King, had enjoyed for two months, and hence for the sake of her own honour and his satisfaction he had given his assent to the seizure of Rizzio. 'Is it then the wife's duty to seek her husband?' answered Mary. 'It is your own fault if you deprive yourself of my company.' He retorted that whenever he had come, she had either not been at all ready to receive him, or had feigned illness. 'So be it, then' she replied, 'but now you have had your last of me and have made your farewell.' – 'That would be grievous', said Lord Ruthven, 'for he is Your Majesty's husband and you must do your duty in return.' 'Now why should I not leave him just as your wife left *her* husband?' Lord Ruthven answered that his wife was lawfully separated from him and indeed not on account of such a matter as the King complained of here. 'And apart

---

[66] [Though Mary was Queen Regnant, Darnley had been proclaimed 'Henry, King of Scots' the day before his marriage to her.]

[67] *Ruthven*

from that this was a common, lowborn man, an enemy of the nobility, a disgrace to you and a destroyer of the national wellbeing.' – 'Very well, but his blood will cost you dear if you spill it.' 'God forbid that,' said Lord Ruthven. 'For the more **your grace** shows herself insulted, the harsher will the world sit in judgement.'

Meanwhile her husband spoke little, and during the whole time she shed hot tears. Lord Ruthven, who felt ill and weak, let himself be brought a draught to drink saying 'This I must do by Your Majesty's leave!' and tried as best he could to persuade her to calm herself. But nothing then that was said to her proved effective.

In the meantime, when Rizzio's murder became known, there arose a tumult in the castle among the Queen's friends, for they believed that all their lives were at stake, and two of them, Huntly and Bothwell, escaped by leaping out through a window. Lord Ruthven hurried down to pacify the people. The King remained with the Queen, deep in conversation with her, and she invited him to pass the night with her; but he did not accept, excusing himself by saying that he was too sleepy. From this time on the Queen's distaste deepened into hatred and anger against him. She turned her love and favour to Bothwell; he afterwards murdered the King and the Queen married him after some months.

All these happenings, related so animatedly by the above mentioned Earl in his letter, but which of course were reported differently again by others, took place at *this* table, between *these* draperies, beside *this* door, and on *this* carpet upon which we were treading. But since, because of the present tasteful fragility of our factory productions, even the interiors of palaces are no longer provided with such durable furnishings, our own era will not bequeath any such interestingly appointed rooms in such a fine state of preservation to historians of three hundred years hence.

Near the apartments of '**Mary Queen of Scots**' is a long hall hung with an infinitely large number of life-sized portraits of Scottish kings and princes[68]. These, however, possess no great interest, firstly because the facial features are scarcely recognisable on account of the darkness of the colours and of the room, and secondly because many of the kings depicted here never even existed but are mere products of the imaginations of the writers of Scottish history. For it is remarkable that the latter, like writers of Irish history, took over the Celtic traditions of the ancient bards and in part literally believed them (even Buchanan did that). I believe that there are no other nations in Europe which have extended their historical claims so far back into the obscurity of past centuries as the Irish and the Scots, who are in this respect remarkable and unique; no others enumerate such long lines of kings both before Christ and after, or so precisely detail what occurred during the rule of each one of those kings, or know so exactly the character, way of life, the parents, grandparents, brothers and cousins of these fictitious kings. A writer of history can easily ignore their accounts and dismiss them as fables without further ado. But the psychologist and the ethnographer must know them and read them because they are an interesting psychological and ethnographic phenomenon. The Scots have carried this passion for inventing a national history for themselves, and thereafter thinking of it as actual history, so far that they have even made pictures of their imaginary kings and hung them in Holyrood among their Alexanders and Jameses, who were indeed once creatures of flesh and blood. **Maria Stuartus** is also among them, but in a bad copy. The best portrait of Mary Stuart is said to be in the possession of the Duke of Hamilton. Our woman of the palace showed us an admirable and accurate little copy of this painting in which the Queen's eyebrows, far apart and highly arched, impressed me as something striking. It is noteworthy that the Dukes of Hamilton, those powerful ancient Scottish dynasts, who once even came very close to possessing the crown of the country,

---

[68] [The so-called Long Gallery, containing 111 portraits, alleged to be of Scottish kings, painted by the Dutchman Jacob de Wit from his imagination for a fee of £250 in 1684.]

have been **Hereditary Keepers of Holyrood-house and Premier Peers of Scotland** right down to our own days.

Another part of the palace, that was destroyed by Cromwell's soldiers and rebuilt by Charles II, contains the entire long suite of rather uncomfortable rooms which were lived in by Charles X[69] and his family at the beginning of the thirties. Several of these rooms are hung with old woven tapestries from Arras, on one of which Niobe[70] is represented with her children as they are struck by Apollo's arrows. In three or four rooms only clouds are painted on the ceilings. 'They did not know what to paint when pressed for time' my companion told me, 'and so they painted these clouds.' The doomed House of Bourbon might well have felt ill at ease, one would think, in these dismal cloudy rooms, especially as the similarities of their own misfortune to that of the Stuarts, into whose house fate had brought them, lay all too near. As Niobe's children were struck by the arrows of misfortune, so the scions of the Stuarts and the Bourbons fell into a decline. Both families have experienced a revolution in their country that interrupted their reign – the execution of one of their crowned heads – a *first* exile (a Cromwell, a Napoleon) – a restoration, a second revolution and exile – a supplanter (William III and Louis Philippe) – and have both finally left a pretender (Prince Charles and Henri[71] V).

I fully understand why Queen Victoria never visited this somewhat melancholy old palace of the Stuarts when she came to Scotland, and preferred the fine comfortable residences of her wealthy subjects. People do say that Holyrood is now to be refurbished to receive the queen once again, who has acquired a predilection for Scotland. However, even if with effort and money the rooms can be made habitable again, the ancient melancholy memories and the ancient bloodstains cannot be cleansed from the palace. (The palace serving-woman assured me firmly and stubbornly that in spite of every endeavour Rizzio's bloodstains could not be obliterated by any means.) And then what a forbidding effect such a story as that of Rizzio and Mary could have on a young queen! It was claimed at the time that there had been scarlet fever in the palace and that the queen had not visited it on that account. However, at that my old woman of the palace shook her head in disagreement and doubt.

There are numerous other skilfully painted portraits in Holyrood, which in respect of history, as well as artist merit, offer no less interest, especially the portraits of several beautiful English ladies, for example, that of the Countess of Kildare by Sir Peter Lellie[72]. She is feeding a lamb with flowers, holds a garlanded shepherd's crook in her hand, and wears a hat trimmed with roses, which encircles her head like a halo. And Elizabeth Rich, daughter of an Earl of Holland[73], by Van Dyck[74], a beautiful lady from the time of Charles I. She is dressed in white and wears a blue shawl; it cannot rightly be discerned whether she is putting a guitar away or is taking it up. These are quite splendid pictures and one could wish that such enchanting originals as these English ladies might always meet with such painters of genius as Van Dyck and Sir Peter Lellie. There are also some striking pictures here by Sir Godfrey[75] Kneller, such as a young Earl of Breadalbane in Scottish dress, an old laird MacNab, also in Scottish costume, and an Earl of Breadalbane (Duncan

---

[69] [The Comte d'Artois, younger brother of Louis XVIII of France, had taken up residence in Holyrood in 1796, principally because it was a debtors' sanctuary and he was being pursued by creditors. He remained there until 1803, but returned intermittently. In 1824 he became Charles X of France but was forced to abdicate in 1830, whereupon he returned to Holyrood, remaining there till 1832.]

[70] [In Greek mythology, Niobe boasted of the number of her children. When they were all killed by arrows, she wept unceasingly and was turned to stone, but continued to weep.]

[71] *Heinrich*

[72] [Sir Peter Lely (=Pieter van der Faes, 1618 – 80) was appointed court painter to Charles II in 1661.]

[73] [Actually 1st Earl of Holland.]

[74] *Dyk* [Sir Anthony Van Dyck or Vandyke (1599 – 1641)]

[75] *Godefroy* [Sir Godfrey Kneller, originally Kniller, German portrait painter (1646 – 1723)]

Campbell) by Holbein. In a large throne-room, which was prepared for George IV in 1822, hangs a life-size picture of this monarch in magnificent Highland dress[76].

It is noteworthy that the Chapel Royal of the Palace of Holyrood lies in ruins. It is a part of the old abbey founded here by David I. Charles I had it restored, so people say, for the *English* liturgy and James II for the *Catholic*. But the Scots, who did not want either the one or the other, let it fall into ruins. These ruins, which immediately adjoin the palace, are very picturesque, especially the gate, which is an ancient Gothic piece of work, and the pillars which are almost all standing upright and surrounded by the graves of eminent Scots. Some still arrange to be buried here from time to time. 'They must pay seventy guineas **'fees'** for that' said my guide to me. On some graves one sees only a sword and a cross scratched on the stone; this must, I think, have been an old Scottish custom, for I have observed it in several other Scottish graveyards. In pride of place they still show Germans the altar in front of which **Mary Queen of Scots** was married to Lord Darnley, as well as '**Queen Mary's confessing room**'. But the most remarkable thing in this chapel is the so-called **royal vault** in which several Scottish kings from the family of the Stuarts are buried. People say that Cromwell's soldiers took the coffins and sold them. The bones were later gathered and laid out on boards. From outside, through an iron grating that was later erected in front of the vault for protection, they can be seen lying there. There are two skulls and some arm and leg bones. I have never seen royal bones exhibited in such a fashion as those of the Stuarts. I also saw a bottle lying among the bones. People say there are '**Records**' contained in it. The vault is painted black on the inside and on the black are sprinkled little patches of white which are meant to represent tears; Catholics always painted such tears on their mourning coats of arms when they displayed them at the death of one of their family members. So all then appears in the appropriate historical and tragic order: in the corridors of the palaces of the Stuarts are bloodstains which cannot be washed away; within the rooms, instead of cheerful pictures on the ceilings, clouds are painted; and, in their funeral vault, tears perpetually rain down on their naked bones – but only make-believe tears.

* * * * * * *

---

[76] [See Introduction, p. xx.]

V
The Forth

Holyrood near Edinburgh, Stirling Castle, Linlithgow Castle and Scone near Perth – these were the principal residences of the former Scottish monarchs. They are situated not far from each another in this broadest and finest expanse of the Scottish Lowlands opening out towards the east, beside the Forth and the Tay; these rivers flow into the sea here as neighbours, enfolding the beautiful county of Fife between them. After I had found myself somewhat satiated with the impressive townscape of Edinburgh, I set out for these other ancient royal seats, and first of all for Stirling, which is best reached by steamer on the pleasant Firth of Forth.

We embarked in the neighbourhood of Leith, the port of Edinburgh, which is reached by an excellent broad, perpetually busy, road. Our little steamer lay beside the *Trident*, an immense, splendid, ocean-going steamship which had just arrived from London and in honour of which a flag had been raised on Nelson's Monument on the Calton Hill in Edinburgh. **'She took her Majesty from this**[1] **to London'** said one of the passengers to me, as he was explaining the remarkable features of the ship. 'She' (that is, the *Trident*) 'was chosen instead of the *Royal George*.' (Ships are all called *she* by the English, even when they have a man's name.) The Queen had come on her, namely the *Royal George*, but she did not go fast enough. Since then the *Trident* has become a very famous ship. It is curious that the English, who as a rule have more neuter genders than we, nevertheless personify many things that we do not. So, for example, they turn every stagecoach into a *she* and even every country as well, for example, speaking of Scotland, they express themselves thus 'She is a very beautiful and interesting country'.

Very close to Leith is another little village called Newhaven which is famous in Edinburgh for its strange inhabitants and in which most steamships now berth. The inhabitants are a small fishing community of a little more than a thousand souls who have quite peculiar customs, build their houses differently from the neighbouring people, dress differently from them, and also seldom intermarry with them. The men are almost constantly occupied at sea, and therefore it can happen that the womenfolk here reign supreme on land and in the house. In Edinburgh, whither they take fish to market, these women are remarked on and feared on account of their strength, and they are so much the rulers in their households that when, for example, one of them marries and she does not appear to be sufficiently active, industrious and energetic, the other women expostulate and cry 'Why did she marry? Is she really in a position to earn bread for her husband and the family?' There is another fishing village near Edinburgh, namely the town of Musselburgh, the inhabitants of which also have many peculiarities, and who are said to be like the people of Newhaven. In the north of Scotland too, near Aberdeen, there are several small fishing villages of which the inhabitants have many oddities, and about whom it is believed that they are old Danish or Norwegian settlers who crossed the German Ocean[2] and retained their peculiar habits.

It is noticeable that fishing villages as a rule stand out from others. On the shores of the Baltic Sea there are, for example, fishing villages with Latvian inhabitants among a German population (in Prussia), fishing villages with Estonian inhabitants among the Latvians (in Courland), fishing villages with Swedish inhabitants among the Estonians (in Livonia and Estonia). On the Black Sea coast there are Cossack fishing villages among surrounding populations of Wallachian, Tatar or other stock. These are either remnants of the old populations of the country, who have remained on remote stretches of coast where they live half on the sea anyway with, as it were, only one foot on the land, or else they are roving settlers from overseas countries, who found it easy to put down

---

[1] [The word *this* was formerly occasionally used instead of *here*, especially in Scotland.]
[2] [Another name for the North Sea, common until the First World War.]

roots there, because they needed only a little land and this was willingly ceded to them. On the German coast of the North Sea too, there are several such ancient idiosyncratic family groups of fisher-folk, for example, the Heligolanders off the estuaries of the Weser and the Elbe, and various Frisian settlements as well.

The whole of the estuary of the Firth of Forth was full of little fishing boats, which we observed bobbing up and down on the water like seagulls. Sometimes they slipped past our steamer at very close quarters. The principal catch here in all these Scottish sea-inlets is herring and salmon. However, it was not yet the season for either fish, and I do not know what creature was the intended quarry of those boats at that time. On account of the situation of their land, the English and the Scots ought to be considered the oldest and best fishermen in the world, yet in fact it is not so long ago that they began to take advantage of the living resources of their seas so industriously. For until the latter half of last century, indeed even down to our own century, it was the Dutch whom the English and Scots allowed to take the fish from under their very noses, so to speak. Even now several kinds of fish are delivered to the market in London exclusively by Dutchmen. The Frisians, the Dutch, the Norwegians are the primeval fishermen and sailors, and probably all those fishing settlements on the Scottish coast that we have mentioned also originate from them.

There is something marvellous about such a lively estuary where the ships so busily bustle to and fro, like insects in a beehive. In the far distance we saw steamers and proud sailing-ships passing. And in between lay several small islands, remarkable for their unusual formation: Inchkeith, Cramond, and others. Some, which we passed close by, could be distinctly recognised as being of volcanic origin, probably formed of traprock or basalt. The little island of Inchmickery[3] looks exactly like a fortress pounded to pieces by a hundred cannon and completely in ruins. On the little island of Inchcolm[4] an old monastery lies between rock-strewn ruins. On several there are large and excellent oyster-beds[5] which, however, unfortunately do not belong to the poor people of Newhaven or similar common folk but to the Duke of Buccleuch and such like.

That monastery was founded by Alexander I when, on a crossing to Fife, a fierce storm drove him on to this island, where he was forced to remain for three days, and where he found no one other than a pious monk who provided him and his retinue with milk and shellfish. The Queen of Scotland too, Mary of Guise, was shipwrecked here at the Firth of Forth by Fife Ness and was there offered hospitality by the owner of Balcomie House[6], an old castle near the foothills. And yet another place on the coast, called 'St Margaret's Hope'[7] is the spot where a Saxon queen, Margaret of England, was also cast ashore.

At its mouth the Firth of Forth is about 10 to 12 miles wide – at Leith about five or six. Gradually it narrows to almost half a mile at Queensferry, only to broaden out again to between two and three miles inland. A distinction could therefore be drawn between an *outer* and an *inner* Firth of Forth. However, since on the far side of the said narrowing the water becomes fresh or at least **'brakish'**

---

[3] *Stone-Mickerey*

[4] *Inch-Colme* [Traditionally, Alexander I was shipwrecked here in 1123. An Augustinian priory was founded here of which the first extant charter dates from 1162. It became an abbey in 1235. The ruins are the best preserved of any Scottish monastic house.]

[5] [See Introduction, p. xvii.]

[6] *Balcomiehouse* [Balcomie Castle is near Crail and was the seat of Learmonth of Balcomie who received Mary of Guise (see Chapter IV, fn. 63) when she landed from France to marry James V at St Andrews. The ship was intended to put in at St Andrews but instead made landfall at Fife Ness; it was not shipwrecked.]

[7] *Margarethens Hoffnung* [Margaret was a Saxon princess who became the wife of Malcolm Canmore, King of Scotland; she was canonised in 1250. The ship in which she and her family had been fleeing to the mainland of Europe following the Norman Conquest was blown north by gales and ran aground in Fife.]

[sic] (half fresh and salt), so the English recognise the River Forth at that point and call this inner expanse of sea '**River**', although little is discernible of a flowing of the water there.

It is noteworthy that the same shape underlies all Scottish firths as a basic form. Thus the Firth of Tay has its narrow part at Portincraig[8] and the Moray Firth[9] has its equivalent at Fort George. Because of these narrowings, they divide into an outer and an inner expanse of water. At the narrow part itself there is always a ferry which goes from one county to another. It is principally steamships that serve these **ferries**. Here it was the Queensberry[10] Ferry between the counties of Fife and Linlithgow. Fife is one of the best, most fertile and most populous counties in Scotland and is depicted by the Scots as a little paradise. Moreover, at its heart lies the Eden Valley which, however, is commonly called '**the How**[11] [sic] **of Fife**'; it is famous for its fertility and the River Eden flows through it.

Fife, which is full of handsome estates, has no large town, though it has a great number of smaller ones that almost all lie on the Firth of Forth; it can be compared with the county of Wicklow in Ireland and Kent in England.

On the other side, towards the south, is the equally flat county of Linlithgow. Only to the west, straight ahead, can the hills of Stirling be seen to emerge gradually. If we compare the Firth of Forth with its brother in the west, the Firth of Clyde, then we must declare first that both are of extraordinary beauty, but that the advantage on the whole probably falls to that of the Clyde, since it leads right into the middle of the Highlands which conjure up more splendid and multifarious vistas on its banks. The Firth of Forth, on the other hand, leads into the heart of the Scottish Lowlands, and therefore proffers charming and delightful scenes of a different character on its banks: the country seats of the Earls of Moray[12], the Lords Elgin, and an old castle of the Stuarts, Rosyth Castle[13], in which also Cromwell's grandmother, who was a Stuart, was born.

As soon as we had passed the strait at the Queensberry Ferry we saw a large number of ducks on the water. The ship's captain told me that at this time of year the sea ducks (of which there are very many different types) and other sea birds begin to withdraw into the inner bay behind the rocks of the strait, and that later in winter so many follow them that often the small bays are completely covered with birds.

On board we had numerous passengers of every conceivable station in life and we set them down in the little towns and villages of the County of Fife and the other counties. In the time since steamship travel has penetrated into every river, into every bay, into every inlet here, all things in the country have changed, a multitude of new interconnections has evolved, innumerable human undertakings have been instituted, and therewith immense, unpredictable prospects have been opened up – all this to such an extent that any desire to speak of such things is lost: one has not the courage to embark on an analysis where every step leads directly into the imponderable. The world is in the grip of such tremendous progress that to observe this progress and describe it becomes almost impossible;

---

[8] *Portoncraig*. [This is the author's version of *Portincrag* or *Portincraig*, from the Gaelic *Port na Creige* 'harbour of the rock'. The word *Ferry* was added to the name and the whole later reinterpreted as *Ferryport-on-Craig*. The Edinburgh and Northern Railway Company bought the ferry rights in 1842 and created the name *Tayport*. When the town became a burgh in 1887, it took this name, *Ferryport-on-Craig* remaining as the name of the parish.]
[9] *Frith von Murray*
[10] [*Queensberry* is presumably a slip or misprint for *Queensferry*.]
[11] I have never been able to find what this word means, either in Johnson or anywhere else. I suppose it must be a provincialism. JGK [It is cognate with *hole* and *hollow* and means 'a hollow'. As a Scottish geographical term it is now spelt *howe*.]
[12] *Murray*
[13] *Rossyth-Castle*

is not needed.

the development of humankind more and more eludes historians, who must gradually acquire massive fists and a hundred arms and a thousand fingers, if they wish to keep hold of all strands.

Among our passengers, two above all interested me: an Italian by the name of Ortelli, from Rivolta[14] near Lake Como, and a Scottish preacher. From the former, the Italian, I realised for the first time that the remarkable spreading of Italians over the islands of Great Britain is continuing even into the north of Scotland. There are many places in Great Britain where the Italian incomers are much more numerous than the German, which is surprising, since Germans are much closer and more kin to the English than are Italians. There are also, I believe, far more Italians in English cities than in German (at least if we except the Austrian ones), which again is surprising, since we Germans have always had much more to do with the Italians. In some sectors of business this is quite definitely so, for example in music and in the making of barometers. For neither Italian musical performers nor Italian makers of barometers and thermometers in Germany are as numerous and as unexceptional as in England. Furthermore, the Italians in England are also teachers of music, makers of plaster of Paris figures, dealers in Italian merchandise, as they are in Germany. My friend had decked himself with barometers[15] from head to toe, back and front. He told me in his Italian-English that he was travelling across the whole of Scotland in this manner and was going '**up and down in the country**'. An Italian in Edinburgh assured me that there were a hundred Italians in the city, whereas scarcely half as many Germans live there.

The preacher was from Fifeshire, a man of powerful build and penetrating voice, who appeared to me to be a prosperous tenant farmer rather than a preacher. The others had already drawn my attention to him and told me he was a '**highfligher**' [sic]. Every fanatic in England is designated by this name, and especially those of the Scottish Presbyterian church who insist vehemently on the rights of this church and its inviolability. Since the Tories have been 'in' again, it is well known that there has been no amicable understanding between the Church of Scotland, '**the Kirk**'[16], and the government of Great Britain[17]. '**The Tories are broken in the church**'[18], 'we must stand up to them' said my cleric, as I started to speak to him about this animosity. 'They want to take from us **the power of the keys**, which, however, was given to us by God himself, and we cannot tolerate this; for that would mean that we would suffer people **to deprive him of his glory**.'[19]

I do not know how it comes about that from my youth I always imagined – and I think this is true of other Germans – that Presbyterian simplicity is accompanied by a certain modesty and tolerance, and even though long ago I learned otherwise from history, nevertheless I still cannot always properly reconcile myself to the contrary. And yet it is by no means the case. The Scottish Presbyterians, who wanted to re-establish in themselves the character and condition of the earliest

---

[14] [Presumably Rivolta d'Adda, about 62 kilometres south of Lake Como. Coincidentally, at this period a D. Rivolta was a barometer maker in Edinburgh.]

[15] [The area round Lake Como had for many years been a centre of home industry barometer manufacturing in winter for peddling to more northerly countries in summer. From the end of the eighteenth century very many Italian barometer makers had settled in the countries of the United Kingdom. This Signor Ortelli was one of at least seven by that surname making and/or selling barometers in England in 1842. Illustrations from that time show barometer pedlars carrying several barometers of almost a metre in length.]

[16] It is usually named in this way with the old Scottish (Saxon) word, while the Episcopal Church is called '**the church**'. In old documents the Scottish church is never called anything but '**the kirk**'. Now in the latest documents apparently it, itself at least, prefers to call itself '**the church**'. *JGK* [The word *kirk* is Scandinavian in origin, not Saxon.]

[17] [See the Introduction p. xxii.]

[18] [This alleged English 'original' would appear to be a back-translation of the author's German version *Die Tories sind in unsere Kirche hereingebrochen* (= 'The Tories have broken into our Church').]

[19] Since this was written, it has become known that that complete, quite utterly remarkable split has occurred, as a result of which 600 ministers with their supporters have constituted themselves as the separate **Free Kirk**. *JGK* [In fact a final total of 474 ministers (out of 1203) left the Church of Scotland in 1843 to form the Free Church of Scotland. See Introduction p. xxiii.]

Christians, have, however, by no means reproduced the humility, love and gentleness in their souls that we discern as the essential characteristics of Christian doctrine, and which manifest themselves in their clearest light in the founder of our religion. On the contrary, they are so far from it that they have imitated the first Christians in outward things only, while adopting great narrowness and harshness in respect of doctrines of faith and completely papal principles in respect of clerical power and rights. In this connection they describe their church as an apostolic church and demonstrate that the apostolic power to loose and to bind (**the power of the keys**, as they call it in all their writings) has come down to them directly from Peter. They contrast the power of the keys with **the power of the sword**, that is, the power of the state and their '**General Assembly**', with the Moderator at its head, regards itself as equally sovereign in Scotland in spiritual matters as is the state in secular matters; they fight for the inviolability of these rights just as fiercely, intransigently and ceaselessly as did the Pope against the Emperor of the Holy Roman Empire.

Apart from the Papal church there is no other in Europe that is so independent of the state, so sovereign, as is the Kirk of Scotland. In Russia and Poland the Tsar is also the head of the church, and likewise in Prussia and several other Protestant countries. In most Catholic countries the state exerts a significant influence on the church. In England and in Ireland the monarch is at the same time the spiritual head of the church, and his decisions and those of his parliament are binding on the church. In Scotland, on the other hand, the sovereignty of the Scottish church has been recognised since the last revolution and even since the Union of England with Scotland. The English kings repeatedly made the attempt to impose in Scotland too the principle that the sovereign of the state is also the supreme head in secular as in spiritual and ecclesiastical matters, but have no longer insisted on this principle.

However, it is naturally easier to put forward something in general terms than to implement it in detail and in particular to delineate the realms and the boundaries of secular and spiritual matters exactly. Several points have therefore always remained contentious in Scotland between secular and spiritual claims; these have never been definitively dealt with by Parliament and at various times have given rise to incidents of friction between church and state.

One of these points is, for example, the question how far the right of patronage goes: whether a minister nominated by a patron must be accepted unconditionally by the parish and ordained by the higher ecclesiastical authorities, or whether he can be rejected, and whether the parishioners have the right that no minister can be imposed on them against their will.

Since almost all benefices of ministers in the Presbyterian church have such patrons the question is very important. In many cases the Crown exercises this right of patronage, in a few the town councils (most of these are in Edinburgh), in others, equally few, **the communicants** themselves, but in the definite majority the great landlords, the marquises, dukes and earls. Thus, for example, the Duke of Argyll and the Duke of Buccleuch have the patronage of an extraordinary number of churches. So the Earl of Zetland has the patronage of 29 parishes on the islands of Orkney and Shetland and only six out of the 35 **parishes** on this group of islands do not lie in the patronage of this Earl.

People in Scotland have naturally been contesting this enormous power of the patrons for a long time, not only through the formation of so-called '**Antipatronage-societies**', of which there is one in Edinburgh and 26 others in association with it in other towns in Scotland, but also through repeated petitions to Parliament for the past 80 years, that the right should be legally granted to parishes to reject a clergyman nominated by the patron. Although this right has never been given so far, the understanding between secular and spiritual powers, especially under the Whig ministry, has nevertheless been reasonably good, either because the patrons (who, it is still worth noting, belong in part to the English episcopal church) nominated such candidates as were pleasing to the parishes, or because the courts of law decided more in favour of the communicants in cases of disputes arising.

Now, however, since the Tories and the English High Churchmen are at the helm again, the patrons have gained in stubbornness and insist strictly on the acceptance of their candidates. At the same time the highest court of justice of Scotland, the so-called '**Court of Session**', which follows the political colour of the government, is deciding disputes which come before it in favour of patrons and against the church. And not only in those cases in which the right of patronage was involved, but also in other cases this '**Court of Session**' has allowed itself intrusions on the rights and entitlements of the Church of Scotland and **has encroached upon the spiritual Privileges of the kirk**.

Just as the highest secular court is the '**Court of Session**', so the highest ecclesiastical court is the General Assembly of the delegates of the different synods and presbyterians [sic[20]], under the chairmanship of the Moderator and in the presence of a commissioner of the government, a **Lord-High-Commissioner**. This General Assembly has made objections to the '**Court of Session**', concerning the cases in which this court of law has enforced its decisions with the arm of the secular power; but these objections have been in vain. Equally futile has also been a request for a hearing in Parliament. Last year Sir Robert Peel made a speech which was very unfavourable to the claims of the Scottish church, and which was bound to displease the General Assembly very much. And since this latter body has now no further means at its disposal, it has appealed to the general public of Scotland and England (**they have brought their case before the country at large**) and passed – under the famous title dating from ancient Scottish revolutionary times, '**Claim of rights**' – a declaration and protestation against the arrogant assumptions of the '**Court of Session**', and of course of the government standing behind it. This document is so outstandingly remarkable and characteristic, not only of the spirit of this church itself, but generally of the Scots and especially of the nature and behaviour of its ministers, that here, where my desire is to contribute to the description of the country and nation, I could find almost nothing more typical to quote than the entire declaration, if the text were not far too long.

This '**Claim of rights**' is dated from 24th of May of last year (1842) and since it not only addresses itself to the Scottish nation (often also called '*the Presbyterian nation*') but generally to all reformed churches in the whole world as well, so it has naturally had a very extensive resonance, for there are Scottish Presbyterians scattered widely over the entire globe. There are seven presbyteries in England, 23 presbyteries in Ireland, several congregations in Holland, six presbyteries in Canada, four in Nova Scotia, two in New Brunswick, two in Australia, one in Guiana, several congregations on the foothills of Good Hope, in the West Indies, in the East Indies, in South America, in the North American free states. The Declaration begins as follows:[21]

'The General Assembly of the Church of Scotland, taking into consideration the solemn circumstances in which, in the inscrutable providence of God, this Church is now placed ... resolve and agree on the following Claim, Declaration, and Protest: ...

'WHEREAS it is an essential doctrine of this Church ... that "there is no other Head of the Church but the Lord Jesus Christ"; and that while "God, the supreme Lord and King of all the world, hath ordained civil magistrates to be, under him, over all the people for his own glory and the public good, and to this end, hath armed them with the power of the sword"... as

---

[20] [*Presbyterianer* 'presbyterians' in the original, presumably a slip for *Presbyterien*, 'presbyteries'.]
[21] [The author translates into German a catena of extracts from the Claim of Rights. These are given here in the original English wording of this document. As usual, words and phrases printed **in this type-face** are those quoted in English by the author.]

distinct from the "power of the keys" or spiritual authority ... yet "The Lord Jesus, as King and Head of his Church, hath therein appointed a government in the hand of Church officers distinct from the civil magistrate" ...

'AND WHEREAS the above mentioned essential doctrine and fundamental principle in the constitution of the Church, and the government and exclusive jurisdiction flowing therefrom ... have been, by diverse and repeated acts of Parliament, recognised, ratified, and confirmed; ... and thereafter unalterably secured by the Treaty of Union with England[22] ... ` (All points of English and Scottish statutes that pertain here are then specified and criticised.)

'AND WHEREAS ... the **Court of Session** ... have, in numerous and repeated instances, stepped beyond the province allotted to them by the constitution ... in violation of the constitution of the country, in defiance of the statutes above mentioned, and in contempt of the laws of this kingdom ... ' (All these decisions and prohibitions are then enumerated.)

'AND WHEREAS the government and discipline of Christ's Church cannot be carried on according to his laws and the constitution of his Church, subject to the exercise, by any secular tribunal, of such powers as have been assumed by the said Court of Session:

'AND WHEREAS this Church, highly valuing, as she has ever done, **her connection** on the terms contained in the statutes ... with the State, and her possession of the **temporal benefits** thereby secured to her for the advantage of the people, must, nevertheless, even at the risk and hazard of the loss of that connection, and of these public benefits – deeply as she would deplore and deprecate such a result for herself and the nation – persevere in maintaining her liberties as a Church of Christ, and in carrying on the government thereof on her own constitutional principles, and must refuse ... to consent that her people be deprived of their rightful liberties:

'THEREFORE the General Assembly ... DO, in name and on behalf of this Church, and of the nation and people of Scotland ... CLAIM, **as of** RIGHT, that she shall freely possess and enjoy her liberties, government, discipline, rights, and privileges, according to law, especially for the defence of the spiritual liberties of her people, and that she shall be protected therein from the foresaid unconstitutional and illegal encroachments of the said **Court of Session** ...

'AND they DECLARE that they cannot, in accordance with the Word of God ... and the dictates of their consciences ... carry on the government of Christ's Church, subject to the coercion attempted by the Court of Session as above set forth; and that, at the risk and hazard of suffering the loss of the secular benefits conferred by the State, and **the public advantages of an Establishment**, they must, as by God's grace they will, refuse so to do ... "**notwithstanding of whatsoever trouble or persecution may arise.**"

'AND they PROTEST, that all and whatsoever Acts of the Parliament of Great Britain, passed without the consent of this Church and nation, in alteration of, or derogation to, the aforesaid government, discipline, right, and privileges of this Church ... as also, all and whatsoever sentences of courts in contravention of the same government, discipline, right and privileges, are, and shall be, in themselves void and null, and of no legal force or effect; and that, while they will accord full submission to all such Acts and sentences, in so far – though in so far only – as these may regard civil rights and privileges, whatever may be their opinion of the justice or legality of the same, their said submission shall not be deemed an acquiescence therein, but that it shall be free to the members of this Church, or their successors, at any time

---

[22] [At this point the author inserts words meaning *and by the oath, which the sovereigns of these kingdoms swear to maintain the constitution of the same and of that Treaty of Union.* In doing so he is paraphrasing rather than quoting.]

hereafter when there shall be a prospect of obtaining justice, to claim the restitution of all such civil rights and privileges, and temporal benefits and endowments, as for the present they may be compelled to yield up ...

'AND, FINALLY, the General Assembly call the Christian people of this kingdom, and all the Churches of the Reformation throughout the world, who hold the great doctrine **of the sole Headship** of the Lord Jesus over his Church, to witness, that it is for their adherence to that doctrine, ... that this Church is subjected to hardship, and that the rights so sacredly pledged and secured to her are put in peril; and they especially invite all the office-bearers and members of this Church, who are willing to suffer for their allegiance to their adorable King and Head, **to stand by the Church** ... and to unite in supplication to Almighty God, that he would be pleased to turn the hearts of the rulers of this kingdom ... or otherwise, that he would give strength to this Church – office-bearers and people – to endure resignedly the loss of the temporal benefits ... and the personal sufferings and sacrifices to which they may be called, and would also inspire them with zeal and energy to promote the advancement of his Son's kingdom, in whatever condition it may be his will to place them; and that, **in his own good time**, he would restore to them these benefits, the fruits of the struggles and sufferings of their fathers in times past ... and thereafter give them grace to employ them more effectively than hitherto they have done for the manifestation of his glory.'

I maintain that this document is truly one of great interest since it stands as a phenomenon of our time, one in the series of many other **Claims of right** that have emanated from the same church. Furthermore, anyone who now travels in Scotland without being acquainted with it would not comprehend the ferment that is seething in the land. To those who would like to have a clear picture of the Scots and their character, it also gives a very good idea of the way in which a large number of Scots are wont to think and express themselves. For it must not be imagined, for instance, that the expressions that occur in that proclamation are chosen because of the seriousness of the subject and are not found elsewhere. No, on the contrary, just as papal phrases have been repeated always and unchanged in all papal bulls for a millennium in the same way, so in this document many Presbyterian phrases appear which are found in every record of the Scottish synods and General Assemblies. And not just there – one can multiply such phrases a thousandfold and imagine that they are heard in everyday life, daily and continually, from clerics as well as from the laity. From the laity too, I repeat; for it is fundamental to the nature of the Presbyterian church that the laity is not at all so sharply distinguished from the clergy and that all of them have, so to speak, a certain priestly tincture. I must abstain from making this even more graphic with some intriguing examples from life, since I believe I would run the risk of giving my readers the impression that I do not wish to treat sacred objects with the solemnity due to them; that is certainly not my intention, for, as an ethnographer, I merely want to depict what I saw and heard.

Only in this way could I correctly understand such expressions as my clerical friend used to me on the steamship. **'The tories will break in the church, and we cannot bear it, -- and now we are fighting'** (in Scottish pronunciation this sounds like 'fechting') **'together.'** The same man had been in Germany too, and he called the Germans **'simplehearted creatures'**. He had also seen Sundays in Dresden, Frankfurt and other German cities (**I saw the sabbath at Dresden**) and murmured with a look of regret and despair towards heaven something to the effect that there was not the slightest respect for the Sabbath there. About the Rhenish towns he expressed himself thus: he had been surprised as to the extent that he had found them **high in catholics and popery**. The goal of his journey, however, had been **Geneva**[23], and he counted himself lucky to have seen this city of Calvin, which is a kind of Zion for Scottish Presbyterians. (In the course of my travels I heard many Scots expressing the pious wish **'I should like to see Geneva'**.) On the way this **'Highfligher'** of ours

---

[23] [This form would appear somewhat exotic to German readers, since the German name of the city is *Genf*.]

left us in a small place in Fife. However, another clergyman, pleasant and educated, remained behind for our consolation and he invited me to visit him in his **'manse'** and **'glebe'**, as they call in Scotland the minister's house and the arable land with which the parish is endowed.

We travelled up the majestic Forth as far as the point where it becomes a completely narrow river and where a lack of water – it happened to be ebbtide – compelled us to leave our steamship and continue our journey to Stirling in a small boat. This steamship was called 'Victoria' and its sister ship, which sails up the Forth in rivalry with her and belongs to the same company, is called 'Prince Albert'; this pair of names is now encountered everywhere among English steamships. The river winds in numerous semi-circular bends up to Stirling, and town and castle and hills slipped by us, now to the right, now to the left, now behind, now in front. The banks presented the most enchanting variety of scene. This last stretch of the Forth as far as Stirling is also wondrously beautiful. As one travels along it, the most delightful diversion is afforded by the splendid abbey of Culross (where the river is still broad), by the little town of Kincardine[24], by the town of Alloa (with its old tower and the seat of the Earls of Mar), by many reminders of Robert Bruce (whose trail is incidentally to be found almost everywhere in Scotland), by all kinds of remains of Roman forts (which one stumbles across in abundance, at least in the Lowlands), and by a host of other things; it would not be so easy to expatiate here on their multifarious historical and romantic interest.

'What a magnificent country this is, what a wealth of the most interesting things in one small area!' I remarked to my Scottish companion. 'I cannot comprehend why your compatriots do not prefer to travel in this country, constantly traversing its length and breadth, rather than giving themselves the trouble of seeking out other lands that in actual fact are far less beautiful.' 'The truth is this', replied my friend, **'in a philosophical point of view, men like variety'**.

* * * * * * *

---

[24] There is another Kincardin [sic] in Perthshire. *JGK* [In fact, there are numerous Kincardines in Scotland.]

VI
Stirling

We finally landed at Stirling and walked through the town to the inn, where we all very much enjoyed a small nourishing luncheon.

There is a remarkable low range of hills that extends through the Lowlands here near Stirling in the direction of south-west to north-east, parallel to the Grampian Mountains. It begins not far from Dumbarton near the Clyde Valley, runs past Stirling and Perth and ends near the sea not far from Montrose, and it has a length of some 80 miles. The highest points of these hills rise to between 2,000 and 2,400 feet. In two places the range is broken by wide gaps, which are much broader than the **Porta Westphalica**[1] of the Weser, firstly by the waters of the Forth (and in this opening the town of Stirling lies on and beside the remaining fragments of mountain and rock) and secondly by the Tay. The latter opens into the Firth of Tay and on its banks, in the gateway of the breach, lies Perth, the Fair City.

Although without question this range of hills forms one geological unit, it has nevertheless various names. The middle portion between Tay and Forth is called **'the Ochill-Hills'**, the part beyond the Tay **'the Sidlaw-Hills'**, and the third part to the south beyond the Forth **'the Campsie-Hills'**[2]. Between this series of hills and the Grampians, parallel, as we have said, to them, stretches a large flat valley called **'Strathmore'** ('the great valley'). Several parts of this valley again have their special names. Thus the plain by Stirling to the north of the hills is called **'the Carse of Stirling'**, and the plain to the south of the hills, which, however, no longer belongs to Strathmore, is called **'the Carse of Falkirk'**. There are a great number of such so-called 'carses' (small plains) in Scotland.

In Stirling I was fortunate in that a keen, patriotic, helpful and knowledgeable guide and friend escorted me to all the beautiful and interesting places in the town and its surroundings, and with his observations and tales made every ruin and stone, every prospect and vista, even more enjoyable and pleasant than nature herself had made it.

First and foremost we climbed up to Stirling Castle, for this castle with its splendid outlook is so much the pre-eminent point of interest that one must give it pride of place above everything else. What was striking to me, as we went up through the main street of the town and across its marketplace to the castle hill, was its extraordinary resemblance to Edinburgh, which is so strong that one can call Stirling a complete smaller copy of that royal seat. However, the similarity mostly concerns only the old part of Edinburgh; for although Stirling certainly has been blessed with not a few pleasant new houses in the outer periphery of the town, not such a great influx of new residents has taken place hither as it has to the capital of the country, and the miniature version of an adjoining New Town is almost completely lacking.

As in the High Street and the Castle of Edinburgh, so there are also several old mansions in the High Street of Stirling, built in a solid style, in part with ornate architectural decorations. These buildings include: the mansion of the Regent Earl of Mar[3], whose descendants[4] were the **'Constables'** or **'Keepers'** of Stirling Castle; the mansion of the Earl of Stirling (Sir William

---

[1] [A gorge, 800 metres wide, on the River Weser between the towns of Bad Oeynhausen and Minden.]

[2] [Modern names and spellings are *Ochil Hills, Sidlaw Hills,* and *Campsie Fells.*]

[3] *Marr*

[4] [This must be a slip for *ancestors* since the building in question was begun in 1571 by John, 5th Lord Erskine and 6th Earl of Mar. The Erskines had been hereditary keepers of Stirling Castle since 1360.]

Alexander[5]), the philosophical poet at the court of James VI and the tutor of Charles I, who made him an earl; the tower, in which Buchanan[6], the Scottish historian famous throughout all Europe, lived and wrote. The last was also tutor to James VI. What sage teachers, what unlettered pupils!

Between these remains of the past and the ruins of an abbey we wandered up to the Castle itself. This sits on a basalt rock which, like the cliffs of Fairhead in Ireland, falls abruptly away on one side in mighty pillars. A path which runs along at the foot of this precipice offers splendid vistas. The ancient basalt columns, which bear the remarkable decoration of huge ivy bushes that partly conceal them – a decoration which we are otherwise accustomed to see only on man-made columns – rise vertically upwards on one side, and on the other the attractive plain opens out. On this plain the many beautiful meanderings of the Forth can be seen stretching away in the direction of the sea. The river appears to find it difficult to take its leave of the broad valley, and it vacillates to and fro until it delivers itself up to the salty waves of the ocean which comes to meet it here, so expansive and so majestic.

On the top of the rock, which itself has different levels, higher and lower, stands the castle; it actually consists of various sections. It is one of the four castles of Scotland that, in consequence of the Treaty of Union, must still be kept on defence alert, and so we were not permitted access to many batteries of cannon, many wall projections. We would otherwise fain have gone up to every one of them, so inviting did every corner, every view, every sight appear to us.

It is a thousand pities that so many reports of travels are being published, for, while each one of us has a few words to describe what he has observed, no one any longer trusts himself to compose an extended account, from fear that the same may have been better said elsewhere. One often finds places, for example Stirling Castle, where one would like to indulge in a flow of eloquence and describe everything very clearly and accurately and painstakingly. However, one is then afraid that it has already been written about too often, one does not then dare to rely on the patience and the interest of his readers, so much of whose time has already been taken up and who perhaps have been disappointed; and so the reader, who perhaps would like to hear something more graphic and in greater detail, loses his gratification. Because of these many descriptions that we encounter, the art and science of portraying countries and journeys is suffering almost total decline.

Professor Thibaut[7], the mathematician from Göttingen, always wished that his students had never heard anything of mathematics, or that they had forgotten again what they had acquired of it, so that he could erect the beautiful edifice of mathematical theorems in their minds on an even and unprejudiced foundation. The Scottish traveller too could equally well wish that his readers had never heard anything of Stirling Castle, of the Forth, of Strathmore and indeed of Scotland. Then certainly he would best be able to set to work and describe. However, since one does not have the confidence to assume this, and since one is always concerned not only to present old things in a novel way, but also above all else to present new and unknown things, so the undertaking remains but a sorry patchwork. So one has to make a virtue out of necessity and hope that the writer nevertheless will still occasionally encounter an uninvestigated fact or at least an unenlightened reader.

The foundations of the oldest buildings and fortresses in Stirling Castle are so old that it is impossible to discover a time in which a castle has not stood on this hill. The greater part of the

---

[5] [(Sir William Alexander (ca. 1567 – 1640) moved to London after 1603 and became Secretary of State for Scotland in 1626.]

[6] [George Buchanan (1506 – 82), 'the finest writer of the tongue of ancient Rome since the age of Augustus'.]

[7] [Bernhard Friedrich Thibaut (1775 – 1832) had been one of Kohl's teachers at Göttingen and was renowned for the elegance of his lectures and for his kindness to his students.]

fortifications, however, as they now are, dates from Mary of Guise, who took refuge here with her French troops, and later from Queen Anne. A Parliament House[8], built by James III[9], a palace of James V and a Chapel Royal of James VI are the most notable buildings.

The Parliament House very typically stands beside the king's Palace, as a part of it, as it were, and in that fact can be recognised the character of these parliaments; they were no more than the king's households and they also never dissented from the sovereign – every dissension that the kings of Scotland encountered in their country attacked them from quite other quarters, never from their parliament houses. Incidentally, Scottish parliaments were held in Edinburgh, Stirling, Perth and also in other towns. For these assemblies were no more tied to one location than were the residences of the German emperors and the imperial Diets in Germany.

James V's palace is a model of tastelessness – which is to be counted a rarity in a king's palace. It is incomprehensible how such lack of discrimination could prevail at a royal court (especially at one where a French princess became queen) that out of it could come such abominable mythological figures as adorn the wall of this palace. But it is right that these grotesqueries should not be destroyed, for as a specimen of the history of taste they too are interesting. Naturally, however, it would be more agreeable for us if the destructive reformers who came after James V had preferred to choose such buildings as these for their depredations, rather than so many splendid abbeys.

In the Chapel is still to be seen **Knox's pulpit**. Such Knoxian pulpits are exhibited in several Scottish towns, as in Germany several pulpits of Luther, Zwingli and other reformers are still seen and cherished. These pulpits are the veritable relics of the founders of our religion, who founded their new edifice simply with the Word and on the Word.

As in Holyroodhouse there is the Rizzio Corridor, so here in a part of Stirling Castle is the '**Douglas-room**', a closet in which King James II (1452) stabbed the Earl of Douglas because he refused to be dissuaded from the alliance against the royal interests which he had formed with several other barons. It is seldom, on the whole, that kings themselves have been murderers. However, in Scottish history this has been the case several times.

> '**Ye towers, within whose circuit dread**
> **A Douglas by his sovereign bled,**'[10]

Sings Walter Scott in his '**Lady of the lake** [sic]' about these rooms in the castle. In fact, murder committed by the consecrated person of a sovereign is an especially horrible deed. For firstly, the sovereign imperils the sacredness of his person by employing physical force against physical force, and secondly, all his subjects and household are filled with terror, since, if the *sovereign* himself does not shrink from committing a crime, they will all feel themselves unsafe in the face of his enormous power. This explains why the murder of a subject, perpetrated by the king's own hand, remains almost as long as the murder of a king, committed by a subject, in the memory of the masses, whilst one might think on superficial consideration that, on the contrary, they would tend to forget it as something unimportant and ordinary, given the magnitude of royal power.

The Stuarts had great affection for Stirling Castle, and more Stuarts lived there than in Edinburgh. James V is especially remembered here, as is Mary, Queen of Scots, in Edinburgh. This king had the habit, like Haroun al-Raschid[11], of going down in disguise from the eminence of his castle to his

---

[8] [The Great Hall.]

[9] [It was still being built in 1500 in the time of James IV.]

[10] [Also translated in a footnote.]

[11] [Harun al-Rashid ibn Muhammad al-Mahdi ibn al-Mansur al-'Abbasi (766 – 809), ruler of an empire that stretched from North Africa to Central Asia. He figures in many of the tales of *The Arabian Nights*.]

subjects, and of not only appearing among the people but of also carrying out acts of charity among them. There is a path down by the incline of the castle rock which James often trod on this excursions and which is called the '**Ballochgeich** (that is, 'the windy pass' in Gaelic[12]). Since people were accustomed to see the unknown gentleman coming down on this path, so they called him, when they spoke of him among themselves, '**the Gudeman of Bollochgeich** [sic][13]' (the good man of the windy pass) or also '**the Laird of Ballochgeich**'.

Now the whole castle was full of Scottish troops (mountain Scots), for whom several buildings served as barracks. They were almost all tall, well-proportioned, indeed handsome men. Some squads were drilling, other guards were standing sentry, still others were amusing themselves in the ancient halls of the castle with the '**Bagpipe**'. For the evening they had announced a play that was to be performed by some **Amateurs** from their number in the castle hall and about which I read badly written advertisements in every corner.

I saw here for the first time the striking Highland dress which we have not seen in Europe for many years. In Napoleon's time it was as familiar in Spain and even in Germany as was the costume of the Cossacks[14], the Bashkirs and other nations. In the comprehensive European peace of the present day each nation is forgetting how other nations appear, and such things should therefore now be called to mind afresh.

It is well known that the Scots pride themselves that their national dress is inherited from the Romans. Roman soldiers are said to have introduced it into Scotland and caused it to be adopted among the Pictish dwellers of the mountains. However strongly most Scots believe this and however many of their respected historians affirm it, nevertheless the matter seems rather improbable. For, in the first place, the Scottish national dress has only a somewhat slight similarity to the Roman military uniform. Secondly, *that* part of Scotland in which this mode of dress especially, indeed almost exclusively, prevails or rather prevailed, is the Highlands; yet the Romans did not occupy the Highlands at all, or occupied them only to a limited extent. It is difficult to believe that the Picts, who were so inimically disposed towards the Romans and were engaged with them in almost uninterrupted combat, would have renounced their old national costume in favour of the Roman way of dress. In fact, a nation which had borrowed nothing, absolutely nothing, other than clothing from another – neither language nor customs but only and alone the outer covering – would be a peculiar phenomenon; and it would be an equally great phenomenon to find that it was in these most distant Caledonian mountains that the Roman dress had been preserved complete and almost unchanged, and that there remained no further shred of it in the whole of the rest of Europe. The similarity of the Roman [sic] chlamys[15] with the Scottish kilt may be, and will probably in fact be, a purely coincidental one. That it can be otherwise is not easily conceivable. However, the possibility is certainly there. Only, the matter would now have to be demonstrated somewhat better. If this proof were forthcoming, that fact would indeed be interesting for the ethnographer, and then, faced with this Scottish costume, he would remember the Latin language, which has remained, in equal isolation, at the other extremity of the Roman Empire, among the eastern barbarians, the Wallachians[16].

---

[12] [Spelt *Bealach Gaoitheach* or *Bealach Gaothach*.]

[13] [Usually quoted as 'The Gudeman of Ballangeich']

[14] [Cossacks were Russian and Ukrainian peasants who had fled to the southern borders of the Russian Empire and had come to regard themselves as a separate social group. Bashkirs were a Turkic people from the Ural Mountain region. Both groups had provided regiments in the Russian army that had fought in the German-speaking territories against the French during the Napoleonic Wars, as had Scottish soldiers in the British army (see Introduction p. xxii), not only in Germany but also in Spain and elsewhere.]

[15] [The chlamys was a short cloak worn in Ancient Greece by men.]

[16] [Wallachia was a principality between the Danube and the Transylvanian Alps; it became part of Romania in 1861. The Romanian language is a descendant of the Latin spoken in that area, namely the Roman province of Dacia.]

The essential thing about Highland dress is above all this, that a lady is never presented with the embarrassment of having to utter the word *trousers*, for the good reason that the Highlanders have no trousers at all. This circumstance imparts to the costume its attractiveness, for there is no doubt that because of trousers the legs, more than other parts of the body, usually lose their natural shape and are transformed into two very ungainly posts. The outer garment of the Highlander is very short, but it falls in many folds and therefore lends the middle portion of the body a certain fullness and breadth. This outer garment is called 'kilt'. Since it is of very heavy material and, as mentioned, has many folds, it cannot easily be lifted up by the wind and so the wearer feels himself very warm under it, especially since in addition a large heavy leather purse, made of goatskin, hangs down over it in front.

Over the kilt is usually worn the 'plaid', which, like the kilt, is made of the colourful checked Scottish cloth, the tartan. This plaid is simply a large shawl, which is thrown over the shoulders and fastened over the chest and the back. It is the only piece of Scottish clothing that is in use among all classes in Scotland instead of the overcoat, and it is also worn universally in Northern England among the common people. I did not see it on soldiers and I do not know whether the plaid belongs to their uniform[17]. The cap is a very attractive piece of headgear, which as a rule is decorated with an eagle's feather or even with a whole fluttering crest of feathers, and finally the footwear consists of sandals, which, like the Roman ones, are tied with coloured laces that criss-cross on the calf[18].

I think that there are two regiments in the English army which are dressed in this way[19]. Among the people in the Highlands themselves, however, this national dress is being increasingly lost, just as generally every European national costume is becoming more and more rare. It is said that there are only a few valleys in which the Scottish kilt is still commonly worn. As a rule it is only a few old people who favour the kilt. Usually, however, the young are made to wear the national apparel up to a certain age, not only almost universally among peasants, but frequently among the nobility, partly because the costume is cheaper, partly because it is held to be beneficial, healthy and toughening for children.

We went into one of the castle halls in which we heard the sound of the bagpipes. These Scottish bagpipes sound much louder and shriller than the Irish, especially those that are intended to drown out the thunder of battles. They are also constructed after a different pattern from the Irish. Those that serve as regimental instruments for the soldiers are naturally especially elegant. There are twelve martial bagpipes in every regiment and two in every company. The Scots adore the sound of this their national instrument to an extraordinary extent. In Edinburgh the bagpipe is heard being played at every street corner. 'When we hear the bagpipe in battle, **then we go through the very Devil**', said the corporal to me who showed us the bagpipes hanging on the wall and performed some melodies on them for us.

At the foot of the castle hill towards the south lie the royal gardens that are said to have been laid out as early as 1315; under the Stuarts they were the scene of many a knightly joust, about which the Scottish chronicles tell. Now they are completely covered with grass. However, in the shading of the lawn the old plan of the gardens is still clearly recognisable: in the middle the hill called **'King's knot'**, the paths radiating from it, the perimeter line of a circle that surrounded the hill etc. Then there is also **'the Ladies' hill'** from which the fair ones watched the knights' **'Tournament'** and many other interesting things. But the ear has no time to listen to all the instructive anecdotes of the

---

[17] [The plaid was in fact part of the full uniform of a Highland regiment at the time.]

[18] [This was not so; it may be that the author was misled by the short stockings that were worn. Alternatively he may be describing pumps worn for Highland dancing.]

[19] [At least three are shown in contemporary illustrations as dressed in this way: 42nd (Highland) Regiment of Foot (the Black Watch), 91st Argyllshire Highlanders, and 93rd Sutherland Highlanders.]

kind guide, for the delighted eye leads it astray, continually returning to the beautiful landscape which lies open in front.

It seems to me that there is no doubt that the prospect from Stirling Castle is the most entrancing of its kind that the Kingdom of Great Britain offers, and since this kingdom itself is one of the loveliest countries in Europe, so this castle deserves one of the most highly-valued accolades. The great beauty of the scene is the reason for presenting my apologies to my readers for returning to the subject yet again. Here, before this broad gateway to the hills at Stirling, described above, three rivers unite into one, the Allan, the Teith[20] and the Forth. The meanders of the last in particular are fascinating, for it forms one loop after another. The tongues of land resulting from this are called '**Links**', and since these fluvial peninsulas are fertile in the extreme, there is the following old rhyme about them in Scotland:

> **'A link o' the Forth**
> **Is worth an earldom o' the North'.**[21]

Although the time of year was already quite far advanced, nevertheless all these links were covered with the most beautiful, freshest green. The black basalt rock of the castle rises up amid this green sea like a high throne, designed by nature for the master of the realm. The immediate vicinity of it is flat. At some distance away stand, like the bearers of high office of the realm, the pillars of the gateway to that castle, crags that are in part equally precipitous and even higher. The realm itself stretches out further in the direction of the sea and into the interior of the land. Towards the sea the view dissolves into blue. Towards the interior, however, the great pyramids of the Grampian Mountains loom in the distance like gigantic frontier guards, one after the other adorned with green and now also with snow and dark boggy ground, uniformed like a regiment of mountain Scots in their '**Highland-Garb**'.

The level floor of Strathmore, the great valley[22], is scattered with a number of hamlets and villages, whose inhabitants one imagines to be fortunate. There remained to us one more day, a not very pleasant one, as is unfortunately all too common in these districts, which, against all justice and fairness, Apollo treats somewhat unkindly. If we had met with a sunny day, I think Stirling Castle would have been the very spot to make the traveller give up all plans of journeying further. But in the end the rain descended upon us and drove us off from that incomparable scene.

* * * * * * *

---

[20] *Teth*

[21] [Translated in a footnote in the original.]

[22] [*An Srath Mòr* in Gaelic, literally 'the great strath'. Strathmore is commonly taken to extend from Perth to Stonehaven, but sometimes from Dunbartonshire to Stonehaven. The author seems to adopt an intermediate interpretation. See Chapter VII, p. 60.]

VII
Drummond Castle

I therefore took my leave of my friend in Stirling and sought refuge under the roof of my hut, namely my travelling hut, by which I mean the stagecoach[1]. In it I journeyed that evening in the company of my amiable Presbyterian parson into the middle of that beautiful valley of Strathmore to view the Drummond family's castle, which is outstanding on account of its grounds and gardens. The road thither leads first up into the valley of the Allan, at the foot of the Ochil Hills, past the villages of Lecropt[2] and Dunblane[3]. Six miles after Dunblane we passed an old Roman camp, which is said to be the finest and most complete of its kind that exists in Scotland[4]. It has a length of over 1,000 feet and a breadth of 900 feet, and is surrounded by triple ramparts and ditches. It is called 'Agricola's Camp' and is said to have been built by that commander for 20,000 of his world conquerors in 83 AD. The ramparts and camp sites, overgrown with grass, are now grazed on by cattle, and in one of the portals that are still distinctly recognisable we saw a triumphal arch, decorated with foliage and erected in honour of our German Prince Albert. This gate stands directly facing the edge of the Highlands, and Agricola had without doubt often entered through similar triumphal arches when he returned victorious from his incursions into the Highlands. Quite recently Prince Albert had similarly entered the camp, but for a peaceful exploration of this scene of warlike tumult.

From this Roman camp to the Drummonds' castle extends a flat stretch of countryside called **'the Moor of Ochill'**[5], and on this moor on a low piece of ground stood a small hut; perhaps it stands there still. As Mr Chambers tells us, this hut was inhabited until 30 years ago by an old woman who was commonly called 'the Empress of Morocco's mother'. This woman's daughter had, like many Scots, wanted to emigrate to America but, some 60 or 70 years ago, on the voyage thither had been taken prisoner by a Moroccan privateer. She was made a slave and taken to Morocco into the harem of the Emperor, who became so enamoured of her that he elevated her to become one of his spouses. As Empress this person entered into a correspondence with her relatives in Scotland, and thus what had happened became known. Her two sons whom she bore to the Emperor are even said to have later claimed support from the English on one occasion, quoting in favour of their request the fact that they were of British blood on their mother's side[6].

Not far from the said Drummond Castle there is a little village called Muthill. Since my **'Reverend friend'** lived in its vicinity, I determined to pass the night here, and in a little inn found every desirable amenity: a helpful and talkative old woman innkeeper, a pleasant, clean room, a bed (as usual in England half an acre in size), and milk, whisky, **'Porridge'**, a hot **'Brose'** (meat soup)[7] – in

---

[1] [Stagecoaches were closed carriages, usually drawn by four horses, which plied between two places along a series of stages, hence the name, though the coach itself came to be referred to as *the stage*. These stages were usually ten miles apart and at them horses were changed. Stagecoaches came into use in the late 17th century and, as roads improved, stagecoach routes became increasingly numerous, thus the first stagecoach service between Glasgow and Edinburgh was introduced in 1749. As railways were built, the number of stagecoach routes decreased. See also Chapter X, fn. 2.]

[2] [Lecropt was a village between Stirling and Dunblane with some 500 inhabitants in 1800. Due to rural depopulation and the growth of the adjacent town of Bridge of Allan (see Chapter XXI), it became abandoned in the early 19th century.]

[3] *Dumblane*

[4] [Ardoch Fort, Braco]

[5] [Properly *Muir of Orchill*]

[6] [Helen Gloag was born at Mill o' Steps in Muthill parish in 1750, daughter of the village blacksmith. Her mother died and her father remarried. Helen sailed for America but the ship was attacked by pirates from Morocco; she actually did become the favourite wife of the Sultan Sidi Mohammed bin Abdullah and hence Empress of Morocco and did have two sons. Presumably, therefore, *Empress of Morocco's stepmother* would have been a more accurate description.]

[7] [This inaccurate gloss suggests that the author was confusing the words *brose* and *broth* and that it was with the latter that he was served. Broth is soup; brose is made by pouring boiling water or milk on to oatmeal or peasemeal.]

short everything agreeable that can be wished for in Scotland. However, since I found that all these things satisfied my mouth etc. but not my heart and my head, I therefore had them show me the way to the schoolmaster[8] of the village; I found him sitting alone by his fireside and he hospitably permitted me to sit the evening with him.

Village schoolmasters are a class of person whom a traveller eager to learn must not neglect in any country. For they belong to the outermost edge of the educated class and, of those who think, compare and reason, it is they who are nearest to the basic population. They have knowledge of the people and their customs at first hand, just as foresters, hunters, fishers, farmers etc. have knowledge of the nature of land, animals, plants, climate at first hand. Thus there has generally accumulated among village schoolmasters such a considerable treasure-house of folklore, especially a greatly detailed knowledge of their rural locality and the customs of their village inhabitants and neighbours, as is not found even among clergymen, who labour in far higher and more remote spheres. The ethnographer and the statistician can, if they proceed critically, extract immeasurably much from the small treasure-caskets of village schoolmasters, and if these small hoards in every land could only be amassed together, then a veritable exchequer would result.

First of all, my pedagogic friend was in himself an instructive phenomenon to me. For I found him, as later I found several of his colleagues, to be very intelligent and well-informed. His rooms were hospitable, tidy, and, more than this, elegantly furnished, and I silently compared them with those of our village schoolmasters in Saxony; I found the latter much more modest, and was surprised that Scotland had made such progress in such a short time, since we know that until the middle of the last century its financially comfortable village schoolmasters could still be counted on one's fingers.

I expressed to my friend my happy astonishment at his circumstances and he said that he was indeed truly content but that on the whole there prevailed a great dissatisfaction among the Scottish **parish-schoolmasters**, especially on account of the salaries that they received. I remarked to him that the same complaint is also common among our German village-schoolmasters, because their salaries are likewise very meagre.

'How high are they?' he asked.

'They vary,' I replied. 'Some have perhaps 100, even 150 thalers, but many only 50 thalers and many even still much less than this.'

'How many pounds are there in a thaler?'

'Seven thalers make up a pound', I said.

'So 50 thalers are about...?'

'Seven pounds!'

'What?' he cried in horror and sprang up from his seat, 'seven pounds emolument for a teacher?'

'Yes, seven pounds!' I said. 'How much do you receive, then?'

'I know no one in Scotland who would have less than 40 to 50 pounds. However, the average income is 70 to 80 pounds and many go up to 150 pounds[9]!'

---

[8] [Most likely William Davidson mentioned in the June 1841 Census; he was then aged 35.]

[9] [These are impossible figures. Forty pounds would have been a very high salary and many schoolmasters existed on less than twenty pounds.]

'What?' I said, horrified in my turn and now also jumped up from my seat. We stood in front of each other both utterly confounded. '150 pounds, that is 1050 thalers? In Germany a baron is content with this income! And you dare grumble about it?'

'Yes, he said, 'we complain! But just consider how expensive everything is here. Coffee (**best Jamaica**) costs (**rosted** [sic]) 2 shillings, **row** [sic] **sugar** 8 pence a pound, chocolate is even dearer, and tea is not cheap either, and then how dear are joints of beef and pork, raisins and pudding and everything that goes with that?'

'Yes, of course,' I answered, sitting down again, 'that is true.' But our schoolteachers are content if they simply have bread in the house, I thought to myself.

Among Scottish ministers, too, complaints about their scanty income have always been loud, for almost everywhere the Reformers who destroyed the abbeys and monasteries let the associated property and income slip away from them, and it fell into the hands of the secular lords; later, in spite of all remonstrations, they were able to gain back nothing of any real substance. However, there is no doubt that none of our German village preachers would imagine that he had grounds for complaining, if he had as much income as the worst paid minister in Scotland. The humblest of them of whom I heard, had as much as 150 pounds annually, apart from a '**Manse and Gleb** [sic[10]]'. Among the Scottish clergy there are neither such rich incumbents nor such poor vicars as among the English.

It is well known that popular education in Scotland is making extraordinary progress, and my friend told me that in his district there prevailed the greatest eagerness among the people to learn something themselves and to have their children well taught and educated. People are not compelled to send their children to school, and it excited the greatest astonishment in my friend when I remarked that this happened in Saxony. He said they came of their own free will, and it would be accounted a disgrace if anyone did not send his children to school. Indeed, it would simply not cross anyone's mind not to do so.

'People,' he said, 'would in no wise tolerate such an obligation here, and it would certainly be the best means of creating an aversion to school and education.'

He was of course speaking principally only about the Scottish Lowlands, on the borders of which we now were.

In the Highlands, the Celtic language, Gaelic, is still a great hindrance to the dissemination of good education, which can only progress on the wings of the Norman-Saxon tongue. For only in the latter is life, intellectual keenness, activity; it is the language for writing and higher thought. All people of culture conceive a liking for it of their own volition. It is almost impossible that in the same country two languages and two literatures could flourish together to the same extent. One *must* oust the other – none more strongly than the authoritative English language the Gaelic tongue! – and everything that Celtic societies and Highland patriots now do for it will not stop its complete ruin.

Indeed, for a hundred reasons one must wish, however much it is to be regretted, that the extirpation of Gaelic should be completed as soon as possible, for the good of the people themselves[11]. Now in point of fact this extirpation seems to be making speedy progress. My friend named for me several

---

[10] [Properly *glebe*.]

[11] [Other opinions are clearly possible. This question was a source of debate in the nineteenth century in the wider context of changes to the educational system and it obviously figured in the conversation between the author and the schoolmaster.]

glens in the neighbouring **Comrie-parish** (already part of the Highlands), in which Gaelic was almost universally spoken 40 years ago and in which English is now spoken almost everywhere. Later in my journey I myself found a number of similar examples and traces of the, so to speak, recently eradicated Gaelic language.

If one considers the antiquity of the Germanic language and race in Scotland, it appears as a sheer miracle that the Gaelic language, which never had a written literature[12] to support it, resisted the inroads of the Germanic speakers for so long. Even Tacitus tells us that the Caledonians (in the Lowlands) were of Germanic race! What battles might these Germanic Lowlanders have joined with the Highlanders even before Roman times![13] What victorious struggles of the Germanic Danes and Norwegians[14] with these same Celtic Highlanders ensued afterwards! And then followed the whole long development of the Saxon[15] settlements, which established themselves here, as in England and, uniting with the previously established Germanic elements, formed a powerful force against the Celtic Highlanders. Yet it required the entire dynamic energy of our own times, armed with primers and schoolbooks, with journals and newspapers and literary equipment of all kinds – the entire unconquerable energy of our own thousand-resourced times – to seize ancient Gaelic, like so many other remnants of language, by the root and tear it from its saddle [sic]. Nevertheless, even so it will still require much time before the Gaelic babble has completely ceased in every glen and on every ben.

Very much, I think, has been contributed to the victory of English in the Highlands by the improvement of agriculture, and especially by the introduction of sheep farming, which, like so much else, dates from the middle of last century. The fact is that formerly, scattered everywhere in the glens of the mountains, many small hut-dwellers lived, who, between quagmire and rock, as in Ireland, worked a little plot of land for their oatmeal-bread and pastured a tiny patch of bad grassland with scrawny cattle. In more recent times a large number of these remote glens have been **cleared**[16] of their inhabitants, often with force. In ancient times, when clans existed, the wealth of a nobleman was assessed according to his adherents (**followers, retainers**) and such a small hut-dweller was still worth something to his lord, the owner of the land, even if he could produce food only for himself. After the dissolution of the clan system, however, the lords had to seek other sources of income. They therefore pushed out of the way these small hut-dwellers, who brought no profit and who could no longer be of service with their persons, and drove them from their miserable little farms; the latter were given over to sheep-grazing, along with the neighbouring stretches of mountain that had been little or poorly used by the hut-dwellers' cattle.

In the meantime the manufactories in the Scottish towns had arisen, trade in the ports had quickened, and even in the larger agricultural villages an improved system of agriculture had been established which therefore not only could sustain more people, but also needed more manpower. Hence the Highlanders, driven by the sheep from their lonely mountain homes, found accommodation in these places of manufacture and of trade, and in these villages. The population of the country moved, in short, from the dispersed sites in which it had found itself until then into more densely populated locations; and it is just this change, I maintain, that has contributed

---

[12] [It is not clear what exactly the author means by *written literature* or to what period he is referring, but an increasing amount of printed Scottish Gaelic had appeared from the mid-18th century onwards so that by 1842 this statement was certainly not true.]

[13] [There is no evidence to support this. Speakers of Gaelic, the author's 'Highlanders', did not begin to arrive (from Ireland) until the 4th or 5th century, by which time the Romans had left. The 'Germanic Lowlanders' came even later.]

[14] [This is misleadingly oversimplified. Suffice it to say here that the Norwegians were in fact finally defeated at the Battle of Largs in 1263 by the Scots. There were no Danish settlements in Scotland.]

[15] [There were no Saxon settlements in Scotland. The incomers in the southeast spoke Anglian.]

[16] [For a note on this view of the Clearances, see the Introduction p. xxi]

especially much to the victorious progress of the English language, as it has to education in Scotland generally.

That abolition of the clans in the Highlands took place in 1746 after the defeat of the last Scottish revolution[17] and of the last Stuart Pretender, and it introduced into Scotland a new spring with a thousand blossoms, which have now ripened to the finest fruits – a spring, of course, with violent and bloody storms (as is well known, it was Cumberland's cavalry[18] whose incursion marked the beginning of that spring). All clans were thereafter abolished by the English, and one of them, which had characterised itself by unrestrained savagery and cruelty, Clan MacGregor, was even proscribed completely at that time[19]. Many MacGregors – the well-known Rob Roy was a MacGregor – were shot, executed, killed, and it was ordered that thenceforth no MacGregor at all should exist. The name was completely forbidden. Thus at that time the MacGregors fled in all directions and hid themselves and concealed their name. Some went over to the Campbells and called themselves Campbell and others to the Drummonds, whose name they took. Here too, in the village of Muthill, so my village school master told me, there were several who were still known to be MacGregors, although they called themselves otherwise in public. Some had recently come out with their old name again[20], but many had still retained a double name; thus he knew of one man who always signs himself 'James Drummond', but in his family and by his friends he is called 'James MacGregor'.

The other clan names still continue to exist. And, of course, through the abolition of the clans the members of the same, who formerly dwelt together in one district, became scattered throughout the wide world, and there now scarcely exists any place in Scotland where MacGregors and MacDouglases and MacPhersons and other clan names are not found among the inhabitants. In spite of that, however, the former situation has not become so indistinct that in particular districts particular clan names are not the most predominant and most common; indeed there are still many glens in which the old clan name is unquestionably that which is found among the most inhabitants. So, in the district in which I now found myself, most people bore the name 'Drummond' and are descendants of the members of that famous old clan which, throughout the entire county of Perth, was, beside the Stuarts, one of the most important and respected. For the head of this clan of the Drummonds, or their **'Chief'**, or, as it is in Gaelic, their **'Cean'**[21] (which word the English write and pronounce **'ken'**), this **'Cean Drummatich'**[22] (the Chief of the Drummonds), was, at the same time, Earl of Perth. However, since 1716 this venerable title has become a so-called **'extinct peerage'** or a **'forfeited title'**. It was taken away from them because of their allegiance to the Stuarts. However, the Drummonds are still called by many **the noble family of Perth**, and there is still said to be a Drummond **who claims and represents this title**. Of such forfeited titles Scotland has more than England, and Ireland more than Scotland.

The heads of the Drummonds, the Chiefs of the clan, always resided in Drummond Castle, that castle near Muthill. This direct line died out recently in the male succession and the surviving

---

[17] [As has been pointed out, this was a dynastic uprising; it was only partly supported in Scotland. See the Introduction p. xix]

[18] [See Introduction p. xx. The appropriateness of the metaphors *spring*, *blossoms*, and *fruits* is, to say the very least, highly questionable]

[19] [This had in fact been a reimposition in 1693 of a proscription of the MacGregors originally imposed in 1603 but repealed in 1661. The MacGregors had obviously attracted attention for their behaviour before 1746 and indeed before the Union.]

[20] [The penal statutes against the MacGregors had officially been repealed in 1774, almost seventy years before the author was writing.]

[21] One of the Scottish kings, Malcolm III, is also called '**Cean mohr**', that is, 'the big head' or 'the big chief'. *JGK* [*Cean* is properly *ceann* and *cean mohr ceann mòr*.]

[22] [Properly *Ceann nan Druimeineach* or *Ceann nan Druiminnich*.]

female **Heiress** was Clementina Drummond, who married Lord Willoughby de Cresby, the **Lord-Great-Chamberlain** of England. When the Queen of England visited here on her journey, this English gentleman represented the 'Cean Drummatich' and the Drummonds, under their flag, stood in order, dressed in their clan colours (which are red, green and black) to greet the Queen. The mother of King James I, Queen Anna Bella[23], was also a Drummond.

The Drummonds of Drummond Castle are the principal bearers of this name. However, besides them there are a number of other important families who bear the name 'Drummond', such as the 'Drummonds of Strathallan', the 'Drummonds of Comrie', the 'Drummonds of Blairdrummond', the 'Drummonds of Hawthornden', the 'Drummonds of Keltie, the 'Drummonds of Kinnoul'. These are mere so-called '**Cadets**' of the principal Drummonds in Drummond Castle, that is, the younger lines who probably – and in some cases also demonstrably – branched off from the main Drummonds. Several Scottish peers are also from these Drummonds and belong to the most prominent families of the realm as for example, the Earls of Kinnoul and the Earls of Strathallan. Besides these noblemen, many **commoners** also have the name 'Drummond'. In London there is a famous Drummond Bank[24]. I met several **Dr** Drummonds in England, and round Muthill and Comrie there are many farmers called 'Drummond'. And so from this account my readers will have a quick survey of an entire Scottish clan of this kind. Just as all these Drummonds have the same surname, so they all bear the same coat of arms.

Before surnames and family coats of arms were generally common, there was, as Robertson says, within each clan a patronymic or local description of some kind that was common to all and which everyone adopted who had made themselves subservient to a leader, either by virtue of blood or through free choice and vassalage. By this acceptance of a common name, an association that was at least in part artificial, became gradually transformed into a natural one, while the blood-relationship, which at the beginning was, at least in a great measure, quite imaginary, was after one or two generations taken for a real one. Everyone then of their own free will followed a chieftain, whom they regarded not only as the owner and lord of their estates but also as the head of their lineage, and they therefore served him not only with the loyalty of vassals but also with the love of kindred[25].

Not far from this district which the Clan Drummond controlled and controls is the land of the Campbells, to which I journeyed after some days. Both clans, the Drummonds and the Campbells, were included by that pious man, the husbandman Maxton of Cultoquhey[26] in his prayers every morning. He added the following words to the Lord's Prayer:

> '**From the greed of the Campbells,**
> **From the ire of the Drummonds,**
> **From the pride of the Grahams,**
> **From the wind of the Murrays,**
> **Good Lord, deliver us.**'[27]

---

[23] [Annabella or Arabella (ca. 1350 – 1401), wife of Robert III.]

[24] [Founded in 1717 by Andrew Drummond (1688 – 1769), a member of a cadet branch of the family. The business was acquired by the Royal Bank of Scotland in 1924 and the premises became known as 'Drummonds Branch, The Royal Bank of Scotland'. Among its eminent clients were King George III, Lord North, Humphry Davy, Whistler and James Smithson (founder of the Smithsonian Insitute).]

[25] [See Introduction p. xxi concerning this view of the clan system.]

[26] *Caltoguey* [This 'Cultoquhey Litany' was written by Mungo Maxton (1687 – 1763) with reference to four powerful neighbouring families bearing these names who unsuccessfully coveted the Cultoquhey estate in Strathearn.]

[27] [In the original text there follows a translation into German. *Wind* is translated as 'tempest' (*Sturm*) rather than 'bombast', which seems to have been the original intention. However, Mungo Maxton was noted for various humorous interpretations of *wind*.]

The next morning at nine o'clock I went to breakfast with my friend, the parson. In England such invitations to this first meal of the day (or early morning coffee) are very often received; in Germany, we take it so very early – as soon as we rise from bed – that as a rule we really cannot expect to see company at it in our houses. In England, however, where breakfast is taken at nine or ten o'clock, there are often very numerous gatherings at it. In Scotland such a breakfast is once again a quite singular affair. Firstly, the family worship that forms part of it is much longer and more solemn than in England. Secondly, as far as food is concerned, meat is not so plentiful at it; on the other hand, fish, sweet things and bakery goods play a correspondingly larger part. Fish is almost never absent from a Scottish breakfast, and I must admit that I find this dish somewhat insipid as the first morsel of the day, especially as it is prepared in Scotland without a flavoursome sauce, simply roasted dry on the griddle. Equally unbelievably tasteless are the so-called '**Barley-skones**' [sic]. These are flat, round cakes which are made of barley and water and on which the fire seems scarcely to have even flickered from afar; for the dough is so undercooked that the flour remains sticking between one's teeth. On the other hand, I found the honey in this northern land as sweet and as aromatic as in other countries that are richer in flowers. The parson told me that during this fine, splendid, mild, dry summer a rare marvel had taken place in his bee garden, namely that the bees had swarmed twice.

A young man breakfasted with us, a relative of the minister, of whom they said **he is before the Presbytery** now, that is, he had finished his studies and was now awaiting his placement. As far as I could tell, my friend was an '**Antipatronage-man**' or, as the Scots also say, a '**Nonintrusionist**'. This last party name refers to the principal question of dissent within the Church of Scotland, touched on by us above, namely whether a minister can be imposed on the parish (**intrude on the congregation**) by patrons and the secular authorities, or not. To the afore-mentioned people are opposed the '**Patronage-men**' or the '**Intrusionists**' who maintain that the patron has this right. Moreover, to the Intrusionists belong many ministers who do not want to set themselves against the distinguished patrons and the secular power, or act so energetically. They are therefore also called '**Moderates**'. A third name for their opponents is lastly that of '**Evangelicals**' because in evidence for the independence of the '*Scottish Apostolic and Missionary Church*', they refer to the Gospel, the Evangel. The name '**Highflighers**' is only a '**Nickname**' that is given by others particularly to some very zealous members of these Evangelicals. Incidentally, as is already apparent from the account we have given above, there are two ecclesiastical parties, which can be traced through the entire history of the last three centuries in Scotland. The Evangelicals of our days are the descendants of the Covenanters against James[28], just as, for their part, these Covenanters of James at that time were in turn the successors and imitators of the Israelites, who, at the Red Sea in dangerous circumstances, made a '**covenant**' among themselves[29] to defend their religion.

After breakfast we went out into the open and sought the way to Drummond Castle, which stands a few miles distant. The weather was splendid, the mountains in their glory encircled the fair plain in which we found ourselves, and round us there were even poetical dogs barking. The reason for that is that my friend, the minister, had received from the '**Ettrick-Shepherd**', shortly before his death, a fine '**Colly**' [sic] (Scottish sheepdog) that was bounding beside us. The collies of Scotland are famous in Great Britain for their intelligence and their other good qualities; like all sheepdogs in the world, I believe, they have long hair, a bushy tail, a pointed face, and a greyish colouring, and the Ettrick Shepherd, from whom our collie came, is famous for his poems. He was a young shepherd,

---

[28] [This may refer either to the King's Confession of 1581 by which the young James VI denounced all forms of Papistry or to the National Covenant of 1638, from which the Covenanters took their name, drawn up during the reign of Charles I.]

[29] [In fact, according to the Hebrew Bible it is the God of the Israelites who makes a covenant with them at Mount Sinai, promising that they will be a holy nation on condition that they obey him; see Exodus 19: 5-6. The crossing of the Red Sea is described earlier, in Exodus 14:21-22.]

by the name of Hogg[30], who lived in Ettrick, a village in the Borders between England and Scotland, and died there in 1835, on a small farm which the Duke of Buccleuch had let him have rent-free. His poems are known throughout the whole of Scotland, though he is not so esteemed and praised here as is the still greater poet of Caledonia, Burns, who also came from the peasant class and remained in it until his life's end.

'**At half two o'clock**' – an Englishman would, as we know, say '**half past one**' while the Scots, who have still preserved so many old Saxon turns of phrase, say, just as we Germans do, *um halb zwei Uhr* – we arrived at the boundary of the park and gradually walked up a beautiful long woodland path, which in part was a sort of dam between two lakes, to the ancient seat of the Drummonds.

When Queen Victoria told her Chief Chamberlain who, as we explained, is the present owner of this castle, that she would also visit this residence of his on her journey, he was beset by apprehension and assured her that his castle was actually nothing but an '**old shooting-box**' and was scarcely suitable for receiving such illustrious guests. But the Queen and her consort would not be dissuaded from visiting this beautiful and romantic country seat situated at the entrance to the Scottish Highlands and they even spent several days there. They also had certainly not come to Scotland to enjoy royal comfort and luxury, which they could obtain for themselves in sufficiency at home. They arrived here on a Saturday at seven o'clock in the evening and did not leave this lovely spot until Tuesday. It was the custom in olden times on the occasion of visits by the monarchs to their Scottish subjects that the '**Clan-men**', dressed in their clan uniform, marched up as a bodyguard; this happened also on this occasion. The owner of the castle had fitted out his Drummonds in their ancient colours and tartans, and they had garrisoned the castle as a '**body-guard**' of the Queen and her consort.

On Monday the master and mistress held a '**Clanshow**', as my friends called the military review of the clansmen, and thereafter they arranged a great stag-hunt for the Prince. '**And a keen huntsman he is**', added my companions. The stag-hunts of Scotland are as famous in Great Britain as are those of Ireland. In England there are now only a few of these noble beasts. '**Deer-stalking**' is what they call these hunts. For since the rugged and rocky mountain glens in which the deer live here do not allow hunting with hounds and horses, they must be 'stalked' on foot, like the chamois in the Tyrol. In Cooper's story 'The Smugglers'[31] an interesting and accurate description of such a Scottish '**Deer-stalking**' can be read.

The Drummonds' coat of arms, three red stripes on a golden shield held by two men armed with clubs[32], is emblazoned on the gate of the castle courtyard that leads to the gardens, and under it is the motto of the family and the clan: '**Gang warily**' – one of the many remarkable ancient Scottish family mottoes that are very characteristic of these mountain dwellers and that could as well be borne in coats of arms by foxes and wolves as by owners of mountain castles and chieftains of clans.

The precipitous rocks on which Drummond Castle sits afford on their surface space enough, probably artificially levelled, for the various parts of the castle. In the first courtyard, on a sharply protruding part of the rock, are the ruins of the oldest portion of the castle; in this the Drummonds

---

[30] [James Hogg, called 'the Ettrick Shepherd' (1770 – 1835.]

[31] [This must be an allusion to James Baillie Fraser's *The Highland Smugglers* (1835) in which Chapter IV consists of such a description. On the title page the author is not named but described as 'The author of "Adventures of a Kuzzilbash", "Persian Adventurer" &'. This anonymity and the fact that James Fenimore Cooper wrote *The Deerslayer* (1841) may account for the author's misattribution.]

[32] [The heraldic descriptions are 'Arms: Or, three bars wavy gules. Supporters: Two wild men wreathed about the temples and loins with oak-leaves, each holding a club resting on his exterior shoulder, proper.' There is in fact no such thing as a clan coat of arms. These arms belong only to the chief.]

resided when they were still Earls of Perth; and on these ruins was set the noble flag of the family, flown here in honour of the illustrious guests. The owner had also contrived some rooms for himself there in order to give the new part of the castle completely over to his guests. On the opposite side, surrounded by the wings of this new castle, another open square reveals itself; this goes down almost to the steep descent of the rocks, affording an incomparable view into the lowlands of Perth. In the distance we even made out, distinctly, the conical **Dunsinnan hill**[33] not far from Perth. Many a young person in Germany is deeply affected by reading Shakespeare's or Schiller's 'Macbeth'[34]; what would they not give to be able to see this hill from the distance in reality as well! My companions told me that to this day people still show, under a large stone, the grave of a man killed by a person who was not born of a woman. They now call it **'the lang Man's graff'** (the tall man's grave). King Malcolm's troops seem to have completely used up Birnam Wood in storming Macbeth's entrenchments. For it is said that there is nothing left to be seen of it.

Other enchanting views into Strathyre[35] and Strathmore present themselves, and then into various neighbouring glens of the Highlands. No Scot has actually been able to give me a precise definition of the difference that they make between a 'strath' and a 'glen'. However, I believe that the main point is this, that by 'strath' a broad, long, low, level expanse of land is understood, extending between two sets of mountains that remain visible on both sides for some distance. On the other hand, by 'glens' are understood the narrower valleys where the level ground in the middle of the valley is more constricted.[36] The straths, long stretches of land between two high ranges of mountains, also often include even hilly and undulating terrain. And in this respect 'carses' are distinguished from 'straths', since by the latter is meant the quite flat alluvial ground near rivers and sea-inlets. Here they also sometimes call these **'Carses'** (depressions) by the name common in North Germany, namely **'Polders'**[37].

The most remarkable strath in Scotland is that flat area stretching between the Grampians and the chain of hills from Stirling to Perth that we have already described. Actually at the widest extent it continues across the whole of Scotland. Often, however, they take this word **'Strathmore'** in a narrower sense as well and then understand by it only that part of the whole that extends on both sides of the Tay in the east of Perthshire. Parallel to Strathmore in the south runs Glen More in the north, or, as it is called in full, **'Glen-more-nan Albin'**[38] (the Great Glen of Albin, that is, Scotland). By this is meant that remarkable, completely straight fissure across the country that is occupied by the elongated lakes Loch Ness, Loch Lochy and Loch Linnhe[39], and through which the Caledonian Canal runs.

'We like to assist nature as much as possible, but it must not be seen', the gardener of Drummond Castle said to me as we stepped on to the magnificent terrace on the rock which leads down from the lofty castle to the garden. And indeed that is very true. The English have brought the horticultural art to the highest degree of perfection, which, as for every art, means that its products are all as artistically contrived as possible and yet appear as natural as possible[40]. This is the triumph of art, that it is totally art and yet appears to be totally nature.

---

[33] [Now usually spelt *Dunsinane*.]

[34] [Schiller translated Shakespeare's *Macbeth*. The first performance using this translation took place in Weimar on 14 May 1800.]

[35] *Strath-Eare*

[36] [The author's distinction is accurate.]

[37] [*Polder* is not listed in the Scottish National Dictionary with this meaning, but John Thomson's *Atlas of Scotland* of 1832 shows *W. Polder* and *E. Polder* on the River Forth, so it may be that the author had seen and misapprehended this or conceivably had heard a usage in Scotland that did not find its way into writing.]

[38] [See Chapter II, fn. 34]

[39] *Linche*

[40] [A classic statement of an aspect of Romanticism, see Introduction p. xv.]

Most of the trees in the park were planted and tended by the gardener, and yet it appeared as though nature had scattered them by chance here and there, casually and picturesquely. The lawn was in great measure artificially planted and yet seems to have been spread out by the Leimoniades[41] themselves for their midnight frolics. Even the stretches of water (**Ponds**) in the park had been allowed to accumulate artificially and yet they were the very image of natural lakes. The ivy that twined round the black rocks of the castle, the old yew-trees that spread out on the various levels of the garden terrace with their twigs like thatched roofs and under which attractive seats offered themselves – all were supervised by artful skill in every stage of their growth, and yet it appeared as if they had been completely left to themselves from the very beginning like unrestrained children of the forest.

The most remarkable part of the grounds is the flower garden, especially because here several plants have been brought to a perfection that can seldom be seen in other places, namely types of heather. This garden lies in a quite flat broad area between a hilly part of the park and the high castle rock, and if one stands in this beautiful floral plot, then all around the most entrancing views present themselves of the splendid park trees, the castle, and its ivy-twined terraced rock. The plan of the garden is, so to speak, patriotically Scottish. The principal paths cross in the form of the Scottish St Andrew's Cross, and between them are the flowers and the shrubs, like the jewels of the insignia of the Order of St Andrew[42], and other paths lead round about them like the setting of a precious stone. On a pillar in the middle of the garden are 60 sundials mounted in a sixtyfold arrangement. And from the bushes many statues gaze out, representing Spring, Summer, Bacchus, Pomona, Winter etc. Only in their flower garden do the English occasionally allow themselves such artifices, and what the gardener told me above concerning nature and art applied least to this part of the grounds. It even seemed to me as though this flower garden of Drummond Castle was an imitation of some Italian garden. I was sorry that I had not asked whether the originator of this garden had brought the idea for it from Italy. Many northern shrubs were trimmed like orange-trees, others, for example holly-bushes, were trained in pyramidal form like cypresses, as though by this means a reminder was to be given of these southern plants which the climate here does not tolerate.

'**The standard-flowers**' (the principal flowers[43]) of the garden, as the gardener put it, are roses, of which they have a splendid abundance. A particular variety, called '**Madame Desprey**', has even been bred here, or, as the gardener, said '**is worked here**'. Most roses here are grown as trees, as is usual in Great Britain generally, and not as bushes, as is more often seen in Germany. Incidentally, in these northern districts they always obtained, and still obtain, the most beautiful and most numerous roses through the London '**Nursery-men**' (commercial gardeners). From Germany too the import of flower-seeds is considerable. In particular and almost exclusively they obtain asters and stocks from there. For stock-seed they have to pay horrendous prices. For one '**Ounce**' (two German *lots*[44]) they pay 12 shillings, which means that they almost treat it like gold. Many flower-bulbs too come via Hamburg to London, and from London to Edinburgh, and from Edinburgh to the gardens in the Highlands. Holland, however, is even more important in this respect. It is well known that this is the age of dahlias and georginas[45] in every garden in the world. The gardener told me that they had about 6000 of these flowers here, and that he had noticed that all the georginas that came from Germany produced larger flowers and longer petals, but that the English ones had fuller heads.

---

[41] [Meadow nymphs.]

[42] [This may refer to Scotland's premier Order of Chivalry, The Most Ancient and Most Noble Order of the Thistle. Knights of this Order wear a dark green velvet mantle with a silver breast star on which is superimposed a Cross of St Andrew bearing a thistle surrounded by the motto of the Order *Nemo me impune lacessit* (= 'No one assails me with impunity').]

[43] [The author seems to have misunderstood the word *standard* here: it refers to the tree-like shape of the plants.]

[44] [An obsolete German weight, varying from 14 to 18 grams.]

[45] [A type of dahlia from Central Europe.]

The oranges cannot be taken out into the open air at all, because even in a good season there are still some night frosts to be feared. They remain in the greenhouse all year round. What interesting gradations there are in the cultivation of this plant! In Berlin they can be in the open air for the summer months, in Dresden even somewhat longer. However, they must always stay in a well sheltered container. In northern Italy they put them outside completely, but still cover them for several winter months. Only in southern Italy and Spain are they completely left to care for themselves. If the orange has to be tended so attentively here, the bay-tree in contrast stands up well in the open air. We saw a bay-tree here that was one hundred years old; it twisted its way up the rock like a enormous snake covered in leaves.

The other standard[46] flowers in the garden are, as I have already indicated above, the varieties of heather, which have been developed to an exuberant size here. The principal paths of the garden are also bordered with heather; the splendour of its red flowers shows up well against the green of the paths. I say 'against the green of the paths', for the latter are covered with an extremely short velvet-like lawn, which for me was not one of the least wonders of the garden. The English, as we know, are the only people in the world who, in furnishing their houses, never forget how tender and sensitive we human beings are on the skin of the soles of our feet, and they take this circumstance into consideration everywhere. I heard of an Englishman who was so little able to tolerate the bare floors on the Continent that in France and Germany he had a floor-covering prepared from mats or other patches of material for every room that he entered, and, if he could not obtain anything else, provided himself with at least a horse blanket under his feet. In their gardens too they love above everything else a soft terrain to walk on, and I understand this passion completely. They have therefore created the beautiful lawns in their gardens on which the grass is kept so short and compact that it almost resembles the wool on Brussels tapestries.

The grass patches in our gardens are generally forbidden territory, since there the long grass grows mostly only for cows and goats and not for human beings. In English gardens, on the other hand, the lawns are usually full of people walking while the stone and gravel paths are, in contrast, empty. Only if the grass is too wet do they use the latter. On German gravel paths there is always the time-honoured toil of eradicating the grass. On English garden paths, on the other hand – as was the case here in Drummond Castle – the grass is often allowed to grow vigorously and it is tended with care, so that on the paths themselves an even finer carpet of short lawn comes into being. This grass was maintained so short and firm that even in the rain it was certainly quite possible to stride out on it with ease.

The pines in English parks are wonderful to behold: their lower branches are always excellently retained and they droop down on to the lawn with a wealth of needles and twigs. I do not know whether this is a peculiarity of the climate and the trees, or, as I suspect, a result of art. In Germany the lower branches of pines have usually fallen to pieces, or broken off, or withered away, and it is only towards the middle of the tree that the unblemished, totally developed branches begin. Because of this, our trees appear to be mutilated. But in the English parks the lower branches trail on the ground like the long tail of the peacock (that is, if it is not displaying its fan) and stretch out behind the tree like the long train of a lady's dress. In this way the pyramid of the pine is intact and the whole form of the tree seems to rise out of the lawn, so to speak. There are a surprising number of things of which one truly becomes aware only in English gardens.

It is remarkable that although Scotland is not so well endowed with gardens as England, either in absolute or relative terms, nevertheless a large proportion of English gardens are cared for by Scots. The Scots are very esteemed gardeners in England. If an Englishman from the middle, or even from

---

[46] [Again the author's misapprehension of the word *standard* as meaning 'principal'.]

the end, of last century, could rise again from the grave, he would in no small measure be amazed that in so short a time these so barbaric Scots have come so far. 'There is no country in Europe', the English are wont to say, 'which has recently made such immense progress as Scotland.' When I spoke to my gardener about this, he pointed over the **'fences'** of his park and said that the reason for it lay hidden on the other side of these fences in the fields. The extraordinary progress that had been made in their cultivation had also brought improvements to the gardens, and from them had proceeded the majority of improvements in the country[47].

'For, Sir,' he added, 'if we have science in the fields first, then we have it in the nation's hearts, and afterwards it finds its way into everything.'

'Indeed,' I remarked, 'I find your garden here delightful. Your master, Willoughby, must be a modest man, if he calls this an **'old shooting-box'**, and I can scarcely understand how your Queen could leave such a splendid estate so quickly.'

'Yes, her time was limited,' he replied, **'and then, having a mother's care about her'**, he added, 'for after all her little ones had stayed behind in England.'

In one of the rooms of the old part of the castle, they then also showed me the arms and uniforms that the owner of the castle had had made for his clansmen who formed the Queen's **'body-guard'**. They were the Scottish Highlanders' garb described above, to which additionally pertain, as ancient Scottish weapons, first a straight sword, called **'clay-more'** (which likewise strangely resembled the ancient Roman one), a **'Battle-axe'**, and a small round shield.

However, the most remarkable piece of all this equipment was the dazzling snuff-box (**snuffmull**[48]) which the leader of the guard had worn; it likewise belongs to his complete Highland national uniform. It plays a larger part in Scotland than in any other country known to me. It consists of a long, spiral ram's horn. The point of the spiral ends in a silver thistle fashioned by one of the famous goldsmiths of Perth, and its lid is usually ornamented with a fine cairngorm. Since its shape is one of the most awkward in the world for the fingers, the work of the latter is usually carried out by several small silver instruments which hang around the horn on silver chains. These are: a small silver hammer to tap on the walls of the horn and to loosen the snuff which might have adhered to them; a small scoop with which to take out the snuff; a small scraper to loosen it even more if necessary; a small hare's paw set in silver, which serves as a brush on appropriate occasions; and other such things. The whole is carried like a powder-horn on a silver chain round the body, and this brings to mind the chieftains of several savage tribes to whose complete uniform a pipe belongs in a similar way.

It is remarkable how it is the Scots, of all the nations of Europe, who are the only ones to have fashioned this so insignificant accessory so elaborately and painstakingly. For among all other peoples the method of taking snuff amounts to much the same thing, and is more or less equally simple everywhere. Only the Scottish snuffmull differs essentially from all other snuff-boxes in the world. In front of snuff shops in England there usually stands a Scottish Highlander in his national dress and with a snuff-box in his hand, just as in our tobacco shops one can occasionally see a black man smoking.

* * * * * * * *

---

[47] [In fact the opposite had occurred. Improvements in Scottish horticulture had led to improvements in agriculture.]

[48] [Snuff-taking became very popular in Scotland during the 18th century. Snuff mulls were often, as here, made from curly sheep or cow horns but others were made of ebony, ivory, or silver.]

VIII
Crieff

I took leave of my Drummond friends here and walked through the splendid, very extensive park of Drummond Castle to the little town of Crieff. It was a pleasant, calm day. No breath of air stirred and the only noise that I heard was the quiet falling of leaves from the trees and here and there the rustling of a pheasant in the dry foliage. And, even if not decked with flowers, then at least covered with withered leaves and fallen spruce needles which had clung to me everywhere, I arrived in Crieff.

Crieff is a pleasant little hill-town that, like Drummond Castle, is situated on the edge of the Highlands. It occupies the top of a little hill which, with another lying opposite, forms one of the various gateways to the Highlands. Through this gateway the River Earn flows out from the mountains into the plain. A famous MacGregor who, however, could only use this proscribed name of his in secret and who called himself 'Mallet' in public – in fact the well known English poet of this name[1] – was born in one of the small houses of this town; he was the son of an **innkeeper** there. I arrived just on a market day, and there were gathered here many men who hitherto had been the best friends of Robert Peel – only recently they have become somewhat dubious about this friendship[2] – I mean the tenant farmers. Formerly large cattle-markets were held here as in many small towns bordering the Highlands, but they have now been transferred to Falkirk.

Over their French clothing, now characteristic of every European, all these farmers (and there were fine-looking men among them) wore a Scottish plaid as well, that is, that rectangular woollen shawl I mentioned above and which serves Scotsmen instead of cloak, instead of greatcoat, instead of tunic, mackintosh, or fur. It is a cause for wonder that the Scots, in such a cold climate, have not invented a warmer outer garment. The Russians, Poles and other nations wear thick bear furs, even in a much more southerly latitude, but instead of this fur the Scots for their part wear a rectangular, loose woollen cloth, and even – instead of under-trousers and over-trousers – no trousers at all. Can such contradictions be understood? And yet it is said that each nation knows its country and climate most accurately and knows best what is appropriate for it. The Scots, on the other hand, *praise* their plaid and say it is **'very handy'** and that one can always immediately wrap in it any part of the body that is cold, and that one can always make out of it whatever one wishes. If the wind blows from the left, then the plaid is pulled over the left; if it rages from the right, then all the wool is crammed on to the right shoulder; if one's whole body feels cold, the plaid is completely unfolded and one envelopes oneself totally in it, like a baby in swaddling clothes; if one feels too warm on the other hand, then the plaid is rolled up, laid across the neck and the ends allowed to hang down under the arms. All this, I say, is very true and would also be very effective and fine if we were thinking of a Spanish or Italian climate and the cool breezes that sometimes waft there. But here, where it is a question of **'Highland-Gales'** I find that too many benefits are sacrificed for the sake of beauty.

It gave me much pleasure to observe the various ways in which people had fastened their plaids round themselves. The usual one is to throw it over the left shoulder and then tie the corners together under the right, wrap them round the arm, or conceal them in some other way. The plaid belongs on the left shoulder as naturally as the sword on the left side, since the right hand is that which plays the principal part in arranging clothing, and it naturally cannot put the cloth so

---

[1] [David Mallet (1705?-1765). He had adopted the Scottish name *Malloch* which he subsequently anglicised to *Mallet*.]

[2] [It is not clear what the cause of this dubiety was. It could have been any or all of the following: Peel's law relating to the import of foreign cattle (see Chapter XIV), or his reduction on the duty on imported corn, carried out in 1842, or his re-introduction in March 1842 of income-tax of seven pence in the pound, or his speech unfavourable to the claims of the Church of Scotland (see p. 42).]

comfortably in position on its own shoulder. On the high column erected to Walter Scott in Glasgow, on which his statue stands in life-size, by a strange oversight on the part of the *native* artist, he has his plaid on the *right* shoulder. However, many people, who had muffled themselves well, wore it also over both shoulders, chest and back and then also again as a belt round the body, in this fashion:

In the hands of an ingenious dandy the plaid provides its most striking effects, and in Edinburgh there are enough of them who study the matter and play about with the plaid, as do many in Germany with their Spanish, or allegedly Spanish, cloaks.

The plaids of my friends and those of Sir Robert Peel in Crieff were all of a black and white check. Black and white is the usual '**Shepherd's tartan**'. (I think that my readers will now be sufficiently initiated into the matter of Scottish dress to be able to distinguish '**Tartan**', the material, from '**Plaid**', an item of clothing, which not all Englishmen yet understand.) In the whole of Scotland and also in the whole of the north of England[3], this black and white tartan is the usual one among all shepherds and most people generally, and it seemed to me that everywhere it is made precisely and exactly in the same way. Since the black and white stripes are very narrow, and moreover give rise to a grey colour where they cross, so from a distance it actually appears more as grey. We could therefore add to our two main types of tartan indicated above, the 'clan tartans' and the 'fancy tartans', a third type, the 'shepherd's tartans'.

Every stretch of road that I travelled in Scotland I found to be full of delights, and hence that from Crieff to Perth too. Campbell calls this country. '**the land of the mountains and the flood**'[4], and that is exactly the most beautiful feature of it, that the mountains, which one is accustomed to see only in the interior of continental countries, are here always surrounded by sea and commingled with the sea-inlets. Here Vulcan and Neptune have had their workshops in the closest proximity everywhere. Now we came to the sea again, namely to the Firth of the River Tay, which is Scotland's pride and joy as much as is the majestic Shannon the pride and joy of Ireland.

The Tay is the most beautiful and the longest of the Scottish rivers, and so signifies to Scotland what the Shannon signifies to Ireland and the Severn to England. It rises in the Highlands and has at its estuary the flourishing trading town of Dundee, which in 90 years has expanded from being a small fishing village to become one of the most admirable commercial cities in Europe, with close on 70,000 inhabitants. The Tay breaks through a range of hills twice, once out of the high mountains (Dunkeld is situated at this point), and once through the Ochil Hills[5], and in this opening lies Perth. Finally, there, where it once again narrows before it joins the sea, is the city of Dundee.

* * * * * * *

---

[3] [The Northumberland or Shepherd's Tartan has a history dating back at least to the fifteenth century. It is of course not a clan tartan, as the author points out.]

[4] [Although the author attributes this phrase to Thomas Campbell (1777-1844), it is in fact from Walter Scott's 'Lay of the Last Minstrel', Canto Sixth, and is correctly 'Land of the mountain and the flood'.]

[5] *Ochrill-Hills*

IX
Perth

Perth is another place of which enthusiasts would say that one would have to write about it in hexameters if one wishes to do justice to the town and to be satisfied with one's efforts.

Admittedly, like Stirling it is situated in the Lowlands, but there is more **'Highland-scenery'** round about it. Although it is situated on a plain, as soon as one steps outside its gates one can see the range of snow-covered Grampians rising in the distance. **'Perth is rather a highland town'** said several Scotsmen to me for this reason, 'although strictly speaking it is not actually in the Highlands.' The Scots really regard it as the capital of the whole of central Scotland, and although it has far fewer inhabitants (in fact only 20,000 souls) than its commercial neighbour, Dundee, nevertheless it is much more distinguished than the latter by virtue of its antiquity, its celebrated name, and its noble aspect. In popular opinion, it bears much the same relation to Dundee as does an old, not overly wealthy baron to an immensely rich city-dweller. **'Noble Perth'** I heard it called several times.

Only later did I discover that another name of the town is **'the fair City'**, but it is impossible that the traveller would not himself give it this name at first sight. The avenues to the town, its interior, its exterior, its near and far – everything is equally beautiful and attractive, and the visitor encounters a wealth of romantic and historical memories of the most fascinating kind. Some miles from the city is Scone House, a seat of the Earl of Mansfield; it stands on the site of the famous old Scone Abbey in which the Scottish kings were crowned. In the garden are still some ruins of the ancient royal palace. Unfortunately I did not see them because, they told me, the present owner no longer permits entry to anyone. The insensitive public, avid for souvenirs, had stolen the fringes and other decorations from the curtains of his bed of Mary, Queen of Scots.

Still nearer to the town is the seat of the Kinnoulls, Dupplin Castle, which presents a high, abrupt frontage to the town and contains a famous dragon's cave; and then there is Kinfauns, the seat of the Lord Grey, one of the most resplendent mansion houses (or, as the English say, **'showhouses'**) in the country. Unfortunately I did not see them. And besides these there are still several other castles, estates and country seats, worthy of attention by virtue of interesting happenings, for example the murder of James I, the imprisonment of James VI, and many other events. I did not see them, unfortunately, simply because one cannot look at everything.

From Perth the river proceeds with the breadth of an inlet of the sea down towards the ocean, and it is generally agreed in Scotland that this stretch of water is the most beautiful in the land. Unfortunately I did not see it, simply because time is so limited and the area round Perth is so rich in interest. And it is precisely this last point that I wished to make obvious and understandable to my German reader, by citing all the things that I did not see. I now come to the things that I really did see.

From afar I had already heard of the two famous Inches of Perth, the North Inch and the South Inch. This name is applied to two flat pieces of ground that lie on the River Tay, one to the north, the other to the south of the town, and they are probably alluvial land washed up by the river. 'These Inches are splendid, Sir!' people had said to me, 'wonderful, matchless, and we have no other sites for games or races in Scotland that can compare with them. The Inches are beyond all praise!' Hitherto I could understand praise applied to a beautiful mountain in a monotonous plain; but I was now curious to see what could excite people to emotion and enthusiasm for a featureless flat piece of land. Consequently, when, on our arrival in Perth, we discovered a great commotion among the populace, and when we heard that they were pouring out through the gates to witness a cheerful spectacle on the North Inch, we let ourselves be carried along with the crowd so that we could see this place for ourselves.

The cheerful spectacle that was awaited was the clown of a troupe of acrobats, who was going to sail down the beautiful river in a small skiff to which were harnessed four geese. The troupe was going to give a performance in the evening, '**and they wanted to get up an excitement for their benefit**'. Every event in England has to be preceded by such a flourish, and even for the best and greatest they always have to '**get up an excitement**' among the public first of all. This time the means were certainly well chosen, especially for an English public which loves comedy more than any other public, and the clown here would certainly not have caused as much 'excitement' if he had announced that he was going to fly through the air with peacocks like Juno or with doves like Venus, as he now caused, dressed in motley, sitting in a wash-tub and drawn by four gabbling geese. After some time he really did appear, and to the shouts of applause from the crowd floated down the river, very skilfully balancing his wobbling craft[1]. Of course the geese were not pulling him, rather they themselves were being carried along by the river. The whole North Inch was covered with people. I looked down on it from the splendid bridge over the Tay which arches high above the river and above the beginning of the meadow, and now fully understood the praise that had been bestowed on the Inches, especially when I took into account the passion of the British for '**sports**'.

Beside each of their towns the English have sought out several flat fields or pieces of ground for the different sports, ball games, races etc., enthusiastically indulged in by their inhabitants and by the clubs that exist among them, just as we Germans make an effort above all else to create some pleasant gardens beside each of our towns in which to enjoy coffee and music. These sports and racing grounds of the various British towns are now frequently compared with one another by connoisseurs and enthusiasts, and then in some cases all favourable circumstances and all requisite features for such grounds coincide to such an extent that they gain a great reputation and fame in the English sports world. Thus the Curragh[2] of Kildare, as we have said earlier[3], is the most famous racing ground in Ireland, and so now these Perth Inches – we could possibly call them 'river-islands' – are the most famous sports grounds in Scotland. Their surface is completely even and, though low-lying, nevertheless usually dry.

The North Inch is devoid of bushes, trees, ditches, and equally without houses, paths, etc., and so to some extent is like a fine big billiard-table. And it is this that makes this river-island so rare and valuable for people. The South Inch is an equally beautiful meadow-ground, but intersected by paths, rows of trees, and patches of bushes. The contrast of these two low-lying Inches, closely hemmed in by the high river-banks, of the mountains and hills round about and of the likewise somewhat high-lying town gives it in addition a picturesque charm.

On the bridge over the Tay I was not a little diverted by eavesdropping on the conversations of the young Scottish boys, who already *prattle* Scots as well as their parents *speak* it. '**Look, the folks,**' they shouted to each other, '**are coming duhn**[4] **to the brigg**[5].' '**Yea, yea**[6], **look the folks on baith**[7] **sides o'**[8] **the Tay.**' This is all Scots and at the same time also more German than the English forms.

---

[1] [This was a clown from Cooke's Circus who went in this way from the Fishing Lodge to the Bridge in November 1842.]

[2] *Currach*

[3] [Presumably in the author's *Reisen in Irland* ('Travels in Ireland').]

[4] '**duhn**' instead of '**down.**' *JGK* [The author's spelling indicates the pronunciation 'doon'.]

[5] '**brigg**' instead of '**bridge.**' *JGK*

[6] '**yea**' instead of '**yeas.**' [sic] *JGK* [It is not inconceivable that the author had actually heard *aye*.]

[7] '**baith**' instead of '**both.**' *JGK*

[8] '**o''** instead of '**off.**' [sic] *JGK*

Travels in Scotland (1840) by J.G. Kohl

From my inn I had obtained as my guide and companion an inhabitant of Africa, a Negro named Bob. Nowadays, even in this remote Thule, people are as much in contact with Libya and generally with the whole world as could formerly be the case only in the Roman towns of Italy – the mother of the Empress of Morocco lives on a marsh in Perthshire, Sir David Baird[9], the victor of Srirangapatnam[10], lives [sic] in Ferntower quite near to the city, poor dusky Red Indians[11] beg in the streets, and black children from the Sahara Desert show one the way through the streets.

My Bob was now persecuted by the boys with their Scots idioms. '**Do you kenn**[12] [sic] **that muckle**[13] **man, that swart karl**[14]**?**' they asked each other, '**do you kenn him?**' 'Bob, you are so black, why do you not wash yourself?'

'**Very ba' folks, Massa!**' began my Negro, in half African, half Scots dialect.

'**You ocht**[15] **to kenn better English!**' my boys replied to him. 'Just look at the soles of your servant's feet, Sir! They are as thick as wood, for earlier he danced about for years on glowing coals and molten lead while he was still with the troop of tight-rope walkers who brought him over here from Africa or the West Indies.'

When the boys came out with this, my Bob (the soles of whose feet, though said to be as hard as wood, seemed to be his sensitive point) became quite furious and poured forth such a wild African Scots-English at the laughing boys that it was not possible for me to bring his sounds into legible words, however much I would have liked to have had a specimen of this style of language. And now in order to save my poor black guide, who had fallen like a big llama among young jaguars, I retreated with him from the bridge and from my observations of dialect.

The Scots are as much in love with those antique Saxon speech-forms of theirs as are the Austrians with some of their own ancient peculiarities of language, and they are especially fond of them in their poems. And a song, in which very often '**duhn**' instead of '**down**', '**baith**' instead of '**both**', '**fecht**' instead of '**fight**', '**bauld**' instead of '**bold**', '**wi' me**' instead of '**with me**' and the like appear, moves them much more than one where these words are all written in the usual general English manner. In a similar way our Alemannic speakers in the Black Forest are affected much more by a song by Hebel[16] in the Alemannic dialect than by any classical German poetry. I also find this quite natural; for, if a person like those boys of mine on the bridge has spoken in this way from his youth, there are many childhood memories, many patriotic allusions, which become bound up with these dialectal characteristics. In short, there is contained in them such a great part of the person and the land, that I would find it perfectly natural, if a Scot in the East Indies or in Africa were to hear someone say '**come duhn**' instead of '**come down**', he would be moved to tears simply by the sound of this word.

In particular, one can comprehend this well from the many Saxon forms which are to be found in the Scots language, because in them the soul of the Scottish people dimly becomes aware of its

---

[9] [Sir David Baird (1757 – 1829) as Major-General in the British Army commanded the final assault on Srirangapatnam in the Fourth Mysore War. He had been dead for some thirteen years at the time of the author's visit to Perth.]

[10] *Seringapatnam* [This appears to have been a general misapprehension of the name.]

[11] [Perhaps slightly unexpectedly, the author writes *Indianer* ('Red Indians'), not *Inder* ('Indians').]

[12] '**Kenn**' instead of '**know.**' '**To kenn**' is also used for *wissen*, as is '**to know.**' '**I do not kenn**' means throughout Scotland *ich weiß nicht. JGK*

[13] '**Muckle**' instead of '**great.** *JGK*

[14] '**Swart**' instead of '**black**'. – '**Karl**' instead of '**man.**' *JGK*

[15] '**Ocht**' instead of '**ought**': many letters, which in English are merely written now, are also pronounced in Scots, for example, English '**fight**', Scottish '**fecht**'. *JGK*

[16] [Johann Peter Hebel (1760 – 1826), Swiss theologian and author of dialect poems.]

ancient German origin, its profound connection with the great Germanic mother soul. But it is remarkable that there are also several words in Scots of French origin which are not found in English; consequently, they are very popular among the Scots, who like to hear them just as much as those old German ones. Such a word is, for example, the expression '**bonny**' (from the French '**bon**'). This French word has, as tends to be the case with such imported words, taken on a quite special, somewhat different, meaning. It is, in fact, used to praise not only the goodness, but also in particular the beauty of a thing and of a person, and hence it has become a general word for praising and flattering. Everything that the Scots find good, beautiful, splendid in their native land is called **bonny**, especially if it is something Scottish, thus, for example, '**our bonnie** [sic] **lasses**' (our pretty girls), '**bonny Prince Charlie**' (that is, Charles Edward, the Pretender), '**our bonny town Perth**'. They also say of a district or a building: '**that is very bonny**'. As a term of flattery it rather comes close to the English '**sweet**'. A whole number of poems by Burns could be cited in which the word '**bonny**' is used with special fondness. The Scots have made it so much their own that for them there is no longer anything foreign and French about it.

Thinking such thoughts, I walked with my Negro Bob to the other side of the town, to the South Inch which, because of its trees, is almost more beautiful than the North Inch. On this South Inch in 1746 camped the German (Hessian) troops who helped in quelling the uprising of **bonny Prince Charlie**. For it is noteworthy that on several occasions we Germans had to help the English fight against the uprisings in their half-Celtic countries. Once in Ireland in 1798[17] it was the Hanoverian troops and once in Scotland in 1746, as was said, it was the Hessians. At the Battle of the Boyne[18], too, in Ireland, German troops stood up to the Irish, as though we Germans still had to work for the victory of the Germanic race over the Celtic, as at that time, when likewise from the north of Germany, from Hanover and Hessen etc., Hengist and Horsa crossed over to Great Britain.

But the most remarkable camp on these Inches – I think it was on the North Inch – was set up in 1390[19]. In that year King Robert III reigned in Scotland; he was pleased (sic) to see the wild, unmanageable clans wearing themselves out in their eternal squabbling, and he therefore proposed to two hostile clans, Clan Chattan and Clan Kay, that they should settle their disputes in the following way. They were to choose their most capable men and come down with them to the Inches of Perth. There, in the presence of the king and his court, they were to fight against one another, and the winners were to be in the right, but, for the defeated side, everything was to be forgiven and forgotten.

Thirty selected valiant men of the lineage of Kay (MacKay) came down from the north, and thirty of the lineage of Chattan[20]. As they arrayed themselves in battle order, however, one of the latter was missing; he had withdrawn through fear or sickness. Now one of the Kays ought also to have withdrawn, but they were all so eager to fight that none was to be persuaded to this, and hence the proposal of Henry Wynd, a Perth saddler, had to be adopted; he had volunteered to fill the gap and to fight in place of the missing man if they would give him half a gold French thaler. Because of this brave and pugnacious man Clan Chattan won. All the men of Clan Kay were slain except one, who jumped into the River Tay and fled into the hills. Ten of Clan Chattan and Henry Wynd remained alive. Although we have all read this story already in **the Fair Maid of Perth**[21], which is

---

[17] [An uprising, inspired by the Society of United Irishmen (a body which wished to establish an independent Irish parliament with religious equality) was defeated at the Battle of Vinegar Hill in that year.]

[18] [In 1690, the forces of William III (of Orange) defeated those of James II in this confrontation near Drogheda in Ireland. This confirmed the Protestant succession to the throne of England.]

[19] [Actually in 1396]

[20] Chambers calls them MacIntosh instead, but in the Encyclopaedia Britannica they are called Chattan. *JGK* [In fact, the Clan Chattan was a confederate clan, embracing Farquharsons, McCombies, MacGilvrays, Macbeans, and Macqueens.]

[21] [The reference is to *The Fair Maid of Perth*, the novel by Walter Scott published in 1828.]

based on that escaped Mackay, nevertheless, here in the very spot, one cannot help reflecting on it once more, especially if at the same time one bears in mind the Circassians in the Caucasus and the ancient stories in the Bible of the Philistines and the Carmelites and other mountain peoples. In their customs they all correspond so remarkably, and among them all we find again these clans, these **'Clans-feuds'** and **'Clans-fightings'**, and indeed these are so similar to each other that they often resemble each other down to the smallest incidents.

This warlike racial and clan spirit, this primitive, crudest form of human society, merely the extended family, was in existence in Scotland for no less than two thousand years or even longer. Not until the middle of the last century was it eradicated utterly, and only since that time did Dundee and other such large peacefully inclined communities of citizens begin to flourish. If it is only so recently that so savage a cause of discord and strife, such sources of the combative spirit, have been removed from the bosom of the European nations, and if such important places as Dundee and other commercial and manufacturing towns have been playing their part in peace for only such a short period, then the peaceful societies of Paris, London and New York can still witness some great and bloody wars without, however, despairing of the hope for the future establishment of a long, deep, general peace.

Until the most recent times, the belligerence of the feudal system was still growing like a weed among us everywhere, and the progress of a new Enlightenment[22] and an accompanying peaceful cast of mind is still so young, but nonetheless so great, that hope must not be abandoned, even if such progress does not yet lead to the goal immediately. It cannot escape any observer of the present that, daily and in all glens and corners of the earth, the world is revealing things never before seen or heard, and that it is still ever-pregnant with such marvels. What is happening, though carried out in silence, is everywhere so great, so extraordinary, that one could not impute fantasy even to a person who is able to believe in universal peace and calm progress and bright sunshine after those storms, which, for the moment, we perhaps still see looming here and there.

Towards evening I made my way through several attractive **'Nursery-Gardens'** back to the town, and there made the acquaintance of some men who, with heart and soul, were **'Sports-men'**[23].

The two main games that Scotland regards first and foremost as the national games are curling and golf. Curling is the more interesting of the two and, since it must be played on ice, is on this account almost exclusively Scottish. For neither in England nor in Ireland, but only in Scotland, is there enough lasting ice. For this reason, this game has emigrated with the Scots only to the northerly parts of the world, and has been spread in Canada, Nova Scotia etc., but not in the West or East Indies.

The fine smooth sheets of ice that form on the smaller Scottish lochs and flooded river-banks were the stimulus for the invention of this splendid game, which consists principally in the skimming of a smooth round stone towards a certain goal, and it not only exercises the strength of the men, but also gladdens and delights the soul, with all the intriguing minor occurrences and scenes that accompany it. Unfortunately I have never myself been present at a **'Curling-match'**; however, my Perth friends were so enthusiastic, indeed I might say so passionate, in instructing me properly in the matter that I feel as though I had actually once witnessed such a game and that I, as though somewhat infected by my friends' passion, detect a little curling-passion in me even now.

---

[22] [See Introduction p. xiii]

[23] **'Sports-man'** does not simply mean a hunter, but generally a lover of all country and gymnastic games and entertainments. *JGK*

Indeed I see very distinctly in my imagination the beautiful stretches of water, transformed by winter's magic wand into transparent crystal – a splendid frozen loch in the middle of a wild Highland landscape – the snow-covered Grampians round about – only here and there steep black walls of rock glinting through. The '**Curlers**', as the participants in this sport are termed, have come down from their mountains and gathered on the '**Ring**'[24] from their various villages and towns. They are all fine-looking, or at least agile and strong fellows, and some of them have perhaps donned their patriotic Highland garb for this national sport.

They all come with their '**Curling-stones**' in their hands. These stones, which can be seen and bought in many shops in Scottish towns, are fashioned in the following way. They are circular, squat stones of 40 to 50 pounds weight. They are very exactly made, well polished, and mostly composed of two kinds of granite, a reddish and a blackish. I imagine that this is so in order that the stones are not so easily shattered by the various knocks that they have to withstand. On top is affixed a neatly fashioned iron handle by which the stone can be gripped for heaving. The whole looks rather like this:

'Our '**bonny Queen**' also had a curling-stone shown to her when she was in Perth,' my friends told me, 'and, though it was so heavy, she lifted it up high.' Among curlers, however, the game amounts to somewhat more than this. A distant goal is marked on the ice, and the task is to heave the stone in such a way that it should come as near to this goal as possible and remain there without moving. Because of the weight of the stones and the smoothness of the ice, the solution of this problem demands therefore not only a high degree of strength but also considerable dexterity, calculation, and keenness of sight at the same time. And it is precisely the best popular games that require eye and arm, body and mind in equally great measure.

The mark or goal is called '**tee**' or '**toesee**'. This goal consists of a small hole in the ice, round which circles of different diameters are drawn to measure the distances. These circles too have their own special names, just as likewise has a particular zigzag line that is drawn at an angle across the course of play and which the stones must at least have passed in order to be counted. The entire length of the course is usually from 120 to 150 feet. Now it is necessary to slide the stones as close as possible to the goal and, in doing so, wherever possible, to push out of the way one or several opponents' stones that are lying near it. Since the game is often played by 20 to 30 people and the goal is therefore quite surrounded by stones, it is often a very difficult task to slither one's stone through the narrow gaps between them and yet at the same time pick out the correct stone that could be given a small push in passing. With a little imagination, even without having seen the game, one can easily see what wonderful shots can occur that give all the onlookers occasion to cry **Beauty! beauty! magnificent! stupendous!**'.

The players are divided into two teams who play against one another, and one of whom is then declared the winner when it has made 31 points, that is, has had 31 stones nearest the goal. Further

---

[24] [Properly *rink*.]

particulars about the rules of the game can be consulted in **'Blaine's Rural sports'**[25] or in **'Tegg's Dictionary of Field sports'**[26], where the reader will be amazed at how carefully and in what detail the English have elaborated everything in this branch of human ability, as in so many others.

The rink, which of course must be smooth and level like a mirror, is always selected, cleaned and swept with great care. Most importantly, it must have no lengthwise cracks, which naturally make the stones deviate from the straight more than do crosswise ones. My friends told me that many men even had their own **'Curling ponds'** which had been prepared for this game and on to which it was possible, after the old course had been used and damaged, to pour two or three inches of water and let it freeze again. Many of these curling ponds are ponds over the winter only, for they are drained in summer and become **'Bowling-greens'**. Sometimes darkness overtakes them before the game is ended, and my friends told me that they often had been so keen on those occasions that they had played on under the light of torches until late into the night. High and low, lords, burghers and farmers are equally avid for this splendid pastime, and there on the rink they are all equal. It is a peculiarity of the English that the same people, who in some particular respects stand poles apart from each other, nevertheless under certain circumstances regard themselves as completely equal. So too in the curling clubs people of all classes are found to have entered into brotherhood with each other.

Curling clubs have been formed in towns throughout the whole of Scotland[27]. The largest and most famous of them is the **'Grand Caledonian Curling-club'** in Edinburgh. It was founded in 1838. The **'Duddingston Curling-club'** is older[28] and likewise very famous. But there are also very ancient clubs. These clubs have men of the highest rank as presidents, and each one even has its own **Reverend Mr** So-and-so as captain who offers up the prayer on ceremonial occasions.

As we said, the Scots have also taken the game to North America, and on the St Lawrence River apparently several enviable rinks can be laid out from time to time in winter. My friends told me that recently a great revolution in the constitution of these societies has taken place. The plan is to unite the **'keen Curlers'** of all clubs **'from baith sides o' the Tweed'** (for there are also some few curling clubs founded by Scots on the other side of the Tweed, in England) and from the other side of St George's Channel, as well as from the other side of the Atlantic Ocean, into one large single society and a great **'Brotherhood of the Ring** [sic]. This is to be held together by correspondence, by common enterprises, and by journals. Ninety different clubs have already entered into this union.

In an **'Annual Report'** of the year 1842 of the big **'Caledonian Club'** I find it noted that the descendants of Scots in the North American colonies go so far in their enthusiasm for this game that the curlers of Toronto sometimes challenge those of Montreal **'to play a roaring game'**, though the two cities are 400 miles apart. **'They meet in friendly bonspiels'** and afterwards over **'beef and greens'**. 'Perhaps,' continues the report, 'we will soon also have the pleasure of seeing our brethren from the other side of the Tweed coming over to see us at some time, from **'famous Londontown'** to **'Auld Reeky''** (my readers know what is meant by that) 'in order to warm their hands **'at Scotland's ain game o' Curling'** and afterwards to gladden their hearts **'wi' ae nicht of true Scotish** [sic] **Curling conviviality'**. At these curling soirées there are also particular old **'Curling-songs'**. The great Caledonian Club and, I think, probably other clubs as well, even have their curling antiquities, for

[25] [Delabere Pritchett Blaine *An Encyclopaedia of Rural Sports; or, A complete account, historical, practical and descriptive, of hunting, shooting, fishing, racing and other field sports and athletic amusements of the present day*, London 1840. The article on curling appears in Book III, Part I, p. 118-9]

[26] [Harry Harewood *A Dictionary of Sports; or, Companion to the Field, the Forest, and the River* [etc.], London 1835. Printed for Thomas Tegg and Son, Cheapside. It contains an article on curling on pp. 92-5. Blaine's article on curling (see fn. 25) refers to this dictionary by the name quoted by the author.]

[27] [This is an exaggeration: curling was virtually unknown in the north of Scotland.]

[28] [Founded in 1795.]

example old curling stones, that were used in times past. One of the oldest of which I heard was from 1613. They told me that they had found it in a marsh.

I tell this to my German readers only as an example of how far these things are taken in England, and of what an interesting occupation the study of the customs and character of this great nation is.

Incidentally, it is noteworthy that it is also true of this game, as is generally true of most pursuits and inventions, that the British were not their originators but their improvers. The Flemings are said to have introduced the game to Scotland 400 years ago. In Paris too a quite similar game can be seen being played with clay balls; however, it resembles more the English '**Bowling**'.

The curlers have brought me on to the subject of golfers. For, as we said, the second great national Scottish game is golf. This game too they pursue as intensively and as avidly as they do curling. For golf there are also large and famous clubs in Edinburgh: the '**Burnstfields-Links-Golf-Club**'[29] which was founded in 1761; the '**Edinburgh-Burgess-Golfing-Society**' founded in 1735; and the '**Company of Edinburgh Golfers**' which, I think, is the same as the celebrated '**Edinburgh Thistle-Golf-Club**'. The year in which the last society was founded is no longer remembered[30]. It bears almost as distinguished a title as the East India Company; for it is also called '**the *Honourable* Company**', which concomitant appellation I have not otherwise found applied to a mere sports club. The members of this club, like some of our shooting clubs, have their own uniform – scarlet, green and white are its colours – and the club has its own coat of arms. The small traders and shoemakers of Scotland were devoted to this game in as great a measure as were the kings of the realm, and Charles I and James II are mentioned as outstanding golfers. The latter is said to have been so proficient at this game that no one could equal him in it except a certain Patersen [sic][31], a shoemaker in Edinburgh.

Although the kings personally were often passionately devoted to golf, the authorities of the State, however, attempted from time to time to cool this passion among the people by prohibitions. Such a ban dates from as early as 1457 'in order that the exercise of archery, which is much more important to our youth, should not suffer'. But such prohibitions little availed. For in 1744 the City of Edinburgh voted a silver cup, annually to be played for by golfers, and now, from to time, the clubs offer medals that are worth up to 200 guineas.

Anyone simply reading and hearing all this will certainly be somewhat astonished to learn that this entire sport of golf is about nothing more than driving a hard little ball with a stick into a certain hole, made at a great distance, taking the least number of strokes possible.

'Yes, Sir, if you wish to think so, the matter is certainly not significant. But the great pleasure in it is the mutual excitement of the two parties playing, their enthusiasm, their skill, their exertions. '**And then the grand thing is,**' he continued, 'the changing position of the ball and the different obstacles offered by this or that position; and the player, who may only play his ball where it has fallen, must take all of these things into account and overcome them with an adroit stroke. – Look, Sir, come here! You want to get to know the subject. I am glad; I will show you everything. Now here are some of the balls that we use. They are made of strong leather. *Which* leather we use is not a matter of indifference; but I will tell you something more about that later. The leather is soaked beforehand, and this is done in boiling water. For only in this way can a solid ball be made from it.

---

[29] [Modern spelling is *Bruntsfield*.]

[30] [It played its first competition for a Silver Cup in 1744.]

[31] [John Paterson, a shoemaker and early leather golf ball manufacturer, who successfully partnered the Duke of York (later James VII and II) in a golf match on Leith Links ca. 1671 against two Englishmen from the Court at Holyrood Palace.]

The inside of the ball is stuffed with feathers which are packed very tightly into it by means of a very cunningly devised little piece of machinery. But you can best see this at one of the ball-makers of the Edinburgh clubs. When you go back to Edinburgh, you must not fail to visit one of them. Go to Messrs. W. and S. Gourlay[32], they are the ball-makers of the Brunstfield [sic] Links Golf Club. They are very obliging people, and they will show you everything punctiliously. But I can give you another address as well. But look. Afterwards the leather of the ball first has to be covered all over with different layers of white paint. White lead is used for this. White shows up best against green and the other colours of the course. And then it is this covering of paint that gives the ball the correct degree of hardness desired. The white lead must be very pure **'and exceedingly well laid down'**. The ball must be covered with it several times. However, every previous coat must be quite dry, before a new coat is put over it. This is absolutely necessary, otherwise the ball is completely ruined! But Messrs W. and S. Gourlay will explain the whys and wherefores of it more thoroughly. We have a lot to do here! – Oh, good Lord! Mary, close the sitting-room door! This gentleman wants to learn about golf, and the children are making such a noise that we can scarcely hear our own voices.' (In fact, I was with my friend in his house – Mary was his wife – and I would point out in this connection that I am writing no fiction but simply and exactly drawing things and persons from life.)

'So! So much for the ball. Now you must get to know what we hit it with, the **'Clubs'** or, as we Scots say, the **'Kolbes'**[33].' (Regarding this, I remarked to my friend that we had the same word in German, about which he became extraordinarily pleased and put forward the suggestion that probably the name **'Golf'** itself is nothing more than **'Kolbe'** in a corrupt form.) Look, I have a great number of them here. Although they are all different, they all, as you see, have the main outline of their shape in common. Each of them consists of a three to four foot long stick with a somewhat curved head, which we call the **'Knob'**. So that you will not forget it again, I can draw the shape for you with a few lines on a piece of paper. Just look here:

'That is simple. But good Lord! to make the thing properly is enormously difficult. The knob must have the correct curve, must not be too heavy and not too light, and the stick must combine a certain elasticity with great strength. The pieces of wood, of which the shaft is composed, must be very well chosen. Inside, the shaft is filled with lead, and on the back of it another strip of thick horn must be fixed to increase its strength. I have, as you see, ivory on it, on account of its greater elegance. I am very fond of the game, am used to my clubs, and therefore am not afraid of spending something on them in order to have them as good as possible. The shaft itself where you grip it must be strongly spun round with silk. I have mine trimmed with velvet and gold braid on top of that as well, as a decoration. Your hand would lose its grip on the bare wood.

'Now pray observe the different shapes of my clubs. Several are plain bulbous knobs. They are used when the ball is lying on completely level ground. Others are somewhat spoon-shaped, hollowed out at an angle to a greater or less extent. They are used if the ball has to be taken out of a furrow or some other cavity. With one stroke it must be very skilfully not only lifted up out of the cavity but

---

[32] [The brothers John and William Gourlay were makers of feather-filled golf balls in Musselburgh between 1810 and 1855; their father Douglas had been a golf-ball-maker in Bruntsfield in the 1780s.]

[33] [This form is not found in the Dictionary of the Older Scottish Tongue or in the Scottish National Dictionary. The author's host may perhaps have said *clubbies*. 'The same' German word *Kolben* means 'thick end', e.g. a rifle-butt.]

driven further on its way. Some, as you notice, are shorter and have a thicker head, and several of these are even completely made of wrought iron. These last are used on those occasions when a very heavy stroke is needed, for example if the ball is lying slightly buried in sand or something like that. They all have different names. However, afterwards I will give you the address of the best club-maker in Edinburgh, that of Mr D. MacEwan[34], who is also the club-maker to that club already mentioned to you. When you return to Edinburgh, do not fail to visit him. The man actually knows many another thing about the rules of our game.'

'If a small loose stone is lying in front of my ball,' I interrupted my friend with a question, 'is it then permitted by the rules of golf to push this stone a little to the side?'

'Ah, splendid! – That is well asked! There are various opinions and customs about this very point. Some clubs allow this; on the other hand, others strictly forbid it, so that the objects must remain exactly where they are. – According to the rules of some clubs it is even permitted, in certain circumstances, to use one's hands to take the ball out of a hole or a furrow if the latter is so deep that it would be impossible to take it out with the club; the ball is then thrown vertically into the air and then hit, naturally with certain penalties. Other clubs, however, are more strict and do not allow this, even if one wished to be subject to those penalties. – But now come! come!' (I had already been long there.) 'Now I will show you the game itself, while there is still light in this room. Ah, good Lord, what a pity! Can you not remain here a few more days? I would invite some friends for tomorrow, and we would go out tomorrow to the North Inch and demonstrate a game for you. Just now there are some of our '**leading men**' here. And our golfers from Perth are without doubt among the first in Scotland. But you are being drawn to our Highlands? Well, we must make a virtue of necessity. However, when you go back to Edinburgh, do not fail to go out to Musselburgh immediately. There are superb players there, and if you stay there a few days you will certainly have occasion to witness some good game or other. On the '**Links**' (a large playing-field near Leith) much good golf is played too, and likewise on the links in Edinburgh and also on the '**Green**' in Glasgow. Nevertheless, our Perth Inches surpass all other playing-fields.

'Now take a club in your hand. I will take one too, and you imagine that we two are the two sides playing. Each side can consist of as many players as it wishes. Every participant has his caddie following behind him with all his different clubs. From them he then takes out the one that he needs for his shot. – Now imagine that this room is the Leith Links or the Perth Inches. That can be the hole over there' (he drew one with a piece of chalk). 'But oh! the chairs and tables are in our way. Ho Mary! just get the boys in. – Boys! move the chairs, tables and the sofa to one side!'

'Oh pray, do not go to so much trouble!'

'No, no, no, please, please, please!'

We emptied the whole room, and it bore a relatively close resemblance to the North Inch, apart from the grass. In addition, the doors to several adjoining rooms were also opened, and so we had an appropriately long course, which then was illuminated by lights everywhere.

'So, now play a shot! right up to the hole. But we must do everything here a little **en miniature**, and hit the ball only gently as well.'

The whole demonstration was now to start in real earnest. But I have to admit that it almost ended with this beginning. My first ball flew straight into the peat ashes in the fireplace and there it was in

---

[34] [Douglas McEwan, a member of a famous golf-club making family. In 1836 he inherited the firm founded by his grandfather James in 1770. This firm remained in existence until 1920.]

a very critical position. My friend invited me to imagine that the ashes were a patch of sand on the field of play and the lumps of peat round about pieces of rock. And he had very much to comment about this episode – what advantage or disadvantage it offered me – with which club I could best bring the ball out – whether I had the right to push the ashes a little to the side, or not, and under what penalties – what would now be better for me, to accept the penalties or to chance the stroke, trusting to luck – and his observations were larded with a profusion of Scottish and golfing expressions, the meaning of which I could not fathom, such as **'tee'**, or **'holing'**, or **'caddy'**, or **'putters'**, or other similar words. The result of all this was that in his enthusiasm he finally became quite heated and the sweat broke out on his forehead. To the eyes of my understanding everything became more and more obscure. In the end I curtailed my enquiries and conceded that my friend was perfectly correct, that the game was certainly not as simple as I had believed at the beginning, and we both sank tired and weary on to the sofa, which the boys had brought in again in the meantime.

Finally, in spite of my protestations, he wrote several letters of recommendation to famous Scottish golfers, and gave me some references to reading material from which I could teach myself about the game in detail.

Such people can be found everywhere in England; they impart the most comprehensive and accurate information to anyone who is honestly looking for it. This is due to the fact that those who occupy themselves with a subject here are usually completely acquainted with it and pursue it with total commitment. Yet it is remarkable how people guard against voicing their opinions about or explaining things of which they do not possess perfectly expert knowledge. Thus I went on to pose some questions to my golfer about curling. However, although he probably knew ten times more about it than I, yet he avoided giving an answer, saying **'In curling I have done but very little!'** 'I would not dare to pronounce on it. However, if you so desire, I will take you to several experienced curlers in our town.' This he did, and I learned much from them, of which I have already shared some part above with my readers.

The goldsmiths[35] of Perth are famed for their neat pieces of work, and I visited some of them. I found these artists no less obliging and eager than the golfers and curlers in showing me the secrets and products of their craft. The presence of the Queen and the celebrations given in her honour had taken up their working-time very much during that period, and they had then filled their shops with all kinds of interesting specimens of their art; this was a result of the mania for Scottish clothing and national Scottish jewellery which seized the whole of Great Britain after the return of the Queen from Scotland, and was also a result of the various commissions for pretty things which still were to be given as presents to this one or that one. Like Ireland, Scotland too prides itself on having once possessed goldmines that were not insignificant. For every country generally attributes a certain distinction and glory to the fact that gold is found in it too, although in reality this is nothing out of the ordinary, since gold, one of the most widely occurring and commonest metals on earth, is found in nature almost everywhere, unfortunately only seldom in the desired quantity. Pearls are also found in several Scottish rivers, as likewise in the rivers of many other countries.

However, of the native national resources of this kind, that which the Scottish goldsmiths use most are the various beautiful stones and crystals which lie hidden in the Scottish mountain-ranges, and especially the cairngorms that we mentioned previously. The finest agates, amygdules, carnelians, jasper and smoky quartz are found in various districts of Scotland, for example very near Perth on the hill on which Kinnoul Castle stands, also high on Ben Lawers in the upper valley of the Tay,

---

[35][Silver had been worked at Perth since the late 1100s when a Royal Mint was established there. Over 175 silversmiths and goldsmiths were active in Perth from 1714 to 1901.]

and lastly especially on the mountain called Cairn Gorm, further to the north. The mountains are full of them.

However, the people have no means by which to extract these pebbles in the mountain for themselves, but they look for and collect only those that have already been loosened by nature and which lie under stone debris in the little clefts in mountain and rock. These clefts are evident in great numbers on many Scottish hills; they arise through the rain draining off, or from little springs and streams, and are called by the Scots '**Burns**' or '**Brooks**', as are the waters themselves that flow in them. In addition, many beautiful topazes and beryls are searched for and collected in the disintegrated fragments of granite in these books.

The beryls of Invercauld, the goldsmiths told me, are the best. Invercauld is the seat of the chieftains of the famous Clan Invercauld[36] and lies ten German miles[37] from Aberdeen. The shepherds that live in the wild mountains usually collect these pebbles on their lonely walks among the burns, while their sheep graze alongside on the fresh grass. Beryls are often found together with cairngorms, and one of my goldsmiths showed me the most charming little curiosity which he had used for an attractive piece of work. It was a beryl that seemed to have penetrated into a cairngorm or rather around which the latter had partially formed. An interesting and noteworthy observation that I heard from these goldsmiths is this, that the smoky quartz crystals (namely these cairngorms) have more colour in the east of Scotland and are often quite dark, whereas towards the west, or rather the south-west, they become paler. At Killin on the Tay, the most westerly location in which they are found, they are completely white.

At the ball which the Marquis of Breadalbane gave for Queen Victoria at his castle, she wore a large fine cairngorm as the clasp to fasten her plaid on her shoulder. '**Highland-Brooches**' are the pieces of jewellery seen most frequently in these goldsmiths' shops. These brooches – at least those now fashionable – are contrived in the following way: a small golden St Andrew's Cross, on which is placed a thistle in bloom (the symbol of Scotland), sits in the middle of a circle of Scottish pebbles set in silver. But there are also some very old-fashioned brooches worn by those Highland ladies of whom **Dr** Johnson related that as the customary dowry they received a certain number of cows, the rich ones 20 or 30. 'But even ten cows or even two,' says **Dr** Johnson, 'are regarded in some districts as not so a bad dowry.' – Such ladies must still exist here and there since, as my goldsmiths told me, those old brooches are still bought here and there. Among these old Highland brooches one appears very frequently, the '**Mary Queen of Scotch** [sic] **Brooch**'. It is a golden, roman M flanked by a thistle and a lily and also surrounded by a similar circle of stones. I think there must still be some patriotic hearts that tenderly beat for that Mary. Most probably, though I have not seen them, there will be Prince Charlie brooches as well. For although we read in our history books that both the Stuarts and the Scottish resistance to England came to an end with the Battle of Culloden, and although, in these years that follow, we are no longer mindful of the story of Prince Charlie and everything that is connected with it, nevertheless we must not believe that that is the case in Scotland. In this country there is continual talk, with tenderness and love, of '**bonny Prince Charlie**', and a traveller here cannot avoid remembering him daily.

Prince Charlie is for many patriotic Scots to some extent the last ray of the sun of Scottish independence, and since he did not become king[38], so he shines more gently, more mildly, and more steadfastly into Scottish hearts than the radiance of many earlier royal crowns.

---

[36] [This was not a clan but a branch known as the Farquharsons of Invercauld.]

[37] [About 64 kilometres.]

[38] [Had he become king, he would not have been the king of Scotland only, nor would he have been king of an independent Scotland. See Introduction p. xx.]

Travels in Scotland (1840) by J.G. Kohl

> 'Fareweel to a' our Scotish [sic] fame,
>   Fareweel to our ancient glory!
> Fareweel e'en to the Scotish name,
>   Sae fam'd in martial story!
> Now Tweed rins to the ocean
>   To mark where England's province stands![39]

so sings Burns of the union with England[40]. And although such songs have no further practical value, like similar songs of Thomas Moore in Ireland, they nevertheless possess a great poetic and, so to speak, ethnographic meaning.

I also saw here some very splendid '**Highland-Dirks**' here, which belong to the complete Highland dress of a Scottish chieftain. Generally a set of cutlery of knives and forks accompanies such a dagger, a peculiar accompaniment, and one that is very characteristic of the Highland chiefs, who very often won their bread and meat with dagger and sword. I have already mentioned those resplendent ram's horn snuff-boxes that are also commonly seen in the goldsmiths' shops. At gatherings of Scottish Highlanders, these '**Snuff-mulls**' customarily are put on the table and are passed around in company, like drinking-horns. I can also add that Scottish regiments also have such native snuffmulls in their mess-rooms. The same people who busy themselves so lovingly with these snuff-boxes nevertheless very often speak of the tobacco-pipe as though it were the most abhorrent thing on earth.

All these magnificent things, and many others too, can be bought by the noble and not so noble inhabitants of the Highlands in the Scottish town of Perth, the shops of which are splendidly stocked with every luxurious article. The next morning, I must say with the greatest reluctance, I said a farewell to all these fine things that I saw, and to very many other interesting things that I was unfortunately not able to see in Perth. For if a town is worth a more prolonged stay, then that town is Perth, '**the Auld**', '**the Fair**', '**the Saint**' – for it is also called '**Saint Johnston**'[41] from the principal church which is dedicated to St John. Like Perth, many Scottish towns have a double name. Mostly, however, the one name has arisen from a contraction of the other. Thus, for example, Aberbrothock[42] is usually called only Arbroath[43] and Linlithgow only Lithgow.

* * * * * * *

---

[39] [A footnote by the author gives an accurate prose translation.]
[40] [The poem is actually a diatribe against those noblemen in the Scottish Parliament who accepted bribes from England to vote for union in 1706: the title is 'Such a Parcel of Rogues in a Nation'.]
[41] [In a parenthesis, the author translates *Saint* into German but repeats *Johnston* unchanged without explaining that this was originally the phrase, dating from the Middle Ages, *John's Toun*; the St John to whom the parish church is dedicated is John the Baptist.]
[42] *Aberbrothwick*
[43] *Arbroth*

X
From Perth to Dunkeld

'**Weel**[1], **sir, have you seen fair Perth-town?** ha! ha! ha!' began an Irishman the next morning, imitating the Scots dialect; he had sat down beside me on the coach that was to carry its '**Out- and inside passengers**[2]' off to the north.

'**Have you seen the bonnie lasses of Perth? Garls**[3] **call them the cockneys. Ha! ha! ha! – Bless my heart! and weel they are!** And godly and religious as well; for these Scots girls, when they meet the young Scots boys, talk of nothing but the '**unity of peace**', of the '**glory of heaven**', of the Bible, of the Kirk, and yet love sneaks up on them and they soon have a wedding. Ha! ha! ha!'

'Sh! sh! Do not speak so loudly! There are some Scots sitting beside us, and they could take offence.'

'Oho, that doesn't matter! The Scots know anyhow that we Irish are half heathen by nature and lost to this world and the next. We have grown up in the darkness of Catholicism and amidst the '**errors of popery**'. Nothing we say offends them. Ha! ha! ha! It is cold, sir! **Will you not take a dramm** [sic] **of Toddy? A splendid stuff is toddy! Is it not, sir?**'

Perhaps, when I heard his offer, my face failed to express agreement.

'**Bless my eyes! In the name of wonder!** What a face you're making, ha! ha! ha! Oh sir, we are allowed to take toddy today and drive in a coach out into the world; for, as you know, today is a '**lawful morning**[4]', ha! ha! ha!'

I did not have my troubles to seek with this Irishman who was continually blessing himself, his eyes, his heart, in the name of wonder and in the name of other things still, and he must have been very shocking to my solemn Scotsmen; for the less they laughed, the more this seemed to excite my Irishman's hilarity. The Irish are instantly recognisable in Scotland, like white sheep among the black.

In front of us, on the place beside the coachman, sat a Scotsman, a grey plaid over his shoulders, quite silent and stiff and without uttering a word. Only when we passed some wayfarers or workers in fields did I see him make a movement and throw on to the road a few little pieces of paper, which these people picked up. At first I thought that he was a surgeon, a doctor or some such person who was making his address known to people in this fashion. But after he had also given me some of his pieces of paper, I saw that they were little prayers and short religious reflections, each printed on a separate little sheet. They were of varied content, and each kind was put together in a different bundle. According to how people seemed to him, he reached now into one pocket, now into the other, and brought out now one bundle, now another. At each village he prepared himself in advance and laid his bundles on his lap in readiness. And where he noticed people in front of their

---

[1] Scots for '**well**'. *JGK*

[2] [See Chapter VII, fn. 1. Both stage and mail coaches carried four 'inside' passengers. A stage coach could carry up to 12 'outside' passengers seated on top of the coach, while a mail coach (as this was, according to the author's list of Contents) could carry one on top beside the driver and perhaps as many as six behind them. Mail coaches made fewer stops than stage coaches and so completed their journey quicker.]

[3] Instead of '**girls**'. *JGK*

[4] '**A lawful morning**' in Scotland means one on which, according to the law, one may work and travel, that is, a weekday. Sundays and holidays are not '**lawful**'. '**Every lawful morning goes the coach from Perth to Dunkeld**', thus Scottish postmasters announce the timetable of their conveyances. *JGK*

doors, children on the street, or poor toiling pavers by the roadside, he would begin first by calling their attention to himself with a loud shout, and then let a few papers flutter out. The workers roused themselves from their heavy labours to pick up the papers and see what they were, the children jumped happily in the air and grabbed at them as though at blossom showering down, and then seemed to study everything through avidly.

I likewise read some of those tracts and kept them for myself. And I will refrain from reproducing any of them here, because they treat of sacred things in a way that is truly excessively odd, and because it could give the impression that I wished to ridicule them; nevertheless, I must freely confess that I was not a little astonished by their content, and that I am not in the least convinced that such pamphlets can promote even the smallest degree of good. The things discoursed upon therein were so completely unintelligible to me, that, if I will not immediately describe them as the work of darkness, I must nevertheless say that not the least common sense was to be found therein, and that consequently the basis of any enlightenment was lacking. I believe neither that God looked down on these things with pleasure, nor that by them any tiny drop of heavenly consolation was trickled into the cup of sorrow of those poor hard-working people and those small ragged children.

Since my travelling companion had so many little tracts, I remarked to him that I supposed that his liberality must cost him very dear. 'Ah Sir!' he answered, 'I can roughly reckon that a hundred of the sheets do not cost me more than a sixpence on average.'

It was the Inverness coach with which we were travelling, and the road it takes goes first of all a good way up in the valley of the Tay. The ancient Scottish place of coronation, Scone, looked out from wooded and parkland surroundings on the higher opposite bank of the river. We passed several battlefields that are so old, I believe, that even ghosts and Manes[5] of the fallen heroes no longer dwell on them. And finally we reached the **'Highland-mouth'** of Dunkeld. Here I left the coach, which travelled onwards to the north, in order to continue my expedition from Dunkeld into the mountains in a gig and later on foot.

However, before we reached that town, we passed near a wood, which is famous even in Germany[6], namely **'Birnam-forest'**, from where Malcolm's soldiers, they say, provided themselves with branches in order to march against Macbeth. I would very happily have gone walking for a little in that wood, if only there had still been a wood there. However, people assured me here too, that there was almost nothing left of this forest than the name. The district that is called Birnam Wood is situated near the above-mentioned mouth of the Highlands and stretches up to the foothills of the Highlands. There is still a hill there, called **'Duncan's Hill'** because that unfortunate king is said to have held court there.

After Birnam Forest the valley of the Tay narrows significantly. The journey leads for a good distance through a kind of defile or narrow mountain pass, which, however, people call **'the mouth'**. This is the spot where the Tay, forcing its way through a gorge, leaves the Highlands and flows out into the plain to continue its way. In the course of the Tay, here in Dunkeld there is the same feature as in the course of the Tay[7] at Crieff, which we remarked on above, and as in that of the Shee[8] at Blairgowrie[9], and in that of the Teith[10] at Callender above Stirling. At all these towns are different **'Mouths of the Highlands'**. The traveller makes his way through the above-mentioned defile and

---

[5] [Roman spirits of the dead.]
[6] [Presumably from Shakespeare's play *Macbeth*.]
[7] [Obviously a slip for *Earn*.]
[8] [The Shee Water is actually one of the tributaries of the River Ericht which runs through Blairgowrie.]
[9] *Blair-Gowrie*
[10] *Teth*

comes into a small open area among the mountains, and in the deep attractive bosom of this, right in the middle, is situated the little town of Dunkeld. We have now entered through the gateway and are in the Highlands, in the country of those Scots who appear on the coat of arms of the Perth antiquarian society[11] accompanied by the motto '**a Romanis invicti**' ('undefeated by the Romans').

Indeed, the thought that is expressed in these few words is the first that always powerfully grips me, albeit from such a remote, obscure distance, whenever I cross the frontier of the Roman Empire at any point. These 'intrepid warriors', as I once found them described in an old German book of the last century, founded an empire, the contemplation of which, it appears, is bound to excite the admiration of historians forever. For several years now I have been journeying round the far-flung boundaries of their empire, which extend from the Black Sea to these **Highland-mouths**, over Wallachia, through Hungary, Austria, German and Belgium, and I have been searching out with keenness the remains of their frontier ramparts and camps, and yet there is no question but that a traveller would have to have a long life if he wished to complete such an inspection of the frontiers of the Roman Empire in their entirety. There is only one other race, to travel round the boundaries of whose area of settlement would be even more difficult. These are the people who rose up beyond the Roman frontier ramparts and who began by conquering the whole Roman Empire; but in addition they also conquered the regions of the world which the Romans did not possess[12]. These people, the Germanic tribes, conquered the Highlands of Scotland as well, and when the Scots said '**a Romanis invicti**', then, in so saying, they probably secretly thought '**a Germanis victi**'[13].

My merry and godless Irishman took his leave of me in Dunkeld, saying to me '**Well, sir, now you are in the Highlands, the Cockneys say the ilands, as if it were Islands**'. The London Cockneys do indeed leave out the H almost everywhere where it is written, and, strange to relate, insert one where it does not belong. Thus, for example, they pronounce '**Islands**' contrarily like '**Highlands**' and say, for example, '**the Highlanders of Newzealand**', as though they were referring to Scottish mountain-dwellers in New Zealand. It is a curious, but almost inexplicable phenomenon that there are a number of peoples who omit the H as regularly where it belongs as they put it in where it does not belong. The Latvians, for example, persistently say 'der Err vom Hause'[14], but on the other hand, 'her (instead of 'er') ist nicht zu Hause'[15].

It has been said that the division of Scotland into Highlands and Lowlands is rather an arbitrary and unnatural one, since in fact the whole country is intersected by mountains, and since in the part that we understand by 'Lowlands', ranges of hills run this way and that, in height and diversity only slightly inferior to those of the Highlands. That is certainly true. What we understand by Lowlands, particularly southern Scotland, is a very hilly country as well, and in no wise does it deserve the name to the extent as do the German Lowlands, which present a completely flat landscape.

Nevertheless, however, first of all the boundary line between the Highlands and the Lowlands of Scotland is on the whole remarkably clearly identified both popularly in Scotland and by Scottish geographers, and therefore it is, with some exceptions, by no means a vague concept; secondly the division has always made itself very perceptible and been drawn distinctly, both in the appearance of the country and throughout its history.

---

[11] [The foundation of a 'Society for investigating the History and preserving the Antiquities and Records of Scotland generally' was suggested by Mr James Scott, Senior Minister of Perth. It was inaugurated on 26 December 1784.]

[12] [If the author is referring to Germanic tribes immediately after the fall of the Roman Empire, he is guilty of gross exaggeration. However, it is possible that he is referring to the British Empire and is including English-speakers among *Germanic tribes*.]

[13] ['conquered by the Germanic tribes']

[14] [Instead of *der Herr vom Hause* = 'the master of the house']

[15] [*er ist nicht zu Hause* = 'he is not at home']

Travels in Scotland (1840) by J.G. Kohl

I will, in the first place, describe this Highland Line as it is understood in Scotland.

In popular opinion and in that of geographers, the Scottish Highlands begin in the west at the fissure which the Firth of Clyde makes in the land. The country to the north of this firth is, and was always, reckoned to be the Highlands, including the islands of Arran and Bute, and the long peninsula that ends in the Mull of Kintyre[16]. This appears very natural when one sails into this firth. For all the islands and mainland mentioned are mountainous, while the counties of Ayr and Renfrewshire situated to the south seem from the sea to be completely flat, and to a great extent are so in actual fact.

Things continue thus as far as Dumbarton, which is the last hill to appear close at hand on the north bank of the Clyde. The steep bluffs, between which the waters of Loch Lomond flow out, form a great mountain gateway, and this is regarded as one of the entrances to the Highlands. From Dumbarton onwards the land becomes level on both sides of the Clyde, and the Highland Line recedes into the interior of the country; there it faithfully follows the range of mountains which from here onwards as far as Dunkeld stand in striking contrast to the plain known for its greatest part as 'Strathmore'. From Stirling and Perth mountain ranges can be seen everywhere, extending in a long line; and here Kilmarnock[17], Callander, Crieff, Dunkeld and Blairgowrie are to be regarded as **'Highland-mouths'**, as they are generally termed both popularly and by Scottish scholars.

From Blairgowrie on, however, it seems that the boundary becomes somewhat undecided. Some geographers virtually trace a straight line from here to Aberdeen or Stonehaven[18] and say that everything that lies to the north of this line is to be included in the Highlands. Others, however, (I believe, decidedly the majority) draw their Highland Line to the east at an angle along the outermost foothills of the mountains and then bring it round in a curve to the Moray Firth[19] and to Inverness, thus reckoning as still part of the Lowlands the entire more or less flat and low stretch of coast in the east of this area of Scotland. In a very striking, but I believe perfectly correct way, the whole narrow strip of coastland that surrounds the Moray Firth and the Cromarty Firth, and likewise the little peninsula of Cromarty that lies between both firths, are then also accounted to the Lowlands. This coastal strip, which is not included in the Highlands, is here and there scarcely an English mile broad; it extends from Nairn by way of Inverness, Kirkhill, Dingwall[20], Hill of Fearn[21], Tain[22], and finally becomes quite narrow and disappears into the Firth of Tain[23] behind Edderton.

This is the characteristic Highland Line as it can be observed not only on Scottish specialist maps, meticulously indicated, but also in the popular mind. All parts of Scotland which lie to the north and west of these lines are Highland, including even the Western Isles, the Hebrides. And all people who inhabit these areas – whether they live on the mountains, or in valleys or the plains that exist here and there, or on the islands – are called Highlanders.

---

[16] *Cantire*
[17] [This cannot be the town of Kilmarnock, which is in Ayrshire, south of the Clyde. The author may be confusing this town with Kilmaronock in Dunbartonshire, about 1 kilometre south-west of Drymen. It appears in John Thomson's *Atlas of Scotland* of 1832 as 'Kilmarnock' in the map of Stirlingshire but as 'Kilmaronock' in that of Dumbartonshire [sic]. (For a note on this spelling, see Chapter XX, fn. 3.)]
[18] *Sconehaven*
[19] *Murray-Frith*
[20] *Dingwale*
[21] *Kiltearn*
[22] *Taiw*
[23] *Frith von Taiw* [Nowadays ' Dornoch Firth']

If we now glance at the history of Scotland, this Highland Line, as we said, makes itself obvious everywhere here. The so-called Lowland districts described are those areas which not only the Romans but also the Saxons chiefly occupied, and in which they disseminated themselves the most[24]; on the other hand, everything that lay to the west and north of this line was retained by the Celtic primeval inhabitants of the land, and was defended in a series of countless battles which they fought with the Romans and Saxons in front of those Highland gateways of theirs.

As in the history of this land, so also in its physical characteristics the division described above shows itself to be of importance. Firstly, the Highlands lie more towards the north, the Lowlands on the other hand lie more towards the south. Secondly, the Highlands face more towards the great ocean in the west, the Lowlands on the other hand face more towards the German Ocean. (Both these circumstances significantly impart a difference in climate and in the whole constitution of the two parts of the country.) Thirdly and finally, the southern parts of the country actually have a quite different appearance to the northern mountain ranges encompassed within the Highland Line. For even if the southern hills are not so remarkably much lower than the northern – the highest of them rise to almost 3000 feet while the highest in the Highlands rise to something more than 4000 feet – they nevertheless without exception have a completely different character. The southern ones have green, rounded, grass-covered tops, not so many wild, steep rocky gullies, chasms, precipices and glens – more forest – less moorland and morass.

All these circumstances and conditions show clearly and distinctly that, not only in the history of the country but in its appearance, a noticeable and characteristic difference exists between the part of Scotland called the Highlands and that called the Lowlands. And there can only remain the problem, firstly whether this term for the difference between Lowlands and Highlands has been correctly chosen, secondly whether its boundaries had to be drawn precisely along the line in which they have been drawn – all in all, two trivial questions. For once the difference itself is correctly recognised, the name chosen matters but little. In that connection, since after all '**Lowlands**' means only that one piece of country is lower than another, since this description is not intended to indicate that a perfectly flat land is meant, and since in point of fact neither the plains nor the hills in the Lowlands are so high as those in the Highlands, there can be no serious objection to the name. As far as the Highland Line is concerned, certainly with regard to the southern portion at least, it could not have been better drawn, since it is precisely along this boundary that the contrasts between southern, lower Scotland and north-western, higher Scotland confront each other most clearly.

Several writers have completely rejected this division of Scotland, which did not come from scholars, and, simply looking at its outward shape, divided the country into three parts, into a northern, a southern, and a central Scotland. Although the persuasiveness of this segmentation is also not to be totally rejected, it is important that the first-mentioned popular method of division be held primarily valid, and it is therefore still worthy of note that the difference in appearance between the Lowlands and Highlands is completely thoroughgoing. That is, the Lowlands are without exception greener, more fertile, richer in grass and forest, flatter or at least more rounded and hence more Germanic than the Highlands, and, conversely, the latter are without exception less fertile, less populated, more covered with bog and heath, more barren, rockier, wilder and more Celtic than the Lowlands.

In these two names are expressed the two greatest and most extraordinary contrasts that Scotland offers. The division that is derived from the outward shape and from the splitting of the land from Inverness through Glen More can be regarded only as a subordinate one. This valley divides the northern Highlands from the southern. Then again from these southern Highlands can be distinguished the western Highlands, by which is principally understood the mountains of the

---

[24] [The Romans did not actively occupy any part of what later became Scotland, nor did the Saxons.]

islands and long peninsulas of Argyleshire. **'The western Highlands'** is a name that is very often heard, likewise **'the northern Highlands'**. There are no **'Eastern Highlands'**, that is, this name is not used as a **nomen proprium**[25], because everything is flat in the east of the country, because the Highlands gradually merge with the plain here, and because therefore their appearance here in the east does not emerge as a definite and distinct entity. The southern Highlands too do not separate themselves off as a segment of the land that can be so easily characterised, and thus one rarely hears any mention of the 'southern Highlands' as a distinct area of its own, although it is surely natural that not only are there people in the north of the country who speak of the more southerly parts of the Highlands, just as there are also inhabitants in the west for whom some parts of the Highlands lie to the east and who therefore describe them as such.

The division of Scotland into Highlands and Lowlands is still by no means a pointless one even now. For apart from the topographical difference, which will always exist, there is at the present day still a marked difference in the inhabitants of the two parts of the country.

As soon as one sets foot in the Highlands, one meets with a different kind of person, still hears here and there the Celtic language, and sees people who have only just begun to germanicise or anglicise themselves. Immediately one becomes aware of the memories of the old clans in the country, hears tell of chieftains and comes into uncultivated and wild tracts. Although the Highlands occupy by far the larger half of the country, they contain, however, a population sixfold smaller than the Lowlands, namely only 400,000 souls, and therefore are on average probably seven or eight times more sparsely populated. In a political respect, too, the Highland Line has still a particular meaning, namely with reference to the distillation of spirits, which is subject to different laws in the Highlands from those in the Lowlands. The so-called **'Boundary of the Highland Distillery'**[26], which is to be found indicated on most Scottish specialist maps, differs only slightly from the actual Highland Line.

* * * * * * *

---

[25] ['Proper noun']

[26] [The Wash Act of 1784 (and the Distillery Acts of 1785) divided Scotland into two excise zones and the resulting 'Distillery Line' closely follows the accepted division into Highlands and Lowlands. The restriction that the produce of licensed stills from the Highlands should not be allowed to pass into the Lowlands was a stimulus to smuggling.]

XI
Dunkeld

Dunkeld – straight away an old Celtic name[1], and a place surrounded on all sides by mountainous country that now is no longer in the distance but in the immediate vicinity, and already the seat of a clan chieftain, namely the Duke of Atholl, who is the head of the great Clan Murray. One Duke of Atholl, I think the third last, was an assiduous planter of trees[2]. They say that he sowed 45,000 acres of land with trees, and the number of trees planted by him amounts to no fewer than twelve million. Others maintain it was fifteen million. It is therefore no wonder that the neighbourhood of his domicile in particular reveals itself as shaded all around by magnificent trees. These splendid trees, the mountains which encircle the town, the dark rocks which leap out from them, the enchanting crystal-clear River Tay which winds its way through with greenswards on its banks, the Highland mouth which leads both the way and one's gaze into the Lowlands – all this gives the place an exceedingly magical charm.

The town itself is very pleasant and pretty. The park and the mansion-house lie behind it. As is customary with British barons and dukes, on the gateway of the park hangs resplendent the family coat of arms, and under it can be read the remarkable motto of Clan Murray '**Furth fortune and fill the fetters**'[3] (that is, 'kick as many prisoners and slaves as possible on the head and thus become great'). The Dukes of Atholl are very famous in Scotland. Only the Dukes of Buccleuch and of Argyle are on a par with them. Perhaps it will be interesting for my readers firstly to learn all the hereditary titles of such a Scottish aristocrat, in order to be able to compare them with our countless Bohemian and Austrian hereditary titles.

The most ancient title of the family is '***Baron* Murray of Tullibardine**', for generally in Scotland the baronial titles are always older than the ducal. (The most recent barons are as ancient as the oldest dukes. The most recent baron dates from 1690 and only one duke is older than 1643.) The other titles are the following: '***Earl* of Tullibardine, Earl of Atholl, Marquess of Atholl, Viscount of Balquhidder, Baron Murray Balvenie and Gask, Duke of Atholl, *Marquess* of Tullibardine, Earl of Strathtay and Strathardle, Viscount of Glenalmond and Glenlyon**'. These are the titles which the Murrays possess in the peerage of Scotland. In the peerage of England, that is, by the act of the King of England, they were created '**Barons Strange of Knockyn**'. **In the peerage of Britain**, that is, after the union of the two kingdoms, England and Scotland, they became '**Earls Strange and Barons Murray of Stanley**'. At the very heart, under all this load of hereditary titles, is concealed none other than 'John Murray'; this is the original and primary name of the first duke. This is the name under which he appears in the baptismal register and before God – in ordinary life he is commonly called the 'Duke'.

I went walking in the Duke's park with an old man of the Clan Murray who guided my steps as my companion. This man spoke of nothing else but the '**Duke**'. For the Murrays their duke is the be-all and end-all of the world. 'That is natural, Sir!' said my old guide. '**For every Duke of Atholl has a great swing in this country, in carrying elections, you know, gentlemen getting in situation and in such things.**' The Duke seemed to them so great that they were not even very knowledgeable about the heads of the kingdom. Thus my old companion insisted stubbornly that Prince Albert was a prince of 'Wämir' or 'Wehmir'. He had once heard tell of Weimar. Finally I persuaded him that he was a Prince of Coburg. 'Well, the name is not important, Sir;' he said, 'the best thing is **that this**

---

[1] [In Gaelic *Dun Chaillinn*.]
[2] [John, 4th Duke of Atholl, known as the 'planting Duke'.]
[3] [Properly 'Furth Forth and Fill the Fetters'. This dates from 1475 when the Earl of Atholl was sent by James II on an expedition against a rebellious Lord of the Isles.]

country is so very much pleased with your countryman. He is such a quiet, nice and gracious man. He does not meddle with politics at all. And a gentleman he is too.'

The celebrated **Dr** Johnson, who made a journey through Scotland and to the Hebrides in 1773, says that a tree in this country is as great a rarity as a horse in Venice. Now, thanks to the Duke of Atholl and several other such avid planters of trees who have lately appeared on the scene, that is no longer true. **Dr** Johnson adds that almost all the trees he had seen in Scotland seemed to him to have been planted quite recently. During the last century, therefore, extraordinary activity must have been widespread in this connection, since beautiful woodlands are now found in so very many places in Scotland. Even in the very northernmost tip of the country there are now great forests, such as Dirry-Meanach Forest [sic][4] and Tarfe Forest [sic][5], which latter extends as far as Cape[6] Wrath.

In Scotland, as in Ireland, a twice repeated afforestation and a twice repeated dearth of trees can be discerned. At first, the land was naturally bare when it arose out of the sea. Then it became seeded all over with splendid forests and thus wooded the Romans found it. As evidence for this we have not only the reports of these Romans but also the circumstance that even in those districts of Scotland most denuded of trees, even on the almost completely barren Hebrides, the most magnificent tree-trunks can still be found in marshes and quagmires, as in the bogs of Ireland. That ancient afforestation disappeared, however, in the course of the centuries through bad husbandry and cultivation on the part of human beings, until our present era – this goddess with a hundred breasts, this nurse with a thousand skills – has once again spread woodlands over Scotland. It is clearly the most splendid thing with which the countryside can be endowed. For even if **Dr** Johnson's dicta are no longer completely accurate, nevertheless there are still quite large areas everywhere to which they are applicable to the letter, and so the land could still have need of several dozen such Dukes of Atholl, patriotic and passionately devoted to planting woods.

In the small part of the Highlands through which I passed, I saw no tree as commonly planted as the larch. To begin with, the Scots believed that this tree could only grow in a southern climate, until the Duke of Atholl demonstrated the contrary to them. The first larches that were introduced here were brought in 1737 from Austria where there are the most superb woods of these beautiful and useful trees, especially in the Etsch Valley. At first they were kept in flower pots and then planted out on the lawn in front of the Duke's residence, where I saw them now grown to fine great high trunks. My guide told me it had been calculated that one of them contained no less than 396 cubic feet of timber. On seeing these two larches I remembered the two cypresses in the Crimea that were the progenitors of all the cypresses in that territory. That selfsame Duke of Atholl lived long enough to see several of the larches planted by him sailing into the world as ship's timber in a frigate of 36 cannons. Unfortunately, the tree-planter is seldom granted such a pleasure, wherefore it is regarded by private persons as an unrewarding enterprise, and so it is a thing that must above all be undertaken by the state, which enjoys a longer life than the individual. Like the larch, most trees in Scotland have been introduced from abroad; of the indigenous trees there are very few, and of these few only few species, and of these few species only few examples.

Dunkeld was formerly the seat of a bishop, and quite near to the modest house that the Dukes of Atholl possess here can be seen the ruins of a beautiful cathedral. Dunkeld and several similar towns lying on the border of the Highlands and Lowlands were the centres of culture whence the

---

[4] [*The Art of Deer-Stalking; Illustrated by a Narrative of a Few Days' Sport in the Forest of Atholl, and with some Account of the Nature and Habits of Red Deer, and a Short Description of the Scotch Forests* by William Scrope 1838, p. 368, lists the Dirrie-Meanach Forest as a 'detached forest in Sutherland', in other words near Cape Wrath.]
[5] [The Duke of Atholl (see this chapter, fn. 2) created a deer forest in Glen Tarf (near Blair Atholl) at the end of the 18th century. It is nowhere near Cape Wrath. One assumes that the author has erroneously written the names of these two forests in the wrong order or has written the German for 'latter' instead of that for 'former'.]
[6] *Cap*

beacon of religion and learning shone into the Highlands. There is mention of bishops of Dunkeld who sent missionaries with a knowledge of Erse[7] into the mountains to preach there, as had the monks of Iona, who, coming from Ireland, had settled on that famous island off the west coast of Scotland, on the other side of the Highlands, and had undertaken excursions and missionary expeditions from there into the interior. However, the bishops often had no small difficulty in maintaining their properties and rights in the face of the neighbouring clans. 'Nevertheless, it is at the same time interesting' says Mr Chambers, 'to note how the terrors of the church at that time did not fail to exert their influence on the superstitious and half-educated chieftains of these clans. Often, only a short time after they had attacked the prelate and his vassals with sword in hand or stolen his cattle and burned down his barns, the bishops compelled them to come to the altar in hair shirts and to beg for the forgiveness both of heaven and of his lordship.'

I could wish that at some time someone would bring together all the various extremely remarkable and fascinating peculiarities and episodes from the annals of the clans. To write the history of every single clan would be not only impossible but also not sufficiently important and interesting. However, a classification and compilation of all the known incidents from clan history would be engrossing in the extreme, and a quite individual portrayal of this unusual state of affairs in human society could result therefrom.

For example, characteristic incidents come to light, such as the following. A certain clan lived with another in irreconcilable hostility, while conversely another clan was allied to another by eternal friendship. In the case of one clan, it was enough to bear the name of a certain clan to be warmly welcomed in all circumstances. A situation could be seen where one clan brought all the members of another clan into hereditary slavery. Many clans had an extremely despotic framework, such as those in the Hebrides, others had a looser organisation. In such a dissertation it would be highly worthwhile to investigate how it came about that, amid all the quarrels among the clans, one never gained supremacy over all the others, and so no larger political units were formed. Can this simply have arisen from the mountainous nature of the land in which they lived?

The clans that live in the vicinity of Dunkeld are the following: the 'Mackays', the 'Mackenzies'[8], the 'Stewarts', the 'MacInroys' and the 'Donnachys'[9] or 'Robertsons'. ((I should like to know how it comes about that some clans have Germanic-English names.) All these clans came down from their mountains when the Queen and Prince Albert were here. On the beautiful large green area near the Atholls' little house a tent was erected for the Queen, in which she partook of luncheon. '**Aecht**[10] **pipers**' were also present. '**Lord Glen Lyon, who had capital spirits, had hundred men of his own.**' This lord is the future Duke of Atholl. The other clans, each with its chieftain, were all in '**Highland- dress**'. Every group had its pipers. On the splendid bridge, built by the old Duke of Atholl, pipers were also positioned to greet the Queen. '**The Queen reviewed all the clans most famously**' and went down the whole line, greeting people amiably. It must have been a wonderfully delightful sight, this lively, colourful, royal scene set against the beautiful green of the park. Now everything was deserted and silent as the grave. The leaves were falling from the trees, the clans dwelt peaceably in their mountain ravines, and the Duchess of Atholl, only a few weeks previously the occupant of this house, had passed to her eternal rest. A short time after the Queen's visit she had taken ill and died.

At the inn in Dunkeld, a fine hostelry, I took a one-horse '**Gig**' and in it followed the trail of the royal couple up the Tay. I could have done nothing better than this. For the route that Queen Victoria and Prince Albert followed on their journey in the Highlands offers some of the most

---

[7] [i. e. Scottish Gaelic, see Introduction p. xxii, fn. 3.]

[8] *Mac Inzies*

[9] [In Gaelic *Donnchaidh* or *Clann Dhonnchaidh*; the author's Anglicised form has now replaced by *Robertson*.]

[10] Scots for 'eight'. *JGK* [This German spelling indicates the pronunciation 'echt'.]

beautiful spots in the Highlands; many Scots say, unquestionably *the* most beautiful. The way led through Aberfeldy, Kenmore, the noble seat of the noble Marquis of Breadalbane, past Loch Tay, through Killin to Loch Earn, and then back. This is one of the fashionable itineraries in Scotland, or in fact '*the* **fashionable rout**' [sic]. And now, since the Queen has traversed it, it will become even more so, and from now on without doubt, as all the people along this road hope, in this year and in the coming years a *stream* of visitors will pour hither. The County of Perth, to which all these places belong, is one of the three biggest in Scotland, as County Cork is the biggest in Ireland and as Yorkshire is the biggest in England. Of the 16 million acres of the surface of Scotland it covers no fewer than two million, and within this area it affords the most beautiful and the greatest diversity of Lowland and Highland scenery.

* * * * * * *

XII
From Dunkeld to Taymouth Castle

I had myself provided with a driver who had a good command of Gaelic and on the journey this man instructed me a little in this language, which has far less written literature than its sister language, the Erse of the Irish, because the Irish formerly possessed a culture and literature peculiar to themselves, while the Scottish Highlanders have always lived in their barbarous wilderness and are only now being civilised with the assistance of the English language.

My driver told me that the clan from which he came was called '**Dschuer**'[1] and that there were only a few of this family and clan in existence. I asked him whether perhaps he knew some old Erse songs, and as we journeyed, he recited several of them to me. Naturally I did not understand a word of them, and when I asked him what the subject-matter was, he answered '**All these songs contain a great deal about love and in that way** [sic]. **Now they do not make up so much poetry as in the olden time.**' I further asked him how they called the Duke of Atholl among themselves in Gaelic. He replied: '**Kean na Murrich**'[2] ('the great Chief of the Murrays').

Potatoes, which like turnips have only recently been making significant progress in the Scottish Highlands, they call '**puntaht**'[3], probably the English word '**patatoes**' [sic] distorted. The little pits that are seen beside every house here and in which they store their potatoes are called '**Tohl-puntaht**'[4]. In English they are called '**Patatoes' pits**'. Sugar, in English '**Sugar**', has been changed by the Highland Scots into '**Suchkars**'[5].

It was very interesting for me to come upon the track of the origin of the word 'punch', now so famous in the whole world. For my friend maintained that 'punch' is a Gaelic word. '**Believe me, sir!**' he said, '**punch is right out of the bottom of the Gaelic.**'[6] I do not know whence the word comes. The many similar words in English ('**punch**' a clown, '**punch**' a chisel, '**puncheon**' a wine-cask etc.) could lead us to suspect that it belongs to the family of words which derive from the French '**poinçon**'.

Foyer[7] in his *Travels* maintains that '**Punch**' (the drink) is an Indian word that refers to the number of ingredients. However, it is thus certain that the word '**Punch**', like the drink itself, is known here in every Highland bothy, while in Germany both are common only in those superior circles in which Schiller's *Punschlied*[8] is appreciated. Incidentally, here the drink itself does not consist of as many ingredients as Schiller's punch. It is nothing more than perfectly simple warm water and spirits, and, in addition, instead of lemons and sugar, **the smell of the peat-reek**[9]. This '**peat-reek**' (Scottish for 'peat smoke') comes from the malt in it, and this is due to the fact that the malt is dried over peat.

What especially amazed me was that according to popular assertion – I have unfortunately no authority for it apart from this – the names usual in the Scottish Lowlands for the Highland costume are not Gaelic at all. I was given the following Gaelic words for those terms. I write them exactly as

---

[1] [Presumably *Dewar*.]

[2] [Properly *Ceann nam Moireach*]

[3] According to Armstrong's Lexicon written '**buntat**'. *JGK* [Nowadays *buntàta*. See Introduction, p. xxv-xxvi.]

[4] According to Armstrong written '**Toll-buntat**'. *JGK* [Nowadays *toll-buntàta*.]

[5] According to Armstrong written '**Sucar**'. *JGK* [Nowadays *siùcar*. See Introduction, p. xxv.]

[6] [In his German gloss, the author translates *bottom* as *Busen* (= 'bosom').]

[7] [It has not been possible to identify this reference. The theory in question derives the word from the Hindi *pāc* 'five', the ingredients being spirits, water, lemon juice, sugar, and spice.]

[8] [As its name (= 'punch song') suggests, a poem in praise of punch.]

[9] [In his German gloss, the author translates this as *etwas Torfgeschmack* (= 'some taste of peat').]

Travels in Scotland (1840) by J.G. Kohl

people pronounced them. I observed their lips closely and had them pronounce the words distinctly half a dozen times. The plaid, they said, is called '**Prächk-kan**'[10] in Gaelic, the kilt '**Fehl**'[11], but tartan '**Catha**'[12]. However, I have not been able to find these words in any Gaelic lexicon[13].

Every mountain slope that we were now passing in autumn was covered with reddish and yellowish larch trees – all the splendid achievement of the Duke of Atholl. Previously everything here had been totally bare. Furthermore, we were bowling along a truly magnificent avenue.

I cannot cease to marvel at how great a change has taken place in Scotland when I compare the country as it now is with that which it was formerly. In this connection there is no more interesting reading than **Dr Johnson**[14]'s previously mentioned description of his journey; he made this journey seventy years ago and depicts the country as virtually barbaric, speaking of it more or less in a tone such as we use about the Crimea or a similar region. He travelled mostly on horseback, bothies were his nights' lodgings, oat-bread his sustenance, quagmire and rocks his roads, ignorant simple mountain-dwellers his travelling companions. Now there are good roads everywhere, good inns aplenty. Not only all points on the coast but also the islands – the Hebrides, Orkney, Shetland, even since 1834 the extremely remote St Kilda – have been brought into a remarkable network of links with the mainland of Scotland by steamships.

If we consider Scotland as it was at the beginning of last century and compare it with the Scotland of our days, and if we take any facet of human activity, any facet of human domestic and national economy – whichever we choose – then we will find things so paltry then and so impressive now that we almost have trouble in believing not only in that paltriness but in the present impressiveness. If we compare the size of the population, the amount of national revenues, if we compare the state of national education, agriculture, horticulture, if we examine every single aspect, the construction of roads and canals, prosperity, architecture – in short, let us select whatever we wish, and we will discover that everything now is at least ten, and many things twenty, times greater.

We find Scotland as it was a hundred years ago so puny and insignificant that, looking at the matter from our present statistical point of view, we can scarcely grasp why this country was even then considered worthy of a mention in history at all. It steered a zigzag course behind all the countries of Europe, yet now it sails forth, like a swift steam frigate, amidst the first nations of the world and many a great European regular service ship must observe the tactics of this frigate and copy them. For over seventeen hundred years Virgil's words '**Penitus toto divisos orbe Britannos**'[15] could apply in fullest measure to the Scots. It is only a hundred years ago that these words suddenly sank into complete meaninglessness.

On the other hand, it goes without saying that there are also in Scotland many things still that have not been swept along by this rapid steamship progress, and remain exactly as they were and as they will be. For in every country we encounter a similar situation. It would not be difficult, I believe, to find in the middle of Germany farmsteads such as the Romans saw. In the Apennines near Rome robbers and shepherds doubtless live not a fraction differently, or perhaps only one fraction differently, from those in the time of Horace. If one goes into the interior provinces of France, one will see there ancient Gaulish things that are probably identical to those that Caesar saw there. Thus

[10] [Modern spelling *breacan*. The transcription illustrates a stronger degree of preaspiration, see Introduction, p. xxv.]
[11] [Modern spelling *féileadh*.]
[12] [Modern spelling *cadadh*.]
[13] [In fact Armstrong includes them as *breacan*, *fèile*, and *cadadh*.]
[14] However, this scholar is not to be trusted in every detail, since, like many Englishmen, he was a great Scotophobe. JGK
[15] ['Amongst the Britons quite sundered from all the world' (Eclogues 1, l. 66)]

90

on our journey among the mountains we glimpsed little huts that looked exactly as the dwellings of the ancient Ossianic Picts and Scots might have looked. They were thatched with clumps of heather that here and there hung down very untidily. Heather, in Gaelic **'frooch'**[16], is without exception the usual roofing material here. The houses are thatched with it, and likewise the **'Stacks'** (stockpiles of hay and grain), and likewise the ceremonial arches that had been erected for Queen Victoria and Prince Albert along their route, all similarly built of heather and the initial letters of both royal personages fashioned from twisted heather.

Here and there in front of the little bothies a well-trimmed little **'spruce fir'** (as the Scots call them) can be seen standing, similar to the clipped hawthorn bushes in front of the huts of the Irish. Beyond the frooch-bothies here and there lay snow (Gaelic **'snechk'**[17]). This word, strange to say, is one of those which people have in all the languages of Europe, in the Romance as well as the Germanic, in the Celtic as well as the Slavonic. Only sometimes the sibilant at the beginning or the palatal sound at the end is left out.

When I arrived in Aberfeldy, dusk was already beginning to fall, and I had no longer enough time to see the celebrated waterfall near the town. However, there was enough light available to read the delightful song that Burns wrote about that waterfall. This song is called 'The Birks of Aberfeldie'[18] and its beauty principally consists in the fact that the poet, while he actually depicts the waterfall, continually turns to the birches that hang over it, and so in a way shows us the principal object of his gaze framed in the green of the birches. Naturally in the poem is also included a **'bonny lass'** with whom the poet sits under those birches beside the waterfall and to whom he turns after every stanza with a recurring refrain. Not only the birches of Aberfeldy, but also Kenmore and Killin and several other pleasant spots on this road up the Tay are praised in enchanting songs by Burns, whom Walter Scott calls the best Scottish poet.

Here, and generally throughout Scotland, we can manage without those poems of Burns as little as we can without those of Thomas Moore in Ireland. Both are lyric poets, both love their native land, both in a short time have achieved an extraordinary popularity. In Ireland, some song or other of Moore's has become so interwoven with every beautiful scene of nature, with every historical memory, that they can scarcely be thought of without immediately evoking that song. No Irishman recalls the ruins of Glendalough without beginning with Thomas Moore[19] **'On the lake, whose gloomy shore'** or **'Let Erin remember the days of old'**, and none can hear King Brien[20] mentioned without thinking of Moore's song **'Remember the glories of Brien the Brave'**. In the same way, if, in a company in which a Scot is present, you happen to mention the Battle of Bannockburn, immediately the eyes of your Scottish friend become transfigured and with a smile he immediately asks you 'Ah, do you by chance know the splendid poem by Burns:'

> **'Scots, wha hae wi' Wallace bled,**
> **Scots, wham Bruce has often led'**[21].

If perhaps you would sometime like to hear the attractive Burns poem, which begins:

> **'Nae gentle dames, tho' e'er sae fair,**
> **Shall ever be my Muse's care;**

---

[16] [Spelt *fraoch*]

[17] [Spelt *sneachd*. The transcription reflects the pronunciation well, including the final consonant.]

[18] [Although *Aberfeldy* is the modern spelling, Burns wrote *Aberfeldie*.]

[19] [Thomas Moore (1779 – 1852). The titles of the three poems are exactly the same as the lines quoted. The ruins in question are those of the early mediaeval monastery of St Coemgen (Kevin) in Co. Wicklow.]

[20] [Brian (or Brien) Boru , High King of Ireland 1002 – 14.]

[21] [Translated by the author in a footnote. The title of the poem is 'Scots Wha Hae'.]

> **Their titles a' are empty show;**
> **Gie me my Highland lassie, o'**[22],

then you need only lead the conversation skilfully on to the subject of Highland girls, and you will soon hear some Scot or other in your company humming this song to himself. But if perhaps you have heard the Burns poem too often, the first stanza of which runs:

> **'The heather was blooming, the meadows were mawn,**
> **Our lads gaed a hunting, ae day at the dawn**
> **O'er moors and o'er mosses and monie a glen,**
> **At length they discover'd a bonny moor-hen'**[23],

or if you have doubts, as many critics have, about whether this poem is really by Burns, then certainly avoid walking over heather moors with a Scot – which is of course difficult if you happen to go walking in Scotland itself – for otherwise he will immediately recite the whole poem once again for you.

A parallel could be drawn between the Scottish Burns and the Irish Moore and, very fittingly, the English Byron[24] too. For all three are recent lyric poets, who are treasured almost in the same way in the entire British nation and honoured and deified, particularly in the respective region of Britain that is especially their own. All three are without doubt geniuses endowed by the Deity. A principal difference is that Byron is such a bad patriot, which is perhaps connected with the fact that England stands at the head of the Union, sovereign, dominant and prosperous, while Ireland and Scotland as repressed or even conquered nations arouse more especially the tender love and sympathy of a poet. It is also remarkable that Byron, just as he can call the more dominant native land his own, is also the most powerful and comprehensive genius of the three. All three have hearts tormented and lacerated by grief and melancholy. The most fervent is Byron, the most sweetly melancholic the Irishman, but the Scotsman too is often quite fervently aroused. Most British poets have had mournful and heavy-hearted natures. This is the characteristic of British literature. It is strange that in that country the divine gift of Apollo does not seem to gladden hearts.

Byron and Burns were most unhappy in themselves, through their stormy, passionate disposition. Thomas Moore seems to be more cheerful, when he is not plucking the strings of Erin's melancholy lyre. Thomas Moore was also luckier than Burns in respect of material circumstances of fortune. Of all three, Burns was decidedly the unhappiest. For although his poems, right from the very beginning and while he still lived, had an extraordinary success, nevertheless his countrymen did nothing exceptional for him. One may dispute this or not, as one will, and one may blame the unruly Burns himself as much as he really may deserve, nevertheless it remains a mark of shame against the Scots that they let the poet that delighted them the most die in want and misery. Even on his deathbed Burns was obliged to write several letters in order to raise five pounds sterling which he owed to a '**Haberdasher**' who was threatening to have him put in prison.

Burns made such splendid use of the material with which the Scots language furnished him, so skilfully elaborated it, and cast it in such completely impeccable forms, that without any doubt his poems must be accounted among those which are '**aere perennius**'[25]. One can foresee that all the millions of people from future generations will long refresh themselves from them still, even as

---

[22] [Translated by the author in a footnote. The title of the poem is 'My Highland Lassie, O'.]

[23] [Translated by the author in a footnote. The title of the poem is 'The Bonie Moor-hen'.] Of course this moorhen is again a **bonny highland lass.** *JGK*

[24] [George Gordon, 6th Baron Byron (1788 – 1824) is sometimes reckoned to be a Scottish poet, for example by the editors of *The Oxford Book of Scottish Verse*. His mother was a Scottish noblewoman and he himself attended Aberdeen Grammar School before becoming heir to the Byron peerage at the age of ten.]

[25] ['more lasting than bronze'. Horace Odes, Book 3, 30, l. 1]

those of the last fifty years have done. And such a man was allowed to become ruined and suffer all manner of deprivation. Future generations will not comprehend the lack of action by his contemporaries, and if these latter allude to the poet's failings, the former will say to them: 'For our sake and that of the world, could you not bear with the failings of this spirit even a little? Was there not one single benevolent, generous soul among you who attended to him, the turbulent spirit, and made provision for him when he himself was not in a state to make provision for himself? Yes, was it not a holy duty for you to do this? – You all knew what you, and the world, had in him,. He did not live unknown among you. It was before your eyes and ears that he sang.' But the world is so fashioned that it is an open question whether or not, when the occasion arises, these so right-thinking future generations will in turn one day again sin against a Burns of their day, in the same way as did their ancestors.

What makes Burns stand out in particular from the two other poets mentioned alongside him is that he did not belong to the so-called cultivated classes, that he had not enjoyed any education. In earlier times in Scotland, when there were no cultivated classes and no literature[26], this would have been no disadvantage to him. He would have gone with armies into battle as one of the most impassioned bards. Now, however, it inevitably brought him into conflict with the world and with himself. For he was now drawn into scholarly and literary circles for which neither his manners nor the extent of his learning could fit him, yet in which, from the pinnacle of his gifts, he was forced to observe so many people beneath him.

As a genuine national Scottish poet, and as one with his origins in the very heart of the nation, he also made use of the Scots dialect in his poems. Naturally this may here and there be somewhat detrimental to him in the eyes of the English, while his standing with the Scots is heightened by the appeal to their ears. For just as the Londoners find an infinite and indescribable delight in the works of Dickens, in part solely because every now and then certain people (the Cockneys) are depicted in them who instead of '**I have**' say '**I 'ave**', and instead of '**fellow**' '**fellor**', similarly the Scots also find an infinite and indescribable magic in the poems of Burns, in part solely because instead of '**with Wallace**' he says '**wi' Wallace**'; instead of '**so**', '**sae**'; instead of '**girl**', '**lassie**'; instead of '**fine**', '**bonny**'; instead of '**who**', '**wha**'; instead of '**all**', '**a**'; instead of '**brave**', '**braw**'; etc. I say 'in part', for I would not dream of imputing a lesser value to the truly outstanding treatment of the English language in Burns's poems.

It is indeed impossible not to be seized with admiration for this untutored man, who renders the not exactly very malleable material of the English language so smooth, so mellifluous, so musical and powerful, that it seems as though the most prodigious and refined art governed his choice of words and in the composition of his verses, while, however, it was only sheer nature that guided his steps. Among a hundred even better examples which we could have chosen, let us examine the sequence of vowels, so pleasing to the ear, in these four lines:

'**Farewell to the mountains high cover'd with snow;**
Farewell to the straths and green valleys below;
Farewell to the forests and wild hanging woods;
Farewell to the torrents and loud-pouring floods.'[27]

The alternation of sounds in the first line is splendid, and the repetition of the same sound in '**loud-pouring**' is powerful and effective, because it depicts the repeated roaring surges of the waters.

---

[26] [The author seems to be referring to some Romantically imagined preliterate 'Ossianic' period, see Introduction p. xix.]
[27] [The first stanza of the poem 'My Heart's in the Highlands'.]

Travels in Scotland (1840) by J.G. Kohl

Here in the north Burns has now surpassed all else with his poems. For as far as the English language is known on the northern isles, so far are his poems known also, and there are said to be places on the Hebridean and Orcadian islands where nothing more of literature exists, apart from the Bible, than – the poetry of Burns.

* * * * * * *

XIII
Taymouth Castle

'**Follow me!**'[1] the Breadalbanes have inscribed imperiously on their coat of arms. We obeyed this call on the most direct route from Aberfeldy and, when it had become dark, arrived at the famous seat of this family. When the Queen was here, they had erected a triumphal arch at the point where she crossed the boundary of the estate; it was made from twigs of the birches of Aberfeldy and on it stood these proud words: '**Welcome to Breadalbane Queen Victoria!**'.

The castle is situated not far from the eastern end of Loch Tay in one of the most beautiful districts of the Highlands of which, however, we were able to see nothing in the evening. Its English name is '**Taymouth-Castle**'[2] but its Highland name is '**Kenmore**', or, as it should be written in the proper Celtic manner, '**Ceanmore**'[3], meaning in fact 'the great chieftain' or 'big head', if you wish[4]. Both names seem to be equally well known, and not only in everyday life but on maps as well now one, now the other, appears. There are a large number of such Scottish places that bear a Celtic and a Germanic name at the same time. This is fairly natural. However, I find it strange that there are also some clans in which an English name has gradually taken the place of a Celtic one. Thus, for example, the '**Clan-Donnochy**'[5] ('Children of Duncan') is nowadays called '**Robertson**'. Another English clan name is that of the '**Royal-Stewart**'.

Again it is very explicable that the English or the Scottish Saxons of the Lowlands have altered or anglicised many Celtic clan names after their own fashion; for they did likewise in Ireland, in Wales. So, for example, they call the '**Kaimbel**' or '**Caimbel**'[6] of the Celts '**Campbell**', in order to be able to think of it as meaningful to themselves to some extent.

It is in fact the clanspeople of Kaimbel or Campbell who live here round Loch Tay, and the Marquises of Breadalbane are themselves Campbells. John[7] Campbell is the name of the present Marquis. He is not the **Chief** of all the Campbells, the chiefs being rather the Dukes of Argyll, whose family name is also Campbell. The Breadalbanes are therefore called only the most powerful branch (not the trunk itself) of this great house of Argyll[8] and are the chieftains of a branch of the Campbells[9]. Incidentally, almost the greatest part of Argyllshire now belongs to them as their personal property.

Quite near on the loch is a small, pretty village, also called Kenmore, in the hospitable inn of which I found lodging. Unfortunately the news that I received concerning the viewing of the park and castle was very unfavourable, for it was said that these were being shown to no one. Furthermore not the Marquis but only the Marchioness was in residence. However, through similar reports I had already forfeited something important once, namely the fine castle and the ruins of Scone, and I was now resolved not to lose the splendid Taymouth Castle so easily as well. Hence I immediately sat down and composed the following letter to the Marchioness:

---

[1] [Strictly speaking, the motto of the Campbells of Breadalbane.]

[2] [Also translated as *Schloß Taymund* in the original.]

[3] [Properly *Ceann mòr* or (as a place name) *A' Cheannmhòr*.]

[4] '**Cean**' does not mean only 'head' but also 'end', and therefore the name can be interpreted as 'the large end', namely of the loch. *JGK*

[5] [Properly *Clann Dhonnchaidh*.]

[6] [Properly *Caimbeul*.]

[7] *Johann*

[8] The Scots themselves write both '**Argyll**' and '**Argyle**'. *JGK*

[9] The Scots distinguish between '**Chief**' and '**Chieftain**'. The former is the head of the whole clan, the latter, however, only the head of a section or branch. *JGK*

'My Lady,

'Permit a stranger to approach you with a request, and pray grant a gracious hearing to a traveller who, at this late time of the year and of the evening, is knocking at the gates of your castle.

'I come from the distant banks of the Danube and from the most remote shores of that great water which is called the Black Sea. I wish that I could say that I came from even further afield.

'An irresistible urge to see the dwelling places of mankind – the humble, unfortunately often also miserable, huts of the poor and the imposing palaces of the great – impels me to carry a not always comfortable wayfarer's staff through the world, as far as my limited strength allows.

'I have now visited the three[10] large and beautiful islands over which Her Britannic Majesty rules, and have now arrived here, among the poor inhabitants of the little village of Kenmore, who pride themselves on belonging to the illustrious family of Breadalbane, as subjects and bearers of the same name from times immemorial.

'I chose this spot as the furthermost destination of my journey in romantic Caledonia, a spot beyond which my desire carries me no further now, because near it rise the battlements of the renowned castle, under the roof of which, as they tell me, a lovely altar is erected to the sacred Penates[11] of your ladyship, and because round about lie outspread the green carpets of the enchanting park, in which, as its fame proclaims far and wide, the elves and water-nymphs, the Dryads and gods of the forest have exerted themselves in an especially glorious manner to devise a picture of nature that would be worthy of being unfolded before the windows of your castle.

'Now, to be sure, night covers the whole valley with possessive darkness, and several disquieting persons have even wished to arouse in me the fear that day will never dawn for me in the Elysium in which Your Graces dwell.

'However, I cannot renounce hope completely, and I venture herewith to appeal to your magnanimity and to address to Your Ladyship the plea that at your command the locked gates be opened to me, and that the hundred-eyed Helios may show me everything, even that which the interior of your palace contains. For the gracious granting of this request the heart of an itinerant philosopher, filled with gratitude, will remain ever devoted to you.'

I sent this letter into the dark grounds of the castle, paid meanwhile a visit to the schoolmaster[12] of the village, and as I returned, received, by the hand of a captain of the troops of Don Carlos V[13], an amicable and favourable reply. I had in fact had no doubt at all about such consent, and I believe one can always give the foreign traveller in England the advice that on all occasions when he is told that it is completely impossible to see something, he should do nothing but immediately address himself directly to the owner by letter. The wealthy among the British have often denied access to their palaces and treasures because as a rule the stream of native residents inquisitively thronging thither is much too great. Those more infrequent visitors, however, who arrive from distant lands are always granted, with great generosity and kindness, what is often denied to the natives, since as a rule the former are already credited with something more than sheer curiosity – or at least, so to speak, with a somewhat more refined degree of curiosity – and since in any case visitors enjoy some privileges in every country.

---

[10] In several English books Scotland is also called an '**island**'. *JGK*

[11] [Roman household gods, protectors of the house.]

[12] [William Armstrong. His age is given as 40 in the June 1841 Census.]

[13] [Younger brother of King Ferdinand VII of Spain, and Pretender to the Spanish throne, Carlos (1788 – 1855) was forced into exile in 1840 after his troops, the Carlists, were unsuccessful in a civil war of succession.]

I tranquilly therefore anticipated a pleasant and enjoyable morning, I invited together a small company for the evening – as best I could do such a thing in the village of Kenmore – namely my landlord and his family, the local schoolmaster, and a farmer from the neighbourhood, whose acquaintance I had made on the way hither. The last was **'a real Häland-man'**, that is, he had above all a command of Gaelic. For, people said to us, **'speaking more particularly, who *has the language*, is a Highlander'** ('strictly speaking, only one who has the language -- namely Gaelic -- is a Highlander'). I adduce this in order to show what the Scots understand by a Highlander.

The Highlanders themselves call themselves **'Galach'**. Their country, the Gaelic Highlands, they call **'Kaltach'**[14]. In contrast, they call the Lowlands **'Machair'**, which they pronounce rather like 'mächir'. As in Ireland the English are likewise called here 'Saxons' (**Sass'nach**) and England itself **'Sachsen'**[15].

It is really very striking that of the two German tribes, the Angles and Saxons, that came over to England and merged together there, the English kept the name of the Angles for themselves, because, as we now read in their books, the Angles were the more powerful and dominant of these two tribes; quite conversely the Celts in Wales, Ireland and Caledonia chose the other tribe, the Saxons, as the appellation of their enemies who came from Germania, thereby seeming to suggest that it was actually these Saxons that had been the more important of the two. This last seems in fact to have really been the case; for we have a *'Saxon'* but not an Anglian Heptarchy, we have in England a so-called *'Saxon'* but no Anglian period of art. Furthermore in the ancient writers these people, whom the Normans conquered and subjugated, are called Saxons and not Angles; – and it therefore remains rather mysterious to me how, nevertheless, for the Anglo-Saxon-Norman mixed race the name 'Angles', apparently less important and less highly regarded initially, later triumphed. Did this come about perhaps since the name of the Saxons was discredited because of the Norman Conquest, and the name of the Angles was plucked from obscurity, as one that was to some extent neutral and untarnished?

It is also extraordinary that the name for the Highland family-alliances, **'clan'**, now so generally common in Scotland, is not Celtic but English. **'To clan'** in English means 'to gang up together' and hence **'the clan'** is a gang, a tribe[16]. In Gaelic a clan is called **'fine'**[17] and what the English call **'clansman'** (members [sic] of a clan) is called in Gaelic **'finneachan'** or **'ciennich'** (pronounced kinnich)[18], which probably comes from **'cien'** or **'cean'** ('the head') and means 'those who are united under one head'.

One subject about which I asked my schoolmaster in particular was the decline of the Gaelic language among the inhabitants of his neighbourhood. He told me that he certainly had command of Gaelic but that now he no longer had occasion to teach it. On the other hand, his predecessors had taught it, and the schoolmaster in Killin at the west end of Loch Tay still taught it even now. At the eastern end it was now to be accepted that Gaelic was almost completely extinct as the customary language of conversation, while at the western end one could still meet people who, if addressed in English, would reply **'I ha' no English!'**. However, even there, as everywhere, it was to be regarded as in the process of dying out. This is all the more remarkable because this present period of the decline of Gaelic is precisely the selfsame one in which the Gaelic tongue is being intensively studied by scholars as never before, and because only now methods for learning and teaching the

---

[14] To my ear it seemed that the people pronounced these words exactly in this way. Armstrong writes these words as **'Gaidhealach'** and **'Gaidhealtached'**. *JGK* [These are now written *Gàidhealach* and *Gaidhealtachd.*]

[15] In Armstrong's Lexicon these words are written **'Sassunach'** and **'Sagsunn'**. *JGK* [The latter is now written *Sasunn.*]

[16] [Gaelic *clann* 'offspring' is cognate with Latin *planta* 'shoot' and is not derived from English.]

[17] Likewise in Armstrong. *JGK* [This is also the modern spelling.]

[18] [Properly spelt *fineachan* and *cinnich.*]

language are being elaborated and put forward. As recently as 1822, **Dr** Armstrong, the brother of my friend the schoolmaster, published the first Gaelic lexicon. Already there are several more. There also exist many grammars now. However, the complete study of this language, which already stands on the edge of its grave, is still in its infancy.

I remarked to my schoolmaster that up till now on my brief journey through Scotland nowhere had I come across Gaelic manuscripts that could still be found in the possession of the population, while on an equally brief journey in Ireland I had repeatedly seen poetry written down in the Irish language. He told me that he too, as long as he had been living in the Highlands, had, however, nowhere ever come across such poetry in writing. On this point, I have been as little able to find out more information, and more positive, as I have been on the matter of why the Gaelic of Scotland does not have its own alphabet, as does the Gaelic of Ireland, but is written with English letters. Certainly this is the case now. However, whether this has always been so I could not discover with certainty. Many assured me that it was true. This would presuppose a great underdevelopment on the part of the Scottish Highland Celts as compared with the Irish.

There was a general conviction among these guests of mine that the Highland national dress had been introduced into the country by the Romans. They told me that they had all worn the kilt until their fourteenth year. Only then had they put on trousers. The crucial thing about the kilt is precisely its lack of trousers, which is already indicated by the word itself. For it comes from a Scottish verb '**to kilt**' ('to gather up')[19], which girls still use when they gather up their clothes when washing. I heard a girl say: '**I kilted my gown**'. I spoke out against the kilt as a very inappropriate garment in such a cold northerly mountain climate. But my friends told me that for them the kilt was far warmer than the English style of dress with trousers. The abdomen and the chest were much better protected with it, which was the main thing. But the legs, once they had become accustomed to it, ultimately felt the cold as little as did the uncovered hands or the naked face. It was a usual occurrence, they said, that if boys had discarded the kilt and put on English clothing they always shivered at first, indeed sometimes even caught cold. On that account, old men, who had been accustomed to the kilt all their lives, would not be able to adopt trousers, in other words, discard the national costume. After the suppression of the last revolution in 1746, the English government had proscribed the kilt and ordered trousers to be worn; from the beginning, the people were so much against this law that it cost much trouble to implement it (and incidentally it was later repealed). Sometimes, in order to comply at least with the letter of the command to have on trousers, and in order not to incur the statutory penalty, people on the mountain range had carried their trousers on their backs. On hearing that, I thought of the Tatars and Gypsies in Russia whom the authorities wished to turn from their nomadic life by building them houses, but who pitched their tents in the courtyards of these houses and left the houses unoccupied.

In another connection the Tyroleans came to my mind again as well. The cut of their clothing has a certain remarkable similarity to that of the Scottish Highlanders. Moreover, the Tyroleans have their legs at least half uncovered. Their short leather trousers do not extend even down to the knee and their knees remain quite bare. I have already mentioned the checked cloth among the Tyroleans. Are these all relics of the common Celtic origin of both groups of people? – My friends were all decidedly of one mind that their children should wear the kilt until their fourteenth year; for it was generally agreed that children *with* trousers were much drowsier and duller, whereas those *without* trousers were much brighter and more active. A pity that custom forbids our schoolteachers to employ this simple means to make pupils lively.

It is impossible to sit with Scots for any length of time without the conversation immediately turning to topics of agriculture. For this is a branch of human activity in which Scotland has

---

[19] [The word *kilt* is of Norse origin and the noun is recorded in English as historically preceding the verb.]

recently made such massive progress that, even though there might be some, though not much, exaggeration in my friends' assertion that **'the Scotch farmers beat the English three times over'**, yet it is not great. The most important thing in Scottish farming is **'Drainage'**. And in Scotland I have had to hear so inconceivably much about **'drainage'**, about **'draining-system'**, and about **'drains'**, that my readers too may have to bear with me and learn something of it here; they will not object since the subject moreover is very interesting.

Just as entire areas of arid Persia are burrowed under with channels to distribute water through the country, so Scotland's fields are almost completely burrowed under to dry out the land and lead the water away. These channels are very narrow, about a foot broad and about three to four feet deep. Towards the bottom they become somewhat narrower. Stones are placed on the floor of every channel and these are covered with tiles on top of which a looser layer of pebbles is spread. Then on top of this very loosely filled trench the earth of the field is tipped back again, so that the whole thus forms a hidden narrow subterranean conduit, the cross-section of which looks rather like this:

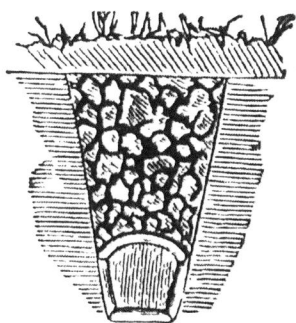

The purpose of these channels, which are called 'drains', is to lead off underground running springs, or flowing surface water and wetness from marshes. Since there is a great excess of all these in Scotland, it is very necessary to equip every field with such drains, or, as the Scots say, **'to drain it'**. In each field it is naturally important to investigate meticulously where and how it should best be provided with drains. The water trickles down through the stones loosely lying on top, and since the covering of the drain is also not completely unbroken and impervious, so the water comes down into the channel and flows away in it. The smaller **Branch-drains** convey the water into larger **Head-drains**, and this combining or merging of drains continues until the water is discharged into a brook or river somewhere. These drains in the English and Scottish fields are therefore rather much the same as are the galleries of our mines, but smaller in scale. The Scots and English regard the **'Draining-system'** as of such importance for agriculture that they cannot conceive how there could be fields without such a system.

As their drainage works excited my curiosity, so it aroused their astonishment that I had never seen their like in Germany. It is perhaps less necessary in our country. However, I believe that there are districts enough in Germany in which such drains would be very beneficial, since they are naturally more effective than side-ditches and more economical of space. Courland and Livonia, which lie on much the same latitude as Scotland and North England, and whose soil moreover always suffers more from moisture than aridity, would certainly gain extraordinarily from the introduction of such a British system of drainage.

If the drains are appropriately installed and solidly constructed, then they last for perhaps twenty, thirty and more years without it being necessary to renew them. However, in time they naturally become choked. And the mole, too, causes people much trouble every now and then. If the ground is properly surveyed, then with one drain twenty different springs can often be drawn off at once. Incidentally, depending on the ground, the drains are often constructed in a very different way. Of course, different farmers consider now one, now another style to be preferable. They have already devised a host of names for the different kinds of drains. Naturally there are also drains that are open on top, like our ditches. A hundred years ago nothing was as yet known about drains in Scotland, and only for the last fifty years have the Scots been burrowing under their country like moles. The extraordinary progress and momentum which has entered Scottish agricultural affairs is a phenomenon the more remarkable, given that this branch of human endeavour is, as a rule, that which makes the most laggardly advances of all. Usually, it is bound by the fetters of ancient legal customs that are hard to change, and is in the hands of uneducated people who live alone and are far from the towns, those centres of civilisation and progress. It would be very well worth the trouble to demonstrate how it comes about that farming, in spite of its slow-moving nature, has advanced in Scotland with a rapidity of development that in other countries has hardly been achieved by even the most enterprising and least antiquated of pursuits.

When we were finally retiring to bed, my schoolmaster offered me in parting, from his elegant silver snuff-mull, the last pinch of snuff, or, as it is called in Scotland, the last **'Snufchen Tabac'**[20]. The word **'Snufchen'** is Netherlandish. In Dutch and Low German they likewise say a 'snufchen'. Since the Saxons who crossed over to Scotland and England did not bring snuff-taking with them, and therefore just as little introduced the customary technical terms for it, so this word seems to strengthen us in the supposition that in Scotland the language continued to develop according to its Lower Saxon nature and, though separated from the body of the mother tongue, hit upon the formation of expressions in the same way as the latter itself. On closer investigation many other words would probably be discovered that have been fashioned in a very similar way on both sides of the German Ocean without, however, having been evolved in mutual contact. My schoolmaster's silver snuff-box was a gift from his Highland pupils who had presented it to him, as the inscription testified **'in respect for his private and professional character'**. The expression **'professional character'** cannot adequately be translated into German.

Although I had permission to go to the castle and the grounds the next day at whatever time and hour would be convenient to me, I nevertheless remained true to the resolve that I had previously made, to see both in the early morning before breakfast in order not to be a nuisance in any way to their fair mistress. It was a splendid, fresh autumn morning. The sun rose clear and bright over the snow-covered mountains and, throughout the park, on the River Tay burbling on its way, and in the small glens on the sides of the mountains, it covered everything with cheerful and lively light and shade. Johnson observes in his journey through Scotland that the countless enchanting nuances that light forms with shade are unknown in this country. I must confess that in its comprehensiveness this sentence does the country an injustice, and that, while there are certainly large stretches of which it is literally true and in which shade – dark brown of the earth and grey of the sky – predominates, nevertheless on the other hand many areas are to be excepted from that judgement; in these the abundance and the attractiveness of both shade and light is certainly impressive enough to fill the human eye with delight. One such spot is this stretch of the Tay valley with the castle and park of the Breadalbanes.

'How grand!' – these were the words of Queen Victoria she uttered to Breadalbane when she stepped from her carriage and cast her eye over the scene round about her. Breadalbane, a handsome, strong man, greeted her as the chieftain of his clan in dazzling full Highland dress (**plaided and plumed in his tartan-array**[21]), and three cheers resounded from the meadow, on which, clothed in the bright colours of their clan, Breadalbane's clansmen were positioned, while groups of young girls stood in welcome under the garlanded ceremonial arch and along the paths beside it. These girls were

---

[20] [This phrase is neither Scots nor English while *Snufchen* is not Dutch, though there is a Dutch word *snuiven* 'to take snuff'. Perhaps the author was thinking of the German *Schnupftabak* 'snuff'.]

[21] [Properly 'All plaided and plumed in their tartan array'. The quotation is from 'Lochiel's Warning' by Thomas Campbell (1777-1844) and was used as a heading to Chapter 7 of Walter Scott's *A Legend of the Wars of Montrose*.]

dressed in white and fluttered coloured '**Scarps**' [sic] (sashes or shawls) in the air. At the same time, the band – I do not know of which Highland regiment – played the Highland greeting and everything was reflected and echoed in the clear waters of the River Tay and in the high mountains round the valley. It must have been a wondrously magnificent scene, and it is also said that it made such a great impression on the Queen and Prince Albert that they declared that they had not seen anything more beautiful in Scotland. For me too the sight of Taymouth Castle and its surroundings is unforgettable, and the poet Burns, who was equally enchanted by it, sang a fine song in honour of this spot[22]:

> '**My savage journey, curious, I pursue,**
> **Till fam'd Breadalbane opens on my view.**
> **The meeting cliffs each deapsunk glen divides,**
> **The woods wild scattered cloth their ample sides;**
> **Th' outstreching lake, imbosom'd 'mong the hills,**
> **The eye with wonder and amazement fills;**
> **The Tay meand'ring sweet in infant pride,**
> **The palace rising on his verdant side;**
> **The lawns wood-fringed in Nature's native taste,**
> **The hillocks dropt in Nature's careless haste;**
> **The arches striding o'er the new-born stream;**
> **The village glittering in the noontide-beam;**
> -- -- -- -- -- -- -- -- -- -- -- -- -- -- -- -- --
>
> **Here poesy might wake her heav'n-taught lyre,**
> **And look through Nature with creative fire;**
> **Here, to the wrongs of Fate half reconcil'd,**
> **Misfortune's lighten'd steps might wander wild.**[23]

The palace is a solid grey building of ashlar, with many towers, and, although new, it is designed in the olden style and embellished with many Gothic additions and excrescences. In front of it lie the beautiful green '**Lawns**' of the park. On these grassy carpets the Highlanders were encamped during the Queen's visit, and in the shimmering of 60,000 coloured lamps that had been ordered from London and which illuminated the valley, they performed their national dances on the first evening of the visit of their Majesties here; for this ten bagpipes provided the music. Even now, and in general throughout the whole year when the noble master and mistress are in residence, daily, at the time of the midday meal, a piper marches up and down on those lawns here in front of the palace windows and walks round the house, playing ancient Scottish Highland folk melodies. The Breadalbanes attach some importance to this old custom of the clan chieftains and their domestic piper is said to be one of the most excellent in the country. The Scottish bagpipes sound extraordinarily shrill and penetrating, for, as already indicated, they were first and foremost intended to be played in the noise of battle and in the desolate valleys of the high mountains. Hence such a piper is audible even when he is standing outdoors, and in the house itself he would be too noisy. Unfortunately I did not make the acquaintance of the man and his pipe since, several days before, a stag had wounded him during the hunt and he was confined to bed in his remote cottage. There are still several other Scottish families who consider such a domestic piper just as indispensable to their household as a head gardener or equerry.

The first thing that I encountered on entering the elegant apartments of the palace of the Breadalbanes was a bull's skull. It was written on it that it had been a '**Dun Bull of the purest Westhighland breed, a good figured and a brave looking animal**'[24]. There were several other similar

---

[22] [From 'Verses Written with a Pencil over the Chimney-piece, in the Parlour of the Inn at Kenmore, Taymouth'. The spelling is as given by the author in his German text.]

[23] [The author gives a prose translation in a footnote.]

[24] [The author's otherwise accurate gloss translates **dun bull** as *Dünenbulle* (= 'dune bull' or 'bull from the dunes').]

bulls' heads on the wall, and I do not recall ever having seen the like in such an elegant setting. I do not believe that the love for particular outstanding individuals of this branch of the animal kingdom is carried as far in other countries. The West Highland stock is incidentally one of the oldest in Great Britain and one that has been least altered by selective breeding. They are the original inhabitants of the land, have the characteristics that are most in demand, and when they come down from the meagre grazing in Argyllshire[25] to the lush pastures of the Lowlands, then they give the best roast beef in the whole of England.

The interior of the rooms and halls of Taymouth Castle presented me with one of the most admirable and most opulent examples of domestic furnishing that I have ever seen[26], and to encounter such an abundance of exceptional luxury and taste, assembled here in the centre of the Highlands amidst the little **Reekhouses** of the mountain Scots, aroused our astonishment in the highest degree. With every step that I took I observed that people had presumably not exaggerated when they told me that the Breadalbanes' estates extend a hundred English miles in a straight line uninterruptedly from the eastern to the western ocean. That there are such estates in Russia is quite understandable, because the country is sufficiently large to be divided into a thousand similar properties. But it must excite our amazement that such estates can exist in little Scotland. Perhaps there is no country in the world that has had, and still has, an oligarchy as powerful and as landed and as restricted in numbers as Scotland.

However, it was not so much the *magnitude* as the *individuality* of the luxury that seized my attention. I believe that it is understood more aptly in Great Britain than in any other country how the antiquity of the furniture-design and room-furnishings from the Age of Chivalry can be combined with the taste and the luxury of the present day, and how mediaeval baronial halls can be decorated with all the splendour and elegance that the our modern state of art and wealth affords, without, however, thereby in any way diminishing the interest of the authenticity and antiquity of the style. Especially remarkable are the richness of the splendid woodcarvings on the ledges of the furniture and in the room, the abundance of curtains and tapestries of the most exceptional quality, several paintings by the most outstanding artists, and a collection of books of most excellent choice. At the same time, everything is perfectly genuine. Even the armour exhibited in the '**Banquetting-hall**' does not consist of bad imitations, but in fact one piece had been worn by a French king, another by an Austrian archduke. The ball in Highland costume, which was given for the Queen in these rooms, must have presented a magical spectacle. The colours of Scottish tartans look magnificent; outdoors among the populace they are seen only in coarse wool, but here, in stately homes, one can behold these colours executed in fine velvet and covering the furniture.

The most remarkable book that I saw in the library was a large *de luxe* work on the different Scottish tartans; it had been quite recently published, probably on the occasion of the visit of the royal couple. A certain John Sobieski[27] Stuart was the editor of it. All the different little coloured threads, to which the individual clans remained loyal during the period of their existence, were reproduced here in brilliant colours in each tartan in which the clans wore them, and continue to wear them, and beside every tartan was a short account of the clan to which the tartan belonged.

Among the paintings that grace the different rooms is a splendid *John* by Rubens[28]. However, I was more interested in the portrait by van Dyck[29] of a Lady Mary Rich, the same woman as can be seen

[25] *Argyleshire*
[26] [See Chapter XVI, fn. 6]
[27] *Sobiesky* [See Introduction p. xxi]
[28] [i.e. 'John the Baptist'. This is almost certainly 'The Feast of Herod' by Peter Paul Rubens (1577 – 1640), bought by John Campbell, Earl of Ormelie (later Marquess of Breadalbane) in Naples in 1830. It is now in the National Gallery of Scotland, Edinburgh.]
[29] *Van Dyk*

in Holyroodhouse. Two hundred years ago this lady was the chatelaine of this castle. She was the daughter of the famous Henry Rich, the Earl of Holland, brother of the even more famous Earl of Warwick, the so-called '**Kingsmaker**' [sic][30]. This lady was, so they say, one of the most beautiful and richest **matches** of her time. For she possessed no less than ten thousand pounds sterling. Among the many knights who sought her hand John Campbell (the first Earl of Breadalbane) was the fortunate one. After the wedding celebrations he withdrew with her to his castle on Loch Tay, which at that time must have appeared quite other than it does now. Chambers describes his journey and his entry into his castle thus: 'On one of the two '**Highland ponies**' which he brought back from London, the Earl himself sat, and he had his lady behind him. On the other pony his ten thousand pounds were loaded, all in pure gold and packed in leather sacks. On each side of the pony walked a Highlander from Clan Campbell, fully armed, as guard. So all arrived safely at Balloch, as the castle was then called, and there, after a long time, a small room was pointed out that was at the same time living room, reception room, and bedchamber of the happy couple.'

Since everywhere I seek out only that which is characteristically Scottish, I shall indulge in no further description of the present royal splendour of the castle, but only relate that the small hand-held looking-glass which Queen Victoria used on her dressing-table here was set with Scottish river-pearls, and that a small '**Stirrup-cup**' was shown to me that had been fashioned for Prince Albert from a beautiful Scottish pebble and in which the farewell drink had been served to him. A '**Stirrup-cup**' actually means[31] the goblet from which one toasts the departing guest when he already has one foot in the stirrup.

Both Queen Victoria and Prince Albert immortalised their presence in Taymouth Castle by planting two trees, an oak and a spruce, which they set into the ground to the accompaniment of music and the cheers of the crowd on the green lawn beside the castle. As already said, in Scotland one cannot immortalise oneself better than by planting trees, and perhaps it was out of consideration for that fact that the royal couple chose precisely this kind of memorial. How greatly must this stimulate others to imitate the example of these illustrious planters of trees! And this is certainly the most lasting and most beautiful kind of memorial that monarchs can bequeath to their subjects in that therein the wish, as it were, lies expressed: 'May your line long be fertile and blossom and grow and flourish, as will these trees, which we, your sovereigns, have planted for you!'

In the park itself I was particularly pleased by the little **dairy** that sits here on a hill among beautiful trees. It is true that in many English parks can be seen the most attractive and exquisite '**Dairies**' in the world. However, this dairy in Kenmore had the peculiar feature that it was entirely built of snow-white calcite stones which are found in abundance in the vicinity, so that therefore the neat little building itself seemed, so to speak, like a palace of frozen milk. The milk bowls were made of white porcelain and were placed in a faience trough through which clear, cool water trickled. To study the absolute perfection of this delicate branch of rural economy one must come to England, even from Switzerland and Holland. I say 'this delicate branch of rural economy'. For indeed the whole process of producing milk and handling it has an especially satisfying and attractive aspect, I believe, because of the colour of the beautiful white milk which immediately comes into being quite clean and palatable, has to undergo no such distasteful processes as do wine and beer, as even grain and other farm produce. Butter too is golden yellow right from the beginning, and even cheese is instantly pleasant and agreeable when it is made. In short, all the processes that are carried out with milk lead automatically, as it were, to cleanliness. And the peaceful and well-contented fat tribe of cows, their sweet-smelling sustenance of plants, all this brings about charming associations of ideas. Admittedly, the dung etc.! – ah well, everything indeed has its weak point too.

---

[30] [The author mistakes Robert Rich, the twenty-second Earl of Warwick, the Lord High Admiral of England, who died in 1658 for Richard Neville, sixteenth Earl of Warwick, known as the 'Kingmaker', who was killed in 1471.]

[31] [Before giving the explanation, the author translates *stirrup-cup* literally as *Steigbügelbecher*.]

In Scottish cattle nothing was more noteworthy to me than firstly their smallness, and secondly the circumstance that occasionally animals without horns are found among them. As concerns the first, it was striking to me that these so-called Scottish **'Black cattle'**, as the ordinary cattle in the Highlands are called, are even smaller than the Welsh mountain cattle which in their turn are already noticeably smaller than the English grassland cattle. Since now cattle are said to be even smaller in the north of Scotland, and on the islands of Orkney and Shetland even smaller still, a gradual diminution in the size of cattle from southern Great Britain to the north can be accepted as a definite fact. It has been said that not only does a larger type of cattle exist on the broader plains than among the high mountains, but also that on the larger islands larger cattle are found than on the smaller, as though cattle on the smaller islands were afraid of occupying too much space. One might ask whether all this depends simply on the better and more luxuriant pasturage which is found on the larger plains and islands, or whether it could be that at the same time other forces of nature are also at work.

British lords love to surround themselves with wild animals in their parks. Hence they always have stags and roe deer near them. Here in the copses of the Kenmore park even buffaloes have been introduced. There are said to have been twelve at one time. They have also tried to acclimatise llamas here, as well as American bison. Unfortunately, as I strolled, I was able to see none of those animals; they always know to make themselves invisible whenever one is looking for them. The owner of the castle has also tried to introduce the capercaillie, which the English call **cock of the wood**, and we were told that the attempt seemed to be succeeding and that the birds were increasing in numbers. Since it is well known that the capercaillie inhabits fir and spruce woods and lives principally on the young needles of these trees, it is probable that with the increase of coniferous tree-planting in Scotland the numbers of this noble bird will increase also[32]. In Gaelic they call the bird **'Capercallie'**[33] [sic]. Several were shot on the hunts that were held here in honour of Prince Albert, and the queen, when she was inspecting the game that had been killed, asked that a capercaillie be shown to her. The **'Headgamekeeper'** brought one to her, and when she asked who had shot it, the answer was: 'Prince Albert'. This capercaillie was stuffed and sent to London.

However, the most remarkable examples of conservation and preservation of wild animals in Great Britain are obviously the descendants, still protected here and there, of the original type of wild cattle that filled the forests of Great Britain before Caesar's time. As we have already indicated above, there are also several parks and woods here in Scotland in which this original breed is still found at the present day. Here too, as in England, they are distinguished from the present tame type of cattle by their milk-grey colour, by black ears and a black muzzle, by long legs and horns that project upwards. These animals, they assured me here also, are so very much used to the natural freedom allowed to them here in the parks that they cannot exist in cattle-sheds. I know of no country – apart from Lithuania, where in the Bialowyser Forest[34] wild oxen (aurochs) are likewise still looked after – in which anything similar is taking place. It can be reckoned a credit to the English that, amidst all their prodigality of cultivation, they have still found themselves a little place for their wild oxen. Every country ought to endeavour to preserve for itself such a specimen of any creature that is becoming extinct in it. I was also told that Breadalbane is said to keep a small herd of wild Caledonian cattle somewhere, though I am no longer able to recall the place. It is the Duke of Hamilton who possesses the greatest number of them in Scotland.

---

[32] Formerly it was thoroughly native to Scotland, Ireland and England, but the entire population was gradually eradicated. In the attempts at its gradual re-introduction, which have been made recently in various places in Scotland, the birds were brought from Sweden. *JGK* [The Marquis of Breadalbane had introduced fifty capercaillie from Sweden into his estate in 1837.]

[33] [*capull-coille* (= 'horse of the wood')]

[34] [Now the Białowieski Park Narodowy, a national park in present-day Poland.]

The letter mentioned above, received by me the previous evening, had been written by the secretary of the Scottish lord to whom I have so frequently alluded. This secretary was a Spanish captain who had been obliged to leave his native country. The most interesting thing that I learned from him was this, that not even the tiniest similarity existed between the Gaelic and the Basque languages. He himself was a Basque and had a complete command of Gaelic. At the same time he was a refined young man of breeding and education, and possessed of the most remarkably sharp and intelligent eyes. And since probably it may be extremely seldom that a Basque, by virtue of his circumstances, is obliged to learn Gaelic, so his observations on both languages were not unimportant to me. I requested him to express my thanks to his gracious master and mistress, and that very same morning I continued my journey on foot after I had first enjoyed a goodly portion of roast meat, even if not quite as much as the Highlanders in the grounds of Kenmore, who during the three days that they entertained their Queen with dance and games, were treated to no fewer than one hundred and sixty-three sheep, eleven oxen, and I cannot remember now how many calves. During the hunts in the surrounding countryside no fewer than eighty deer and nine hundred and fifty hares were killed, and so many 'grouse' and other game birds that they had to be taken home on carts. These figures will, I suppose, for long re-echo in the neighbouring glens, and will even be handed down to the children. For long will it be said still: 'These were great days, when the Queen of England visited our master, Breadalbane. Then there was nothing but lights and reels, and they slaughtered eleven cattle, not to mention the sheep and the eighty deer and the capercaillie.'

* * * * * * *

XIV
From Taymouth Castle to Loch Tay

In these lonely and beautiful regions, where there are still no especially good roads, there is no better way of travelling than walking in the company of a cheerful Highlander, because on the entire journey, unlike on the great high roads of the Lowlands, the wayfarer is not inconvenienced by carriages but rather always encounters only other pedestrians, and therefore can examine for himself the countryside at close quarters everywhere along his path. I chose the road along the southern side of the loch, which is admittedly less good than on the northern side, but is more picturesque. For from here can be seen the most attractive views of Ben Lawers on the other side and of other mountains, and then immediately in the neighbourhood such beautiful scenes as, for example, those offered by the waterfall of Acharn Den[1]; this was the next destination on our journey. The name 'Acharn' reminds me of the Achernsee[2] in the Tyrol, which is perhaps likewise of Gaelic origin. '**Achern**', my guide informed me, 'means "waterfall"'[3]. Without doubt the word has something to do with water, as is indicated by the syllable '**Ach**', a sequence of sounds that occurs in all the Celtic and also in some other languages of Europe and which means 'water'. In Scotland low-lying meadows, pieces of damp ground, in particular, are habitually called '**Ach**'[4]. '**Den**'[5] in English means roughly an opening, a cleft, between bare cliffs, and so, on the grading of different descriptions for depressions between hills, it ranks even lower than '**Glen**'. Hence '**Achernden**' means 'cleft of the waterfall'.

At first I had no especial desire to be tempted from my way by this waterfall, and to climb the steep hill-path that leads up to it. However, I did not regret having decided otherwise. For it is in truth beautiful, and has its own quite unique characteristics; indeed I have not yet seen a single waterfall that was not worthy of examination by virtue of features peculiar to it.

The first remarkable feature is the approach to this magnificent spectacle. Since the water cascades down, as I have said, into a '**Den**', and since almost on all sides precipitous rocks rise round about it, it is difficult to come close to the scene itself. Neither upwards from ground level, nor from the top of the rocks, would it be feasible to accomplish this successfully. There remains no other possibility but to work one's way between the very rocks. This is achieved by means of a subterranean passage-way; this passage is, I imagine, partly artificial, partly natural, and at its extremity it broadens out into a room-like cave that lies on the vertical rock-face exactly halfway up the waterfall. Hence the beautiful sight of the latter meets one's eyes, with all its splendours, as soon as one comes out of that dark passage and into this small cave which has the aspect of a pleasant, mossy hermit's cell. The English, who are always very clever at finding the appropriate vantage-point to view anything, were well aware that the place to admire a waterfall is opposite it, exactly halfway up.

The second curiosity of this waterfall is this, that there is a break in the middle, and that it then does not, as most waterfalls do, continue to drop vertically, but rather deviates to the side and falls obliquely, somewhat like this:

---

[1] *Achern-Den*

[2] [A slip on the part of the author. Achensee is in the Tyrol. Achernsee is in Germany near the east bank of the Rhine opposite Strassburg.]

[3] [*Àth a' Chairn* means 'ford of the cairn', not 'waterfall'.]

[4] [The names of these meadows contain the Gaelic word *achadh* 'field' or 'meadow'. It has nothing to do with water.]

[5] [As the author implies, this is not Gaelic. It is probably the Scots *den(e)* (= 'a small narrow valley) and so *Acharn Den* could have been used by a Scots speaker to mean 'the narrow valley in which the Falls of Acharn lie'.]

In fact, at mid-height a slanting, flattened stone blocks its path, which makes the water shift to the side. This does not, of course, make the waterfall more beautiful, but, as I said, gives it originality and individuality. In addition, the whole disposition of rocks and trees round about is so beautiful that the totality presents an enchanting tableau. The entire waterfall is two hundred and fifty feet high, but the last oblique slope is one hundred and forty feet in length.

Unfortunately the traveller can see such things only for himself, and can bring little of them back for his readers. The only thing that I found for them in my hermit's cave was a little curiosity of Loch Tay which I shall describe here, because I have never before seen it in any other country, and because it could perhaps be a peculiarity of this district. These were namely several '**natural clooses**'[6] ('tangled balls'), as my Scots called them, of the needles of larch-trees. These balls, people explained to me, come about from a natural compaction of the larch-needles which fell into the loch and were pounded together by the winds and the waves. Several of these balls, among other oddities of nature, had been hung up in the hermit's cell. I requested permission to appropriate one of them for myself, and picked it to pieces to discover what lay inside it. The ball was about three inches in diameter and, like all the others, was completely spherical, like the large balls of matted hair found in the stomachs of cattle. The little needles were in a certain order and quite tightly stuck together, so that it was not particularly easy to tease them apart. At last, in the middle, we found a tiny piece of wood. They told me that in all these balls there was something similar, either a scrap of wood, or a leaf, or a seed of corn, or a blade of grass. These balls, they said, were found especially frequently in November, when the loch was severely whipped up by the wind. It is incomprehensible to me how waves and wind, or water-nymphs and wind-gods, can fashion them so spherical and regular, and besides it is remarkable that these balls are formed in water, where, one would think, their resinous sap must lose its adhesiveness.

Here too one can hear and read (for the relevant verses are also inscribed on the wall of the hermit's cave) what Burns has said of this waterfall. The following are his words[7]:

> '**Poetic ardours in my bosom swell,**
> **Lone wand'ring by the hermit's mossy cell,**
> **The sweeping theatre of hanging woods,**
> **Th' incessant roar of headlong tumbling floods**'.[8]

Making a short detour over the hills, we descended to the loch, along which our way led onwards. I made use of this detour in order to look at the interior of one of the Highlanders' small smoky cottages on the way; these had been built on slopes that could be cultivated. 'All these cottages, explained my companion, an old Highlander as already mentioned, 'are built in the usual Highland style. Furthermore, they are all nothing but '**thatched houses**'.' I must confess that I did not then

---

[6] [Cf. English *clew* (= 'a ball of thread or yarn']
[7] [From 'Verses Written with a Pencil over the Chimney-piece, in the Parlour of the Inn at Kenmore, Taymouth'. The spelling is as given by the author in his German text.]
[8] [The author gives a prose translation in a footnote.]

know what every English lexicon could have told me, namely that a **'thatched house'** means a house roofed with straw; I asked my old companion what it meant, and he gave me the following definition of the word. 'To thatch a house, sir, that means, for example, if someone is thatching a house, and you then go past him and, as you greet him, you enquire **"Well, you are thatching, good man, to day** [sic] **?" that means to thatch a house, sir!'**

Our straw-thatched house was built of wood. Inside, by the fire, sat an old man who was warming himself, as the old usually do. Over his fireplace was fastened a large wooden box. It was the salt barrel of the house. I believe that in no other country is such a significance and a so central and commanding a place given to the salt barrel of the house as here in Scotland. On the sides hung a kind of chicken coop in which, however, instead of chickens, the cups and plates of the house were stacked up. In front of the door stood a large cheese-press which was but very simply constructed and in which heavy stones functioned as best they could. Everywhere in Scotland a similar cheese-press is seen standing in front of houses as one of the most important pieces of household furniture. For these regions provide, if not especially excellent, yet fairly numerous cheeses.

Our old man and a young man who was just arriving had completely black hands, like Moors, and since I was somewhat surprised at that, they told me that **they had tared** [sic] **the sheep** just then. And on this occasion I came upon a quite extraordinary ritual that is performed here, and as far as I know, *only* here in Scotland, with the sheep. In fact they tar the latter, partly so that the animals, as they told me, might be less cold in winter, partly to protect them against vermin. To this end they mix the tar with some butter and heat this mixture until it has completely blended. Then they take their sheep, or rather the year's lambs – for it was done only to them, they told me – and rub in that mixture on them in the following way. With their fingers they trace a line over the lamb's back, making a slight parting in the wool. Into this little furrow they then pour a small portion of tar, and rub it well in on the sides. Then they make similar partings on the animal's flanks and work the tar in here too, and finally likewise on the legs, where the wool is long. From this extraordinary procedure the men acquire such dirty hands that, for the whole winter until Christmas, they scarcely need buy themselves gloves for the dance-floor because they are wearing perfectly natural ones. Tar is used occasionally for the avoidance of vermin in man as well as beast. Here I remembered, for example, the Ukrainian shepherds, who soak their shirts with tar in the summer and then, after they have dried somewhat, don them, and then wear them for all eternity, it being rightly assumed that such a shirt could never become dirty.

However, during the winter, they keep only some of their sheep on the mountains here round about Loch Tay, driving most of them down into the Lowlands, where they can be wintered better, more safely and more cheaply, since the fodder there is more plentiful, and especially since it can also be supplemented with carrots, turnips and such vegetables which are grown there in quantity for this purpose. They told me that a shepherd with five hundred sheep would send about three hundred of them down into the Lowlands, after he had carefully tarred the lambs among them. The other two hundred, however, would graze the poor Highland pastures even during the winter. The time for their departure is usually about Martinmas (the 15th [sic][9] of November), and they generally come back up on the fifteenth of May. I can speak only about this district in which we are at the moment. For other areas of Scotland – since almost everywhere in Scotland a similar migration of sheep takes place – different dates may be customary.

Last summer in Great Britain it was impossible to sit down with an owner of sheep or cattle without the conversation straightway turning to the policy that Sir Robert Peel had followed with his new tariffs relating to sheep and cattle. The opinion of my two experienced old friends about this was that Sir Robert Peel was admittedly one of the best politicians in England, 'but now he is **wrong**' in

---

[9] [Martinmas is in fact the 11th November.]

one point, they said, 'and it is this, that he also wants to let foreign cattle in, and thereby is spoiling the market for us completely. It is really an incomprehensible blunder on his part. For there was never talk before of changing the tax on foreign cattle. People complained only about dear corn and bread. England was supplied with the best cattle in the world from Ireland and Scotland, and was very content with that. For fine roasting-meat is bought only by the more affluent, and for them it is somewhat immaterial whether they pay several pence more or less for it. By letting in foreign cattle, Sir Robert has therefore won himself no friends, but on the contrary many enemies. The corn and bread, well, that was something different. The poor rightly demand these as cheap as possible, and hence the importing of them could not be made easy enough.'

So spoke my '**Graziers**', as cattle-breeders are called in Great Britain. That reminded me of similar comments by an Irish farmer; he too declared that Sir Robert was one of the foremost politicians in England, but that he was **wrong** only in one point – namely, relating to free trade in corn. With this, he said, Peel had attacked at its very root precisely the most efficient section of the population of England, namely the farmers who, trusting in the existing legal protection, had made the most strenuous efforts to improve their crop-growing. The result of Sir Robert's clumsy measures would be a total ruin of agriculture, and, before the year was out, probably all tenant-farmers and landowners would be left with no alternative but to go bankrupt *en masse*. – We know that the manufacturers in turn use, for the sake of their pockets, some different arguments.

From out our smoky little hut we had a wonderful view over the water, or, as the old man put it, '**a bonny peep on the loch**'. I crawled out through the low door of the house and sat down for a little while on the stone bench in front of the house to enjoy this '**bonny peep**'. The heather and the straw, with which the house was thatched, hung down long and straggly from the edge of the roof. The little projection of the roof, which was above our heads, was held up on roughly hewn tree-trunks on which some branches still had remained as supporting forks. On the branches of these half natural, half artificial columns hung several dried fish. Beside these columns stood the cheese-press. My two old friends sat down by my side, puffing away on small, stubby pipes, and in front of us a pair of long-haired '**Collies**' ('sheep-dogs') lay down in the grass. To the right of the house a small grey Highland horse was grazing, and to the left several black-headed sheep were also grazing. Looking down we could see the long, narrow strip of Loch Tay, and, on the other side of it, the high hills, that mark '**Glen Lyon**' (so called from a river, the name of which is '**Lyon**'[10]), and, in pride of place, Ben Lawers, which is one of the highest mountains in Scotland. It is 4015 feet high[11], and hence is exceeded by Ben Nevis[12], the highest Scottish peak of all, by only 350 feet. On the green slopes, over which we looked across to Lawers, numerous flocks of sheep and herds of cattle were grazing in the distance.

While I was looking at this whole scene, it seemed to me as though I had seen the same thing somewhere, just like that, once before in my life. I pondered a little, and, sure enough, I found the answer. I had seen exactly the same scene once before in Berlin, where for the first time I had come across a splendid copper engraving of the outstanding picture by Edwin Landseer[13], which is famous under its name '**the Highland Drovers**'. For becoming acquainted with Scotland, this splendid painting is at least just as valuable as an entire Scottish novel in three volumes – by which comparison, incidentally, I by no means intend to detract from the praise of these novels, which are

---

[10] [The author gives alleged German translations of '**Glen Lyon**' and '**Lyon**' as *Löwenthal* (= 'valley of the lion') and *Löwe* (= 'lion') respectively. The English names are a version of the Gaelic (*Gleann*) *Lìomhann*.]
[11] In MacCulloch we find its height given as 3945 feet, but 4015 feet is the result of the very latest measurements. *JGK* [Ben Lawers was 3982 feet high in 2001. John MacCulloch (1773 – 1835) published *The Highlands and Western Islands of Scotland* (1824) and produced the first Geological Map of Scotland in 1836.]
[12] *Newis* [Ben Nevis was 4408 feet high in 2001.]
[13] [See Introduction p. xvii-xviii. For the name of the painting see this chapter, fn. 15 and Chapter XV, fn. 1.]

just as masterly in their own way. The picture is now in the possession of Mr J. Sheepshank[14] in London, through whose gracious kindness I was able to enjoy it to the full. In fact it ought to be exhibited on the boundary of Scotland so that everyone who is journeying to this country in order to get to know it, can prepare himself a little.

If all the things that can be painted in Scotland were painted as masterfully as the drovers in Landseer's picture, then the German traveller who wanted to tell his compatriots something about Scotland could do nothing better than to collect small copies of all these paintings and supply a commentary on them, since in this way his readers would be best instructed. However, because this is out of the question, so, with the use of the writings by an anonymous English author on the same subject, I will try to give at least a small commentary on Landseer's drovers[15] which perhaps will explain some things to those that have seen the picture in Germany, and which may stimulate those that have not seen it to seek it out.

* * * * * * *

---

[14] [John Sheepshank (1787 – 1863) English art-collector; in 1857 he presented his collection to the nation. The picture is now in the Victoria and Albert Museum in London.]

[15] [*The Art-Union: a Monthly Journal of the Fine Arts*, No. 1, London, 15 February 1839, p. 6 contains an account of the engraving by J.H. Watt of Landseer's painting, here entitled *Highland Drovers departing for the South* (see Chapter XV, fn. 1). This account praises the engraving and the original painting, of which a brief description is given. It is possible both that this is the engraving seen by the author in Berlin and that this account is part of the 'writings by an anonymous English author' on which Chapter XV is based.]

XV
'The Highland Drovers'[1]

In earlier, savage times, the glens and hills of the interior of Scotland – even the highest mountains are simply called **'Hills'** by the Scots – sent out bands of armed men under a Campbell[2], Cameron or MacGregor into the Lowlands, or even into the neighbouring English counties. They were to seize by armed force what their own poor land could not give them – money, grain, clothing, and other good, useful things, and even cattle, in order to make good the deficiencies of their own herds. They called such an expedition to the rich south **'a raide'** [sic][3].

In recent times, especially since the Union of England with Scotland and more particularly since the dissolution of the clans in 1746, the place of such warlike raids has now been taken by peaceful **'Droves'**. Nowadays those valleys and hills send out annually, through the north of England and through the southern plains of Scotland, the cattle, which they rear for the busy markets of England, 'where a tasty morsel is always welcome'. The most welcome here are the **'Galloways'**[4] and **'Argyles'**, which are the best varieties of Scottish Highland cattle and are those that can be fattened up most easily and successfully on the luxuriant pastures and in the good stables of England (**they are superior to all other Highland-varieties *in their capacity to fatten*,** an English grazier said to me). For these lean Highlanders must still be fattened up in England, just like the Irish cattle, with the fattening of which the English are likewise not satisfied. – In this connection, England and London stand in the same relationship with respect to Scotland and Ireland as do Northern Italy and Milan with respect to the Alps and Apennines, – as do Austria and Vienna with respect to Hungary and Galicia, – as do the Baltic provinces and Petersburg with respect to the Ukraine and the steppes of Russia.

The cattle which form **the drove** are gathered together on a determined day and at a specified place, – at the foot of a range of hills, on the shore of a loch, beside an old castle or near a big village, and probably also in the vicinity of an old famous battlefield celebrated in song; for the drovers are still drawn together to the old fields by the same local circumstances as were the fighting men in ancient times. **Herdsmen** are chosen to lead the various sections into which the drove is divided, while a kind of chief leader, a **'Topsman'**, as they call him in Scotland, is put in charge of the whole.

This topsman controls all the movements of the drove, concludes all items of business, and is responsible to the owners of the cattle for the profits. He gives the orders and the agreed signals, indicating when the sections are to stop or to proceed. He is always active and busy, now at the head of the whole drove, now at the rear, and his subordinates consult him about all difficulties. He knows the safest routes, even in the wildest parts of the mountains. **Shapfell** is as familiar to him as **Shehallion**[5]. If a choice is available, he prefers the grassy paths, which are easy on the hooves of the animals entrusted to him and at the same time ensure mouths full of fodder. Therefore he usually

---

[1] [This painting is catalogued in the Victoria and Albert Museum under the title *The Drover's Departure - A Scene in the Grampians*.]

[2] *Kaimbel*

[3] [There is some truth in this. Cattle *reiving* (i.e. 'cattle rustling') had been practised over much of Scotland, including the Highlands, where cattle tended to be regarded as communal property. However, from the 17th to the 19th centuries, the export of cattle became an important feature of the Highland economy. Cattle were driven in the autumn by drovers to markets in Crieff and Falkirk where they were bought to be driven further afield to be fattened in the Borders, Yorkshire, and East Anglia.]

[4] [The description 'Highland cattle' is not accurate for Galloways, for they originated in the south-west of the Lowlands. They are hornless and often black animals. 'Argyles' may be an error for Angus cattle, more generally known as Aberdeen Angus. Highland Cattle, properly so-called, are long-horned beasts with shaggy, indeed wavy, coats. Galloways, Aberdeen Angus, and Highland Cattle are all bred for their beef. Highland Cattle and Galloways were mainstays of the droving trade.]

[5] [Shap Fell is a mountain in Cumbria, England while Schiehallion is a mountain in Perthshire.]

chooses the by-ways, since the dusty and hard public military roads[6] damage the hooves of the cattle and afford them little to eat.

As a rule these topsmen are paid for their work and trouble, and since there are now bankers everywhere in Great Britain, the financial transactions which are involved in the payment are mostly attended to by the bankers in the small towns. But previously, in the not very distant past, the Highland cattle-owner himself accompanied his drove to the south and then returned to his mountains with the money gained. There often occurred such things as the following incident, related about just such a Scottish owner of a herd and a famous English highwayman. This latter, dressed like an elegant gentleman, fell in with the former on his way back to his native heath, with his well-filled money belt round his body, with his '**Wallet**' ('crosswise bag') on his back and with his '**Staff**' in his hand, and beside him his faithful dog, called Bran. Both went a little way together, and the gentleman expressed his surprise that a poor Highland herdsman could dare to travel alone on the hazardous English military roads with so much British gold.

'Now, sir,' answered the Highlander, 'I am not quite alone. For if I have English gold in my belt, I also have Scottish steel in my sheath, and' – touching the hilt of his '**Dirk**' ('dagger') – 'with an Andrew Ferrara[7] and with Bran there' – he patted his wild shaggy wolfhound beside him on the head – 'I fear no highwayman.'

'Really?' exclaimed the other, 'Is your dirk a real Ferrara? Blades like that are rare.'

'See for yourself, sir', said the Highlander, taking out his dirk and showing his companion the date on it and the name of its maker.

'Indeed, it is as you say', replied the other, touching the blade of the dagger.

'But take it by the hilt, man!' said the Scotsman somewhat sharply. 'Upon my word, you should know there is a right and a wrong end to it!'

The Englishman now grabbed the dagger by the hilt, and inflicting on poor Bran, who was heedlessly trotting in front, a crippling wound in the stomach, he at once threw himself on his companion, seized him, and shouted 'Your money or your life! You see now that a Highlander too can be outwitted!'

The Highlander, seeing no other way out and considering resistance useless, despondently handed him his purse, and sighed 'Who will believe it in Breadalbane that with such a good dog and with such a strong arm and such an excellent blade by me, an English highwayman was able to rob me!'

'Oh, think nothing of that!' answered the Englishman, who was still holding him tightly, 'For I have trounced better men than you. And furthermore I will give you a proof to go with you, so that people will believe you that you have been robbed by me. The whole world knows that I chop off the right hand of everyone from whom I steal. Lay your right hand on that tree-stump!'

'He is as solemn as a Spaniard, as sly as a fox, and as slippery as an eel! – said Mackay, an English spy, in 1716 about that old Earl of Breadalbane, who in that year still lived in his castle, an eighty-

---

[6] [These paved roads had been built to help to subjugate the Highlands. Field Marshall George Wade (1673 – 1748) oversaw the construction of 240 miles of military roads between 1724 and 1740. Damage to hooves on them necessitated cattle-shoes (hence blacksmiths and money), consequently drovers instead used grassy paths wherever possible.]

[7] [So-called after Andrea dei Ferrari of Belluno, Italy, a famous sixteenth-century swordmaker]

one year old man, and whom he had been sent to investigate. One could say this more or less about all Scots. And the last part of that judgement in particular was true of this Highlander, who found himself here in such great danger, as he forthwith demonstrated. For when the highwayman spoke to him in the above way, a thought occurred to him, and a ray of hope began to glimmer in him. He laid his right hand on the old tree-stump. But while he was watching the other's eye, he suddenly drew his hand away as the sword, wielded forcefully, crashed down. This remained embedded deep in the wood, and while the highwayman exerted himself vainly to extract it, the Scotsman seized him by the throat, threw him to the ground, and at the same time dealt him several Highland drover blows so powerfully that he thereby quite stunned him and completely overpowered him. He bound his throat, hands, and legs, took his money bag back, and informed the authorities of the spot where they could find a person for whom the gallows would be a good thing.

Such anecdotes and traditions of the Highland drovers, and obviously even more interesting ones than the foregoing, seem to have been in the mind of artist mentioned earlier when he executed that painting which is famous under this name. But not content with the inspiration which these tales and his own imagination were able to give him, Landseer even came north himself and took his landscape and his scenes from nature and from life. And therefore, in every respect and down to the tiniest details, his picture is not only a masterpiece of poetry, artistic treatment and execution, but also one of ethnographic faithfulness.

The time chosen is morning, when the drove begins its departure to the south. The hills deliver up all their cattle, the glens their sons and daughters, and one might question whether any one of the ancient chieftains,

'when plaided and plumed in his tartan array'[8]

marching to battle in times of old, could have made a deeper impression on northern minds, than does such a day now, when cattle are brought down, and neither sword nor warlike bagpipe ring out. Every incident in life brings its own emotions. Here it is the young lads who, setting out for the south, take leave of their parents, of their cottages, and perhaps of something even dearer, and then there are the old people, sending their worldly possessions to strange parts, uncertain and anxious whether there might come back a small welcome profit for house and home. It is not only the young lads who bid farewell on such occasions. The topsmen are often married and leave behind house and home, wife and child. The artist has felt all this deeply, and hence a certain melancholy is incorporated in the brilliant colours of his picture, and this actually constitutes its basic character, since it is a scene of parting.

The landscape belongs to the central parts of the Scottish Highlands, in fact, those in which I was now sojourning. In the background, a range of hills, dark and misty, is depicted. Beyond them lie the pleasant, level lands of the south to which the expedition is travelling. There is an expanse of loch at the foot of the hills. On its shores, on a spit of land jutting far out into the water, an old uninhabited castle lies in ruins. These tell of stormy times and warlike chieftains, now, however, fortunately banished into the far distance; here and there in a desolate valley, in which no corn grows, a birch or an ash or a dark spruce, struggling for life and nourishment in the cleft of a rock, testifies that there barrenness rules the land and that it is given over only to goats and wild life.

At the foot of this wild landscape, in the background, the leading sections of the drove are seen moving forward on their way to the south, not in a perfectly straight line, but, as cattle usually do when left to their own devices, spreading out a little over the heath, here and there taking a mouthful of food, and going up to the loch to lap the water. They are already so far distant that their

---

[8] [See Chapter XIII, fn. 21.]

different colours are now scarcely distinguishable, and their herdsmen walk behind them, striding out with solemn steps, like men at the start of a great enterprise. A second section follows the first. The two are kept apart by their drovers. Several herdsmen of this last section are still at the very back, and are receiving the last farewell drink at a small building which heather, straw and smoke mark out as the dwelling of human beings. In front of the house stands a small two-wheeled cart, the wheels of which, like the wagon body of woven birch, indicate that society in this landscape is still in a primitive state, which for the painter is entirely felicitous.

The lines of cattle, the mountains, the drovers, the cottage, the cart already constitute a picture by themselves. But all these are still in the receding background, and the artist has not expended his greatest powers on such things of lesser importance. He has kept the main subject and the strongest colours, as is proper, for the foreground. Here in the foreground is now the last section of the drove, with which the topsman himself will set off; he is standing roughly in the middle of the foreground. The canvas is so rich in incidents here in the foreground that if we wished to describe them all, it could almost seem to the reader, as though it were overcrowded. And yet everything is so tastefully and effortlessly combined, and so skilfully grouped, that nowhere does it seem excessive to the viewer; on the contrary, everything appears to form a harmonious whole.

The central point of the picture and the tallest figure is, as I have said, the topsman. From his head the group diminishes to right and left in pleasing undulating lines, just as it does from Joseph's head in Raphael's 'Holy Family'. The topsman is in full travelling apparel, kilted, with his plaid round his shoulders, with sandals on his feet, and with his **'Blue Bonnet'** on his head; this bonnet was probably manufactured in Kilmarnock[9] for, so the Scots say, only in this little factory town do people understand how to make properly these broad, blue caps of thick wool, decorated with a tassel in the middle, which suit their wearers so well, especially those who know how to don them to good effect. He is holding his youngest son in his arms and seems to be taking a last farewell look at him. Perhaps it would not even have occurred to this rough Highlander, little given to sentimentality, to take this tender farewell of his infant, had not his wife put him into his arms, in order meanwhile to fill his wayfarer's flask with refreshment. The little one has taken hold of his father's elaborately decorated dirk and is putting its hilt into the place where children put everything that seems pretty to them – into his mouth.

His wife is, as I said, occupied in filling the wayfarer's flask. This is a curly ram's horn. And the refreshment is whisky. What more welcome and comforting thing can the loving, attentive Scottish housewife give her Scottish master of the house to take with him than a flask of whisky, this splendid drink that offers consolation and life throughout the whole wide cold north? The wife, who is turning her full face to the viewer, is masterfully portrayed. We recognise in her at first glance the mother and the industrious toiler. The third main character of the picture, if not indeed the most distinguished of all, is the topsman's old father, who has emerged from the cottage and sat down on a chair in front of the door, to attend the whole scene and to witness the departure of his son and the cows that perhaps he himself owns in the drove. He is bald, and not only his snow-white hair brushed behind his ears, but also his stooping posture and the features of his lined face testify to his advanced and venerable age. His trembling right hand with its wrinkled stiff fingers rests on the stick on which he is leaning. He even seems to be somewhat deaf; for his unmarried, fresh-faced, black-haired daughter is bending down towards his ear, urging him to keep warm, and doing up a thick woollen shawl on his chest against the fresh morning mountain air.

---

[9] *Kilmarnock* [Kilmarnock was the leading centre for the production of Scottish woollen goods in the 18th century. The circular 'Balmoral Bonnet', worn by the topsman in this picture, was formerly known as the 'Kilmarnock Bonnet'. The name dates back to 1647, when the Kilmarnock Corporation of Bonnet Makers was formed.]

It is perhaps the last time that the old father will look upon this happy scene with his family, but then perhaps not, for in Scotland people attain to almost as advanced an age as in Russia and Norway. It has apparently been noticed that, even if the lifespan in Scotland does not frequently extend, as it does in Russia, beyond a hundred, indeed a hundred and fifty or a hundred and sixty years, nevertheless the number of those between seventy and a hundred years is as great as in any other country. In 1821 there were no fewer than 150,000 who were aged over sixty years among the 2,093,000 inhabitants of Scotland, which therefore amounts to one elderly person of more than sixty years in every thirteen people. We should consider and, if possible, investigate the effect that such a proportion must have on the moral condition of a people. How beneficial must the effect on families be when they are always headed by the old grandmother and the worthy grandfather. It must immensely strengthen the patriarchal structure of families, or as would be said in Scotland, their clan structure.

The old grandmother also appears on Landseer's painting. She is standing stooped between the old man and their tall, sturdy son. She is looking towards the old man, who perhaps has just said something that could be of use on the journey to his son, who as topsman is assuming such a great responsibility. She has raised one hand, and it almost appears to me as though she is about to pat her son on the shoulders and whisper to him 'Do you hear? Do not forget! And do what your father is telling you!'

On the grassy slope to the side of this group – so anxious about the whisky, about the babe, about the old man's health, about the son's departure – sits a loving couple at some distance. They have their backs turned to the others, as in general lovers turn their backs on everyone else, for they are sufficient one for the other. The man is young and strong, with his staff in his hand, and about to go south as a herdsman with the topsman. The poor girl seems to be apprehensive and disturbed by melancholy thoughts. For she is sorrowfully holding her head and is looking out into the distance with a pale face and eyes filled with sadness, while her lover presses her hand, bends over her, and assures her of his fidelity and his return. Her countenance is that of a typically lovely Scottish girl, and certainly in Great Britain have often been seen such physiognomies, not only among the high-ranking but also among the humble.

Just as typical is the small, shaggy, short-legged, thick-jawed grey horse, already saddled for the topsman and which is pulling up its last mouthful of grass on the slope behind the lover's back. This animal is encountered on Scottish mountain paths a hundred times over, exactly as Landseer has depicted it in his painting, and even today I had already seen a dozen of them on my way round Loch Tay.

Horses are usually grey in Scotland, cattle on the other hand are mostly black. Highland cattle are therefore also often called '**the black cattle**'. Some splendidly painted examples of this beast are standing behind the horse. They are not eating, and they seem to be experiencing a certain disquiet about everything that is going on round about them. One is looking out into the distance and is bellowing after the departing herd; another, with erect ears and horns and with that shrewd unwavering stare that is on occasion peculiar to these stupid animals, is looking into the group of people as though it wanted to ask 'What is going to happen now?'. At the edge of the painting some Highland sheep and rams are lying, sunk deep in their thick wool and inveterate stupidity.

Several smaller figures occupy the very nearest part of the foreground, a hen with her chicks, some dogs and a young shepherd boy, all of which are playfully pestering each other to their hearts' content. Even these small scenes are outstandingly executed, and each one of them could constitute a small painting in itself, yet all are splendidly integrated into the composite whole. The hen is being attacked by a small playful puppy who is regarding the matter as mere fun, while the hen is treating it as deadly serious. Her anger is making all her feathers stand up; her eyes are rolling, she is snapping her teeth, or rather her beak. In short, her agitation points the most comical contrast to the frolicking puppy's attacks. Even the chickens are all treated by the painter with great, and yet not over-fastidious, attention to detail. One of them is hopping carelessly and awkwardly quite close to the horse's hoof, and is pecking at a small grain of corn. A shepherd boy with bare feet seems to be performing a repetition of this idea with a small dog. However, here it is the dog that is mistaking playfulness for seriousness. It is a small Scottish terrier, fiercely and viciously barking out from under a chair, jumping up at the little shepherd, who is grabbing at it and making a face at it. Between them sits a large Scottish collie which is carrying out two duties at the same time. For it is feeding a little suckling puppy and is pressing closely and faithfully against the side of its master, namely the old man, the head of house and home.

Of course, one must not judge the picture itself by this imperfect description – all descriptions of pictures are imperfect. However, looking at it for oneself afterwards, then one will realise how all the groups and all the motifs combine easily and pleasingly and work together in harmony. Withal, every detail in it is such a faithful expression and impression of the country that it must be committed to memory detail by detail if one wants to understand the country.

As far as I know, Landseer has not given us a second national Scottish picture as large and as comprehensive as this, his 'Highland Drovers'. However, several other small pictures by him exist that are characteristic of Scotland and are of interest. But unfortunately they are dispersed among the rooms of the great. For example, I saw one above a fireplace in a house of the Marquis of Landsdowne. But in the interest of geography and ethnography one ought to collect copies of pictures like this, depicting a country, just as assiduously as one collects books written about countries, since usually the former are just as instructive as the latter.

* * * * * * *

XVI
From Loch Tay to Killin

I shook hands in farewell with my white-haired, shivering old man outside his door, and took the arm of another old man to continue on my way – as I said, old people are very numerous in Scotland!

This whole area at the western end of Loch Tay, together with the whole valley of Glen Lyon and several other tracts of land belong to the district that is still popularly called 'Breadalbane'. This is one of those names for parts of the country that are no longer recognised by the government as official units, but which in popular memory are lost only slowly or never. Before the division into counties was also completely implemented in the Scottish Highlands in 1746, the latter were simply divided into districts of this kind, over each of which one of the great estate-owners or clan chieftains had jurisdiction. These private jurisdictions have long been abolished[1]. Glenorchy, – Lochaber, – Morvern, – Glenelg[2], – Assynt are names of other such ancient districts which have disappeared only in official reports, but not in popular speech. Moreover they still survive in the titles of lords and barons as well. It is remarkable that the name of a clan remained attached only to individuals and families, and did not pass over to a district or division of the country. There is, I believe, no single example known of a clan name becoming also the name of a district, whereas particular clans are known to have been indeed the only inhabitants of particular districts, valleys, or islands. The little Hebridean island of Ulva was and is inhabited only by people of the name and clan Macquarry[3]. Why was it then not called 'Macquarry' too? Other islands are occupied only by Macleans or Macdonalds, in some glens dwell only Stuarts, in others only Campbells[4], and yet these islands and glens were never named after these families[5]. We find that this question, like many other questions concerning the clans, is not at all investigated by Scottish writers.

The Breadalbane estates, however, extend much further beyond this district; for, as I have already said, they stretch for a hundred miles across, as far as the Atlantic Ocean. Whether they actually do reach from coast to coast, as some people assured me, I have never been able to verify. However, I do not believe it. In the Tay Valley they extend not far towards the east beyond Taymouth Castle, in fact only as far as Aberfeldy. Taymouth Castle itself, initially called Balloch, as we said, was in fact built in 1580[6] by Sir Colin Campbell of Glenorchy at the most extreme eastern end of the Breadalbane lands. Indeed it is said, that this gentleman, when his attention had been drawn to the awkward location of his castle, replied, pointing eastwards, **'Never mind, we'll brizz yont'** ('That matters not, we shall press ahead'). I know not, however, as I said, whether and to what extent this threat or prophecy, reminiscent of a similar remark by Peter the Great, when he founded Petersburg, has been fulfilled.

Loch Tay is, as the English put it, **'a fine piece of water'**; they always have more stock phrases and idioms appropriate for all occasions than do we. Its shape is that of almost all lochs in Scotland, namely extremely narrow, very long, and lying in an almost completely straight line. The following

---

[1] [See Introduction p. xxi.]
[2] *Glenely*
[3] *Macguarry*
[4] *Kaimbels*
[5] Some castles are an exception to this, for example, Castle Douglas, Castle Campbell and Castle Kennedy. *JGK*
[6] [It was probably built in 1550. In 1733 two wings, designed by William Adam, were added; in 1805 the original central keep was demolished and replaced by a four-storey neo-Gothic block; during the 1820s the Adam wings were altered and extended to include extravagantly decorated public rooms (see p. 102) in keeping with the ongoing expensive tree-planting and other improvements to the Breadalbane estates. These ostentatious architectural alterations were reported to be 'almost ready' for Queen Victoria's visit in 1842.]

Scottish lochs have these three characteristics to the same high degree as Loch Tay, namely Loch Ericht, Loch Lochy, Loch Ness, Loch Shin, Loch Rannoch etc. Naturally this is due to the configuration of the mountain ranges. My companion told me, and it was confirmed to me in Killin, that the salmon of the River Tay even come up right into this loch. These creatures owe their lives of course to the Breadalbanes, who possess the fishing-rights for the entire seventeen mile long loch. Previously these rights had been linked to an Augustinian priory that stood on a small island in the loch. This priory had been founded by Alexander I, and his wife, Queen Sybilla, the daughter of King Henry[7] I of England, lies buried on this lonely island[8]. The Reformation probably destroyed the priory and handed over its rights to the Breadalbanes.

Like Loch Ness and most of the Scottish lochs, Loch Tay is of extraordinary depth. This exceeds one hundred fathoms. It is remarkable that all Scottish lochs are so very similar to each other in this respect too. Most of them are deeper than one hundred fathoms. And one hundred and fifty fathoms seems to be the greatest depth that occurs. They are therefore nothing but clefts between mountains, filled with clear water. If the Scottish mountain-peaks are measured from the deepest bed of these lochs – and it is also not uninteresting to know their height measured in this way – then they have a height of about five thousand feet.

'Our loch never freezes', people assured me. **Dr** Johnson had been told the same thing about Loch Ness, and he was careful enough not to believe it at once. However, it is quite possible that the great depth of these lochs, as well as their isolation because of the mountain-ranges that lie along their sides and protect them, keep them from freezing quickly.

In my thoughts I pictured Queen Victoria and Prince Albert gliding along on this lonely clear loch in their elegant little pleasure boat with their royal retinue. For they undertook this portion of their journey by water.

'I believe,' said my old companion, 'that our Queen would have liked to remain even longer with us in Taymouth Castle, and in fact she did stay one day longer than had been planned at first. But her Prime Minister, Sir Robert, would not leave her in peace and insisted that matters of state made her departure necessary. I believe that the Queen by no means felt indebted to him for that, and when she stepped into her boat and the Prime Minister followed, she turned to him and said "**Sir Robert, we are full here!**", and he was forced to go into another boat with the Marquis of Aberdeen.

'The decorated boats,' he continued, 'and all the colourfully dressed oarsmen and other persons in their '**Tartan-Array**' made our loch lively and pretty as never before. The graceful little foreign gentleman, the Spanish captain, whom you met in Taymouth Castle, looked especially elegant. **He was as nice a person, as I ever saw under the kilt. I never had imagined, that he had so nice legs. The only mistake was his bonnet, it was rather a little too large.** But his legs were excellent. They were extremely well-proportioned, not too thin and not too fat. **Thick legs are not always the bonny legs, sir!** and not the ones that look best under the kilt. The knees should be really rounded and strong. The calves should sit just below the knee and begin full and rounded. For there are people, sir, whose calves sit further down; that does not look well! But the calves and legs should then get narrower and look slim and elegant, and they should end really neatly in a small foot. These are the best legs for the kilt, sir!'

---

[7] *Heinrich*

[8] [Queen Sybilla (1092 – 1122) died on the islet of Eilean nan Ban-naomh on Loch Tay and Alexander I was said to have founded a priory on it in her memory. She was in fact buried at Dunfermline Abbey.]

I had never thought that the very wearing of the kilt would have occasioned among humble people in Scotland such an acute and accurate disquisition on the beauty of legs. In this old man's stories about the Queen's visit, it was also very remarkable and striking to me that he was so precisely and minutely informed about everything, and that, for example, he could even give the time of each occurrence to the very minute. The Queen arrived in Taymouth Castle on Wednesday about six o'clock in the evening. From nine o'clock until eleven the Highlanders[9] performed their dances in the park. The next day, Queen Victoria went walking in the park with the Duke of Sutherland between nine and ten o'clock and visited the attractive dairy. That same morning, Prince Albert had already gone hunting with the Marquis of Breadalbane before nine o'clock. After two o'clock, Prince Albert came back from the hunt. After luncheon, they went into '**His Lordship's vegetable garden**'.

On the second day, Prince Albert came down as early as at half past one, namely from the hills, where he had been hunting. Queen Victoria had taken a walk with the Marchioness until eleven o'clock. It had been '**soft weather, wet in the afternoon**'. From three to five o'clock the ladies and gentlemen were on the balcony to watch the Highland dances, and then went for a drive to view various beauty spots in the vicinity. Two of '**his Lordship's servants in Highland dress**' rode in front, then came the carriage with Her Majesty and Prince Albert, behind them two '**footmen in scarlet dress**', five carriages with '**several parties**' of the invited guests, with the '**Duchess of Sutherland**', the '**Duchess of Norfolk**' '**and such as that**'. At nine o'clock the ball began in the hall. That evening there were only ten thousand lamps lit in the park. **His Lordship** – the old man always mentioned him first – and Queen Victoria, Prince Albert and the Duchess of Norfolk opened the ball, which ended at twelve o'clock.

The next morning the trees were planted at half past ten. And at 11.15 the whole company had embarked. The band of the 92nd Regiment were in a boat of their own. In another boat the Queen also had two pipers, of whom **His Lordship's Piper M'Kinzie** [sic] was the best. He played wonderfully on the loch upon a '**silvermounted pipe**', which he had won as a prize from the Edinburgh Pipers' Company. I think that if all the foregoing were compared with the most detailed reports of the most detailed English journals, it would be found that my observant old man's accounts corresponded completely with them.

The heads of the mountains on the other side of the loch were all coiffured in the outdated fashion of last century, that is, dressed with a wig of snow and powdered white, especially Ben Lawers, which resembles a fairly regular pyramid. This is the case with most Scottish mountains of the greatest size. Even Ben Nevis[10] rises fairly regularly to the point of a pyramid. Most of these highest pyramidal mountains in Scotland are called '**Bens**'[11], or rather, properly written in the Celtic manner, '**Beann**' or '**Beinne**', for example, Ben Nevis, Ben Lawers, Ben More, Ben Ledi, Ben Lomond, Ben Avon etc. This is probably a Celtic word, which has also remained in use in Germanic Scottish and in English as the term for the highest mountain peaks. Several, though only a few of the highest mountains, do not have this epithet, for example, not Cairn Gorm (4095[12] feet high) and Cairn Toul (4245 feet high).

For the lower peaks in Scotland they have the word '**Hill**', which without doubt is the German term 'Hügel' abbreviated; we have, for example, Wisp Hill (1830 feet high), Soutra Hill (1716 feet high).

---

[9] [There were in attendance men of the 92nd Highlanders, 6th Carabineers, Royal Breadalbane Highlanders and Dragoons.]

[10] *Nevis*

[11] This Celtic word is also found in the 'Pennines'. *JGK*

[12] [Collins *Scotland Atlas and Gazetteer* (1999) gives the following heights: Cairn Gorm 4084 feet, Cairn Toul 4234, Wisp Hill 1952, Soutra Hill 1207, Ben Clach 1748, and Ben Armine 2309.]

However, since neither in nature nor in human language is there anything without an exception, there are also some mountains that are always called '**Hills**' and which nevertheless are higher than some '**Bens**'. Thus Baltock *Hill*[13] is 2611 feet high, while *Ben* Clach rises to only 2359 feet. So too *Dunrich Hill*[14] has a height of 2421 feet, *Ben* Armine[15] on the other hand a height of only 2307 feet. However, even these names are not completely arbitrary nonetheless, but there is usually a particular and rational underlying motive for them. So, for example, Ben Clach is the highest mountain in the Ochil range and hence rises there among its lower neighbours as the dominant *ben*. Apart from that, as a general rule, the word '**Hill**' – 'Hügel', 'collines' [plural sic] – has attained such a high degree of importance as in no other country. For in this country, they usually apply no other expression than that of '**Hills**' to entire mountain ranges. Thus they speak of '**the Ochill-*Hills*', the Grampian-*Hills*'** which are ranges of hills that far exceed our Harz *Mountains*, Thüringer Wald *Mountains* and Black Forest *Mountains* in height and surpass them even more in wildness and starkness of character. In the whole of Scotland I know of no '**Mounts**'[16] and '**Mountains**'. These expression occur of course in English books about Scotland, but not in the nomenclature of Scottish geography as it exists in popular speech.

Many small brooks run down from the mountains on both sides of Loch Tay. As a rule their beds are cut remarkably deep into the rocky ground. The English call them '**Rivolets**' [sic], the Scots '**Burns**', as we have said, and the Gaels '**Uilgh**'[17] (pronounced 'ültsch'). On our side we jumped and strode across several of them. On the other side, however, their number seemed to be extraordinarily great, indeed uncountable. All the hillsides were furrowed with these burns like ploughed fields.

On the way, we passed through small mountain hamlets, by the names of Achianich[18], Skiag, Margmor. In the last, which lies approximately in the middle of the lengthwise stretch of the loch, we partook of our midday meal. This consisted only of a piece of Highland cheese, a glass of toddy, which was a mixture of hot water, whisky, and some syrup, and, to accompany these, '**Oat's cake**' [sic] **à discrétion**. This was somewhat simple, I think, and yet we had to pay for it no less than ten pence (that is, almost one-third of a thaler) per person which I believe was, relatively speaking as dear as anything one could imagine. Everywhere in these miserable, uninhabited Highlands prices are a phenomenon which I cannot rightly understand. For a breakfast, for which one usually pays two shillings in English inns – one shilling in elegant London clubs – we were charged three shillings here in the Highlands. Even in the most modest inns, a night's lodging cost likewise three shillings every time, which is as much as one pays in the best inns in English towns. There the customary price is from two shillings to two shillings and a half. To a guide I was obliged to pay from six to eight shillings per day, and although I was the only traveller at that time of year, and no competitors were available to them, they usually showed themselves very displeased, if I did not wish to offer above eight shillings. A one-horse, two-wheeled gig costs at least one shilling per mile. At the same time the road tolls and '**what the driver expects**', that is, the gratuities, are so high, that a German mile[19] costs the traveller between seven and eight shillings. I could not rightly understand these prices among such impoverished people as the Scottish Highlanders are. It is

---

[13] [Perhaps Mount Battock (2552 feet) or Meikle Balloch Hill (though only 1201 feet).]

[14] [Perhaps Dun Rig, near Peebles (2437 feet).]

[15] *Ormen*

[16] [John Thomson's *Atlas of Scotland* (1832) shows Mount Keen and Mont (sic) Battock. But the author is correct in the main: there are very few. Collins *Scotland Atlas and Gazetteer* (1999) lists only nine hills or mountains prefixed by *Mount*. In some at least this is a corruption of the Gaelic *monadh* 'mountain (range)', thus Mount Keen (Monadh Caoin 'smooth mountain'), Mount Battock (Monadh Biadhtaich 'mountain of the raven'), Mount Bouie (Monadh Buidhe 'yellow mountain').]

[17] [Properly *uillt*, plural of *allt* (= 'stream')]

[18] *Achimig*

[19] [A German mile was roughly 7,420 metres, a statute mile is 1,609 metres.]

improbable too, that such prices are found only on this so-called *fashionable* tour; for if elsewhere they were significantly lower, then even on the fashionable tour they would be soon be forced down by competition. What a contrast exists in this respect between Scotland and Norway, otherwise similar in so many ways and equally poor!

In order to encourage us in our meagre midday meal, we were told that Queen Victoria and Prince Albert had also enjoyed the same and had tasted this kind of whisky, which is called '**Athol-brose**'[20] (Athol soup), in Dunkeld. There, however, it had been prepared with best honey, as is in fact proper. Here unfortunately they had nothing but syrup.

The Campbells are not very numerous in the hamlets here on Loch Tay. The Stuarts, however, are the most numerous. Everywhere on my way from here to beyond Killin as far as Loch Earn and Loch Katrine[21] I encountered many Stuarts, or Stewarts, or Stewards, or, as they are called in Gaelic '**Stuartich**'[22]. This is again an example of a clan which adopted an English name. For the Stuarts borrowed their name from the English word '**Steward**'. The Norman knight Fitzalan became '*Royal Steward*' in David I's household, and this title (also the position I believe) became hereditary in his family and then also passed over to the clan founded by him. They are still called, if one is talking of the clan as a whole, not simply 'Stuarts' but '*Royal*-Stuarts'. I do not know whether there is another Clan Stuart which is *not* '**Royal**'. I also do not know whether they are called 'royal' because those kings of Scotland came from them, or rather from the family of their founder and chief, or whether this epithet dates from those times when the Fitzalans were '**Royal Stewards**'. Incidentally, from Scottish history I know of several more examples of the transformation of titles into surnames. This may come about because so many titles and offices became hereditary, and hence the official title merged, so to speak, with the family.

All over this area there are also several MacGregors, or as the Gaels pronounce it '**Machk Krekars**'[23]. Most of them, however, are to be found near Aberfeldy. My guide was a MacIntyre[24] himself (Duncan was his Christian name). This clan is not very large. '**The Mac Intires go under the same badge with the Macdonalds**', Duncan told me. Have perhaps these two clans the same colours or the same coat of arms? Are they kinsmen and related? Do such allied and related clans actually exist? Did one clan on occasion emerge from another? Did one clan on occasion perhaps split into several others? Clans present the most remarkable phenomenon in Scotland for the historian and psychologist and it has by no means been sufficiently examined; I can scarcely begin to enquire into it, because I do not know how I can obtain an answer to all the different questions that occur to me.

I said just now that there are no **Mounts** in Scotland. However, I must make an exception to that, namely in favour of those little artificial hills which are to be seen sometimes in Scotland, even if not so frequently as in Ireland. These little conical accumulations of earth were always called '**little mounts**'[25] by Duncan. We saw several of them by Loch Tay. They were very regular cones, usually overgrown with trees, sometimes surrounded by a stone wall. Probably they were burial mounds, such as we have already described in Ireland, or those mote-hills from which in olden times the clan chieftains dispensed justice for their clansmen. At both ends of Loch Tay, both at Kenmore and Killin, there are said to be remains of old druidic temples. At Kenmore there are indeed very significant ones.

---

[20] [Originally Atholl Brose was oatmeal stirred into a glass of whisky. Heather honey and sometimes cream were later additions, but oatmeal was always an ingredient. The author's gloss again shows his confusion of *broth* and *brose*.]
[21] *Katterin*
[22] [Properly *Stiùbhartaich.*]
[23] [In Gaelic *MacGriogair*. The transcription indicates preaspiration and a particular quality of the final r-sound, see Introduction p. xxv.]
[24] *Mac Intire*
[25] [Perhaps Duncan was saying *mounds*.]

It was very strange to me to find, beside almost every one of the mountain farmhouses, a special little limekiln, intended only for the needs of the farm. Lime is remarkably commonly used here, as in Ireland, for the fertilisation of the fields, and in fact generally appears to be the principal means of improving this peaty soil. Often the little **limekiln** is nothing more than a funnel-shaped excavation in the hillside, at the bottom of which a little hole is made to let the draught into the fire.

The little boys in the hamlets all wore the kilt and almost all also spoke only Gaelic.

The small landowners are now also frequently planting trees. One of them, by the name of Marcus, who was mentioned to me on the journey, had planted twenty-five thousand spruce trees here, not far from the loch. So different are countries that what counts as praiseworthy and as a sign of progress in one is regarded in another as a sign of backwardness. Thus, for example, it must be said of the Scottish Highlands: 'This country is still retarded in its cultivation, for it is almost all barren', whereas with regard to Poland the complaint is made: 'The whole country is still barbaric and half of it is forest'. In Poland it is regarded as progress in cultivation when much forest is cleared. In Scotland it is regarded as a good thing, not only when a thriving wood takes the place of a badly cultivated field, but also when well conducted sheep-grazing takes place of such a bad type of agriculture as is practised by the little cottage-dwellers of the Scottish Highlands. On the other side of the whole of Loch Tay, everywhere round about Ben Lawers, the land is either newly planted forest or grazing for sheep; **'all the hills there are under sheep-farm'**, people said.

The hardy little black Highland cattle, the little shaggy white horses, the great black-headed tarred sheep, the low heather-thatched smoky cottages, Ben Lawers to the right, Ben Lawers to the left, Ben Lawers in front, Ben Lawers behind us – for we were walking almost right round it – and finally a countless number of those little carts of woven willow, such as can be seen on the picture by Landseer – these were the things that met us on the remainder of our journey to Killin. These last, the little carts, served **'for taking down the peat from the hills'**, and they were all fully laden with this material which is just as important here in the Highlands as in Ireland. These little vehicles are so small, for the particular reason that almost all the peat is found on the mountains and must be brought down on very awkward paths. In the glens and valleys the peat and bog is now either eradicated by cultivation or has always been absent from there. And even if here and there bog and peat are found in some wild glens, it is not as good as on the mountains, because it is mixed with sand and detritus from the rivers and the stones that come clattering down. Only on the hills is a good, pure, usable peat found.

The Scots call these bogs **'Moss'** or **'Muirs'**. The former are the marshes of moss, the latter the actual peat-bogs. It is a remarkable and inexplicable phenomenon that these quagmires, marshes and bogs have been increasing in size down to the most recent times. At least this seems to be the generally held opinion in Scotland. It is also believed that the climate of Scotland has therefore been deteriorating down to the most recent times. Or, on the contrary, could a deterioration and increasing coldness of the climate not be the cause of that increase of the marshes? I adduce this here only because a quite similar belief is common in respect of the appearance of marsh and peat in Ireland. However, it is most highly probable that the marshes will retreat due to the forests, the improved grazing, and the expanding fields, and that consequently the climate of Scotland will also improve again.

* * * * * * *

XVII
Killin

Towards evening we arrived in Killin, a small town at the other end of the loch, surrounded by woods, foliage and charming mountain scenery. There I paid my usual visits to the local minister[1] and the schoolmaster[2], two very pleasant and well-informed men. On a map of Scotland the schoolmaster had added the ancient Celtic names of many places, and among them I found the ancient Celtic names of Edinburgh, Perth and Stirling, for which I had been looking for a long time. Edinburgh is called 'Tuhneeten', Stirling 'Shruila', Perth 'Perschtj'[3]. I have already mentioned the Celtic names of Scotland, Albin and Alba, as well as that for the Scots themselves, Albanach[4]. However, I thought I noticed that the Gaelic Scots always pronounced these words more or less as **'Allopa'** and **'Allopanih'**[5]. The question also occurred to me whether or not these words could be related to the name of the Alps. Perhaps **'Alb'** or **'Alp'** is an old Celtic word with which mountains in general are denoted[6], and hence in Scottish **'Albin'** means 'mountain-land'. The names of the English kings have also had to suffer slight alterations in the mouths of their Gaelic subjects. Thus, for example, the Georges are called **'Seorus'**[7] (pronounced 'Schorus') by the Scottish Highlanders, for example, Schorus IV, that is, George IV. The last king, William, was called "Uielleam"[8]. For Victoria they had no particular Gaelic transformation, since, of all English sovereigns, this queen is the first and only whose name remains unaltered in the mouths of *all* nations, which is remarkable.

The minister bade me goodnight with the warning that I could not continue my journey the next day, because I would scarcely find anyone who would carry my things, indeed because perhaps on the military road I would not even see anyone from whom I could enquire the way. And the schoolmaster welcomed me, as I stood hesitantly on his doorstep, with the words 'Pray do come in. But I must point out that today is the eve of the Sabbath, and that I therefore have to request you to speak to me only of serious matters.' The Sabbath is more strictly observed in these Scottish Highlands than in any other part of England.

I learned another remarkable fact here that I ought to have learned in Dunkeld, namely that a convert to Roman Catholicism had built a completely new Roman Catholic church there[9]. Here in the Highlands I heard several times of such newly built Catholic churches and thus I commented that this remarkable phenomenon of the increase and spread of Catholics is affecting not only the whole world and Great Britain, but even the remote valleys of the Highlands as well. 'An inclination towards Catholicism is noticeable especially among Highlanders and among the aristocracy,' several people, who were in a position to know this, repeated to me. If this is taken

---

[1] [Alexander Stewart (1811 – 1883); he joined the Free Church in 1843 and ministered to Killin Free Church till his death.]

[2] [D(uncan?) Ferguson; his age is given as 55 in the June 1841 Census.]

[3] [Properly *Dùn Èideann*, *Sruighlea*, *Peairt* respectively. Though literate in English, the schoolmaster was not literate in Gaelic and notated pronunciation using English spelling conventions. Cf. Kohl's procedure, see Introduction p. xxv.]

[4] This means all Scots, while by the word mentioned earlier 'Gaidhealach' only the Celtic Scots are understood. *JGK* [Properly *Albannach* (singular), *Albannaich* (plural)].

[5] [The author's spelling reflects the pronunciation fairly well. See Introduction p. xxv.]

[6] [Since southern central Europe was the Celtic homeland, it is possible that the word *Alps* is of Celtic origin. However, the name has been variously explained as meaning 'high' (compare Gaelic *alp* 'mountain') or 'white' (compare Latin *albus* 'white').]

[7] [Properly *Seòras*.]

[8] [Properly *Uilleam*.]

[9] [There would seem to have been no Roman Catholic church in Dunkeld itself, but *The Statistical Account of Perthshire* of 1844 states 'About two years ago a small chapel [the Chapel of St Anthony the Eremite] was consecrated on the Murthly Estate where the Catholic servis is now performed'. Murthly is eight kilometres from Dunkeld.]

together with the endeavours and reforms of the Puseyites[10], who also wish to carry out reforms in a Catholic, hierarchical spirit, and with other reforms in other countries, then it can be assumed that, just as the Reformation began with Luther three hundred years ago, now a Counter-reformation has begun with the Puseyites and other people. The building of new Catholic churches is spreading out from Ireland across the whole of Great Britain. I would regard the Catholic converts in England – if I may judge from the few that I have seen and heard – as the keenest and most ardent in the world.

Irish Catholics have recently obtained Maynooth[11] as their seminary; similarly the Scottish Catholics have had St Mary's College near Aberdeen[12] as their appointed college since 1829. This is intended solely for young men who dedicate themselves to the Catholic priesthood. There are said to be usually fifty young people there. According to the Edinburgh Almanac[13] there were forty-two students there in 1836. I do not know whether all my readers are aware that, in spite of the fanaticism of the Reformation in Scotland, there are nevertheless Catholic congregations everywhere there. In fact there are about fifty in all; however, in the large towns – if the Irish who live there are not taken into account – there are relatively fewer than in the country, and in the Lowlands there are not only relatively fewer than in the Highlands, but also absolutely far fewer. The so-called Roman Catholic Scottish eastern diocese, or **the eastern District**, contains only about a dozen congregations and includes almost the whole of the Lowlands, while **the western and the northern District**, which, apart from the congregations of Glasgow and Greenock, include almost only the Highlands, contain nearly forty congregations. If the entire population of the last named two districts is assumed to be 800,000 inhabitants, which is probably the highest that one can assume, but the entire population of the first district is assumed to be 1,600,000, which is certainly the minimum estimate, then there is a Catholic congregation for every 20,000 inhabitants in the Highlands, but only one for every 160,000 in the Lowlands. Like education and the Saxon tongue, the Reformation had its focal point in the Lowlands and was most successful there, but nowhere among the glens and mountains of the Highlands could it make inroads to the same extent. On the islands, too, that belong to Scotland, this same phenomenon can be observed; for while on the large islands almost everyone belongs to the Reformed faith, several of the small ones have remained completely Catholic, or at least it is only on the small islands that Catholic congregations are exclusively found, as on Barra, Eigg[14], South Uist.

That evening in Killin I felt a great lack of conversation, since I did not dare trouble my friends there with my company for too long, on account of the Sabbath. I therefore borrowed from one of them an old book about '**Germany**', written by a certain William Guthrie, Esqr., at the end of last century in 1776[15]. I chose this particular book because I had found one of the inhabitants of Killin reading it, and because I was curious to learn what these people read and know about my own native land.

In order to learn about a particular nation, it is necessary to know how other nations are seen by that nation. Of course it could be objected that we could not learn from a book written in 1776 how Germany might be regarded by people in Great Britain in our time, and that for such information we

---

[10] [Followers of Edward Bouverie Pusey (1800 – 82), one of the leaders of the Oxford Movement. Stressing the historical continuity of the Church of England and the importance of the priesthood and the sacraments, they attempted to restore the ideals of the pre-Reformation church to the Church of England.]

[11] *Mainooth* [See Chapter II, fn. 31.]

[12] [St Mary's College, Blairs, Aberdeen, established 1829. It closed in 1986.]

[13] [*Edinburgh almanac, or Universal Scots and imperial register* (published at intervals by Oliver and Boyd, Edinburgh) contained information not only about Edinburgh but about Scotland and the British Empire.]

[14] *Barra-Island, Eig-Island* respectively

[15] [Probably *Travels through Holland, Germany and Switzerland and other parts of Europe but especially Italy* by the late Monsieur de Blainville, sometime Secretary to the Embassy of the States-General at the Court of Spain. Translated from the author's own manuscript by William Guthrie, Esq'., Vols. 1 and 2, Dublin 1743.]

would have to look at present-day publications. To some extent this is true. However, within one nation there is a large number of very different people. Firstly there are those who read periodicals and move with the times, who dwell near the sources, who live in London or at least in Edinburgh. On the other hand, there are those who reside in the Highlands and in the Hebrides, or those who only by chance have at their disposal some ancient book about Germany, inherited from their grandfather; they do not move with the times but remain encumbered with outdated ideas. And such antiquated ideas not only still abide in the heads of unsophisticated people, but long endure in the minds (or, so to speak, in the very blood) of more or less everyone, even of the more enlightened, and sporadically they are still seen to crop up in the country in many forms. Thus many comments by W. Guthrie reminded me of sundry questions that had been put to me concerning Germany. They made me recall then several observations that I had encountered in more recent English books. In England, up-to-date books about Germany are certainly not numerous; for the English have to read about so many countries that lie on the other side of the equator that Germany is but *one* of the countries about which they seek enlightenment only in passing, and about which they then begin to look for guidance in some old Guthrie or other. In short, by no means do I regard this book as so behind the times that it would not be capable of indicating what thousands of people still learn and read about us every day.

It is praise of us with which Guthrie begins. 'The Germans are a people honest by nature, hospitable and freedom-loving, who are not given to pretence and affectation.' This is an old truth, it can be found as early as in Tacitus, and recently I found the proposition in one of the Edinburgh reviews, developed at length and applied to the spirit that infuses all the Germanic peoples.

'The upper classes of the German nation are proud of splendid titles and ancient ancestry in a ridiculous way and to a dreadful extent.' – This German characteristic is found attested in Great Britain too. For there is scarcely another country in which titles, at least hereditary titles, are held in higher regard.

'Industriousness, diligence and tenacity are the principal and characteristic features of the German nation.' This too is found perfectly demonstrated in the example of our English brothers.

'The Germans are brave, and when they are led by skilful generals, especially by Italians, they have frequently achieved great things.'

'No nation has more wedding feasts, funeral ceremonies, birthdays and name days and other celebrations than the Germans.' – I also regard this as true, at least neither in France, nor in Russia, nor in Spain are there so many days for festivals, dancing and country drives, – so many places of entertainment, concert halls, coffee-, milk- and cake-gardens, as in Germany.

'No nation has so many field sports, hunts, bullfights, dog-baiting and bear-hunts and suchlike as the Germans.' – The taste for such things has recently, it seems to me, moved rather to England, – and at least some of the pastimes mentioned are now out of date in Germany. In Austria there were bear-hunts only here and there in the middle of last century; but in England the German traveller is still occasionally asked what German bear-hunts were really like, and whether he by any chance had witnessed one.

'The great passion that the Germans have for hunting **the wild boar** is perhaps the reason why more woods and forests still exist in Germany than in any other country. However, **the Hercynian**[16] **forest is now cut down in many places**. Every count and baron has his forest well stocked with game of every kind, with roe deer, red deer of all sizes and all colours' (thus for example with dwarf deer,

---

[16] [On the mountain region between the Rhine and the Carpathians.]

giant deer, green deer, yellow deer, crimson deer?! – the writer has clearly heard tell of black boars and red deer). 'Then there are a host of hares, foxes, wolves, bears and boars, so many that in many districts the peasants enjoy game as their daily fare. The glutton of Germany is one of the most voracious animals in the world. It eats itself so full that it cannot move, and in this state the Germans' (the whole nation?) 'pounce upon it and kill it. They also kill wolves and bears, but as a rule they do not eat their flesh.' Here the writer could well have added that as a rule we do not eat the flesh of horses or dogs either. Would one believe that as late as the end of last century a book could have been written about us and could still be read towards the middle of this century, which more or less resembles a second edition of the '**Germania**' of Tacitus?

I once spoke to an English squire, who had heard that the wolverine or '**Glutton**' created terrible havoc in Germany, and who said to me '**I had a wonderful idea of your Glutton.** Pray tell me a little about this remarkable German animal.' He would scarcely believe that I had seen this creature nowhere other than in a museum, and still less would he believe that this dreadful animal is no larger than a moderately large dog.

'The two principal rivers in German are the Rhine and the Danube, and the two most important lakes are the Lake of Bregenz[17] and Lake Constance[18]. Besides the lakes and rivers, Germany still contains a number of **large noxious bodies of standing water** as well, **which are next to pestilencial** [sic] and which plague the neighbouring inhabitants with a number of most highly lamentable illnesses.' – As a rule we Germans are accustomed to place these marshes in Hungary and Poland. From the viewpoint of England the picture of Eastern Europe is apparently foreshortened, and the '**bodies of standing water**', which we see gleaming in the distance, appear to the English to be lying static in the very centre of Germany.

'As an antidote to these marshes, however, nature has also given the country a number of curative mineral water springs. Some of these mineral waters intoxicate the drinker, it is said, immediately they are ingested, and therefore they are surrounded by railings and sealed off.'

'**Had Germany before the middle of this century been acquainted with agriculture**, it would be one of the most fertile and productive countries in Europe.' – Ye Heavens! it almost seems the English squires and farmers believed that, until the time of our grandfathers, we were nomads and lived in the forests. Even in the most primitively farmed and wretched districts of Ireland I could sometimes barely make the people believe that we had far better cultivated fields than they.

'Even in its present **rude state**, foodstuffs are cheaper than anywhere else, which can be proved by the extraordinarily large armies that are maintained there even in the most uncultivated parts of the country.'

'In winter, when the different arms of the Danube are frozen over, the ladies disport themselves in sledges of very different shapes, for example, in the form of tigers, griffins, swans, **scollop-shells** etc. The ladies sit in these sledges in velvet clothes, trimmed with expensive fur, and decorated with lace and jewels, while on their heads they wear velvet caps. And the sledges are drawn **by horses, stags, or other creatures**' – perhaps by wild boars, wolves, bears or even by gluttons? – 'And these animals are then decked out with ribbons, feathers, and bells.' – Let us imagine that this book is being read by a clan chieftain in the Highlands, or by a laird on the Hebridean islands, or by an owner of sheep-grazing land, or by a schoolmaster in Orkney or Shetland; how such a person's fantastical notions of Germany will be incited!

---

[17] *Bregentz*

[18] *Constanz* [This and the preceding are the same lake, the German name of which is *Bodensee*.]

'German ladies as a rule possess a fine complexion, and some of them, especially in Saxony, have all that tenderness in their features which is found so enchanting in the fair sex of some other countries. However, they are excessively enamoured of gold and silver finery. In some German courts they appear in costly furs, and they are all cluttered with jewels if they can get them. The middle-class women of many towns are decked out **inconceivably fantastic** [sic], as can be realised from various pictures and engravings.'

'The most unfortunate Germans are the vassals of the small princes who harass and torment them, in order to maintain their own superiority.'

'The printing of books is promoted in an extravagant and imperfect way. Every educated man is also an author. They multiply books without number, and every prince, baron or gentleman in Germany is a chemist or **natural philosopher**.'

'Germany has also produced several good political authors, geographers and historians. But they appear to have no great taste and no talent for works of imagination and entertainment, as for example, poetry, plays, novels and short stories. Their works in these genres are dry, prolix, voluminous and mechanical, and they know nothing of the art of combining the pleasing with the useful.'

They say that when a new star rises in the firmament or an old one sets, it takes a long time before we on earth are aware either of that rising or of that setting, because the rays of the new star penetrate only slowly to our remote planet, and those of the dying one continue on their old course even long after its extinction. And even when the astronomers and wise men have taken cognisance of the new phenomena, it still requires a long time before all the school children and the bulk of the population learn of it. And thus it is, too, with the knowledge countries and nations mutually gain of each other. From this perspective, I believe that Guthrie's book expresses a host of ideas about Germany that will be incorrigible and ineradicable '**Standard-opinions**' of the masses in England for a long time to come.

* * * * * * *

XVIII
From Killin to Loch Katrine[1]

The following day, after overcoming some difficulties, I found a guide, and continued my journey on foot. Since I wished to arrive at Loch Katrine the same day, and there were many hills to be climbed before that, I set out at six o'clock in the morning. It was a wonderfully clear, but cool, November morning. The little ponds in the town and on the country road were covered with thin ice, and the brilliantly white peaks of the mountains were delineated with the most distinct and fine lines against the blue sky, as brightly and clearly as I had scarcely expected to see in grey and foggy Scotland.

Two glens, the valley of the little River Lochay[2] and that of the River Dochart, come together at Killin and discharge the waters that flow in them into the head of the loch here. The famed beauty of the mountain landscape of Killin is the result of this division of the whole area into two main valleys, or actually into three, for the valley of Loch Tay itself can be regarded as the third. Through this valley of the loch one can gaze up at Ben Lawers and through Glen Dochart at Ben More, the peak of which is visible sparkling in the background, while over Glen Lochay Meall a'Churain[3] rises up. All three mountains are situated at roughly equal distances from Killin. The River Dochart is spanned by a rather imposing bridge, which we walked across, for a long time enjoying the fascinating spectacle of the cataracts or rapids of the river which are opposite the bridge.

For a lengthy stretch the waters of the river, split into many arms, rush and tumble over a broad stone ledge and through the midst of an extraordinary number of boulders, in part rectangular, which lie scattered round about at the sides and in the middle on the stone slabs. These great rocks look almost like blocks of masonry, and, remembering the great Nordic Scoto-Irish architect of nature, I asked my guide whether perhaps Fingal had not once been here. 'Yes, sir,' he replied, 'he lies buried not at all far from here, near the western end of the loch, – we need go back only a few steps on the way that you came yesterday evening.' – It is a wonderfully beautiful spot near an old castle, called Finlarig Castle[4] in which the Campbell family (the Breadalbanes) used to reside before they moved to the eastern end of the loch.

Not far from this castle there is an attractively located churchyard, called Inchbuie[5], where different members of Clan MacNab[6] are buried and Fingal too, according to the popular legend. Fingal's grave, like that of his son Ossian, is, however, shown in various places, and Fingal's name comes echoing to the traveller from every cave here, from every mountain, from every extraordinary stretch of scenery. I do not speak merely of such remarkable caves as Fingal's Cave on Staffa. The same holds true even of insignificant ones. If I remember correctly, **Dr** Johnson visited a little known cave on the Hebridean island of Coll[7]. In it he found an extraordinarily large rectangular block lying. This, too, the inhabitants called 'Fingal's Table'. – My guide told me something about Fingal that hitherto I had not heard or read anywhere. Namely, he told me that **'Fin'** was derived from the Gaelic word **'fäun'**[8] which meant 'white', 'pale in colour'. Fingal, he said, thus meant 'the

---

[1] *Katterin*

[2] *Lochy*

[3] *Mealcrum*

[4] [Remains of a seventeenth-century castle at Killin.]

[5] *Innish-Mü*

[6] *Mac Nal*

[7] [This was actually on the island of Mull, in Mackinnon's Cave. Johnson and Boswell had earlier visited Coll, which may account for the author's error.]

[8] [Spelt *fionn*. The guide was not wrong. *Fingal* is properly *Fionn mac Cumhaill*. The first word is a nickname meaning 'blond'; the second and third mean 'son of Cumhall'. His real forename was allegedly *Deimne* 'stability'. See Introduction p. xvii.]

white one' or 'the pale one'. 'Had he perhaps fair hair?' I asked my guide. '**Yes, sir, he was fairhaired,**' he answered, quickly and quite seriously, as though he himself had seen it.

Either the etymology involved in the matter is *true*, and in that case it is interesting, or it is *not* true, in which case at least the people believe it, and that is also interesting. To be '**fairhaired**' is an advantage for the Irish and the Scottish Highlanders, and so I believe that they could scarcely think their Fingal to be endowed with hair of another colour. Furthermore, it is quite usual for the Scots to derive their heroes' nicknames from their hair, thus '**Rob Roy**' (Red Robert), '**Roderic Dhu**' (Black Roderick[9]).

What was remarkable to me were the many pheasants that I saw in the fields on both sides of my road. They were as plentiful there as chickens in chicken-runs. It appears to me that these birds, namely pheasants, are not only more numerous by far in England than at home, but also kept in much less controlled conditions. If I have been correctly informed (as I believe to be the case), they remain in the open air all summer and winter, while we have to have so-called pheasant-houses for our pheasants on account of our harsh winter. In England a feeding-box is put out into the wood or park for them, because the food that they find in the open is not always sufficient. Here in Scotland I saw very neat and ingeniously constructed feeding-boxes for the pheasants. They were of iron that was painted with green oil-based paint. Therefore they could not be easily become spoiled in the open air, nor be easily stolen or pushed over. They consisted of two compartments: one of these was closed, and it served as a small storage space, out of which the gamekeeper took the feed; the other was covered only loosely with a movable hinged lid and contained the portion of feed intended for the pheasants. Iron rods were attached to the front of this latter compartment and the pheasants hop on to them. By means of a simple mechanism, these rods are connected with the lid so that it immediately opens, if the pheasant hops on to the rod and presses it down with its own weight. As soon as it has eaten its fill and flies away, the lid shuts again by itself and keeps the feed dry.

'All these hills here,' my guide told me, 'have been leased out by Breadalbane to different gentlemen, for sheep-grazing, or shooting-grounds, or peat-cutting or the like. There is a gentleman living there who has leased that range of hills for fifteen miles across.'

As a rule, many of these gentlemen, like the Highlanders in general, have supplied nothing more than a so-called '**Shed**' for their cattle in winter. These sheds are often quite without a roof or at least are provided with a half roof only on one side, and they very much resemble those structures that I have seen in southern Russia for the overwintering of cattle.

On our journey we met with many long-haired Scottish '**Black-cattle**'[10], returning from different cattle-markets that are held in autumn on the edges of the Highlands. The people were very little cheered by their market. Sir Robert's tariff[11], for which they blamed everything, left them with sad eyes and melancholy visages. They had wanted to sell but a few of their cattle, because the prices had been too low for them, and now they wanted to overwinter their animals somewhere, to see whether perhaps they would receive better prices in spring. Above all, however, they wanted to celebrate their Sunday in Killin, which they had not been able to reach the previous evening.

After these herdsmen we encountered no other human soul on the entire journey, nor did we see anyone near the cottages which stood here and there by the roadside. 'The time to go to church is

---

[9] *Roderich* [Properly *Rob Ruadh* and *Ruairidh Dubh* respectively.]
[10] [Though Highland Cattle (properly so-called) are now generally reddish or tawny in colour, due to a recessive gene, in former times they were usually black.]
[11] [Sir Robert Peel had revised the general tariff on several imported articles of commerce in 1842.]

not yet here,' said my guide, 'and now they are still sitting all together in their houses, reading their Bibles.'

My guide was a Scottish Highlander, who, as he told me, sometimes played the music for his compatriots' dances. In Killin they had already sung his praises to me as their best violinist. In this capacity, he told me, he had travelled through probably all the glens in Scotland and had been as far as Inverness several times. He assured me that he knew many glens of the Scottish Highlands in which Highland dress was still worn as something ordinary. In many of them the **'Lads'** had two kinds of clothing, an English jacket with trousers and a kilt without trousers, and they donned the latter only for special events.

Since no opportunity had presented itself to me to witness a **'Reel'** (Scottish national dance) in Scotland, and since I had a man in front of me who must needs have been intimately acquainted with it, I asked him what kind of a dance the Scottish reel actually was. Unfortunately, however, I received no clear picture of it from my friend. In English **'the reel'** actually means 'the spool'[12] and **'to reel'** means something like 'to unwind'[13]. If this should have anything to do with the name of the dance, it would certainly not convey an especially favourable picture of its artistry and grace. Neither did the thing appear to me any more artistic from my musician's explanations. He said the reels were danced by four persons, two lads and two lassies, **'who keep constantly tact [sic] to the tune and make their manoeuvres. In fact,'** he said, 'a Scottish reel is nothing more than this.' – I asked in what these manoeuvres then consisted. 'Firstly, as I said, in keeping time, **and then they go through the figure of *ächt***'[14]. I asked him again what it meant to go through the figure-of-eight. He answered that **'to go through the figure of *ächt*'** apparently meant the same as **'to go through the reel'**. So saying, he drew me the following figure in the sand on the road:

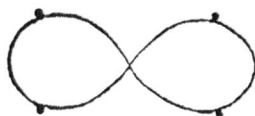

The four dots represent the four dancers and the twisted line the figure-of-eight. Now, by the dancers' always keeping in time to the music as they moved, and by constantly going through the figure-of-eight, each dancer would always correctly return to his place. And so that would be the proper reel. – I think that by this description a fairly correct notion will nevertheless in the end be gained of the rough way in which the Highland people perform this dance[15].

Because I was eager to discover whether the harp, which I had frequently seen in Ireland and Wales and even in the hands of the common people, was also common among the Celtic Scottish Highlanders, I asked my friend, if he perchance knew whether the harp was also found among the Scots in their mountains. He answered that he admittedly knew the harp very well, for he had seen it in Glasgow, but that, although he had grown old in the mountains and had traversed their length and breadth, he had never seen a harp anywhere in the hands of the people. This is strange, and the question therefore arises whether we do not have to imagine the Scottish bards without any harps and also to erase the harp from Ossian, insofar as we understand by that a Scottish and not an Irish Ossian. Those pictures and etchings that we have made of the spirits of Ossianic heroes playing harps are quite apt in respect of Ireland, but not of Scotland.

---

[12] [The author gives the translation *die Haspel*.]

[13] [The author gives the translation *abhaspeln* 'unwind' rather than the more accurate *haspeln* 'to reel in'.]

[14] [This spelling reflects the Scots pronunciation *echt*.]

[15] Now, after I have seen several Scottish reels, I can only confirm this. *JGK*

The transverse valley that leads from Glen Dochart to Strathearn is called Glen Ogle. It is a very wild and completely uncultivated glen. It consists of nothing but black rocks that appear to have been made of cast-iron. The peaks of the mountains as well as the tops of the rocks are covered with high heather. Several small burns run down from the mountains, and by their sides here and there stands a solitary and stunted little birch-tree. Apart from that, there is not a trace of welcoming vegetation there. Fragments of rock cover the mountain slopes in extraordinary profusion. People relate that sometimes quite big lumps and entire broad slabs detach themselves from the rock-face and hurtle away, shattering into a thousand splinters, across field, road and path. My guide showed me a spot where only a few years before such a rock-fall had taken place. There are countless such wild glens in Scotland, and even very much wilder ones. Indeed in the mountains there are quite extensive desolate stretches that are uncultivated or no longer cultivated. I was still to see a small example of that myself that very day. I noticed in Ireland that there as a rule the highest mountain peaks were the haunt of one or several pairs of eagles. My guide said that that was the case in Scotland too, and then made the following observation: 'Everything, sir, that is called a 'Ben' in Scotland, *that* you can without doubt regard as the home of eagles.' I will use this opportunity to add that the Gaelic Highlanders appeared to pronounce this word not as 'Benn' but as 'Behn' (sic)[16]. They pronounced 'Ben Nevis[17]' as 'Behn Nivesch' and 'Ben Lawers' as 'Behn Larrs'.

We toiled our way through our wilderness and finally espied the inn at Lochearnhead on Loch Earn. I know not whether it was this joyful sight, or some other idea, that made me begin to whistle. But, in short, I began to whistle a little to myself. 'Sir, stop whistling', my guide said to me, **'for they will be wondering, to hear a parson**[18] ***chwistling*** (Scottish pronunciation) **at a sabbathday!'**

This whole district has everywhere become classic ground as a result of Scottish history as well as of Walter Scott's masterly descriptions, and the traveller has the double pleasure not only of wandering through romantic wild valleys and gorges that are fascinating in their own right, but also through such scenes as he himself once beheld in the magic mirror of imagination, and which hundreds and thousands still look at every day in the same magic mirror. Thus in the above mentioned Glen Dochart is the scene of the attack on Robert Bruce by MacDouglas [sic] of Lorne[19], his implacable enemy, and of Bruce's heroic deeds against him and his people. Thus here near Lochearnhead in a wild spot among the rocks, called Creag Mac Rànaich[20] – the very name sounds like the shattering of stone and rock – can be seen one of the many **'Robert the Bruce's caves'**; in it this Scottish epitome of patience is said to have hidden on his richly adventurous and lengthy flight. Thus I turned my step away from here inland into the mountains to Rob Roy's grave.

Unfortunately I had to hire a new guide in Lochearnhead. I cast a passing glance at beautiful Loch Earn which led down in the direction of Crieff to the Drummonds and to districts known to me, and in that same moment I bade it hail and farewell. Then I continued on my way with that individual, who was one of the most stupid people that I have ever had as a guide. If I asked him about a man of whom I wanted to learn something, he invariably answered in a monosyllabic stutter: **'that was a very clever man, sir!'**. So about Robert Bruce, he said: **'That was a very clever man, sir, and king of Scotland'**. About Rob Roy, too, he knew nothing more than: **'He was a very clever man, sir, and a great robber'**. And in the same terms he dubbed Mr Stewart, Esq. a very clever man and owner of

---

[16] [An English equivalent would be *bane*. It approximates to the Gaelic pronunciation somewhat better than *ben*.]

[17] *Newis* [Again the pronunciation is indicated as well as was possible for the author.]

[18] [The accompanying German translation makes it clear that he understands his guide to be saying *person*. The author's spelling is either an error or an indication of the pronunciation.]

[19] *Lorn* [Because of a murder committed by Bruce, a blood feud had arisen between Bruce and the MacDougalls. In 1306 John MacDougall of Lorne attacked Bruce in battle at Dalry, near Tyndrum (actually at the head of Strath Fillan rather than in Glen Dochart) and defeated him.]

[20] *Crickmachkranach* [It is printed in emphasized type. The name may mean 'Bellowing rock'.]

Ardvorlich[21] House by Loch Earn. Some men, because of their own cleverness, regard all other human beings as exceptionally clever, but others do so because of their own stupidity. The worst thing was that I soon realised that there was nothing about which my new friend knew less than the footpaths that led directly across the wild mountains to Loch Katrine[22], and that I would therefore probably lose my way with him. This actually happened very soon indeed.

Of course, as far as Balquhidder[23] we found the way perfectly; it was impossible to miss it since a straight road leads directly thither. But not far after Balquhidder we lost it, because soon there was no more road at all at that point, not even the narrowest path, but only rock and mountain wasteland. Balquhidder is famous because its little churchyard contains Rob Roy's[24] grave. The little cottages of this pretty little village lie scattered in the valley of Loch Voil, at the eastern end of this loch. The church stands somewhat higher on a projecting slope of the mountain, and then all of this is surrounded on both sides by even higher and wilder mountains; among them the most celebrated is a steep rocky part called '**the Braes of Balquidder**', the praises of which are often sung in Scottish songs.

The graveyard lies beside the little church on the aforementioned green slope. A service was just being held in the church and so I could scarcely induce my guide to come into the churchyard with me. He said that he was afraid that we could be seen from the low windows of the church, and we could give offence to the congregation by our idle walking about. I thought of Catholic churches, even inside of which idle and inquisitive strangers are often not afraid to walk about during services. I said to my guide that we could after all walk quietly and carefully, and that I had at least to take a look at Rob Roy's tombstone; only on account of it had I in fact come here and he definitely had to show it to me. At that, he very unwillingly laid down my belongings behind a stone at the churchyard gate, for to appear carrying them there was particularly abhorrent to him, and then he crept into the churchyard with me, but with the countenance of a criminal, and showed me Rob Roy's grave.

This consists of nothing more than a rough block of stone, on which the equally rough outline of a large sword is – I cannot say 'chiselled out' but have to say – scratched in. There are several other gravestones of this kind there, most of which appear to date from Rob Roy's time and even from a still later period, in other words from the beginning and the middle of last century. However, they look as though they had been fashioned in the time of the Druids, for they are nothing more than rough, almost completely uncarved, plain stones from the fields, on the top of which just such an outline of a big long sword is scratched with shaky and uneven lines. Never in my life have I seen gravestones as extraordinary as these, or rougher. If the men that lie under them resembled these stones that cover them, then they must have been veritable blocks of stone. On some there were no such outlines of swords, which, I believe, were found only on the graves of chieftains. On one I also recognised the entire outline of a human being, more or less delineated like the shapes that, in spite of police prohibition, our street urchins draw on the walls and sides of houses; for I could not make out whether it was intended to represent a lady or a knight, an old woman or a thief. If the French, in their geographical books until the middle of last century, spoke of the '**Sauvages de l'Écosse**', by which they understood the inhabitants of the Highlands and the Hebridean islands, then, judging by these Balquhidder works of funereal art, they were quite right. On several stones there were also some more hieroglyphic outlines to be seen which I could not decipher.

---

[21] *Ardvoirlich* [Named in the German as *Schloß* 'castle', not *House*.]
[22] *Katterin*
[23] *Balquidder*
[24] [See Chapter II, fn. 6.]

'On the itinerary that you have marked out for yourself in Scotland, you will find a specimen of all those things that make up the typical components and peculiarities of our Highlands: some attractive lochs that resemble more or less all our lochs, some high bens that look like all our bens, some wildly romantic glens from which you can picture the others, some pretty forest scenes that you may replicate with not too powerful a multiplier, some rivers, burns, and waterfalls that can serve you as models for the rest,' – thus I had been advised about my proposed route. And indeed I had already found all those characteristics of Scottish scenery. What was still missing for me was only a barren Scottish expanse of rock and marshland that I could replicate in my thoughts with a very effective multiplier in order to picture all the great scenes of barren country in the rest of Scotland and the Scottish islands. Today I found a splendid specimen of barren country between Balquhidder and Loch Katrine. The direct distance is in fact only ten English miles. But because what lies between the two valleys is a rugged mountain ridge, and the traveller has to clamber back and forth, then it becomes at least twenty, and because he finds himself in utter desolation and sees nothing but wasteland, and every step that he takes is laborious, so the distance becomes as long as fifty miles for him.

At first we still had a decent path and encountered people here and there as well, especially shepherds, who were always surrounded by an extraordinary number of dogs. We went into the last little cottage, in order once more to find out quite precisely about the direction we had to take. We found some people sitting by the fire. Behind the fire was a big stone, up towards which the peat flames were flickering. On the stone stood once again the big Scottish salt jar, which I have mentioned before. It almost looks like a little dog kennel, for there is a round hole in it, as in a kennel. However, this hole is intended only for the cook's arm to reach into it. I asked the people why here in Scotland they always gave the salt barrel such a prominent place by the fire. They answered me that it was partly in order to have the salt always to hand at mealtimes, partly also to keep it dry. 'Does it not also say in the Bible "Ye are the salt of the earth"?' added an old man, 'and is not salt to some extent sanctified through this saying, and therewith is it not meant that it is one of the best things for men? For that reason we place it over our hearth!'

Then began the description of the route. That was a somewhat difficult matter. For since all the land here is either rock or quagmire, and since neither the one nor the other can show human footprints, in consequence absolutely no tracks or footpaths have been formed here, however many people may have walked over the mountains since the formation of this wilderness. Since everywhere is equally difficult, everyone who is familiar with the area strikes out on his own, and therefore nowhere are footprints added to footprints and nowhere does a beaten track come into being.

At last there was nothing else left for us too than to choose our own way after we had more or less taken note of the principal peaks and the saddles that we had to pass. There is nothing more desolate and dreary than these Scottish wastelands. After we had climbed a little, we could look out over a fair expanse of them. The valleys and the peaks each had their name, though they really did not deserve a name. I was given the names of Glen Soinne[25], Gleann nam Meann[26], Glen Finglas[27], as well as of the mountains Ben Ledi and Mealaonack [sic][28]. But I did not give myself the trouble to verify these names and the valleys and mountain tops to which they belonged, because where everything merges together in a wilderness, it is not worth the trouble to make pointless divisions sharply one from another.

---

[25] *Glen Scheini*

[26] *Glen Man*

[27] *Glen Fenlas*

[28] [In John Thomson's *Atlas of Scotland* of 1832 it is spelt *Mealaonach* (= Meall Aonach, 'steep hill') and lies between 'Stob brean' (Stob Breac) and 'Ben venoch' (Beinn Mheadhonach). It is not named as such on the Ordnance Survey map 378 (2007), but from its position it must be An Stuchd (669 m., Ordnance Survey reference NN447146).]

Travels in Scotland (1840) by J.G. Kohl

Since, however, a large part of the Scottish Highlands and decidedly the largest part of the surface of the Hebrides, the Orkney Islands and the Shetland Islands look like this, it may be interesting for my readers to learn some further details about the appearance of the country. The main thing is firstly that nowhere is even one tree or bush to be seen. Not only the tops of the mountains but the valleys and hollows are completely bare and stark. At the same time everything is wild in the most miserable way. To be more precise, all the slopes and glens are covered with innumerable large and small pieces of rock, and these are mostly overgrown and slippery with damp moss and heather, and if one treads among these stones, one steps into a morass. Sometimes a green patch appears here and there. The wayfarer runs eagerly up to it in the hope of being able to set his aching feet on level grass. However, when he reaches it he discovers that the green is not living grass but deceptive reeds under which quagmire has accumulated, and in order to have firm ground under his feet he must clamber laboriously about on rocks above the mud. In addition, the colour of the entire landscape is dark and melancholy. The only thing pleasing to the eye lies on the highest peaks, namely snow, and the only thing of use to human beings on the long mountain ridges is peat bog, '**Miurs**' or '**Muirs**' (I could not rightly decide whether the Scots pronounce it this way or that).

Since, as I said, the largest part of the Hebrides looks like this, it is understandable why Lord Huntly, to whom James VI offered the entire archipelago of those islands for ten thousand pounds Scots (eight hundred pounds sterling), hesitated to agree to the suggestion. An acre of this land affords a person about as much profit as about several rods of land in the fertile parts of the Lowlands. In 1810 the income of an acre of land in the County of Edinburgh amounted to one pound, four shillings and 6¼ pence, or 294¼ pence, while in the same year the income of an acre in Argyllshire (one of those Highland counties situated near the regions through which we were travelling) amounted to one shilling and eleven pence or 23 pence, and that includes both fertile and barren land. However, in Orkney the income of an acre was eight pence and in Shetland merely three pence: in the latter islands, therefore, about one hundred times less than in the Lowlands. This can serve to give an idea of the extraordinary difference in the average crop yield in the Lowlands and the Highlands. However, the contrast would be even greater still if one only were to compare the yield of the *fertile* stretches of the Lowlands with that of the *barren* Highland districts.

After we had continued to torture ourselves onwards for several hours in this dreadful spot on the earth's surface, I finally sat down by a miserable little spring, furious and in the depths of despair, and began to quarrel with my stupid guide, who was quite ignorant of the way. He was called Macpherson or Ferguson, that is, 'son of Fergus'. Several ancient Scottish kings bore the name Fergus, and they could well be the founders of the clan of the 'Descendants of Macpherson', which the English have now changed to 'Ferguson'; for in Gaelic these descendants are actually called '**Machkpherasch**'[29]. However, I paid little heed to these claims of royal origin and remonstrated as vehemently with my Macpherson as the vexation of the moment provoked me.

'Sir, if you are so furious with me, give me my money instead and let me go home! Why are you cursing? What do you want from me then?'

'More than anything, I want a better path from you!'

'Well, sir, can I change the paths, then? I wish they were better myself; for I shall have to have my shoes patched tomorrow!'

'Why did you lead me astray on such a miserable track and why did you not take the right one?'

---

[29] [Properly *Mac a' Phearsain*]

'I swear to you once again that I did not know the right track and do not know it; if I had known it, I would not have hidden it from you!'

'You wretched man, why did you offer yourself to me as a guide here?'

'Good gracious, sir, wages are very bad just now, people want to earn something, and I am doing it as best as I can!'

'If you at least would only enliven this depressing journey a little with stories, but you are as dumb as a piece of wood! Rob Roy lived in this wilderness; could you not tell me something interesting about him?'

'I already told you that people say he was a very clever man and a robber, and I do not know any more about him.'

'You guides know your '**native country**' best; why else would a stranger hire you, but to teach him something about the land and its character!'

'Now, sir, you yourself can see best how the character of the land is formed. Just look over there, and there. It is a miserably wretched land.'

'Could you not tell me something about the life of the people in the mountains?!'

'About the life of the people? Of course, I can; if you had only asked me first, I would have told you a long time ago. People here live mostly on potatoes and milk. They mash the potatoes, and they pour the milk round the pile of mash. On holidays they also cook a piece of lamb for brose[30].'

'Very well! Now be quiet, pick up my things and let us be going again.'

As we resumed our acrobatic leaps from one piece of rock to another, to my great delight I suddenly saw a living figure moving on a hill-ridge in the distance. We stopped to see what it was. The figure now disappeared, now reappeared, and we recognised a man energetically making his way towards us, waving his hand to us from the distance and calling out to us. We greeted him with joy and acquainted him with our unpleasant situation with regard to finding the way to Loch Katrine, or rather to Miss Stuart's inn near the loch.

The man wore an attractive Glengarry[31] bonnet, with a bird's feather on it, which suited him very well, and therefore I took him for a huntsman at first, especially too because of his energetic step and sure foot on the rough rocks. However, it soon emerged that he was a young tailor who had been summoned to some farmers in the vicinity of the lochs. Tailors, who travel about the country from farm to farm, have always a lively aspect to their character. Since they are acquainted with many people and hear many pieces of news, and since because of their quiet and peaceful work they can also indulge in more conversation than, for example, smiths, carpenters or cabinet-makers, they are usually talkative and good travelling companions through dreary countryside. The farmers to whom he was going were called Stuart, since almost everywhere round about here there were Stuarts living, in Glen Soinne, Glen Finglas and by Loch Katrine. He said that we could accompany him thither, rest a little there, and then from there perhaps still reach Miss Stuart's inn beside the loch in the evening. We accepted his suggestion with pleasure, had soon reached the top of ridge,

---

[30] [This may again be the author's confusion between 'brose' and 'broth'. See Chapter VII, fn. 7.]
[31] *Glengarri* [This is a boat-shaped, peakless hat with a pom-pom on top and often two ribbons hanging down behind.]

and now were making our way down on the other side, into Glen Finglas I think. Here too the going was not one whit better, but because of the better company it appeared so to us.

Mr Tytler[32], who has written the most comprehensive and in Walter Scott's judgement the best history of Scotland, gives an account of Scotland's forests at the time of Wallace and Bruce, from which it appears that even then (in the fourteenth century) the country was still covered with large forests. This is a period that, relatively speaking, does not lie far back in the past (only about five hundred years) and it remains a puzzle why and through what circumstances the country could be deprived of timber and forest in such a terrible way. Only when we came somewhat '**laigher**[33] **down**' did we find isolated trees again; these my companions called '**Scotch Mahagony**' [sic][34]. Unfortunately, however, I can no longer remember what kind of trees they were.

The first inhabitant that we came across was Kristy Mac Lara [sic][35]. However, we saw this old woman's cottage only in the very far distance, at **a very lonsome** [sic] **place**, in a low piece of ground, at the entrance to two wild barren glens. They told me that this old woman lived there completely on her own, and that her only companions were a cow and two sheep for which she collected food on the neighbouring rocks. She had leased the rights from the rich leaseholder Stuart, I no longer know for how many pence annually, and from time immemorial had always lived there alone. The little black speck of this old woman's cottage looked almost terrifyingly lonely in the broad desolate mouth of the glens. This was without doubt some old woman out of Walter Scott, in whose cottage the smugglers and the furtive whisky distillers held their meetings and had their hide-outs.

At last came proper woodland again, we made our way through it, and on a beautiful smooth grassy slope walked down the remainder of the hills and straight to the spacious small-holdings of the Stuarts, which lay at the foot of this enchanting slope and in the middle of a lovely widening and clearing in the woodland.

There were no fewer than six 'Stuartich'[36], six Stuart leaseholders, whose families have possessed very extensive sheep grazings for many years. According to what people told me, it appeared to me that all six families were living together in a sort of leaseholders' community. Each, however, had its own house, and their farmsteads all lay close together, forming a little village. I was told that here in the district they were the biggest '**Graziers**' for miles around. Altogether they had between five thousand and six thousand sheep. The lord and owner of the land is Lord Doune. 'Actually, you should say "the Earl of Moray"', observed the old tenant farmer Stuart, whose house we had entered at dusk and by whose fireside we had seated ourselves. 'For,' he went on, '"Lord" or "Baron Doune" is only '**the second title**' of "Francis Stuart". "Earl of Moray", however, is his first and most distinguished title, and he is known to people by that title.' These farmers know about the titles of their lords very precisely. A stranger always makes mistakes in them. Furthermore, the Earls of Moray must not be confused with the Murrays, which is not a title, but the name of a clan. The Scottish Lords Doune must also not be mixed up with the Irish Lords Down. The Earls of Moray are the richest and most distinguished of all the Stuarts, and I believe they are regarded as their 'Chiefs'. But they are not the only Stuarts in the Scottish peerage. The Earls of Galloway, the Earls

---

[32] *Tyler* [Patrick Fraser Tytler (1791-1849), author of a nine-volume *History of Scotland* (1828 – 43).]

[33] 'Laigher' or 'leger' means in Scottish 'lower', just as in Low German, probably from the German 'liegen' [= 'to lie'], 'das liegende Land' [= 'the (low-)lying land']. *JGK* [Scots *laigh*, English *low*, and German *liegen* are in fact probably etymologically connected.]

[34] [Probably alder trees, the wood of which turns red when exposed to light and weather.]

[35] [This may well be Christiane McLaren, mentioned in the 1841 Census as being aged 65 and living in Achnahard (*Achadh na h-Airde*) which was at the entrance to Glen Finglas and Gleann Casaig.]

[36] [Properly *Stiùbhartaich*. It is not possible to identify this settlement from the 1841 Census, although there seems to have been a family of six Stewarts at Drimbowie and one of nine Stewarts at Achnahard.]

of Dumfries[37] and Bute, the Barons Blantyre, the Earls of Traquair are also Stuarts. However, some of them spell their names 'Stewarts'. The Stuarts and the Douglases are, I think, the most frequently occurring name in the Scottish peerage.

Although dusk, as I said, was already falling, Mr Stuart nevertheless showed me house and farm **en détail**. He had, it appeared, built his dwelling-house in two parts, one for the stables, for the manservants and maids and for everyday living, and one for his guests, for Sundays and for festive occasions. Even in the first everything was very neat and proper, but in the latter it was as elegant and attractive as I had seen only in the best farmhouses in England. Not only its rooms, but also its staircases and passage-ways were carpeted and the rooms were so clean and tidy that, dressed as I was in my tattered travelling clothes, I did not dare enter them. Since I had just come from the very midst of the wastelands, where for the whole day even the sight of the humblest cottage would have given me pleasure, I was filled with tremendous astonishment, like a savage brought into the middle of a capital city. Apart from his share in the six thousand sheep, my friend had only nine cows and two horses, since here the cultivation of '**Oats**', '**Barley**' and '**Patatoes**' [sic] was not extensive.

After that, we sat down again by the fire in the large '**Servants'hall**' [sic], where the master, the manservants, the neighbours, the maids, the tailor and my guide were gathering. An enchanting maid – she was called Jeane Fischar[38] [sic] – did the honours with delicious Highland milk, which is much sweeter than that in the Lowlands, and with '**Barley-scone**' (that mush of flour and water that I have described above at Muthill). '**Dschihn**'[39] (thus they pronounced the name 'Jeane') was much prettier than her name, and in addition she had a refinement of facial features such as is certainly very rare in peasant women in many other countries.

The men all wore the gloves of which I spoke earlier at Loch Tay; I mean those tar gloves. For in the previous days they had been undertaking the great task of '**smuiring**' (rubbing in) their sheep. They had still six big containers full of rubbing mixture standing in their farmyard and a whole row of tar barrels, some empty, some full, lying there. For the '**smuiring**' or '**smiuring**'[40] was to begin again the following day. With a flock of between five and six thousand sheep, it can be imagined that this is not an insignificant task, and that a great deal of time, labour, tar and butter must be employed in it. For thirty sheep, they told me, they used one container full, which held ten pints of tar and a **Stone** (that is, fourteen pounds) of butter; three thousand sheep therefore use a thousand pints of tar and one thousand, four hundred pounds of butter every year. Since there are many farms that have three thousand sheep to rub, it is apparent that this matter is not a trivial one. They regard the '**smuiring**' as absolutely necessary; '**the tare** [sic] **keeps them warm and clean**' they repeat to the traveller who protests. In other countries where it is also cold, people know nothing of this tarring, yet here a great business is made of it. In the domestic management of every country in the world similar branches of activity and institutions are found; the native inhabitants give themselves enormous trouble over them because they regard them as indispensable, while in other countries nothing is known of them, yet nevertheless they successfully survive without them, without tarring and without rubbing.

However different in many respects one thus finds countries and their customs, nonetheless on the other hand they are remarkably similar in many other characteristics. So, for example, at one time when I saw the Latvians in Courland fishing at night, using a torch and a harpoon with many spikes with which they stab through the fish, I used to imagine that this was only a Latvian idea. And now

---

[37] *Dumfrees*
[38] [The 1841 Census lists a Janet Fisher, aged 15, at Callander.]
[39] [The author's transcription in German spelling accurately reflects the pronunciation of the name *Jean*.]
[40] In the rules of Scots pronunciation, of course, one finds that the 'ui' is to be pronounced like the French 'u' or the German 'ü'. However, it always sounded to me as I have indicated above. *JGK*

Travels in Scotland (1840) by J.G. Kohl

I learned that this way of catching fish with exactly the same implements is also known in Scotland, and I have since read that in North America too, and in several other parts of the world as well, fish are quite unerringly caught by the same method. Similarly, I once believed that only the Ossetes in the Caucasus and the Tatars in the Crimea have the custom of making their fire by setting a thick tree-trunk alight at one end and then, as it burns away, pushing it into the fireplace. And now I was sitting here this evening in my Scottish farmers' house by a fire that was almost completely identical to that Tatar fire. They had a great long tree-trunk, which lay with one end in the embers and rested on its branches at the other. They had surrounded the burning end with pieces of peat, which always kept it alight. In this way, they said, they made themselves a decent fire when it was truly cold.

Now and then I saw them putting something on a stick and holding a brown rag on it to the fire. At first I could not rightly ascertain what it was, and my first, fearful, thought was that it might be '**Mutton-chops**'; for I remembered that I had often seen people prepare a piece of mutton-chop at the fireside in the same way and that I had had to consume it afterwards, to the displeasure of my teeth. To my relief I soon saw that it was tobacco leaves. The reason is that people here get their tobacco in rolls from which they then cut off a piece. They unroll this piece and dry it by the fireside in the way just described, until it is quite dry and brittle, and then, crumbling it between their fingers, they can easily fill their little pipes with it. This is again a procedure involving tobacco that I had not previously seen anywhere and which circumstances here make necessary. My hospitable host had a '**Dram**' served to my guide, as also to several of his neighbours, and what was remarkable to me was the ceremonious way in which they acknowledged each other and drank each other's health. Before they raised their glasses and downed their drams, murmurs of 'Your health, lad!' – 'Your health, Stuart!' – 'Good fortune to you, Robert!' were always heard round the group. The drinking of people's health is otherwise less usual in the higher classes of Scotland and England than in Germany. Perhaps, too, more ceremony is made with alcoholic spirits than with beer and wine, because they are stronger, and because people are, as it were, ashamed to drink them completely **sans façon**.

It was not long, too, after the dram had been drunk and a certain familiarity had been established that they asked me about my clan and native country. My clan, I answered, was not especially significant, and, in particular, was not royal like their Royal Stuart Clan. By nationality, however, I was a '**Garamaltjach**'[41]. (Thus one of the experts in Gaelic had described my countrymen, the '**Germans**'. Without any doubt this name is only the English word '**German**' distorted.) On hearing this, they embarked on an adulation of the Garamaltjachs, and several, who were acquainted with the loch below, said that of all foreigners the Germans were those who came there in greatest numbers to visit their lochs. 'You Germans are a nation that goes abroad, just like us Scots. You like foreign countries and you travel about everywhere. In that respect you are quite different from the French, our nearest neighbours, whom we could expect to encounter here oftenest, but whom we almost never see. And yet your country is a good seventeen times larger than France, so that you have far more space in it than the French in theirs. Your passion for travelling fills me with astonishment because your own country is so big, and I cannot understand it. Since we Scots have such a narrow country here, it is no wonder that if we take two or three seven-league steps, we immediately find ourselves in the sea. Then of course it is natural to yearn sometimes for other countries across the sea. But where you live all the countries are joined together, and everything, foreign and native, is more of a unity.'

Apart from the '**Germany**' that was seventeen times larger, everything that my Highlander said was reasonable. And even that is not so absurd. I have already explained above that Germany seems to the people here much bigger than it really is, since they also include Hungary in it and in fact all the

---

[41] Armstrong writes 'Gearmailteach'. *JGK* [The author's imitated pronunciation is fairly accurate.]

countries bordering the Danube, because they hear that the Danube is a German river. Germany – for the people here that is the great expanse in the east beyond France, and they often do not know themselves whether the Russians are still Germans or not. Once I was asked by a Scottish merchant, to whom I had said that I was a German, '**are you a Russian or a Prussian German?**' The unfortunate rhyme of Prussia and Russia has, I think, given rise to several errors of that kind in the past.

Incidentally, it must be pointed out that the Scottish Highlanders are without exception a very intelligent and also mostly a very well-educated people. Not only do we find them so at the present but **Dr** Johnson, and even earlier travellers still, found them to be so; they observed that however uncouth and rough their habits might be, and however miserably they generally lived, nevertheless not only the acuteness of their understanding, but also the breadth of their knowledge and the range of their education, were to be described as exceptionally outstanding in relative terms. In several places in his book **Dr** Johnson expresses his amazement that such great understanding and such wide knowledge could be allied to such rough habits, to such a belligerent disposition, and to such great poverty. In a remarkable book, published by the '**Poorlaw Commissioners**'[42] in 1841, dealing with the education of the children of the poor, there can be found very much information about Great Britain in general and, among other things, we can read several interesting reports from owners of large factories about the national characters of the different workers whom they employ in their works. From it I will quote the opinions of several of these gentlemen about their Scottish workers.

'We find that Scottish workers on the Continent make much better progress than the English; this I ascribe in particular to their better education, which makes it easier for them to cope with different circumstances, to be more agreeable to their colleagues and to associate politely with all those with whom they come in contact. Since they have usually learnt their own language grammatically, they also possess a greater facility in acquiring foreign languages. They have a greater fondness for reading and always seek to keep reputable company and to make respectable friends. They are circumspect in their conduct and keen to gain such knowledge as will fit them for the better classes of society.' This testimony was given in London by a Herr Escher[43], who is one of the most important factory-owners in Zürich.

Another manufacturer, a Mr Fairbairn[44] from Manchester, who employed six hundred and eighty people there and five hundred in another establishment in London, expressed his opinion of the Scots in the following way: 'The workers who come from Scotland and from the north of England, from Cumberland and Northumberland, have on the whole received quite a good elementary education. Those from Scotland have usually been taught in the parish schools, they read and write, are in general reasonable arithmeticians, and they often have a good knowledge of the lower branches of mathematics, some of them do not draw badly. The English workers from the northern counties of Cumberland and Northumberland are of a similar standard, but not quite as carefully taught as the Scots, and I attribute this to the lack of parish schools, which in Scotland, in my opinion, are of inestimable value. In respect of education, the workers from Yorkshire, Lincolnshire and the south of England are far beneath those of the north. The workers from the north of Ireland rank in terms of schooling alongside the English from the northern counties, although they are inferior to them in technical skills.'

---

[42] [The Poor Law Commission was a body established in 1834 to manage relief for the poor. It lasted until 1847.]
[43] [It is just possible that this was Alfred Escher (1819 – 1882), a Zürich politician, entrepreneur, 'railway king', and founder of a bank.]
[44] [Sir William Fairbairn, (19 February 1789 – 18 August 1874) was a Scottish civil and structural engineer. His factories in Manchester and London produced locomotive boilers and built ships.]

These indubitably interesting reports accord completely both with that which earlier travellers reported and also with that which the present-day traveller can observe there. Thus among my farmers not only did I too find great refinement in their conversation, but Farmer Stuart showed me his library as well, which consisted of statistical, religious, geographical and philosophical works. He also received a periodical called the '**Gazetteer**'[45]. And yet their farmsteads were surrounded on three sides by desolate countryside, which I have described above, and on the fourth by a wood, which I walked through later. I must indeed belatedly make the observation that in the houses of the different hosts in little villages, with whom I lodged on my journey, I found everywhere a well chosen, presentable and well kept little library. My farmers and their servants, as in fact everyone present, assured me that they could all read and write, and that in general everyone here possessed these skills. However, it may not be possible to infer this of all the wastelands of the Highlands.

What is very noteworthy to me in the report of the last-named factory-owner is the observation that he found the Englishmen from the northern counties to be *better* educated than the other Englishmen, although not *quite as well-educated* as the Scots, and the Irishmen from the north *almost as well-educated* as the Englishmen from the north. It is well known that the northern provinces of England cited had long and often been in the possession of the Scots, and that they are now occupied by a population that is actually half-Scottish. It is equally well known that the north of Ireland is inhabited by people of Scottish origin. It therefore appears that the passion for knowledge and better education is peculiar to the Scottish race and is something inherent in the Scottish blood.

Concerning what has just been said about the wide reading and education of the Scots, we remember too what is reported about the erudition of a nation even more distant from the literary centre of Europe, namely the Icelanders, and at the same time we may draw a parallel with the northern parts of almost all countries. As a whole, northern France is without doubt better educated than the south; it can read and write better than the latter. As far as the Low Countries are concerned, the same can be said about Holland in comparison with Belgium, that it is more enlightened and better instructed than the latter. When we look at Germany, the situation is the same – generally in the north a more refined teaching and a greater literary culture than in the south. In Italy those in Milanese territory have exactly similar advantages over those in Naples. In the same way, in Russia the centre of its intellectual life is situated in the north.

What is thus found confirmed in a striking way about every country in particular is also demonstrable about Europe as a whole. In the entire north of Europe there is a more extensive knowledge of literature, a more academic bent and better schooling everywhere than in the south. This is surely connected with climatic conditions. The long northern winter evenings, the cohesive domestic and family life, the more meagre population in streets, farmland and countryside bring it about that they are more keen to read and write, and also that they communicate more culture and knowledge among themselves. These very climatic conditions may also have caused the light of science to rise for the first time under a southern sky. As long as knowledge was handed down, as in the case of the Greeks and Romans, only from mouth to mouth, it was bound to remain in the south. After the invention of the printing-press, however, it had perforce to move to northern lands where greater opportunity for reading is found.

Doctor Johnson says that he would have reproached himself if had he not asked the Highlanders about the remarkable subject of '**second sight**'. He adduces much of interest about this, which the whole world can read in his writings. I also thought about '**second sight**' when I found myself among such sagacious people as my Stuarts were. But I was not so lucky as to hear anything new.

---

[45] [This might be *Cleave's Penny Gazette*, published weekly between 1837 and 1844. There appears to be no periodical called *The Gazetteer* published in 1842.]

They only answered my question whether there was also a Gaelic name for this phenomenon. They said yes, it was called '**Darschul**'[46].

If this is correct, as I believe it is, then it seems to follow that the remarkable psychic phenomenon of '**second sight**' is very well known not only to the common people in Scotland, but also particularly to the Gaelic population. I even believe now that this mental mirage (for thus could '**second sight**' be very appropriately termed) is of more Gaelic than of Saxon-Germanic origin. It seems to me to accord so completely with the other characteristics of the Gaelic psyche. Unfortunately I do not know whether '**second sight**' is equally widespread in Ireland, as one might well suspect from the examples of the many things that Ireland and the Scottish Highlands have in common.

Like beauty, wisdom too is most attractive in simple garb, and it was therefore hard for me to bid farewell to my intelligent farmers. However, since according to my travelling plans I had to arrive at Miss Stuart's inn near the Trossachs[47] that same evening or at least during the night, I set out by moonlight to cover the last five miles of my day's journey. Since I had no further need or desire to prove my guide's unreliability, I was very glad that some of those present joined us to accompany us down to the lochs, from where I could no longer fail to find Miss Stuart.

Glen Buckie[48] is the name of the pretty little narrow wooded glen that led us down to the lochs, and we were able to discern its picturesque beauties only indistinctly in the half-light of the moon. I say, it was wooded. It is usually the case with Scottish Highland glens that they have a few trees at their entrance, but that higher up barren wasteland is encountered. In the depths of the valleys, at their mouths, along the edges of the lochs, there the honey of woodland in the Highlands is spread only thinly, while the summits, the high ridges, the long lines of hills, the wide plateaux are mostly totally bare. What a contrast in this respect with other maintain-ranges, especially, for example, with those of the Thüringer Wald, where in general all the hills, all the summits, all the ridges are seen to be covered with woodland, while in the hollows and the valleys the trees have been displaced by fields.

After an hour's walking we arrived at the main valley of the lochs. This is a valley similar to that of Loch Tay and to those of the numerous elongated lochs in Scotland, only with the difference that here the water has not accumulated in a single stretch of lake, but in three long portions; the largest and longest of these is situated in the west and is called Loch Katrine, there is a small one in the east, Loch Venachar, and the smallest lies between these two, Loch Achray. High Ben Lomond and the Menteith Hills in the south, Ben Ledi and Maclaonach [sic][49] in the north constitute the boundaries and summits among which the hollow of this lake valley lies. We arrived near Loch Venachar and after my friends had taken a hearty dram in a little whisky house very romantically situated at the head of this loch, they directed us to go up the straight road in the valley that led directly to Miss Stuart. We walked by various pretty scenes formed by wood and rock, and then passed hard by the edge of little Loch Achray, which gleamed in the moonlight, and in the name of which I again found noteworthy that 'ach' (**aqua**) which occurs in so many Highland place-names. Merely in the vicinity of these lochs there are the following 'achs' on my specialist map: the village

---

[46] According to Armstrong it is written: '**darasuil**'. *JGK* [Modern spelling is *dara sùil.*]

[47] *Trosachs*

[48] *Bucki* [This would seem to be an error. Earlier in the day the author had probably climbed up from Balquhidder through Glen Buckie.]

[49] [See this chapter, fn. 27.]

of Ach[50], the villages of Acharn, Achoan, Achirgarn, Achessan, Achinver, Achaltic, Achnagillin, Achenboui, Achnacrieve, Achanellan, Tross-achs, Ben-achar etc.

Miss Stuart's hostelry is generally called simply **'Stuart's Inn'**[51], probably because, like the whole district around here, it has been in the possession of Stuarts for a long time. It is a fine and comfortable large building, and I had the whole house to myself, for I was the only guest, and after the people had shown me to my bed, they locked up the inn behind them and retreated to a neighbouring building. Only the lady of the lake did they leave with me, I mean a copy of Scott's **'Lady of the Lake'**, with the reading of which in my hermit-like abode I passed the hours of the night; they were sleepless ones for me on account of our excessive exertions in the mountain wastelands.

* * * * * * *

---

[50] [Kohl does not name this 'specialist map', though from some of his spellings of place-names, he seems to have used John Thomson's *Atlas of Scotland* of 1832. However, it is pointless to try to identify these places. Each bears a resemblance to at least one Scottish place-name, though not necessarily located near Loch Achray. The initial element *ach* is modern Scots Gaelic *achadh* 'field, meadow'; it is not connected with the Latin *aqua* 'water'.]

[51] [It has not been possible to identify this inn from the 1841 Census.]

Loch Katrine[1]

As is the case with most Celtic names in Ireland and Scotland, there are a number of different English ways of writing the name of this loch. Walter Scott writes it 'Loch Katrine', Chambers 'Loch Katterin', on some maps one finds 'Katherine'. People always pronounce it 'Loch Catteren'. I do not know whence the loch has received this name. The first thing that naturally occurs to me is that the beautiful lady of the lake who is the subject of Walter Scott's poem, and also the object of the royal hunter's love, could have been called Katterin and that the loch could have been given its name from her. However, this does not emerge from the poem itself. It is also improbable that, in naming the loch, people took into consideration the event, on the whole unimportant, that gave the poet the inspiration for his beautiful narrative. The name Katterin occurs several more times in Scotland. Thus, for example, there is also a castle of the Stuarts in Ayrshire called Catrine[2]. And it therefore seems better to think here of the '**Catterens**', those famous mercenaries[3], who played a not unimportant role in Scottish history for a time, and to accept that it was in their honour that those castles and lochs were named.

A Gael gave me another derivation of the name. He said that in Gaelic the loch was actually called '**Loch Cearn**' (pronounced 'kärn'), which means 'the loch of the lords' or 'the loch of the heroes'[4], and later this word was corrupted, as were so many other Gaelic words, in this case to 'Katteren'.

The inn is a mile distant from the loch itself, and between the two rises the remarkable rocky area that is so famous in Scotland under the name of the '**Trosachs**' [sic]. This Gaelic word, according to the explanation of my excellent Gaelic-speaking guide with whom I began my walk to the loch the next morning, means '**a ruff** [sic] **place, a broken and bristled territory**'. And indeed this perfectly describes the Trossachs. It is a high rocky ridge that cuts into the valley at an angle and runs from one high mountainside across to the other. At the same time it is not an unbroken wall of rock, but rather the rocks are intersected and fragmented in various places by ravines and hollows, and out of these project higher pinnacles of rock; and all the ravines and pinnacles are studded with birches, oaks, hazel-bushes, and other trees. In earlier times this ridge may have dammed up the higher loch to form a notably deep basin of water, and its overflowing waters may have plunged over the rocks in beautiful waterfalls. Now, however, a channel has broken through for it, and from its prison, now forced open, it flows placidly out between those cliffs, which are more than a hundred feet high. The place on which Stuart's Inn stands is called *Ardkenkrokran*[5]. I do not know what this name means[6], but without a doubt it also contains some allusion to that '**bristled and broken territory**', and one need only examine this Highland sequence of mountain sounds to obtain a fairly distinct conception of the appearance of the surrounding area; for the Trossachs occupy the same position among the features of the earth's surface as does the name *Ardkenkrokran* among sequences of sounds.

My guide insisted on trying to lead me among the rocks again, because, as he told me, only then, when I myself climbed about among the gorges and on the peaks, would I be able to comprehend

---

[1] *Katterin*

[2] [Catrine House, seat of Sir Matthew Stewart (1717 – 85).]

[3] [The Gaelic name is *Loch Ceiteirein*, the meaning of which is obscure, though according to the Celtic scholar and authority on place-names, W.J. Watson, it is 'the loch of the fiends', from the Welsh *cethern* 'furies'. *Ceiteirein* sounds like *cateran* (caterans being sixteenth-century Highland freebooters who plundered the Lowlands) and this gave rise to a folk-etymology, popularised by Walter Scott, whereby the name is said to mean 'loch of the fighters'.]

[4] ['Loch of the heroes' would be *Loch nan Ceathairn*, which might be what the author heard.]

[5] [In the German text the word is printed in double spacing for emphasis. In Thomson's *Atlas of Scotland* it is spelt *Ardkenenocan*. Properly *Ardcheanacrochan*]

[6] ['Height at the end of the hillock']

why the Trossachs enjoyed such a great reputation in Scotland. Since my feet, however, still bore too unpleasant memories of the previous day's journey through the mountains, I protested against this, and, apparently faint-heartedly, but, in fact, at least most comfortably, we sedately made our way along the fine level track that leads through the defile, beside the wild rocks; then we reached a charming little harbour on the loch where a pretty little boat awaited us, amidst the

> 'Mountains, that like giants stand,
> 'To sentinel enchanted land.
> 'High on the *south*, large Benvenue
> 'Down on the lake its masses threw,
> 'Crags, knolls and mounds, confusedly hurled,
> 'The fragments of an earleer world;
> 'A wildering forest, feathered o'er,
> 'His ruined sides and summit hoar;
> 'While on the north, through middle air,
> 'Ben-An heaved his forehead bare'.[7]

An Italian is reputed to have once said about the Scottish lochs and their attractions, comparing them to the famous lakes of his own country: 'You Scots have black beauty, and we have white.' Many foreigners hold the Scottish lochs in great contempt and refuse to account them among the beautiful and praiseworthy places of this world. But that Italian has decided the question very correctly, I believe. A philosophical observer must not regard African Negro beauties as unworthy of all comment because they are black and have different features from European women. As to all goals, many different roads lead to ideal beauty from all directions. Many of them fully reach this goal; many, however, can approach it to only a greater or lesser extent. Beautiful black women do not quite attain it, and the Scottish lochs too do not advance as far as the lakes of Italy, however much Scottish poets and patriots exert themselves to promote them.

What impressed me most about these lochs was their great similarity to the Lakes of Killarney, which I saw in Ireland. This similarity extends to many small details. The shape of the rocks, the dark colour of the landscape, the grey of the stones, the black inks of the moss and peat covering them here and there, the brown peaty water, the trees clinging to the rocks, the little bush-covered rock islands in the middle of the loch, the eagles on the top of Ben Venue, the narrow pass through which the waters of the loch flowed out, the desolation of the high mountains, even the colour of the sky – all this reminded me again of Killarney, and not only of Killarney, but also of other lakes in Ireland and Scotland, and yet again of other lakes in the northern wild part of Wales. Loch Lomond, too, has these same typical features, as do the famous English lakes of Cumberland and Westmoreland, Windermere[8] etc. And hence one can assume a certain character common to lakes and mountains that is found in all the wild mountain-ranges of Great Britain; beyond any doubt one can speak of typical British mountain lakes, resembling each other often down to the smallest features so remarkably that the traveller is overcome by amazement how similar geological forms and similar climatic and botanical influences have been able to produce such a great similarity over such great distances.

By and large there is nothing of significance at Loch Katrine. For by and large everything here appears too grey and dark. There are not enough different expanses of colour to produce memorable impressions. Moreover here there are also lacking the splendid phenomena of the Alpine and Italian air, by means of which azure, purple and red mountains and bluish distances are produced. All

---

[7] [The spelling sand typography are reproduced as in the German original. The quotation is from Walter Scott's 'The Lady of the Lake', Canto 1, XIV, although in line 4 Scott has *in* for *its*. The author gives a prose translation of his version in a footnote.]

[8] *Winander Meer*

distance – one need only look closely to be persuaded whether it is true what I say – all distance here is dark grey or quite black.

On the other hand, there is in the neighbourhood a host of enchanting and beautiful scenes for the watercolorist's brush and the steel engraver's needle. We landed first on the island on which that banished family of Douglas, which appears in *The Lady of the Lake*, is said to have lived. The traveller is still shown the setting of every incident in the poem – the place where the king clambered down the rocks while he was hunting the deer; the place where he slept the night, wrapped in his plaid; the place where, for the first time, he glimpsed the fair maid of the wild country. My guide knew the whole poem from memory and at each spot quoted the appropriate passage. Although there is scarcely anything authentic in the whole narrative, except beautiful poetic truth, nevertheless every year thousands of people come to look at these different places and, in so doing, to indulge in enchanted daydreams and poetic fancies. Some years ago there still stood a little hut on the island that completed the illusion that this was the island to which was banished the beautiful lady of the wild countryside. But some time ago careless cigar-smokers caused this illusion to go up in flames and smoke.

However, the old oak tree that provides shadow for the landing-place of this little island is wondrously magnificent, with its branches extending far out over the water. Apart from that, everywhere by this lake I saw a host of interesting and picturesque appearances of trees on the surface of the rocks. Here and there thick oak trees protruded, so it seemed, out of the bare crevices. Every now and then a magnificent ash-tree had taken solitary possession of the top of a rock and, regal and dominant, had spread its boughs there. It almost seems as though here, between the rocks and the ravines, the trees, like goats, learned climbing and all sorts of other tricks that they are not seen to perform on their customary terrain. Thus I saw an enormous, massive tree that had grown into the ground again with all its branches, of which I counted more than thirty. There, where the branches had put down roots, new branches sprouted out again on all sides, and those branches again curved down to the ground and in their turn put down roots. Several of these branches had crammed the ground solid with a hundred little off-shoots, every one of which was putting down its roots among the grass. It seemed as though it were an abnormal propensity of the tree, brought about by the configuration of the ground. – Another similar little sylvan curiosity that I had never previously seen was exhibited by an '**Aldertree**' and a '**Mountain-ash**', which were so grown into each other, that the strong roots of the latter pierced through the thick trunk of the former. They went completely through it, and only then attained the ground, in this fashion:

Probably the seed of the mountain-ash had fallen into a little hollow of the alder and had there awakened to life and taken root; thereafter the serpent that the alder had nourished in its bosom bored through its trunk. Nevertheless, the crowns of both trees mingled with one another amicably. The most remarkable thing, however, was that this piercing and embracing had taken place several times. In no forest had I seen anything similar previously. Another phenomenon that I never saw before was what I descried here in the case of an oak, which, as it grew, had forced itself on to a rock to such an extent that it seemed to have completely lost the one half of its trunk. In fact it covered the rock with a broad outpouring of an organic mass of bark and wood; this formed its trunk and it now rose from the rock in a half bow. Had the rock and the tree been cut through, this would have yielded roughly the following cross-section:

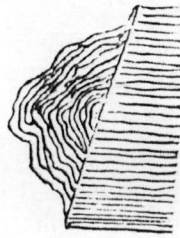

As I said, the trunk of the tree was only half there, or rather it was misshapen and crushed into an amorphous lump. Nevertheless the sap was able to flow through it and above it large, complete, regularly formed and abundant branches again stood out against the rock. These, I say, are altogether odd little tricks which the trees can achieve only in such an extraordinary rocky landscape. Those who live by the loch have given particular names to several of these remarkable trees. Thus one of them, which, on a bare stony peak, leaps out of the rock with many branches like antlers is called **'the Stag's head'**.

There, where the outflow from the loch passes through the rocks, yet another minute loch is formed between the latter; this they call **Loch Lium**[9] (pronounced *lähm*). The most interesting place is actually here, and from this spot one can see a remarkable rocky pass leading through the nearby mountain masses of Ben Venue; it is known as **'Bealoch-Nambe'**[10] ('the pass of the cattle') because the herds of cattle which come down the mountainside can make their way through only at this point.

At last I let myself be persuaded to climb some rocks on the opposite side of the loch in order to gain a view of majestic Ben Lomond, whose white peak commands the whole area. Although it was but a *small* majesty, which in Switzerland would scarcely occupy the position of one of the least important courtiers, nevertheless I could not help but bow before it, for in these surroundings it alone was dominant. The powerful and great of this earth, even the least of the great, everywhere demand that others should bow before them, and a traveller in Africa must show his respect to a despotic Negro prince as much as in Europe to a mighty king.

At the furthest western point of Loch Katrine we saw the mountains which form the pass between this loch and Loch Lomond. 'Yonder on that pass between the two lochs,' my guide told me, 'Rob Roy had his **'property'**. Before he became a **'fribooter''** – thus are Rob Roy and his henchmen always described here – 'he was a drover **'and he came very well on in the droving line'**. He himself, as you know, was a MacGregor but his mother was a Campbell. His wife, as everyone here on the loch says (and they know this from their grandparents), was **'of a very quiet disposition'** and by no means a woman of such ambitious and valiant temperament as Walter Scott depicts her.'

Finally I left the Trossachs and Loch Katrine, happy and content with the prospect of now returning to beautiful Stirling. For though, in so saying, I do not wish to belittle the characteristic merits of the **'Highland-scenery'** and the lochs, nevertheless I must confess that, all in all, I saw nothing finer in Scotland than Stirling and its surroundings.

* * * * * *

---

[9] [Properly *Lèim*. In 1859 a dam was constructed here raising the level of Loch Katrine by five metres so that water could be supplied to Glasgow through a 34-mile-long system of tunnels and aqueducts; nowadays therefore this outflow is not as the author saw it. Neither John Thomson's *Atlas of Scotland* of 1832 nor the Ordnance Survey map 365 of 2010 give a name to this inlet of the loch. However, in the latter an adjacent hillock is marked as *Meall an Lèim*.]

[10] [Properly *Bealoch nam Bò*]

XX
From Loch Katrine to Callander

I returned the same way as I had come the previous evening, then walked by Loch Venachar[1] and so came to the town of Callander[2] which, in a similar way to Dumbarton[3], Crieff, Dunkeld and others, lies on the point where the Highlands open out into the Lowlands. On the way, I met with no particular occurrence. The only thing was that I made the discovery, when my guide offered me his snuff-box, that about this time probably every pinch of snuff in the whole of Scotland smelt of tar; this is due to the '**Smuiring**' which is now general. Then not only do the shepherds contaminate their snuff with a subsidiary flavour of tar, but, since they also dip into their friends' snuff-boxes, this smell travels from snuff-box to snuff-box and probably is never actually absent from Scottish snuff-boxes the whole year round, just as peat-smoke is never absent from their whisky, just as the smell of leather is never absent from Russian merchandise.

On the way we had partaken of nothing more than a little dry '**oat's cake**'. 'That gives you strength, sir!' people told me, 'but it makes your blood hot.' In Scotland, therefore, it seems that our German saying 'He is feeling his oats' applies to people not only figuratively, but also quite literally.

Then several times I encountered old women in long, scarlet cloaks, and I had seen this strange clothing and colour of material not only in Wales, where they had explained to me that it was characteristically local, but also in most of the other counties of England, and now here in Scotland too. This scarlet cloak for old women can therefore be regarded as a garment generally worn in Britain. Those dressed in scarlet in Great Britain are old women, soldiers and students in Aberdeen and Glasgow (but not in Edinburgh). As a result of this, old women were once mistaken for soldiers. To explain – in Wales, they say, when, on the occasion of an enemy landing, the coast was totally empty of troops, the women in their red cloaks had gathered on the hills. The enemy had taken them for soldiers and had through fear retreated to their ships. This is perhaps only a fictitious anecdote. Soldiers, they say, were given this red clothing so that wounds and flowing blood were not immediately noticed and pointless scares were averted. However, why students and women wear this colour, which once used to be the prerogative only of kings, remains incomprehensible.

In Callander, in the good inn of the town, we were given a splendid brose[4] with our oatcake, and I revelled in the enjoyment of both these kinds of food, for they were the national foods of the country in which I was just now travelling.

Callander lies at the foot of Ben Ledi, which means 'God's Hill'[5]. On its peak there is said to have been a place for the worship of a god in Druidic times. Even in recent times people gathered here to light a great fire here in honour of Baal, the Fire God or Sun God. Even now the period of the beginning of May is still said to be called '**Beltein**'[6]. At this I remembered the Bal or Bel Mountains[7] which I had seen in Ireland, and on which likewise they lit fires in honour of the Sun God of the same name, and now in my thoughts I soared across the vast area between Scotland and Ireland in

---

[1] *Venagar*

[2] *Calander*

[3] *Dunbarton* [The town is spelt *Dumbarton*, the county *Dunbartonshire*.]

[4] [See Chapter VII, fn. 7.]

[5] [The name *Ben Ledi* is a distortion of the Gaelic *Beinn Leitir* which means 'Hill of the Slope', a description of its shape. The English form was misinterpreted by Dr James Robertson, the minister of the parish, as *le Dia* 'with god' and so 'hill of God' was published by him as the alleged meaning in the First Statistical Account of Scotland in 1791.]

[6] [Nowadays *Beltane*, Gaelic *Bealltuinn*. It has nothing to do with Baal.]

[7] [It is impossible to know to what the author was referring: there are no mountains in Ireland with that or a similar name. It might be the Hill of Uisneach, on which Beltane fires were said to be lit.]

this extreme north and the towers of Babylon, in which land once upon a time Baal was worshipped probably everywhere.

From Callander I now took with me the last Highlander who accompanied me on my journey. For here I bade farewell to the Highlands:

> **'Fare well to the Highlands high covered with snow,**
> **Fare well to the straths and green valleys below,**
> **Fare well to the forests and wildhanging woods,**
> **Fare well to the torrents and loudpouring floods.'**[8]

Others bid farewell to the Highlands only at Doune, ten miles further on, for they are of the opinion that the boundary of the Highlands lies only there, although here beside Callander is the end of the last range of mountains and the traveller can now make his way out on to the plain. Callander itself is very Highland. Many people here can still understand Gaelic and their children still wear the kilt. There is even said to be an old man still living here who throughout his whole life, all seventy-two years of it, has worn no trousers, but only the Highland kilt, and who on that account received a medal from the **'Highland-Society'** in Edinburgh; he appears in church on Sundays adorned with it. This state of affairs ceases immediately after Callander. I therefore do not know what circumstances inveigle some geographers into extending the edge of the Highlands as far as Doune.

Just beside this pleasant little town I was shown the rampart of a Roman camp. It is an obviously artificial construction, irregularly winding back and forth, which begins at the lower bank of the River Teith[9] and returns to the bank of this same river in an open semicircle. The rampart is studded with trees and an attractive walk leads along its crest. That it is an artificial structure, erected by human hands, and not, as some aver, one formed by the river, is obvious to any observer. However, whether it is a Roman construction may be doubted. The trees that grow on it are very old spruces. The position at the opening out of the mountains and on the edge of the fertile plain could certainly, however, serve military ends very well. And even the name of the town, Callander, appears to echo the sounds of Latin.

Within these Roman ramparts there is now a fine level stretch of grass, which the inhabitants of Callander use as a playing-field. Their principal game on it is **'Football'** which, according to the description of it, must be very similar to golf [sic].

* * * * * * *

---

[8] [This is the second stanza of Burns's 'My Heart's in the Highlands', the spelling and punctuation as in Kohl's German original. He gives a prose translation in a footnote.]

[9] *Peth*

XXI
From Callander to Stirling

My Highland Scot was a merry fellow and, as we walked, he sang an abundance of beautiful songs, all of which I have unfortunately forgotten. I only recall well that there often appeared a '**Mountain-rose**' in them[1]. He was also very knowledgeable concerning the witches and ghosts that lived in the mountains. I was not a little surprised to hear from him almost exactly the same stories about these spirits as I had heard in Ireland. They likewise term them '**good people**' just as in Ireland, or also '**the men of peace**'[2]. 'That is a strange name for such creatures', I remarked. 'Yes, that is true, sir!' answered my friend, '**for they are always leaping and kicking about for some mischief.** In Gaelic they are called "**Funshies**" or "**Kelpies**", and that just means "men of peace". "**Brumes**"[3], sir, are a particular kind of them. They are little dwarfs who thresh the grain for the farmers during the night, so that to their astonishment they find it ready the next morning. Once a funshy came to a poor smuggler in the forest who was just in the act of smuggling his whisky, which he had distilled in a secluded glen, down into the Lowlands. The funshy asked him to set down his cask for a moment, to take his ease, and then to dance with her. The smuggler did that. He danced perhaps a whole hour, or even longer, with her, without becoming in the least tired. Then he went down to the Lowlands, sold his whisky, and returned to his children and his wife. To his astonishment he found his young wife grown quite old, and his children grown up and sturdy. The funshy had kept him with her for a long number of years and thus had robbed him of a great part of his life.'

Very soon there fell upon us again the darkness that, with these short days now, is with us at almost every hour. The people who met us still continued to greet us with '**Fine weather to day, sir!**', just as those who had met us during the entire day, although there was nothing truthful in this piece of news other than that hailstones were not falling nor was beer raining from the sky. In no other country have people so often and so effusively said to me '**Fine weather to day,**' or '**a beautiful day to day, sir!**' as in Ireland and Scotland. It is indeed true that we human beings are inclined to speak most about that which we least possess. I am convinced that in Persia and other lands which lie under a perpetually clear sky it does not occur to anyone to praise the weather.

At seven o'clock we arrived in Doune, just as the '**Bellman**'[4] was walking through the little town and announcing that, in the drawing room of the Moray Arms inn, the famous **Dr** John MacNab would deliver a lecture on the maintenance of good health. (It is a very common custom of inns in England to show the coat of arms of some great family or other on their inn-sign, and as a rule in every town is found an inn that is called after the arms and name of the most important family of the neighbourhood, for example, '**Glengarry Arms**' or '**Mac Donald Arms**' or '**Huntley** [sic] **Arms**' etc.)

I asked my landlord whether he believed that this lecture would be interesting. '**It is very likely,**' he replied, '**he will be capital good hand**' [sic].

After I had put on slippers and otherwise had made myself comfortable, I betook myself to the place indicated, straightway found the tallow lamp that flickered in a little side passage and indicated the

---

[1] [It has not been possible to identify unambiguously which particular songs these might have been.]

[2] [This is in line with scholarly belief. The word *sìth* means both 'peace' and 'fairy' or 'otherworld person', deriving from the Old Irish *síd* which means both 'peace' and 'fairy mound' or 'otherworld'. The semantic connection is the idea of 'settlement', either abstract ('peace') or concrete ('otherworld').]

[3] [*Funshies* may be *banshees*, from the Gaelic *ban-sith*, 'female fairy'. The word *kelpie* is a Lowland term for a malignant sprite in the shape of a water-horse; it may be ultimately P-Celtic in origin, **ceffyl-pol* 'river-horse'. *Brumes* is possibly a misreading of his notes or a mishearing of *brunies* from Gaelic *brùinidh*, an otherworld creature in the rivers of Highland Perthshire.]

[4] In most small English towns such a bellman is appointed by the town council. *JGK*

entrance to the drawing-room, and climbed up the narrow wooden staircase that led from outside to the entrance doorway. Since we in Germany are not acquainted with such a phenomenon as a doctor who seeks to increase his medical practice by travelling round villages and delivering lectures to people on the maintenance of health, it will without doubt interest my German readers to hear what I found there.

The lecture had not yet begun and the lecture-room was still far from full. However, the doctor was standing behind a large table which he had covered with all kinds of papers; only later did I learn what they contained. He arranged these papers, and every now and then appeared to become engrossed in reading a letter. He was not like the Italian quacks who, colourfully and fantastically dressed, travel through the Roman and Neapolitan villages with a small cart, with a host of medicine bottles, and with a companion who behaves like a sort of clown and advertises them, as the bellman had advertised this English doctor. For the latter very well knew that such blatant quackery would not please his solemn Scotsmen. They would have immediately recognised him as a charlatan. He was therefore completely clad in black and exhibited something gentlemanly in his demeanour. Everyone who wishes to win the favour of even the lowest among the common people must be to some degree a gentleman, and I would have taken him for a thoroughly honest man if he had not begun to speak.

Gradually several members of the audience crept in, some workmen, some farm labourers, some weavers, some girls, some old women, some boys. When there were twenty of us, he made to begin the lecture. However, he said, it was necessary to choose a '**Chairman**'. Of course, he went on, he had not the slightest lack of confidence in the refinement of the members of the estimable gathering and he was not in the least apprehensive that anything might occur that was contrary to seemly behaviour. Nevertheless, it was after all according to custom and usage and it was also a principle to which he invariably adhered, not to hold any kind of meeting or deliver a lecture if a chairman had not first of all been chosen. The assembly remained silent. He repeatedly invited them to propose a chairman. Finally a name was mentioned, and scarcely had it been uttered than it was received with loud clapping of hands and stamping of feet. The man nominated hesitated a little at first. But several of his friends gave him some encouraging thumps on the back, and so he strode forward and, once he had decided on assuming the office, took up his position as chairman, with some measure of propriety and dignity, beside the quack.

In the case of English common people I have always noticed that if they are accorded such a public duty, at first they always need to be pressed and they decline as modesty demands, but then, as soon as they have reached a decision and have taken possession of the office, they conduct themselves with all dignity and propriety and with no timidity. In Germany such people would have too much modesty and too little confident dignity. It is remarkable, too, that even in insignificant gatherings such as this, there is observed the striving for a government with responsible ministers or rather for self-government by the nation. Even a quack like this does not dare to take over the command of his gathering of villagers, and he allows them to choose their leader for the evening themselves, to whose requests and orders they defer.

When eight o'clock had struck, the chairman rose – as I said, he was a workman or an artisan – and declared the meeting open, at the same time calling on the audience to listen attentively to Doctor MacNab, who had come from Glasgow to speak to them on a subject of such importance for everyone as the maintenance of health etc. At that, the doctor rose and delivered his speech which was a masterpiece of that characteristic type of charlatanism or **Humbug** which is customary in England. If I were able to repeat it in its entirety, the reader would find in it so much more that is typical of the English and of English habits than even an elaborate analysis of this subject could give him. Unfortunately I can impart only a few points from it.

He began with the creation of mankind, as it is related in the Book of Genesis, at the same time he also quoted some texts from the Bible – in Scotland biblical texts have to be quoted at every opportunity – and on several occasions called Adam the best **'natural philosopher'** in the world. In the description of the human organism, all his metaphors were suited to the understanding of an industrial nation. The organism itself he invariably termed the machinery of our body. He called the heart the **'steam-engine'** of our body, and he compared the stomach to the fire-box of this piece of machinery which must be provided with good fuel, that is, with appropriate sustenance, so that the heart, the **'steam-engine'**, may itself work energetically. 'Many clumsy and inexperienced engineers,' he continued, have meddled in this wonderful piece of machinery with clumsy hands and, if something in it was to be restored to working order, have often ruined and destroyed it! And why? For want of a correct method! A correct method, *that* is the main thing for living and for the maintenance of good health! He who has no method ought rather in no wise to interfere! How many examples could I give you of how sham doctors, in cases where a person's life could have been saved with a mere trifle, allowed all to be lost. And why? For want of method! and, what is even worse, for want of experience, for want of appropriate practical insight! Only this one thing, practical experience, is even more important than method itself, practical mastery and insight, of which I can give you no definition, which moreover no one can acquire through effort and studying; it is a gift from heaven which God himself has given to doctors – and among them to a few only.

'How many examples could I give you from my own experience of life, how many cases could I adduce, in which the doctors erred, not for want of knowledge and correct method, but for want of correct insight, for want of presence of mind, so to speak, as in the case of Lady Elizabeth K-nor, whom you all know. She suffered from a terrible **Pneumasi pulmonicorum**. However, all the doctors were trying to cure her of an **Encheiresis stomachica**' (here he mentioned some Graeco-Latin compound names or other). 'Why? For want of correct insight! They had not recognised the illness. Her Ladyship suffered terribly, and day by day her pain grew worse, her illness more serious. She was at death's door. Then she bethought herself of me. I have always enjoyed the patronage of Lady K-nor. I was first recommended to her by Lord T-by and by the Earl of B-ford, who are also among my patrons. The Earl of B-ford's father had already known my father and been friendly with him; he likewise was one of the foremost doctors in Glasgow, and I hope that the patronage of these families will be passed on to my children. To what extent the Earl of B-ford values my knowledge and talents you may yourselves gather from the following letter, which his Lordship wrote to me, when his Lordship's eldest son had been very ill.' (At this point he now read a long letter from the aforementioned lord, adding a host of explanations and comments.) 'But let me continue to tell you the story of Lady Elizabeth. She was at death's door. She sent for me. I came, I saw, I saved. I immediately recognised the mistakes that my predecessors had made.

'"Milady! Have they made you take too much **Mixtura Wiltenbachii cramboniorum**?"

'"Yes!"

'"Have they even given you **Aqua prulsia piccivi**?"

'"Oh, yes!"

'"You could not help sweating, vomiting, bleeding?"

'"Yes!"

Travels in Scotland (1840) by J.G. Kohl

"'Now, Milady, that is all wrong and is to blame for your present state! For the time being take this to strengthen you and restore you! Tomorrow, continue with it! And the following day complete your cure with it!"

'Much as I held Lady Elizabeth in highest regard and esteem, nevertheless my many enterprises and duties did not permit me to visit her again immediately. Moreover I had complete confidence what I had done. On the third day I visited her again. She met me in her garden, came towards me, shook my hand warmly and said "Doctor, you have saved me." I could tell of ten, a hundred, a thousand similar examples! For I am now sixty years of age and therefore have lived longer and gained more experience than most of you.

'But I now want to come to my subject itself and give you those principles for the maintenance of your health that are the most fundamental ones and which you must bear in mind and obey throughout your lives. They are first: '**good food**', second: '**temperance**', and third: '**ventilation**'' (fresh air). (He had a fourth point, which I have unfortunately forgotten.) 'If you consider what I said, that the heart is a steam-engine that drives the blood through the entire machinery of our body, and that the stomach represents the fire-box of this steam-engine, then you will understand why I have put '**good food**' in first place. It is above all most important that the machinery should be well stoked; for without this there can be no question of its coming into operation. Good, healthy and nourishing food is as essential to our body as are Newcastle coals to British steam-engines. Newcastle coals are not to be had free of charge, neither is '**good food**'. It is bought in exchange for money. Therefore, if I give good healthy nourishment pride of place as a foremost prerequisite for good health, then to that I must also add as a '**conditio sine qua non**'[5] high wages and good pay. A poor man cannot live happily and healthily without high wages. So I repeat: '**good food! cheap bread! and high wages!**' (**hear! hear!** – cheers from all sides!)

Of course this met with approval, and now the speaker took the opportunity to broach the subject of politics, and in doing so revealed himself as such a true radical and anti-Peelite that he was greeted with applause from all sides. I was astonished how one and the selfsame man could at the same time be such a great supporter of patronage, as he had demonstrated in the case of Lady Elizabeth, and such an arrant radical as he had now shown himself for the benefit of his audience.

After a long digression on the politics of the day, he then turned to the subject of temperance and sang its praises in the same manner as is now to be heard echoing everywhere in England. This was without doubt the best and most useful part of his lecture.

My German readers will totally fail to understand why the third item, 'fresh air', occupies the position that it does here as one of the four principal points in the preservation of health and the prolongation of life, unless they know that fresh air is one of the obsessions of the English. By that I do not mean that it is a bad idea, on the contrary, it is to some extent certainly very conducive to health; but I maintain that it is an English obsession, just as the washing of windows and houses is an obsession in Holland. In every English house, winter and summer, fresh air is ensured in the most conscientious and scrupulous way, in that the windows remain open for an age and a slight, but often very fresh and chilling draught constantly wafts through every part of the house. In every English public and private residence, in every hotel and inn, in every hospital and prison the visitor will almost always find the windows a little open and the door to every bedroom, every drawing-room, and every other room in the house (this includes many a place that cannot quite be mentioned) invariably quite wide open, so that everywhere the freshest air prevails, and dampness cannot insinuate itself anywhere. One of the standing complaints of the English on the Continent is the want of fresh air that they discover there, and when they have grumbled their way through their

---

[5] ['indispensable precondition']

list of complaints about our rooms without carpets, about our black bread and our pickled cabbage, about our short beds, about our suffocating stoves, then they finally come to the subject of fresh air. There are people in England who constantly preach, speak and write about fresh air and regard it as one of the most important benefits that one can make known to the poorer classes; there are even people who devote all their energies to bringing this about. And so my quack then included fresh air as well among the four principal prerequisites for the maintenance of good health and the prolongation of life.

Now, after he had well and truly illuminated all these points, he continued, 'See, these are the four most important things with which you will lead a long and healthy life. If you desire to see in a person the effect of following this scheme, then I can quote you my own example. Come to Glasgow and visit me, my house and my family. I live in George Street[6]. This street is the most genteel and fashionable street in Glasgow, and I tell you that that is where the elite of the city live. I have had my house midway along it for thirty years. Here is my address.' So saying, he distributed, from a heap of addresses he had lying on the table, a bundle of them among his audience. 'Come and visit me and my family there. Every visit will be a pleasure to me and I assure you, that, from whatever you suffer, I shall cure you with my method. I shall show you my wife and children, and you will see whether or not they are healthy and flourishing because of my method. I have five boys and four girls. I know that there are fathers of larger families. But my boys are lads like iron and the girls are blossoming like apricots. They are almost all grown up. One girl is married, and I assure you that the others will not lack for a husband either. George Street is two miles long, and I assure you that for the last thirty years we are the only people whom death has spared. All the houses round about us have received other occupants. Death has **cut off** whole families in our neighbourhood and **'no death at all with us'** [sic]. Is this a miracle? Believe me, nothing is a miracle in nature and in our lives. There is no mystery involved in all this. I repeat, it is only a result of my correct method and my strict adherence to the four fundamental principles, which I have commended to you: **'temperance'**, **'ventilation'**, **'good food'** and then fourthly ...' (as I said, I have unfortunately forgotten his fourth point).

'Never in my life have I drunk too much; whisky does not pass my lips. I restrict myself to water and beer, and only when I have good friends in my house do I serve a glass of wine. In my house everything is always well-aired, and my wife – you should see what a splendid woman she is; I thank the Lord that He has given me such a helpmeet! – always attaches the greatest importance to constant fresh air throughout the whole house. Likewise we lay stress on **'good food'**. The Lord be praised, I have never suffered hunger. My extensive practice has always kept me in a position to have good hearty roast beef on my table. Pray visit me and help to partake of a hearty meal of roast beef! **Ladies and gentlemen**, all of you are most sincerely invited to do so. And the more often you visit me, the happier I will be! Is there anyone here who does not yet have my address? There are still some addresses here.

'Now, **ladies and gentlemen**, I thank you for the attention you have given me; follow my method, and you will live happily. And from the bottom of my heart I wish that I can be of help to you in the future. And to you, Mr Chairman, I offer my deepest gratitude for the support you have given me. If you come to Glasgow, you can rely on my friendship there; and pray recommend me warmly to all your friends in Doune, a town which I especially love more than any other town in Scotland and which I will often visit in future. I still have some medicines here created by myself for particular **'diseases'**. Only from me and from my own hands can you receive proper and genuine medicines like these. Ladies and gentlemen, I take the liberty of recommending some more of them to you.' Then he distributed some more leaflets among his audience; these advertised various medicines for

---

[6] [The Post Office Glasgow Directories for 1840/41, 1841/42 and 1842/43 show no Dr John MacNab resident in George Street, nor is any such name listed under 'Physicians and Surgeons' in them.]

various illnesses and again contained the address of the doctor; the latter thereupon took his leave to the stamping of feet and the cheers of the company and closed the meeting.

It is not unusual to meet with such lecturers and quacks in British villages, and I have described for my German readers the speech and the conduct of my MacNab as an example of them all.

In the evening I returned to my landlord, who was an ordinary village landlord and held a few small fields on lease; he could give me nothing more than a '**box-bed**' on which to sleep, that is, a kind of hole in the wall in which the bed is made up, as is frequently found in Scotland, and as the Lower Saxons have in Bremen, Hanover, Friesland etc. and which, if I am not mistaken, they call 'Kujen'[7]. Nevertheless, my peasant landlord had a very fine little library, which he showed me. In pride of place among them I found several copies of the Bible, among others Th. Hawke's [sic] Bible[8] with illustrations and notes on the text, for which he had paid five guineas, then '**the British Cyclopedia**'[9], which had cost him three guineas, and then a large geographical book called '**the Earth**'[10], and yet more religious books, among others Josephus[11], which he had read from beginning to end several times. He also had a large barometer and thermometer in his room, and since he had praised the village blacksmith to me as an '**educated man**' – a commendation that everyone in Scotland now strives to earn and which consequently is very often heard being used – I went with him to visit this blacksmith's library too, as well as the collections of books belonging to yet more village inhabitants, which they showed me with pleasure. The blacksmith had no fewer than two hundred works on religion, natural history and other subjects, among them Josephus again, who seems to me to be very popular in Scotland. The smith had firmly convinced himself that I had come to his books only to make a '**Bargain**' with him. But when he saw that this was not the case, he asked for at least a little money for a dram. I must not fail to point this out, because doing business is something as characteristic of these literary Scotsmen as it is of all Scots, and because among them education has not rooted out the fatal inclination for a dram. With regard to doing business and small trading, as in so many other respects, the Scots are similar to our mountain-dwellers, the Swiss and the Tyroleans. There was a time in Germany when as many Scots travelled throughout the country, with all kinds of haberdashery and small goods for sale, as the Tyroleans and Swiss do now, and if that is no longer the case, it is due to the fact that so many other corners of the earth are now open to the Scots as subjects of Great Britain. Homesickness is as typical of the Albannaich as of our own Alp-dwellers. Once upon a time, too, especially during the time of Gustavus Adolphus, Scots could be found among the bodyguards of every European prince, as the Swiss can be found even now.

Near Doune are the remains of a once-important Scottish castle, called Doune Castle. Probably the village first received its name from this castle. My companions led me up on to the hillock which its now ravaged walls enclose. The way to it is shaded by beautiful old trees, and from the walls and towers, which themselves are disposed very picturesquely, there open splendid vistas into the lowlands to the front and into the Highlands to the back. This castle, Chambers tells us, was built by the Earls of Menteith[12], who were Grahams. Now, however, it is the property of the Stuarts, and in

---

[7] [They are in fact called *Kojen*.]

[8] [This is very probably the Bible with a commentary entitled *Evangelical Expositor or a Commentary on the Holy Bible* by Rev. Thomas Haweis, published by Sommerville, Fullarton, Blackie and Co., Glasgow, in 1818.]

[9] [*The British Cyclopædia of Natural History: Combining a Scientific Classification of Animals, Plants, and Minerals ... By Authors Eminent in their Particular Department*, edited by Charles F. Partington, London 1835.]

[10] [This could be any one of *The Earth: its Physical Condition, and Most Remarkable Phenomena* by W. Mullinger Higgins, London 1836; or *A General Descriptive Atlas of the Earth, Containing Separate Maps of the Various Countries and States from the Original Drawings*, by W. Mullinger Higgins, London 1836; or *The Earth* by Robert Mudie, 1835.]

[11] [Flavius Josephus (ca. 37 – c. 100), author of 'History of the Jewish War and Jewish Antiquities'.]

[12] *Monthith* [It was built by Robert Stewart, 1st Duke of Albany, who was also Earl of Menteith, in the late 14th century.]

particular of the Earls of Moray, who, as I have already said earlier, take from it their second title, that of the Lords of Doune. In the interim, it was for long in the hands of the royal Stuarts as a crown castle and was inhabited by several regents and royal personages. '**Mary Queen of Scots**' also lived here at times. There is '**excellent shooting**' nearby, and the Queen is said to have often gone hunting here. Here, too, several small rooms high up on the ruins were shown to me in which she is said to have lived. The stone doorway which led from her sleeping chamber to a neighbouring small room where her '**ladies of the bedchamber**' slept, was so narrow that in spite of stooping low I grazed my head on the stonework. If this did not happen to those ladies every morning, I assume that they must have been more skilful in stooping than I.

In 1745 this castle was also occupied by '**His Royal Highness**', Prince Charles[13] Stuart – there are Scottish books in which that title is always given very punctiliously to this prince whom English writers often call a mere adventurer, and they appear to regret that the **Royal Highness** never became a **Majesty**. A MacGregor, called 'Ghlun Dhu'[14] by the Highlanders (that is, 'the black knee' or also 'the black shepherd's crook'), a cousin of Rob Roy, defended it for a long time in the Prince's cause. After his time it fell into that decay in which the traveller sees it nowadays. The '**Hall**' of the castle is large and roomy and in its ruined state still manifests something regal. Immediately under this room was the dungeon.

The Morays have now built an attractive country house as their residence, a few rifle shots distant from the castle; this is known as 'Doune Lodge'. 'Some readers,' remarks a Scottish writer in describing this lodge, 'may be interested in the fact that, on his march from the Highlands to Edinburgh, Prince Charles stopped for a moment at the gates of this noble seat and, without dismounting from his horse, drank a glass of wine proffered to him by a young lady who was related to the then owners of the estate.' I mention this as typical, in order to show how the Scots hand down to their descendants even the most insignificant tradition of their beloved last Stuart.

I then walked through fertile and attractive Lowland meadows as far as Bridge of Allan[15], a pretty little village on the Forth[16]. On the way, I encountered large herds of '**Black-Cattle**' from the northern parts of Scotland, from Caithness and Sutherland. The animals were all almost as black as ravens, and on most of them I could not find even a single white stripe on their foreheads or light patches on their feet, as tends to be the case with our dark coloured cattle. The cowherds told me that they had come thither from Inverness in fifteen days, and that this was the usual duration of their journey from Inverness as far as Stirling. Their cattle were all young and fine-looking beasts, only six to eight '**Quarters**' (quarter years) old.

I am convinced that if Prince Albert and Lady Victoria – the British often say '**Lady Victoria, our queen**' (we cannot exactly say it in German in this way, but we can say 'unsere Frau Königin' or 'unser Herr König', which the French again cannot imitate with '**Monsieur le Roi**' or '**Madame la Reine**') I say if that royal couple had had time to look closely at the fanciful triumphal arch which the villagers of Bridge of Allan had erected for them, and under which they rapidly drove on their way, they would have been vastly amused. For above this archway, which I found still in its full finery, there stood, in allusion to the little mineral well which is in the vicinity of the town, a large painted tumbler with the caption written underneath 'This is the beverage from heaven for you!'. And in the middle of the triumphal arch a gilded beehive was suspended, and under it hung the following inscription with beautiful gold lettering:

---

[13] *Carl*

[14] [Properly *A' Ghlùn Dubh* (so-called from a black spot on one of his knees), this was Gregor MacGregor, otherwise called James Grahame of Glengyle, a nephew of Rob Roy MacGregor.]

[15] *Allanbridge*

[16] [It is in fact on the Allan Water.]

'How is the little busy bee improving every shining hour!'[17]

Here one could indeed rightly pose to the honest inhabitants of Bridge of Allan the question, *which* allusions to the journey of a royal couple they had detected in this verse about the bee when they deliberated in their council meeting about the best decoration for their triumphal arch, and in how far a small busy bee, taken from a reading-book, is capable of being the mediator between them and their **Lady Victoria the Queen** and the bearer of the homage offered to her[18].

In spite of every effort, I have not been able to imagine the processes of thought in which the inhabitants of Bridge of Allan might have indulged. Poets often hide their cogitations so deeply that they can in no wise be detected.

But I must confess that I was astonished at the paucity of the inscriptions and poetic effusions that I found on all the gates of honour which stood along the route of the Queen's Scottish journey. Indeed I must confess that this golden precept about the bee in Bridge of Allan was in actual fact the only one. People here must on the whole have less poetical imagination or another kind of it than, for example, in Alpine districts of Germany, where only a year previously I had found all the triumphal arches that had been erected for the Emperor of Austria on a journey through his mountain regions almost hidden under verses and inscriptions.

Now near at hand I glimpsed again the splendid town of Stirling and its castle beckoning to me, and soon, on the two wheels of a gig which I had hired in Bridge of Allan, I returned to this beautiful spot; here, as a matter of first importance, I made haste to take a close look at the magnificent Agricultural Museum of Messrs. Drummond.

* * * * * * *

---

[17] [The author gives a German translation in a footnote. The sentence is a near quotation from a poem by the hymn-writer Isaac Watts (1674-1748) entitled 'Against Idleness and Mischief', the first stanza of which runs 'How doth the little busy bee / Improve each shining hour / And gather honey all the day / From every opening flower!']

[18] [The bee or bee-hive is the crest of Lord Abercromby, feudal superior of Bridge of Allan. This would explain the choice of decoration.]

XXII
From Stirling to Edinburgh

In their histories of Scotland both Walter Scott and **Dr.** Tytler[1] tell of a great Scottish Highland hero, called Donald the Hammer. This warrior lord was so averse to agriculture that he quarrelled with his more peaceably minded son for the very reason that the latter gave himself over to the advancement of farming on his estate of Inverfalla[2]. Indeed, one day, when he was riding along the bank of the river that divided his and his son's lands, he espied several of the latter's men busy with hoes and ploughs and even saw that his son himself was putting his hand to these implements in order to show a worker how better to use them; at that, Donald fell into such a rage that he straightway jumped into a currach, a little boat covered with cowhide, and rowed himself across the river with the intention of slaying his son there and then, since he had besmirched the name of his family in this way by the most demeaning of all occupations. Of course, he did not succeed in this, because his son escaped by fleeing, but his action is nevertheless noteworthy since it demonstrates the great disdain that the ancient Scottish Highlanders had for such a noble occupation as farming, although agriculture is perfectly compatible with a courageous and warlike spirit, as the example of the Romans illustrates, for they knew no more noble calling for men than war and farming.

I know not how old Donald the Hammer might have conducted himself in the Drummonds' Agricultural Museum[3] in Stirling which indeed is perhaps one of the finest and most complete collections of this kind that exists in any country on earth. **Drummonds** [sic] **& Sons** are in fact so-called '**Seedsmen and Nurserymen**', such as are to be found in every town in Scotland, of course not always on such a large scale. They have important vegetable gardens in which they grow a large number of different plants in order to transact business with their cuttings and seeds. In addition, they have a large shop in the town where these products are sold both wholesale and retail. Generally such seedsmen and nurserymen also supply various agricultural implements; naturally, their shop is visited by many farmers and landlords, and so the designers of new threshing machines, ploughs or other agricultural tools also used, with their permission, the Drummonds' shop to exhibit their inventions there. Consequently, after the thunder of battles and of warfare had fallen silent in Scotland and swords had been beaten into ploughshares and spears into pruning-hooks – that is, not until after 1746 – there was always something to see and to scrutinise in their establishment. However, only in 1831 did it occur to Messrs Drummond of Stirling to devote a larger area to these small collections which hitherto had occupied only a limited space in their shop and had to some extent been only haphazard and temporary, and to set up an established, permanent Agricultural Museum; in this would be displayed to the leaseholders and farmers of the region specimens of all produce from gardens, fields and forests, together with models of all farming implements and of all the most recent improvements and inventions; these would be not only for inspection but also for purchase. To this end they fitted out their building and since that year have been enlarging and completing their collection to such an extent that it now occupies three large, broad storeys and offers a diversity of exhibits that can scarcely be equalled by any other museum of its kind in the world.

This museum of the Drummonds was found to be so useful and so important for the development of agriculture and generally so advantageous as an investment, that several seedsmen and nurserymen in Scotland have copied the enterprise, so that now a similar Agricultural Museum has already been

---

[1] *Tyler* [See p. 135, fn. 31.]

[2] [See Walter Scott *Tales of a Grandfather* 1828, second series, chapter VI.]

[3] [Drummond's Agricultural Museum, Stirling, was started by Messrs. William Drummond and Co., Nurserymen and Seedsmen, in November 1831, a fact which points to the importance of horticulture in the history of agricultural improvement in Scotland. It exhibited not only seeds and bulbs but the latest inventions in agricultural tools. In 1840 it was awarded a Gold Medal by the Royal Highland and Agricultural Society of Scotland.]

formed or is in the process of being formed in almost every important town in Scotland. The most outstanding after that of the Drummonds are the museums of Messrs. Lawson[4] in Edinburgh and of Messrs. Dickson and Turnbull[5] in Perth. I have seen them all and took such great and genuine pleasure in these splendid and helpful institutions that I would fain have visited several more. However interesting might be a detailed report on these museums, and specifically about the Drummonds' museum in Stirling, not only for every farmer but in general for every thinking person who observes the progress of agriculture in other countries, nevertheless on account of shortage of space I must deny myself the pleasure of such a report here. However, I will nevertheless pick out some things which, on the one hand, appeared to me typical of Scottish farming or which, on the other hand, illustrate the scope of this museum and serve to indicate how much progress has been made here in Scotland in such matters, and what extraordinary benefits are thereby offered to the farmer in these museums.

First and foremost, specimens can be seen here of all the different types of farming land and soil which the surface of Scotland offers. Here the whole country, as it were, can be seen with all its subtle differences in miniature, all types of terrain from the moorland and the peat bog of the mountains down to the rich and heavy loams of the plain and the sands of the coasts. Thus the visitor has the opportunity of comparing crude natural soil with artificially improved soil, in order to see what changes lengthier cultivation, more thorough systems of drainage, deeper ploughing etc. have wrought; thoughtful Scottish farmers have often provided the museum with entire sequences of types of soil from the same field as these came into being following different types of treatment in different years. How important such information is for the tenant-farmer or landlord who cannot travel about from farm to farm to learn at first hand about the effects of particular procedures!

In addition, all possible kinds of fertiliser are on view, helpfully displayed, in particular a large number of new types which are little known, and about the existence and efficacy of which the husbandman can immediately learn for himself here, since not only are inert samples of fertiliser exhibited, but small experiments are also conducted therewith, and the results achieved are then observed in their subjects. Powdered oyster-shells, bone meal, different kinds of ash, different rape cakes, various salts, different types of gypsum and chalk – all manner of things that no one had hitherto thought of keeping in museums, although the sight and examination of them affords much greater benefit than that of the rarest of molluscs and the most exquisite of snail shells.

After that, there can be seen a large collection of agricultural crops which in its comprehensiveness has no equal. Where it was possible, growing specimens were planted in pots and tastefully put on display (*so* many grasses for fodder!), or otherwise dried and assembled in splendid, profuse groups (*so* many types of cereals!), or in freshly gathered samples, which are constantly changed as they deteriorate (*so* many fruits, carrots, turnips, potatoes!).

First and foremost the turnips – these were introduced only fifty years ago, although southern Scotland lies in the very middle of the typical turnip-growing belt, but now are grown in extraordinary quantities there, since they are commonly recognised as the undeniable basis of a good agricultural economy and as the best means of improving the soil.

Then potatoes – this wonderful crop, which likewise was introduced very late into Scotland, but of which a new variety is brought to light there almost every month. Last year I saw a new Peruvian variety of potato in every Scottish seedsman's shop, but I do not know whether this little monster is already widely known in Germany. It was very long in shape and twisted like a snake. I saw one

---

[4] [Lawson's Agricultural Museum, opened by Peter Lawson in Hunter's Square in 1833.]
[5] [James Dickson laid out nursery grounds east of the Tay and on the north and east sides of Kinnoull Hill in 1766. They are shown on the 1823 *Plan of the City of Perth* as being owned by Dickson and Turnbull.]

that was three-quarters of an inch in diameter and thirteen English inches long. I said that potatoes too came to Scotland very late, yet already there is a range of varieties of this vegetable that have been given the names of Scottish islands and counties, for example, the Manx potato[6], the Perthshire potato etc. Many kinds of vegetables encountered here seem to have come from Germany to Scotland, for they have retained their German names, a fact that cannot be gleaned from the usual lexicons of the English language, thus, for example, 'Kohlrabi', 'Mangoldwurzel', which are written '**Kohl-Rabi, Mangold-Wurzel**' in Scotland.

The most noticeable thing for a German in these Scottish agricultural museums is that rye, our principal North German cereal crop, is often held in little regard there, and indeed in the extensive collections of varieties of cereals is not found at all. Admittedly, Messrs. Drummond had several specimens of it; they told me that a man had brought them with him from France where this kind of grain is widely grown, but that in Scotland its cultivation appeared to have ceased completely. In North Germany, rye is called '*corn*', because it is the principal cereal crop there. In Scotland, however, it is '**Oats**' that are '**the corn**', and if Scots talk of 'corn' without further specification, then by that they mean oats. I noticed this everywhere in the Highlands, where as a rule there was nothing other than oats anyway. In the Lowlands, wheat is gaining the upper hand everywhere and so it is that which by preference must come to be called typical 'corn'. What a denigration of our rye seems to us to lie hidden in the fact that the English and Scots grow it only occasionally, as cattle-fodder!

Besides such collections of plants, a permanent exhibition is maintained of those factory-made products, the manufacture of which often constitutes a branch of agriculture itself. Here, on constant display, can be seen all possible types of flour, sago, pearl barley, malt and cheese.

All these collections are novel and interesting, especially when the visitor has such helpful and knowledgeable men as guides as are Messrs. Drummond or the renowned Mr Smith[7] of Deanston, the foremost farmer in Scotland and the one most active with hand and pen. They immediately make clear how *genuine* Ayrshire cheese, the most superb type of Scottish cheese, can be distinguished from false, and they impart many interesting observations, as for example, that the most vigilant and competent owners of cattle in Scotland now make very sure that in their dairies they have only cows that give one and the same kind of milk, that is, milk of the same taste, fat content, colour, and quality, because they have noticed that the mixing of different kinds of milk neither produces a good butter nor a good cheese. Nevertheless, however interesting these sections of the collection are rendered because of such information, the sections containing the different farm implements are by far more interesting and more useful and also more extensive; the number and diversity of them truly beggars belief.

I would fain eavesdrop on Virgil's astonishment if it were possible to show him a museum such as this, where he could see a thousand implements with which to dig the ground, to turn it over, to crumble it, to pulverise it – implements of which he himself had no inkling even in the most beautiful visions of his *Georgics*[8]. Such a museum must needs be compared with the collections of implements of most European peasant-farmers, in order to grasp to what a great extent agricultural practice is everywhere still in its infancy, indeed, so to speak, is slumbering like an immature babe in swaddling-clothes that has yet to awaken and make its way in the world. A hoe, a spade, a

---

[6] [*Man-kartoffel* in the original, presumably referring to the Isle of Man; this, of course, is not a Scottish island.]

[7] [James Smith (1789 - 1850) became manager in 1807 of a cotton factory in Deanston, a village on the River Teith near Doune and owner of a farm there in 1823. He patented improvements to the spinning of cotton but also invented a reaping machine (which won him a medal from the Imperial Agricultural Society of St Petersburg) and a subsoil plough; in 1831 he published an agricultural pamphlet entitled *Thorough Draining and Deep Working*.]

[8] [In the author's original, *seines Ackerbaugedichtes* = 'of his agricultural poem'.]

Travels in Scotland (1840) by J.G. Kohl

plough, a club for threshing, a harrow, a few graips and pitchforks – these are the principal objects that can be observed in the hands of most of our European farmers. The plough of the same ancient traditional country-wide shape still turns over the most diverse types of soil. The threshing-flail continues to perform its arduous labour exactly as in the time of Adam, though machines could do it much more easily and satisfactorily. One and the same type of hoe, which at one time was adopted by an entire multifarious people, carries out tasks of the most disparate kinds; for these, hundreds of different hoes should be employed in order to perform the work better. Great broad tracts of land can be seen planted with one and the same kind of cereal crop, in accordance with an ancient tradition that extends far and wide, for example, the whole countryside from Finland to Holland is covered with rye, whilst there is no doubt that every one of the infinitely many subtle differences of soil and climate is, according to its character, appropriate for a particular type of grain. Nay more, not only has nature given us a host of different types of grain, but mankind could in addition develop a further range of subspecies of them and make them suitable for every different type of soil and climate.

In that respect, horticulture is far in advance of agriculture. The former possesses no fewer than 1600 varieties of apple, 1000 kinds of pears, thirty types of garden peas, countless sorts of grass with, for example, sixty species of clover alone, all manner of other fruit, flowers, and plants. Equally as many varieties of grain could be developed, and, in part, they have in fact already been developed and classified; but these are still to be found only in the hands of scientists or, at best, of specialists in horticulture. In general, farming still operates with a relatively extremely restricted number of varieties. Even in Scotland, one of the most competently cultivated countries in the world, only about a half dozen types of wheat can be considered as being in use in general farming. Of two hundred varieties of grass, all of which would be suitable for the climate of Scotland, and all of which are found growing wild there, and for each of which a particular method of growing, a particular use, could be found, only two or three varieties have attracted the general attention of Scottish graziers. In short – for it is scarcely worth the trouble to dwell long on this matter, since the target is still so far off – in short, I say, the slightest reflection on this topic will demonstrate that our present age has not only invented rational farming and has taught a group of people to reason and to ponder (people who hitherto had scarcely begun to do this), but it has also inaugurated roads to development and progress that open up infinite vistas. Museums such as that of the Drummonds are particularly suited to reveal, in the distance, the goals of these movements that have been initiated among farmers.

Among the different machines for sowing seed that I saw here, I was particularly impressed by an eighteen foot long device for sowing beans which put in thirty beans simultaneously at every step of the horse, – then there was a machine for sowing turnips that at the same time somewhat pressed in the scattered seed, – yet again, a device for spreading fertiliser which at every movement formed a countless number of little heaps of bone meal or powdered oyster shells, – and thereafter innumerable types of machines for ploughing, harrowing, reaping, and threshing, of the most ingenious designs. I saw here twenty models of diversely constructed drains and a host of various kinds of implements, hoes, spades, shovels, that are necessary for the construction of these drains – numerous little devices to trap the different creatures that are deleterious to crops – then countless machines for making butter (**Churns**). Among the various mechanical contrivances for milk, butter and cheese I found the **Milk-coolers** especially interesting. I saw, for example, one of zinc that was said to increase by ten per cent the amount of butter obtained from the milk, and in which the cream was removed on to a zinc plate in a completely unbroken layer for the churn. Finally thermometers were on display, especially designed for use in the dairies and creameries.

The visitor does not have eyes enough to take note of everything that Messrs Smith of Deanston and the other excellent Scottish agriculturalists have thought out in the minutest detail. They have likewise thoughtfully and critically considered the various barrows and carts for farmers, and like all agricultural equipment in Great Britain, so too first and foremost all farm vehicles are now in the process of undergoing a salutary and thorough transformation, as is the attire that the countryman should wear, and here can be seen a collection of farm workers' smocks that are particularly suited for such and such a task, for such and such a season of the year, for such and such a type of weather.

In Germany, many minor branches of the craft of agriculture are too little or barely taken into account and developed, as, for example, that practice of most profitably enclosing fields, or 'fencing', as the English say. I had hitherto heard so little of this work that to begin with I did not grasp what the English constantly meant by their fencing of which they spoke to me so much, telling me that in Germany it was in such a dreadful state. Later, of course, I understood well enough when I saw English parks and fields and then the Drummonds' museum. In Germany, in some areas there are great stone barriers round the fields, made of immense unhewn blocks of stone, as, for example, in Holstein; these serve equally as a protection against human beings, cattle, hares, wolves and mice. In other localities they have huge wooden palisades round gardens and fields, for example, in Prussia, Courland. A vast amount of good timber is wasted there. In other places, that is, towards Poland, they have stockaded the farmsteads with great thorn walls round them. Then again ditches and tree-covered earthen ramparts, and here and there living hedges, which are of a certain effectiveness, serve to fence off the fields. Certainly, all this to some extent accords with the particular character of the land. However, since in certain districts certain modes of enclosure exclusively predominate, and since these can serve for hundreds of purposes, this betrays some absence of thought. Only in England has the idea of hedging and fencing been grasped with analytical, intellectual deliberation, and for different purposes different types of 'fences' have been developed. The foremost genuinely English fences are those of living plants (thorn bushes of different kinds) and thereafter those of iron. Iron fences take up least room, are the most durable, strongest, and in addition can be greatly decorative. For their manufacture there are important and extensive establishments in London and in other English cities. They make small, delicate 'Hare-' and 'Rabbit-fences', 'Sheep-fences', 'Cattle-' and 'Horse-fences', 'invisible fences' of iron wire painted green, which are simply not noticed in parks, but are very strong and serve their purpose well. These invisible fences are still completely unknown in Germany, or are not yet well known, and so we must needs always surround ourselves with walls and immense gratings which impart to our gardens the appearance of a prison or cloister and completely block our view out into the open country. The entire 'fencing-system' is also undergoing a thorough transformation in Great Britain.

Let us consider how many centuries must still elapse until in all Europe every field and garden is enclosed in the most efficient manner, until every plot of land is planted with the best and most suitable kind of crop according to its character and its climate, until the ancient uncomfortable farm-carts are replaced by more appropriately constructed ones, until farmers are all attired as they ought to be, until every type of ground has acquired its individual plough, until instead of horses' hooves or the threshing-flail, machines everywhere are capable of extracting grain from corn, until instead of the bean-planter, who must laboriously bend down fifty times, a mechanical sower performs the work fifty times more quickly and easily everywhere, until with a zinc sheet we separate in an unbroken layer the cream for butter from the milk in every village. Let us consider, I say, how long it will be before all these inventions and developments have established themselves in every corner of our European farmland, and let us be rendered speechless partly with horror at the barbarism in which we are still sunk, partly, however, with joy at the prospects that are opened to us, and at the paths of progress on which we are now making our way. For it is glorious that our tremendous era is truly advancing with tremendous steps to such a tremendous fulfilment. Everywhere the farmer rubs his eyes with astonishment, and everywhere inappropriate practices, to which mankind has clung since the time of Adam, are being consigned to oblivion.

In the short space of this present century more '**Horticultural and Agricultural Societies**' have been established than in the whole of antiquity and the Middle Ages together.

In Scotland, the moving spirit of all the subsidiary and minor societies, disseminated throughout the land, is the '**Highland- and Agricultural society of Scotland**', founded at the end of last century, at the head of which are now the foremost nobility and most prominent farmers of the country. The Drummonds' Museum and the other institutions modelled on it are in contact not only with every part of Scotland but indeed with the whole world. It was to Ireland and Wales, they told me, that they now exported the most '**Agricultural Implements**', and every year the quantities sent there increased, which was a new proof of the improvement of agriculture in both these parts of the kingdom in which hitherto so little progress had been made. To one single landlord in Ireland alone, the Marquis of Waterford, they had recently had to send four hundred large picks for the digging of drains. They named me several towns in Germany as well with which they were in contact. Nevertheless, their principal business goes over the ocean, to the great landmasses in the South Seas and in the Indian Oceans, now opened up to agriculture, whither now the Scottish farmers and '**Tillers**' transport the altars and mysteries of Ceres, or, to use their idiom, their '**fencing-**' and '**draining-systems**'. To Australia, likewise to Canada, many implements and seeds are constantly shipped.

In these Scottish museums not only is that which is of benefit amassed in such great quantities, but it is also particularly pleasingly displayed and manifoldly embellished – busts and portraits of famous Scottish husbandmen, views of Scottish landscapes enhance the spacious rooms; at times charming collections of beautiful and rare flowers allow visitors to do homage to their beautiful colours and shapes once they have seen enough of the utilitarian turnips and potatoes; Chinese, Indian, Tatar, Russian agricultural implements, which are interspersed, also satisfy other types of curiosity and thirst for knowledge. Moreover, these museums are the gathering places for ladies and gentlemen of all ranks. For all these reasons the most agreeable diversion is always to be enjoyed there.

Now there still remained to me two things to visit in Stirling, firstly the rock that is called Abbey Craig, and secondly the famous battlefield of Bannockburn[9]. My host's swift little gig conveyed us thither. Abbey Craig is a remarkable high rock that takes its name from an old abbey that once stood at its base. '**Craig**' means the same as 'rock', and Abbey Craig therefore signifies 'abbey rock'. It is higher and larger than the rock on which Stirling Castle stands, and bears the same relation to it as do Arthur's Seat and the Salisbury Crags[10] to the ridge on which the Castle and High Street of Edinburgh stand. All these rocks resemble each other strikingly, and there are many other similar ones in Scotland besides. Because of their shape, a Scottish writer called them '**craig and tail**', because they all have a great high precipitous rocky summit in the west and then towards the east either they merge with other hills in a long ridge that progressively becomes lower, or they gradually level out in the plain. This direction from east to west is characteristic of them all, and they are also all of volcanic origin, judging by their basaltic formation.

Just beside Abbey Craig is another '**Craig and tail**' which exhibits the same outline and is called '**Craigforth**'. The general shape of these rocks, which forms such a typical feature of the landscape of the Scottish Lowlands, can be epitomised rather like this:

---

[9] *Bannockburne*
[10] *Salisbury-Craigs*

These hills once projected as small reefs and islands out of the sea that surrounded them, and even though no small ships ran aground on them, since ships did not yet exist at that time, nevertheless whales did so. Several years ago, at the foot of Abbey Craig, twenty feet above sea-level, whalebones were found in the ground. The inhabitants of Stirling themselves, who best have been able to judge how unique the appearance of these black basalt long-tailed rocks is in the midst of the beautiful green Lowland plain, and who inhabit one of these rocks, have therefore also taken from the latter a singular nickname. They call themselves **'the sons of the rock'**. Not only in poems about Stirling but several times in Stirling newspapers I found this poetic appellation.

One could reproach the Scottish traveller for continuing still, at the present day, to talk of the old battles near Stirling; these are long gone without a trace and they seem to possess only an antiquarian and romantic, but by no means practical, significance now, since they lie much further back in time than, for example, those battles by which the individual parts of the Prussian kingdom came together, indeed, almost as far back as, and in part even further than, those battles by which the different provinces of the French monarchy were forged into a whole. Nevertheless, there are battles between different nations that are quickly forgotten, others again that never fade into oblivion. The different regions of France fused together relatively quickly into a close union, and there, as in Prussia (with the exception of Posen[11]), there is no trace of such a blunt antipathy between nations as exists in England between the English and the Scots. As is well known, for six hundred years these two nations fought each other with fire and sword and with the utmost fierceness. King Edward I of England desired that after his death his bones should be gathered up and taken on a standard into battle against the Scots. During his life he rejoiced in the thought that even after his death he would still be able to terrify the Scots. On his tomb in London his nickname can still be read: 'the Hammer of the Scots'. To this very day, in the neighbouring provinces Northumberland, Cumberland, the English still castigate the Scots who come among them for their **'Raids'** of yore, half in jest, half in earnest. The English also sometimes refer with wrinkling of their noses to certain Scottish illnesses, on account of which, it is jocularly claimed, the Duke of Argyle erected specific fence-posts at specific intervals on his land[12], for which the Scots are said to have praised him highly; in a similar vein the English are still affronted by many other Scottish singularities.

In short, if one wished to enumerate all the points that now give rise to occasional minor friction between the two nations, then one would have much to do. Scotland has not become subjugated to the English as a province; on the contrary, after many a fearless battle, after a long glorious defence of its freedom, Scotland has become a partner with England, first in the union of the two crowns and then in the union of the two parliaments and realms. However, as a smaller country she has always to some extent been conscious of her weakness in comparison with mighty England, and every so often, against her volition, has had to make some concession. The union of the parliaments and realms was not so *completely* voluntary, and equally involuntary was the fading away of last century's revolution in Scotland. Just as a little man pitted against a large one commonly tends to

---

[11] [Modern Poznań in Poland]

[12] [This is a garbled reference to the enclosure of the Argyll lands in the 18th century. Sheep and cattle (not people, as the English joke apparently claimed) were observed rubbing themselves against the newly-erected fence-posts to remove fleas and ticks. Popular myth had it that they were saying 'God bless the Duke of Argyll!'; subsequently anyone seeing an animal scratching itself repeated the saying.]

act in a somewhat pugnacious manner, so too Scotland still remembers her heroic deeds against the English with unabated enthusiasm and patriotic excess, continues to rehearse them constantly to herself and to strangers, sings of them – even now a good part of the most recent Scottish poetry marches on the ancient Scottish battlefields of Stirling, Falkirk, etc. – and describes them incessantly; yet on the other side of the Tweed and the Cheviot Hills, all the battles in which the Scots in their turn were defeated by the English are, to a much greater extent, forgotten.

On the battlefield of Bannockburn near Stirling, as the Queen passed in the vicinity last year, there had been hoisted a flag so that she could see, at least from afar, on what spot her ancestors had been defeated by the Scots in armed conflict[13]. On learning that, I was reminded of the Emperor of Austria's journey in Styria. The Styrians too have many battlefields to exhibit on which they repulsed the Austrian archdukes and emperors, but I believe that in that country propriety would not have permitted anything similar to that which it allowed here in Scotland. England and Scotland find themselves in many respects in a like situation to that of Sweden and Norway. The Norwegians, too, boast about their victories over the Swedes more than do the latter about their victories over the Norwegians.

Thus, as long as these petty jealousies continue to exist between the English and the Scots, so long will the memory of the ancient victories and battles be daily reinvigorated there in the above way; so long will the traveller not only be *able* but be *compelled* to mention that it was on the Abbey Craig that Wallace had raised his banner on the thirteenth of September 1297; and so long must it not be forgotten that he came down from this rock in order to attack the English – who, under the command of Sir Hugh de Cressingham, King Edward's general, had rashly crossed the Forth – and to hack them to pieces beside the famous bridge. And so long, too, must an invitation not be refused to go out from Stirling to the battlefield of Bannockburn, in order to examine everything there meticulously and to comprehend thoroughly the various positions of the English and Scots and the astute tactics of Robert Bruce, who vanquished them here on the twenty-fourth of June 1314 and thereby safeguarded his own crown and ensured independence for his native land.

The Battle of Bannockburn is without a doubt one of the most portentous and most important that was ever fought in Scotland, for the Scots led no fewer than thirty thousand men into battle, and the English are said to have had actually three times as many and to have lost thirty thousand soldiers and seven hundred knights[14]. However, in other great battles, for example, that of Leipzig, many more troops were deployed, and many more men fell there. And yet, I believe the Battle of Leipzig will be able to count itself very lucky, if after five hundred and thirty years all Germans were still to know of the details of that battle, to the extent that the Scots, after five hundred and thirty years now, are still familiar with the details and minutiae of the Battle of Bannockburn.

It is as though all the individual events of the battle had impressed themselves ineradicably on the memory of the nation. For although these events were but fleeting incidents of a few moments, nevertheless these fleeting incidents have given all the different places in the surrounding area their names for ever after. Thus one site in the vicinity is still called '**the bloody field**' even now, because here a unit of the English, which was on the point of retreating to join their fellows, was slain to the last man. Thus another place in the neighbourhood is called '**Ingram's Crook**', because here an English general, Sir Ingram Umfraville, was killed. Another place is called '**Randal's field**', because here on the evening before the battle Randal, Earl of Murray, and Sir Robert Clifford fought in furious combat. One hill is called '**Gillies' hill**'[15], because the supply-carriers, whom Bruce had

---

[13] [The victor of course was also an ancestor of Victoria.]

[14] [Modern estimates range between totals of 10,000 and 22,000 for the English combatants and of 6,000 and 10,500 for the Scots. English casualties are estimated as between 4,000 and 10,000 and Scots as between 3,000 and 4,000.]

[15] In the Highlands '**Servants**' are still called '**Gillies**'. *JGK* [Gaelic *gille* 'lad', 'manservant'.]

positioned behind the hill, made their appearance here to support their compatriots, and caused such a fright among the English, who took them for fresh reinforcements for the Scots, that they fled. The great granite stone, too, is still there that is called **'the bored stone'**[16], because there is a hole in it in which Robert Bruce had set up his banner during the battle. It was in this stone that the flag referred to above was put up for Queen Victoria and Prince Albert.

The Scots troops, like the Swiss, were mostly infantry, or at most had only their little mountain ponies (Bruce himself rode such a little mountain pony during the battle), and they had, in all their battles with the English, an especial fear of the heavy English cavalry. Therefore Robert Bruce, like the Swiss against the Austrian horsemen and knights, also adopted safety measures here against the English. It is said that he laid mantraps of some kind in the grass and had a large number of small deep holes dug round the entire edge of the battlefield. I must admit that, since the battlefield of Bannockburn is at least two miles in length, I have never been able to picture to myself the immense number of holes and mantraps that it would take to surround such a very extensive site completely, and in the same way I have never been able to form a clear idea of the success and the effectiveness of these measures undertaken by Bruce which are recounted by all Scottish writers of history. I had hoped that the battlefield itself would enlighten me about this to some extent, but it too has not been able to persuade me to regard his course of action as any less bizarre, blundering and inept than it had appeared to me from the very beginning.

In this very same so historically interesting marsh, round the edge of which those holes were dug and which extends out into the valley of the Bannock Burn, I now saw deep furrows and holes dug out once again; these, however, had a more peaceful purpose, namely the draining of the marsh. The greatest part of it had already disappeared in previous years under the advance of farmland. Now I was seeing the last part of this historic marsh being brought under cultivation. The people who were employed in cutting the drains showed us a sword that they had found under the peat, and for which they without doubt will have received a good price, since swords from the Battle of Bannockburn are somewhat rare and have certainly not been becoming less valuable and interesting to the Scots. This patch of marsh is part of a larger area of bogland near Stirling which survived for a long time, but has now almost completely been transformed into arable land. The owner of it is the Marquis of Abercorn. To the people who clear the marsh he gives, for their lifetime, the fields that they thereby bring into being. They create these fields for themselves in very different ways, depending on the circumstances. Sometimes they dig the peat completely away and then use the good soil that lies under it; sometimes they burn it away, plant seed in the ashes and create a fertile layer of earth on top of the peat; sometimes they only dry it out by means of drains and are able to use it like that straightaway. To carry the peat away they utilise the little streams and burns. To do this, they cut out all the peat and marsh and thoroughly hack it to pieces. Then they dam the flow of water which, when they release it, carries away all the mud and the pieces of peat and moss. Sometimes they make channels by means of which they enable the peat and mud to flow out into the big rivers.

The stagecoach which was to bring us to Falkirk to the railway in the evening, fetched us at the door of the Drummonds' museum, and I made use of the opportunity to return once more to this fascinating place whither we Germans can never return without seeing something new. Here I now caught up with the splendid collection of grafting knives and garden shears of all kinds, of the shape, mechanism, and very existence of which I had earlier had not even the least idea. Above all, I was interested in the invention of pruning shears and secateurs with dual action, which, like our shears, squeeze and compress and at the same time cut and saw with both blades like knives; they thus exert an enormous force on the branches to be chopped off and, with a slight movement of the hands, can cut off the strongest branches. Then there were small delicate knives or hooks on long arms **'to take out weeds for Gentlemen walking about with'**. Then again there were efficiently

---

[16] [*Borestone* on the 1999 Ordnance Survey map.]

contrived grass hoes to weed the grass of lawns and parks and, in particular, to tear off the heads of the little '**Daisies**', so that they might not obtrude on the uniform colour of the green carpet.

In actual fact, not only can each one of these implements (which incidentally without exception are manufactured in Sheffield in vast quantities and of the finest quality) be regarded as a minor illustration of the entire state of English agriculture, but each one of them also affords glimpses into the domestic life and the industriousness of the English.

Usually English seedsmen's shops have also a large number of choice pumpkins in their windows. But it is strange that people do not eat them, for even the poorest here do not understand how to prepare pumpkin and cook it. They plant pumpkins solely as ornament and decoration. Yet how many poor people could satisfy their hunger with mashed pumpkin from time to time, if only someone could get them into the habit of eating this vegetable. If someone were to introduce the cultivation and preparation of pumpkin into Scotland, certainly a dozen more people, at a conservative estimate, could henceforth live in Scotland. And that does not say very much, a whole dozen people. Yet indeed, if only one more person could thereby improve his existence, should not that be important? Did not the Romans give a crown to him who saved the life of even only one fellow-citizen[17], and likewise should not the crown be given to him who created more space for a rational being here on earth?

With this thought we 'stagecoached' through the darkness to Falkirk, and from there we then 'railed' further. '**To rail**', '**I railed**' I have often heard used in England instead of '**I went by railroad**'. It is a short and good word, and if it is not already in general use, it will certainly soon acquire general acceptance. In a similar way, we ought to create from our German word 'Schiene', a rail, the verb 'schienen' ('to schien'). We could thereby save many words, for example, instead of 'I went from Dresden to Leipzig on the railway', we could say 'I schiened from Dresden to Leipzig'. It is strange that our inventions are now proceeding with such speed that the idioms of language cannot keep pace with them. Thus, remarkably, neither in English nor in German have particular expressions been created for journey by steamship. In England they say 'we *sailed* with the steamship from Dublin to Glasgow', although this is manifestly wrong, since often no sail whatsoever is hoisted. We Germans say 'We travelled with the steamship', which is not wrong, but which, however, ought to be better expressed in one word, following the example of 'kutschen' (instead of 'to travel by Kutsche (coach)') or of 'schiffen' (instead of 'to travel by Schiff (ship)'). In short one ought to say 'we steamed'. It is actually a 'paddling', but, however, a kind of paddling other than the usual. Our language nowadays seems to be especially unwieldy and unimaginative.

I travelled through the town of Falkirk twice, just as I travelled across the southern part of the county of Stirling, the county of Linlithgow and the western part of the county of Lothian twice, without seeing anything of them other than night and darkness, indeed without putting my foot on even a single square inch of ground in these counties. By virtue of the railways, there are now thousands of travellers in Europe who take back home with them, from many regions they traverse in utter darkness like birds of prey, no clearer memories than images of fog and darkest night.

* * * * * * *

---

[17] [The *corona civica* ('civic crown'), fashioned from oak leaves, was awarded to a Roman citizen who had saved the life of a fellow citizen in battle.]

XXIII
Edinburgh

When I arrived back in Edinburgh that same evening, I was surprised to see the Old Town, opposite my inn, not so brilliantly lit as previously, indeed almost completely dark. '**It is a great preaching night to day, sir!**', people told me, 'and all the inhabitants of those houses and almost all the inhabitants of the entire city are now in church.' Indeed I saw that only the high windows of the churches were illuminated.

The next morning the illumination in the city was all the more dazzling. The sun came out from behind the Salisbury Crags[1] with a brilliance that was certainly extraordinary for Scotland as well as for this time of year. Just as the sun stood at the sharp vertical edge of this rock, the view was at its most beautiful, as the following figure indicates:

The whole sombre black-tinted wall lay in the deepest shadow, but on the other side of the sharply delineated boundary line there poured forth an immeasurably dazzling torrent of sunbeams. Many coincident circumstances are necessary before a spectacle of such great splendour and of such powerful contrast can come about, as here on the Salisbury Crags. And it may be asked whether there are other town-dwellers who can see the sun rising every morning in such a manner as can the citizens of Edinburgh behind the Salisbury Crags. When the sun comes up over the horizon, the misty atmosphere of the ground has long been suffused with the reflection of its light and the contrast is no longer so great.

I made use of the beautiful hours after this sunrise by taking several long walks in the town and its surroundings.

Edinburgh is the only town in Scotland which has a zoological garden[2], while in England over half a dozen towns possess zoological gardens. These zoological gardens with *living* animals seem to be regarded now in Great Britain more and more as a necessary adjunct of civilised towns, like museums with stuffed animals, like botanical gardens, like municipal observatories, like agricultural museums. In fact, it seems a reasonable notion to place living animals on display to urban lovers of nature and science just as much as living plants. Of all European countries, Great Britain alone is in such a fortunate position as to be able to realise this idea easily.

The zoological garden in Edinburgh has been established for only three years, but it already contains a host of creatures of the highest interest and, moreover, a special building with the skeleton of a whale which, I think, is unique of its kind because of its size and completeness. It contains the smallest as well as the largest bone of this gigantic animal, perfectly cleaned, and the whole is so superbly hung in the room that the visitor here is given the most wonderful impression

---

[1] *Salisbury-Craigs*
[2] [This had been established in 1839 in Broughton, on land bounded by East Claremont Street/Bellevue Road/West Armadale Street. It closed in 1857.]

of this mighty son of nature. The skeleton is eighty foot long, and I doubt whether any European museum can boast of a similar specimen. Whalers cannot undertake the careful anatomical dissection of such an animal during their tempest-ridden voyages in the Arctic, and consequently one must wait until such time as a storm drives one of these creatures into sheltered waters in the vicinity of our museums and causes it to be stranded there. And even then it still may be rare that the stranding happens as providentially as in the case of this Edinburgh example which ran aground here on the Scottish coast on to *sand*, and in which even the little fin ossicle remained intact.

Something new can always be seen in these zoological gardens. Thus I was present at the feeding of a young seal, the whining and cries of hunger of which not every naturalist can pride himself on having heard. This animal had been caught on the northern coasts of Scotland and it had been brought hither in order to make an attempt at rearing it. I have never seen a more remarkable sight than the feeding of this creature, which was as ugly as the night and which lay like a serpent in the dog-kennel that had been constructed for it. Although it was only several months old and was only about three feet long – they had carried it off from its slain mother, on which it was still suckling – yet it proved to be as wild and as ill-tempered a suckling as I have ever seen, and there is no question but that suckling lions and bears of the same age are veritable lambs compared to such a young seal. The people who were to feed it held out a cudgel to it in its cage into which it immediately sank its teeth, and thus they pulled the creature out. It constantly snapped about it whenever anything approached it, and so forcefully that the striking together of its teeth and cheeks resounded afar. Fortunately, like a fish out of water, it was able only to move at a sluggish dragging crawl.

Although it was, as I said, a suckling, it was nevertheless so powerful that three strong men had to strain every nerve to feed it. Two of them seized it suddenly and skilfully by the ears and at the same time threw themselves on to its powerfully beating tail with their knees and, in doing so, had obviously to muster all their strength to keep hold of the little monster. The most unforgettable thing in all this was the frightful shrieking of this creature. For its cry sounded as piercing as that of a little child, but like that of a child that is screaming through an amplifying tube, that is, ten times louder and distorted nauseatingly. The most repugnant things in nature are imitations of the human form and of human sounds. In front of its snout the third man held out a broom handle into which it immediately fastened its teeth. He then poured the milk into the mouth thus opened wide. But as soon as the animal felt the milk, its fury appeared to redouble. It let go of the stick, writhed under the weight of the two big men quite pitifully, and squealed like a stuck pig. I must say that it was deserving of admiration. For it exhausted the strength of the men several times, so that they were forced to let it go, upon which it lay in the grass like a sack and spat out the milk. The men had probably been bidden to make it take some milk **à tout prix**, and they continually renewed their task until the milk bottle was empty. But I did not see that they succeeded in forcing the ferocious creature to keep down even a single drop. They themselves despaired that the attempt at feeding it would be successful. From what I had seen of this youngster, I fully understood what trouble a mother that is defending such a young animal must give to seal-hunters. One would have to travel about in Europe for a long time before one could, with such great ease, witness again the feeding and the wild behaviour of such a **'Seal'**.

A very strange habit while feeding is also demonstrated by a kind of bear from Borneo which the English call **'the sun bear'**[3]. As soon as this animal got its meat, it immediately rose up on its hind legs and with its front paws, with which it was bracing itself against the wall of its cage, held the meat so high up that it scarcely could get at it with its teeth. Then, in this uncomfortable posture it tore off one piece after the other and lay down again in comfort only when it had nothing left to eat. The keepers assured me that it adopted this procedure every time that it fed. I do not know whether

---

[3] [A small black bear, *Helarctos malayanus*, of South-east Asia.]

it was only a particular notion of this individual or whether it is a general habit of its kind to hang the bread basket so high of its own accord. Most other animals, for example tigers and lions, by contrast habitually always make themselves quite at ease whenever they feed.

The most unattractive feeders are eagles. Since they cannot bite meat into pieces with their beaks, they pull and tug it about in a terrifying way. When we chased them away from their food, which they did not in the least defend, there remained long sinews on their beaks and large scraps on their talons, with which they stupidly and inanely moved around in the dirt.

I was filled with astonishment by the great owls which, as long as daylight remained, touched nothing of the food allocated to them, although it lay under their very noses, so to speak, and although they certainly had an appetite. Here in their cage, too, they remained stubbornly faithful to their habit in the wild of eating only by night. The guides told me that they always fell upon their food, quite conscientiously, only when it was dark.

The Edinburgh zoological garden contains the largest, strongest and most magnificent American bison that I saw in Great Britain. Someone had had the idea of putting this mighty beast into one and the same enclosure with a bold, but in comparison feeble, billy-goat. The billy-goat was constantly at pains to tease its powerful fellow-prisoner and to challenge it to fight, and this confrontation afforded me one of the most interesting scenes, which confirmed for me the great general law of nature, namely, that strength is always more generous than weakness. Every now and then, when the billy-goat came bounding and attacked it, the bison simply lowered its immense hairy head. Nevertheless it adopted an attitude of complete readiness to fight, as though to please the other. Only occasionally did it growl and shake its horns, when the not exactly gentle nudges of its opponent met a more sensitive spot on its head. It even appeared to me that it had no little fear for its eyes, for it always blinked them and closed them when the goat butted it. No less was I astonished at the courage and the boldness of the latter. For, like a knight in a tournament, it came up intrepidly charging from the distance and leapt straight at the rough face of the buffalo, the appearance of which could indeed instil fear enough. Lions and small dogs have often been observed together in a similar manner. However, the association of buffalo and billy-goat was new to me.

Edinburgh has also a collection of natural objects that are dead, stuffed, dried or preserved in spirit, indeed so outstanding a collection that it is certainly the best in the three kingdoms after the collection in the British Museum, which it perhaps even surpasses as regards order and effective arrangement. This is the natural history collection of Edinburgh University[4]. The most splendid thing it possesses is firstly a wonderful collection of birds and then another equally very well stocked collection of phocae, for which, of course, the Edinburgh museum is especially favourably located, since the coasts on which those animals are caught lie in greater proximity to it than to any other significant European museum. Here there can be seen the finest examples of sea lions, seals, dugongs, walruses. One could spend whole days among the birds, revelling in natural historical delights. Here I examined the finest example of an eagle that I have ever seen. It is an eagle from Guiana (**Falco Destructor**) with a black nose, a crest on its head, with powerful talons and excellently stuffed, in an impressive pose, the most beautiful and picturesque expression of all that one imagines on hearing the name of this king of the birds.

The museums in the countries through which the visitor is travelling are indispensable to him for learning about these countries, for in them he sees those things that are rarest and most beautiful assembled in one place, whereas to search them all out in their proper habitat would be impossible.

---

[4] [This particular collection had been started in 1804 by Professor Robert Jameson and in 1812 was given the title *Royal Museum of the University* and moved to the newly built University Quadrangle.]

Thus I saw here, all gathered together, the different pelicans, geese and ducks which inhabit the Scottish coastland and the offshore islands round it, and to the nests of which many an arduous rock must be climbed before these birds can be examined at leisure. Here all the pale, white and greyish colours of their northern plumage stand in the most remarkable contrast to the dark and glowing tints of the southern climes, in which as colonists these northern Scots now kill just as many birds as on their own rocky islands. However, nature in the north has in its pale colours a magnificence that is, of course, less conspicuous, but more profound and even almost more admirable. Thus there is here a large snow owl from one of the Shetland Islands, the snow-white feathers of which, lightly speckled with brownish spots, are an unsurpassable masterpiece of gentle colouring and delicate plumage.

Of all the wild animals which Great Britain still nurtures nowadays, the wildest is the wild cat, which can be found in the Scottish Highlands, but the largest is the wild ox. There are specimens of both here. The wild ox came from the Duke of Hamilton's park, and it was the very image of those that I had seen in Staffordshire. The length of the animal, the shortness of its head, the breadth of its forehead, the fineness and the greyish-white colour of its hair – these were the same in both places. In the English ox and in the Scottish, the ears were similarly black. And the black patch, which covers the jaws like a plaster, was here as there outlined in exactly the same way. I find this complete unanimity of detail in both breeds very remarkable, since for many centuries they have lived separated from one another in areas wide apart. It demonstrates that these animals have completely retained their ancient untamed characteristics. Under the domesticating hand of man they certainly would have soon developed in a very different way.

Even now the hunting of the wild cat is still an occasional dangerous pastime of the mountain-dwellers. A Highlander told me that once he had shot off both forepaws of one of these animals with his first shot. Enraged, roaring like a lion, it had worked its way towards him unbelievably swiftly through the grass on its hind legs, and he had scarcely had time to inflict the second shot on the creature snarling for revenge, in order to kill it completely.

The Edinburgh museum is distinguished by so many features. Even the manner of exhibiting its fishes is worthy of imitation. They are not nailed to the wall, as is occasionally still the case in other museums, but pinned on to iron wires, so that they can be viewed in their entirety and from all sides. In addition, in the case of many animals the advantageous system is followed of storing them in a twofold manner, both dried and stuffed or immersed completely in alcohol. There are museums enough that are nothing more than collections of outer layers and skins. How far off are the majority still from having, beside every stuffed skin of an animal, its skeleton as well, and where possible also its intestines, stomach, entrails inflated and dried, and its heart, brain etc. preserved in spirit. By how much could we still improve our museums! How much judicious hunters could still do for our museums! If only it would occur to such a hunter to preserve a lion's stomach or a tiger's heart in alcohol and send it to Europe. That would be so easy! Such an object would excite much interest in every European museum, would find many viewers, far more than the badly stuffed skins. And yet it appears to occur to no one. One could describe a whole host more of such things that are easily obtainable and are nevertheless overlooked, if only the hunters would be amenable to instructions.

From the wonderful halls of the museum I was summoned by the sounds of bells to a university ceremony, to the opening of lectures for the winter term. The bells are in fact rung when the professors begin their procession across the great courtyard of the university building to the hall; at their head is their Principal[5], in front of whom, as a sign of his rank, is carried the silver university

---

[5] [John Lee (1779 – 1859), theologian, Doctor of Medicine, and polymath, was Principal of the University of Edinburgh from 1840 to 1859. He was Moderator of the General Assembly of the Church of Scotland in 1844.]

mace with a thick pommel. This was the first gathering of members of an English university that I had witnessed. In contrast to German students, those students all appeared so seemly and respectable, like a company of gentlemen in comparison with a gathering of frivolous, merry, carefree, boisterous, convivial lads. Many were also there with their patrician papas, who had travelled from the Highlands or Lowlands so that they themselves could induct their sons into the seat of the Muses here. The professors, depending on how popular they were, were greeted with more or less enthusiastic applause. I could see them coming from a distance and just from their physiognomy judged in advance whether they would be applauded or not; I was usually correct and realised that the preferences of German and English students must probably be quite similar. The greatest ovation greeted Wilson[6], the famous professor of political economy. Apart from that, the speeches that were delivered and the ceremonies were of no further interest.

Edinburgh, although now the most important, is however the youngest of the four Scottish universities; it was founded in 1583. The oldest, but now the most insignificant, is St Andrews, founded in 1410. The least important [sic] section[7] of the university is, as is well known, its medical school, while neither Aberdeen nor St Andrews signify much as regards medicine. In the past forty years the number of those **who graduated in Medicine** increased as follows: in 1806 there were only thirty-seven, in 1816 seventy-six, in 1826 one hundred and eighteen, in 1836 one hundred and twenty-three. From here on the number has been decreasing again somewhat. In Glasgow too in the last decades almost one hundred medical degrees were awarded annually. In the course of this century more than six new professorial **chairs** were endowed at each of the two universities. It is noteworthy that all these new chairs, with only two exceptions, were endowed by the Crown and then, of course, the Crown at the same time has the right of nomination to these posts. In general *all* posts at the universities of Glasgow and Edinburgh to which the Crown nominates the professors are of recent date, mostly from this and the second half of last century. I find this remarkable. For could we not discern therein an indication of the growth of the English government's influence on university affairs? In many respects this would not be without significance, for example because the universities also nominate Members of Parliament. The patron and selector of the more ancient professorial posts is either the **Town-council** – as in the case of most Edinburgh chairs – or the University Senate (**Faculty, Rector and Dean**), or a Duchess of Portland, or a Marquis of Ailsa, or Sir A. Ramsay of Balmain, or the College of Advocates or Notaries of Edinburgh.

Among the many fine buildings in Edinburgh one of the finest is that of the '**Royal Institution for the encouragement of the fine Arts in Scotland**'[8]. It is situated right in the middle of the city, between the New Town and the Old Town, quite isolated from other buildings, on the great **Earthen Mouth**[9] that stretches across the deep valley and connects the two parts of the city with one another. The building is executed in the most beautiful Greek style and is built of the most solid stones. The collection of artefacts that it contains is more important than that of the similar institute in London. In the same building is the museum of the Society of Antiquaries[10] of Scotland. If the completeness of our German museums of natural history seems somewhat pitiable, then that of our antiquarian and historical museums is truly lamentable. However, Nature always remains the same, and we can

---

[6] [At that time, Political Economy was part of the Moral Philosophy course. The professor in question was John Wilson of Ellerey (1785 – 1854), Professor of Moral Philosophy from 1820 to 1851. He was also an advocate and a prolific literary critic and author, one of the main contributors (as 'Christopher North') to Blackwood's Magazine. In 1865 a statue of him was erected in Princes Street Gardens.]

[7] [The German text reads *die unwichtigste* (= 'the most unimportant'), presumably either this is a slip for *die wichtigste* (= 'the most important') or a *nicht* (= 'not') has been omitted.]

[8] [Built in 1826, it is now the Royal Scottish Academy.]

[9] [Properly *Mound*.]

[10] [Founded in 1780 and incorporated by Royal Charter in 1783.]

still find most objects and animals just as they existed with Adam in Paradise on the morning of Creation. And if at the present time we are not making a complete collection of things, then our children's children can still hope to accomplish this, for in Nature nothing, or only little, becomes lost since everything reproduces itself again in the same way.

On the other hand, in the history of mankind, almost nothing repeats itself. Almost everything becomes lost, and only sad fragments remain behind. Let us just consider everything that a complete historical museum of a country would have to contain – all those portable things and objects which have any relevance at all for the history of the country and are at the same time capable of being stored, together with facsimiles of those objects that do not lend themselves to storage in a museum. In such a historical museum – as it ought to be, as it in part also could be, as it however nowhere yet exists – one would therefore have to encounter, for example, a sequence of models of the dwelling houses of the inhabitants of the country. From them could be seen how these inhabitants lived at first in caves and huts of foliage, how they later moved into wooden and stone houses, how these houses were furnished in antiquity, how in the Middle Ages, how at the present time, how in the Highlands, how in the Lowlands, how the houses of the common people were furnished, how the houses of the chieftains. Such models would instruct the public better than all the antiquarians' laborious descriptions. Then specimens would have to be available of all clothes and weapons and tools that had been in use in the country from the beginning, chronologically ordered. In how few of the museums that call themselves historical can we find even an attempt at a crude chronological ordering of the exhibits! There ought to be portraits there of all the important men of the nation, of all their kings, military commanders, lawgivers etc. Wherever possible, there should also be preserved a piece of clothing belonging to each of these men or an instrument that he himself used. Those instruments, with which anything at all important and successful was achieved, should themselves be there **in natura**, for example all the daggers, arranged in order, with which kings were murdered – all the warhorses of Cromwell, Napoleon or similar heroes, stuffed – all the seals which were affixed to great peace treaties – all the principal banners and standards that the commanders displayed in the most outstanding battles in which the country was liberated – whenever possible also phrenological cranial casts of all the heads of great philosophers who lived in the country.

If we think thus and reflect even further on everything that a historical museum ought to contain, then we cannot but reproach historians and antiquarians of every period for not having more carefully considered and collected that which could be of interest to posterity, and those at the present time for not being more industrious in at least assembling and storing what there is to be assembled and stored. I believe that such a general historical museum, where for example every room would contain its century, every display table its decade, does not yet exist anywhere. Only with regard to isolated sections, to weapons, to statues, paintings etc. has this been accomplished. And yet it is indisputable that not only certain isolated branches of the sciences and the arts, but also general political and cultural history equally justifiably could have, and ought to have, their comprehensive museums.

I maintain that while we exclaim 'how negligent these antiquaries and historians!', we must also exclaim 'how unfortunate!'. Envious Fate leaves them but few scraps and remnants of prehistory, and the storms that agitate the sea of humanity often greedily engulf all signs of it, leaving only the last vestiges. How many millions of people from different tribes, clad in all manner of fascinating clothing, did not tread on Scottish soil before Roman times? What quantities of woollen and linen cloth, of skins of sheep and other animals, of iron, bronze and other metals did they not use? And if ever, from all the relics of all those primeval Scottish inhabitants, merely an old leather sandal is found preserved in the depths of a Scottish bog, then a great cry of rejoicing goes up on account of it, and thenceforward in the historical museum that old sandal will represent all those periods of history which are lost to our sight.

And after them, the Romans – how long did they not struggle and wreak havoc in Scotland under Agricola and other famous commanders? The uniforms of their Scottish legions, a piece of Agricola's armour, models of their encampments, and many other similar things would be essential components of a historical museum of Scotland. Instead of that, what do we find here to represent or illustrate the Roman period? **'A Roman camp-kettle'**, likewise unearthed in a **'Peat-Moss'**.

All the famous men of Scotland, like all famous men generally in the world – how infinitely many objects did they not sanctify, so to speak, by touching them or by putting them to use? How many rings, how many brooches, how many hats, boots, coats, shirts, scarves did they not use, and how happy would they not have made posterity if only they had once in a while bequeathed to it a few items from their immense wardrobes! **Queen Mary**, for example, that beloved Queen – what immense collections could not her ladies-in-waiting have established of things that would have been invaluable to posterity and a most highly useful gift to their own descendants and heirs? And what remains now of her possessions? Nothing more than a pair of gloves with black embroidery, a key of Loch Leven Castle, which locked her prison door and the door of her prayer-room.

Let us just vividly imagine the battlefield of Bannockburn as it appeared on the twenty-fourth of June 1314 after the conclusion of the battle. Thirty thousand Englishmen[11] lay slain there, seven hundred English knights, the flower of the English nobility, all with their costly armour and weapons. How many thousands of swords, helmets, daggers, arrows were scattered on that battlefield! How many horses had perished, trapped in the holes dug by Bruce! How many English battle trumpets, how many Highland military bagpipes! If a thoughtful Scottish antiquary had walked around there at the right time, what a wealth of precious relics would he not have been able to collect for the Scottish **'Society of Antiquaries'**, for the reliquaries of a host of great English families who here had lost their uncles and cousins or their heirs, so full of promise However, the tempest of time has blown away that whole immense collection of historical relics at Bannockburn even to the last equine bone. And what is to be seen of all these things in the Scottish historical collection? Nothing. At least, I do not recall have seen anything at all of them. And should not we rightly be entitled to expect that something, in chronological sequence, should be shown at least of the most important of those battles that the Scottish bards and historians celebrate and depict as unforgettable – a group of little relics of the Battle of Bannockburn, a group from the Battle of Falkirk, a group from the Battle of Culloden, a group from the event at Killiekrankie etc.? Of all that, nothing.

In our imagination, let there pass before our eyes all the murder weapons by which men of high position in Scotland lost their lives – the daggers, swords, axes, cannonballs, which split asunder the skulls, entrails and hearts of the various royal Stuarts, Wallaces, Bruces, Darnleys, Rizzios, Bothwells, Montroses etc. What an array would this not provide to stimulate our imagination! How solitary and alone therefore stands there in that museum one single, but of course remarkable, instrument of execution called **'the Maiden'**! It is a type of guillotine that the Earl of Morton[12] brought to Scotland from Italy and with which he, who had introduced it, was first put to death, and after him the Marquis of Argyle, Sir Robert Spottiswood and many other persons of distinction.

How many combs were there in Scotland, I wonder, that once held in place distinguished hair, and which we would have liked to preserve? But we have only one, of course one of the most

---

[11] [See Chapter XXII, fn. 14.]
[12] [James Douglas, 4th Earl of Morton (ca 1516 – 1581), Regent of Scotland (1572 - 1580), executed for alleged complicity in the murder of Darnley.]

extraordinary, which is nine and a half inches long and six and a half inches broad, and which kept in place the long hair of Charles I's head, severed under the executioner's axe.

Of course, there are still so many things in this museum that I have not been able to mention even the most interesting. Incidentally, the Scottish antiquaries could probably regard some things among them as antiquated and therefore remove them from this historical museum, for example the splendid family tree of the Scottish kings, which began with **King Fergus I** who **anno mundi 3641**[13] began to reign in Caledonia and was a contemporary of Alexander the Great.

The last exhibition and the most recent source of wonder that I visited in Edinburgh was the exhibition of the '**Highland- and Agricultural Society**'[14]. This society and its extended activities are so remarkable that those of my readers in Germany who as yet know as little of it as I myself knew before I came to Edinburgh, will certainly welcome the account that I am able to give. This extraordinary society was founded in 1784 at a time in which people began to engage in the cultivation of the barbarous Highlands, which previously had formed an isolated area of Europe. Its aim was principally the cultivation of this region; in a like manner, in London at about the same time (in 1778), the **Highland-Society**[15] also came into being; and since then several societies have likewise been formed that direct their attention to the Highlands in other connections, such as '**the Highland Missionary Society**'[16], such as '**the Highland Club of Scotland**'[17], which, let it be remarked in passing, even has its own manufacturers of tartan and its own '**Pipers**'.

Later, however, as a great general movement took hold of Scottish agriculture, the '**Highland and Agricultural Society**' extended its activities and its schemes over the whole of Scotland and over the whole of Great Britain and placed itself virtually at the head of this movement. It is constituted under a President, four Vice-presidents, ten Extraordinary and thirty Ordinary Directors. The President of the Society used to be the Duke of Sutherland. Now, however, it is the Duke of Richmond, one of the most influential agriculturalists in Great Britain. To begin with, the Society had as its aim the promotion of all kinds of beneficial rural enterprise. Since, however, societies for herring fishing and for other similar branches of activity were later formed, it finally restricted itself simply to agriculture, but interpreting this in all its ramifications. Many local associations, which were formed not only in all Scottish towns but also, following their example, in several English ones, established links with it.

In order to fulfil their aim of propagating better agricultural knowledge and practice, the Society has set up a museum which is open to everyone, publishes a journal in which are made public those papers submitted to it, and maintains a constant correspondence with similar associations and leading agriculturalists. In addition, however – and this is its most important activity – it offers annually a series of prizes for appropriate new inventions of agricultural implements, for farming uncultivated land or extending cultivated areas, for developing breeds of farm animals, for the promotion of certain domestic products connected with agriculture, for encouraging industry among the lower agricultural classes and for the improvement of their lot etc.

---

[13] ['in the year 3641 since the world began']

[14] [Established in 1784 as The Highland Society of Edinburgh, it changed its name in 1834 to The Highland and Agricultural Society of Scotland. In 1948 it became The Royal Highland and Agricultural Society of Scotland.]

[15] [The Highland Society of London was formed in 1778 to campaign for the repeal of the Act of Proscription of 1747 (see Introduction p. xx). After this aim was achieved, it continued with the aims of preserving the Gaelic language and Highland culture, and of improving life in the Highlands.]

[16] [No record of an organisation with this name has been found, though organisations such as the Society in Scotland for the Propagation of Christian Knowledge (founded in 1709) and the Northern Missionary Society (1800 – 1843) were active in evangelising the Highlands; perhaps the latter is meant.]

[17] [No record of an organisation with this name has been found.]

These prizes on offer are announced annually in a small brochure so that all may learn about them. Last year's brochure listing these prizes is an octavo volume of no fewer than eighty large pages and hence is a remarkable little object in itself. I cannot help but make known to my German readers some details from it, because they will see to what a degree and in what a liberal manner all divisions and sub-divisions of agriculture are kept in view and encouraged. I believe that in that respect this Scottish society is surpassed by no other in the world. And to give an impression of this, it will suffice to draw attention to some of those prizes that go into most detail.

An award of five hundred guineas is promised to whoever first shows how steam power may usefully and effectively be introduced into ploughing or harrowing.

Twenty guineas for a lotion for sheep which will protect them against the cold and damp of the Scottish climate as effectively as does rubbing them with tar, yet at the same time will not harm the wool.

The Gold Medal, or ten sovereigns, for whoever successfully demonstrates cross-breeding between Leicester and Cheviot sheep, or between Oost'vold[18] and Cheviot. (Since there is a multitude of such breeds of sheep and different results are obtained by cross-breeding between them all, it is obvious from this into what great detail the Society goes in this connection, since no type of cross-breeding is neglected.)

Fifty sovereigns for the best treatise that demonstrates the effect of certain types of fertiliser on certain types of Scottish soil.

Five sovereigns for whoever demonstrates the different use and effectiveness of scythe and of sickle in reaping corn.

Twenty sovereigns for the most satisfactory report on an experiment with farm horses concerning how these can be fed in the cheapest and most effective way.

Fifty sovereigns for the most exact geological description of a Scottish county.

Thirty sovereigns for the most complete mineralogical report on one of the Scottish coal-districts.

Forty sovereigns for the clearest and most accessible report on the most practical construction of farm-carts.

Ten sovereigns for an apparatus with which fattened cattle may be weighed at market most easily and quickly.

Ten sovereigns for the improvement of grazing on fifty acres of moorland.

Five sovereigns for the best batch of early-ripening peas.

Five sovereigns for the biggest batch of late-ripening peas, and then likewise a similar prize for every batch of the best of all kinds of crops and grain is promised. In the same way there is a prize for the best example of not only every kind of cattle, but also of every single breed of every kind of cattle. Indeed there is a prize for almost every age-group of every breed.

---

[18] [i.e. sheep from Oosterwolde in Friesland, The Netherlands.]

Travels in Scotland (1840) by J.G. Kohl

Sixteen different prizes for the best sheep-fleeces of different kinds.

Certain districts that are still very unprogressive are always particularly borne in mind. Thus there are special prizes for the Orkney Islands, special ones for the Isle of Mull etc.

Thirty-two different prizes for the cleanest and best kept farm cottages and farm gardens of which the annual rent does not exceed five pound sterling, in thirty-two different Scottish districts. The annually repeated prizes of this class must be of immense benefit to the country.

Ten pounds for the best report on the best method of heating farm dwellings.

A series of eight prizes for the workers in eight different districts who at a pre-arranged digging competition use the spade most skilfully.

A series of nine different prizes for different plantings of trees, for example for the best wood of a certain size laid out on piece of land that is at least six hundred feet above sea level, another for the best kept nursery of woodland trees.

All these things may give my readers a slight idea of the degree and extent of care with which this remarkable Society includes and promotes in its purview all branches of agriculture. Let us look at the past and reflect that throughout long, long centuries – we can say until 1746 – the offer of no prize was heard of in Scotland other than that of rewards for the bringing in of certain prisoners, alive or dead, for the bringing in of this or that human head, of this or that right hand and the like. And let us now look into the future and at the beneficial influences that those offers of prizes, now common in Scotland, must have. Considering these facts, we surely cannot help but rejoice at such a prospect of generations-to-be that will flourish here; and we shall surely bless the activity of a Society that labours so effectively to improve the foundations of human fellowship, the techniques of farming, and the agricultural classes.

The museum of this Society, in which all the agricultural implements invented in Scotland are deposited either **in natura** or as small models, is full of the most interesting objects. For the German reader who is curious about innovations and thirsty for knowledge and who cannot visit this museum himself, I shall select several of those objects that I myself saw there.

Different types of '**thrashing mills**' as the English call them. Some of these are powered by horses, others by steam. Already there are many leased farms in Scotland where threshing is carried out by steam.

'**Churns**', as the English call them. They can be found in many Scottish farms powered by water or, as I was assured, also by steam.

Very simply and beautifully constructed little '**Lactometers**' which are becoming increasingly common in all Scottish '**Dairies**'. The simplest are hollow little glass balls which sink more or less deeply into the milk, depending on its density or fat content.

Reaping machines which at the same time press down the grain, cut it off with a large number of little shears underneath and throw it to the side in heaps.

'**Sweeping machines**' for chimneys, the effective construction of which is at this very moment occupying inventive English brains, since by an Act of Parliament of recent years it is forbidden to employ for this purpose small boys, who previously were used as machines.

Besides a countless number of similar and other apparatuses, the same things can also be found here to which I already referred in the Drummonds' Stirling museum, displays of fruit and all manner of country produce. The gentlemen who had the courtesy to conduct me around, gave me everywhere the most interesting account of each object. About wheat, for example, they explained that the wonderful, fine and dry year of 1842 – for Scotland and Ireland a *dry* and warm year is always a *fine* one – would play a particularly important role in the increasing cultivation of wheat. They said that in this year a greater area of land had been planted with wheat than in previous years, since the farmers had been encouraged to do so by the weather. Because of this, wheat was therefore also increasingly ousting barley. The latter had also declined further because of some changes in the customs tariff, and particularly because of the decrease in the distillation of spirits for which it had been especially grown. They also told me that, as the establishment of improved Scottish agriculture could be traced to the time of the Union of the two kingdoms (1706[19]) and even more so to the time of the dissolution of the clan system in the Highlands (1746), so too its latest extraordinary development and its most recent progress dated from the Reform Bill[20]. The great excitement over the question of Reform, which had dominated the country at the end of the twenties and at the beginning of the thirties, had deflected the thoughts of everyone from agriculture since everyone was occupied with politics. Only since the resolution of this question and the calming of passions had the majority of the fine Scottish collections that I had seen come into being, together with most of the agricultural museums and the greatest improvements and reforms of the last ten years generally.

Recently many small branches of Scottish agriculture have achieved greater prosperity and importance because of the extraordinary expansion and acceleration of transport, especially because of steamships, which now increasingly link all the large and small Scottish ports with London and the other great English markets and make it possible for them to send to these markets much country produce, even types of vegetables, from such a great distance.

Among the different objects of interest that this museum contained, what particularly interested me was a palm-tree that had been washed up some months ago on the west coast of Scotland in Argyllshire[21] and by all appearances had floated across from South American regions, perhaps from Mexico. It seemed that it must have spent a very long time in the sea, for it was very heavy and hard, and everywhere in the indentations, from which the leaves of the tree grew out, it was studded with small, deeply embedded, shellfish. They told me that it was precisely on the coast of the above-named county that such emissaries, washed ashore from southern climes, were more numerous than in other areas of Scotland. If this is true, as I believe, then a subsidiary branch of that great oceanic movement that the English succinctly call '**the Gulfstream**' must flow towards this part of Scotland. With its far-reaching islands and arms, the above-mentioned county extends as far as the opening of the Irish Sea into which, as I already noticed in Ireland, there flows an oceanic current.

So much for the *practical* arts. Of the *fine* arts I saw less in Edinburgh. The numerous splendid portraits in Holyrood House I have already mentioned, likewise the hundred Scottish kings painted from one and the same insipid paint-box. In the University Library I saw a delightful little collection of paintings[22] by Old Masters which, I think, contains the finest that Edinburgh can offer

---

[19] [The Treaty of Union was approved by the Scottish Parliament in 1706 and by the English Parliament in 1707.]
[20] [See Introduction p. xiii and p. 10.]
[21] *Argyle-shire*
[22] [This was the Torrie Collection which came to the University in 1836 and was hung in the Library, probably on the Library staircase. It is now in the Talbot Rice Gallery of the University.]

of this genre. Among them are several enchanting Hobbemas[23] and Ruisdaels[24]. Then they led me to an **'Ornamental Painter'** whose exhibition, they told me, **'is allowed to be a select collection'**[25]. I believe that the paintings were all by recent Scottish artists. However, I must admit that the little **'knitting girl'** that I saw here left me completely without any interest; painted fruit was shown to me and the last thing to which it tempted me was to bite into it; landscapes revealed themselves to my eyes and by no means did I feel the desire rising in me to dwell in them; I could not have imagined anything less than to hear the smack of the kisses of the loving couple who were embracing. (There are some admirers of paintings who regard it as the highest expression of praise if they hear all the singers portrayed singing, all speakers speaking, all painted cannons firing, all painted rivers murmuring, and all painted kisses smacking.) Indeed I was even hard-hearted enough to refuse the hoary old harpist the little gift of my approbation.

In contrast to these, the same **'Ornamental painter'** had a **'collection of painted woods'** that could be described as unique of its kind. I must admit that in truth I know no country in which this branch of the painter's art flourishes as it does in England. Here I saw different kinds of timber, such as rosewood, oak, pine, and their graining and cell construction so splendidly imitated that the finished products could only be called masterly, and so deceptive that they could scarcely be distinguished from nature. What I saw here was the ultimate in this genre; but as a rule every English house-painter understands how to imitate all natural woods admirably well, and this kind of painting in English houses, rooms, landings, on house doors, cellar doors, banisters etc is more common than in any other country.

No little interest was afforded to me by the different Edinburgh art shops and copperplate engraving shops, in which I found many objects that greatly promised to contribute to the increase of my knowledge of the country, for example a pretty picture that represented Scottish curlers[26] who were playing on an icy surface that favourite Scottish game that I mentioned – a copperplate engraving that represented the Scottish **'Snapapplenight'** or **'All-Hallow Eve'** (2nd November[27]). The amusements on that evening consist principally in skilfully plucking up apples in one's teeth from a bucket of water. And this pastime is equally commonplace in Scotland and Ireland and the North of England. In most shops I found copperplate engravings that depicted Calvin's death. This man is almost more highly regarded in Scotland than in Switzerland itself. Nowadays an unbelievable number of such pictures and portrayals from the time of the Reformation of the Scottish church are made, sold and disseminated among the people in copperplate engravings, woodcuts and lithographs. It is remarkable what pains are taken to avoid in those pictures all such objects as, in the opinion of Presbyterians, could contain an allusion to **'the superstitions of popery'**. For example, no Scottish Presbyterian would buy the picture of an apostle or a saint around whose head was a halo. There are great illuminated popular broadsheets on which is written: **'the witnesses for the truth in the church of Scotland'**. On these sheets are then shown in a series of little woodcuts a great number of scenes from the period of the Scottish Reformation[28] – the burning of Patrick Hamilton,

[23] [Meindert Hobbema (1638 – 1709). His masterpiece 'The Avenue, Middelharnis' greatly influenced landscape painters.]
[24] [Jacob van Ruïsdael or Ruysdael (1628 – 1682). One of the greatest landscape and seascape painters of the Dutch school and Hobbema's teacher.]
[25] [The term 'ornamental painter' usually meant a painter-decorator, one of whose skills was wood-graining.]
[26] [This is most probably 'The Curlers' by George Harvey (1806 – 76).]
[27] [This may be a reproduction of 'Snap-Apple Night', a popular painting by the Irish artist Daniel Maclise dating from 1833 and depicting a Hallowe'en party. In the right foreground five people are ducking for apples. Hallowe'en is celebrated on 31 October, the eve of All Saints' Day. It is All Souls' Day that is celebrated on 2 November.]
[28] [Patrick Hamilton (ca 1498 – 1528) was burnt as a heretic in St Andrews, an event which precipitated the Reformation in Scotland. Robert Lamb was executed in Perth in 1543 on account of his Protestant beliefs. Thomas Forrest, Augustinian canon and vicar of Dollar, Clackmannanshire, was burnt as a heretic on Castlehill, Edinburgh, in February 1539/40. John Welsh may be John Welsh (ca 1570 – 1622 or his grandson John Welsh (?1624 – 81) both Reformed preachers, though neither was martyred. Samuel Rutherford (1600? -1661) was a Presbyterian minister who

of Robert Lamb, of Thomas Forrest and other martyrs who refused to pray to the saints, and who advocated the reading of Holy Writ and went to the stake on that account – John Knox's sermon – John Welsh's prayer – Samuel Rutherford in prison, and the like. Do our members of the Reformed Church in Germany have similar broadsheets?

* * * * * *

(because of the constantly changing politico-religious climate) was successively forbidden to preach, then appointed Professor of Divinity at St Andrews, and finally charged with treason just before his death.]

XXIV
From Edinburgh to Carlisle

My last breakfast of fish and scone was consumed in the company of an old gentleman who had come the previous evening by way of Glasgow from Liverpool and intended to return thither. At breakfast he told me that things in Liverpool were still **'very dull'** ('very ??' – the word 'dull' cannot be satisfactorily translated into German). **'Nothing going on.' 'No movement in the docks.' 'A complete standing still of all things.'** He told me that he had gone as far as Glasgow by ship and had had **'a very rough night and boisterous sea'** (these words too cannot be translated), **'she rolled tremendously'**. By 'she' was meant the ship. He had not yet uttered the antecedent to this pronoun. But the English always speak thus. And if there is talk of a **'She'** on the sea, nothing other than the ship can be intended.

It was five o'clock in the morning. Since it threatened to become a very foggy and rainy day we took inside[1] places, but remained as long **outside** as was at all possible.

There are only two principal ways to cross from Scotland into England. One road leads along the east coast by way of Berwick, and the second to the west coast by way of Carlisle. In fact, that part of the Cheviot Hills[2] that stretches along the very border between England and Scotland has in all likelihood impeded and made impossible any significant development of highways here in the centre of the country, in the same way as have the Pyrenees between Spain and France; around them likewise both main connecting roads lead along the coasts past the extreme ends of that mountain range, one between Bayonne and St Sebastian and one between Perpignan and Gerona. If we just look at a Scottish road map, we will find that all Scottish roads[3] centre either on Carlisle or on Berwick, just as all the water courses join together either eastwards in the River Tweed on the border or westwards in the River Esk on the border[4].

I believe that the majority of travellers between England and Scotland go by way of Berwick. However, I chose the road by Carlisle because I hoped to find something special in the famous cathedral of Carlisle and also because I thought it pleasant to travel by railway across the country from Carlisle to Newcastle[5] by the edge of the ancient Wall against the Picts. Furthermore, it is a wondrously beautiful stretch of land that lies between Edinburgh and Carlisle and even in rainy weather a journey between these lovely valleys and hills affords enjoyment enough.

At first the road completely traverses Midlothian or Edinburghshire which, with its wheat fields and its splendid **'Ayrshire Cows'**, produces milk, butter and bread for the country's royal capital. Through many attractive varying scenes of country estates, factories, villages, fields, meadows, copses, we finally came, at the extreme end of the county, into the valley of the River Gala, the young men of which Burns regards as superior to all the young men of the neighbouring valleys when he sings:

> **'There's braw braw lads on Yarrow braes**
> **That wander through the blooming heather;**
> **But Yarrow braes, nor Ettrick shaws,**

---

[1] [See Chapter X, fn. 2.]
[2] *Cheviots-Hills*
[3] [Not all; only those main roads leading to England.]
[4] [This is misleading: the configurations and drainage areas of the Rivers Esk and Tweed are very different.]
[5] *New-Castle*

Can match the lads o' Gala Water.'[6]

The whole valley of the Gala Water, like most of the valleys in the Cheviot Hills (which now lay before us), has the appearance of a pleasant bright district of pastures and meadows. If farming is not as extensive as farther north in Lothian near Edinburgh, Nature, on the other hand, is not as wild as she is in the Highland glens. Hence there is also an old Scottish song that again, like the poem of Burns, praises the '**Gala-lads**'; it runs:

> '**Lothian lads are black wi' reek**
> **And Teviotdale lads are little better;**
> **But the black eyed lass a Gallashiels**
> **Wad hae none, but the gree o' Gala Water.'**[7]

Galashiels is a small town in which two individuals are said to have been still alive in 1836 who could remember that all the houses in the town, with the exception of two, had been built in their lifetimes. It is woollen weaving mills that have made this pretty little town expand so quickly. A whole host of such towns could nowadays be mentioned that have recently appeared in the valleys of the Cheviot Hills.

Among the reasons that caused me to choose the road to Carlisle rather than that to Berwick was also that I wanted to get out of the coach at Galashiels, and from there visit first the splendid ruins of the famous abbeys of Melrose and Jedburgh, and then Abbotsford. Unfortunately, however, this desire and plan came to nothing. The rain and the mist were too impenetrable, and – as the traveller not only is often forced to make sacrifices on journeys, but also learns to make them effortlessly – I left those beautiful ruins lying shrouded in the mist in which they lay nearby. From everything that I have heard of them, I shall always have to regret that I did not visit them; for they are said to be the finest that Great Britain possesses of their kind.

Abbotsford, too, I had to leave unvisited in order to travel further with the coach on the same day. It lies on the River Tweed at little more than a distance of a few rifle shots from the road. We could see it quite distinctly. Tweed, Gala Water, Yarrow and Ettrick and all the pretty valleys of these rivers meet near here from different directions. All these valleys are celebrated in the history of the border hills, and obviously the area is a kind of notable and established focal point for these uplands. The abbeys of Melrose, Jedburgh and Dryburgh, the towns of Selkirk and Galashiels are situated in the vicinity. Without doubt this influenced Scott in the choice of the purchase and building of his Abbotsford, for which until his dying breath he maintained as ardent a love as he did for the entire surrounding countryside, almost every spot of which he had celebrated in verse and immortalised.

Incidentally – a fact that perhaps may not be known to all my German readers – the Scotts were and are still one of the most powerful and distinguished, extensive and numerous clans in this district. There is even at this moment a famous Walter Scott, who, they say, can without a doubt spend somewhat more money on his country seat than the modest owner of Abbotsford; for he is the richest man in Scotland, and he is estimated to be annually worth no less than two hundred thousand pounds sterling, an income that is surpassed by no other Scottish person of repute. The complete

---

[6] [Burns's 'Braw Lads o Galla Water'. The author gives an accurate prose translation in a footnote. The published version is 'Braw, braw lads on Yarrow braes, / They rove amang the blooming heather; / But Yarrow braes nor Ettrick shaws / Can match the lads o Galla Water.']

[7] [Printed as in the German text. Again, the author gives a prose translation in a footnote. It has not been possible to discover where the author found this 'old song'. The first two lines accord with the version published in Chambers' collection of Scottish songs of 1829, but in that, the third and fourth lines run 'Let them a' say what they will, / The gree gaes ay doun Galla Water'.]

name of this Walter Scott runs as follows: **'Walter Francis Douglas-Scott, Duke of Buccleugh'**[8], and under that last title he is known throughout the length and breadth of Scotland and England. He it was who received the Queen of England last year so dazzlingly at his family seat of Dalkeith near Edinburgh. I think that he is regarded as the chief of the entire House of Scott. However, there are other Scotts in the Scottish peerage, for example, Baron Polwarth.

The Scotts have preserved the original Irish tribal name of the 'Scots', which, originating in Ireland, later became applied to the whole nation. With the exception of the Scotts, the Douglases, and several more, most of the other ancient names of the untamed Border clans appear to be not, like the greater number of Highland clans, of Celtic or Gaelic origin but of Germanic. Indeed, the Gaelic language has, for a long time, not been heard anywhere in these southern Border hills of Scotland, and now but few names of towns, mountains and rivers here are still Gaelic.

I was very upset that circumstances did not allow me to pay a visit to the romantic dwelling of that poetic spirit. 'You may console yourself, Sir!' observed one of our inside passengers to me, after he had taken off his right leg in the interests of comfort and had propped it behind him in the corner of the coach – it was in fact a wooden leg. 'Console yourself, Sir! Indeed there are prettier country seats here in Scotland than this Abbotsford, and if you have seen Taymouth Castle, Dunkeld and Dalkeith, then you may pass by here without misgiving. Walter Scott, whom I myself knew, bought this house as a small-holding on which he built himself at first only a very small and cramped dwelling-house. The greater his means became, the more he extended his living-quarters, and finally it became this irregular and strange little country-house that you see before you now. Furthermore, the house is now no longer even in the condition in which the so-called 'great unknown' (or rather the 'great well known') left it. And at the end of the day I really do not understand why people now are so incredibly avid for mementoes and relics of Walter Scott. Believe me, the fame and adulation of Walter Scott, like the fame and adulation of all famous people, has been exaggerated to an unbelievable extent. What was Sir Walter after all? He was **'Clerk of the Writers to the signet'**[9], that is, secretary of the college of notaries in Edinburgh. Did I not see him every morning coming out of the Parliament House in Edinburgh and down the hill? There was absolutely nothing of the English gentleman about him, nothing so refined and distinguished. On the contrary, he had a truly rough, commonplace, old Scottish face, small eyes, a very round, big, fleshy nose which always appeared somewhat swollen. And he did not at all look as intelligent as people always imagine him. Rather his thick, rather slack lips gave him a somewhat stupid appearance. In addition, he had big feet and limped a little. When he met you, he always gave you a very uncouth Scottish greeting. **'How d'ye *do*, sir?'** he always said quite coarsely, laying the whole stress of the accent on the **'do'**, like the common people. Actually, he could not pronounce **'r'** very well, and he turned it almost into a **'ch'**, rapping it out from deep in the back of his mouth. When he wanted to say **'rock'**, it sounded almost like **'cock'**. In a word, if the good man were not dead, and if you could see him as I have described him to you, striding out in his old rough green overcoat with big metal buttons that he habitually wore at Abbotsford, you would believe you were looking at a farmer rather than a poet.'

Not far from Abbotsford, no more than about three English miles away, we reached the pleasant small town of Selkirk, which is old and quite famous in the Border skirmishes between England and Scotland. Apart from that, renowned were also its shoemakers[10]. From that period dates the ancient custom that, before their admission, the new burgesses of the town have to clean a bundle of pigs' bristles that afterwards is sewn on to their burgess ticket. The sole exception to this unpleasant task

---

[8] [Nowadays *Buccleuch*.]

[9] [See Chapter IV, fn. 33.]

[10] [The shoemakers of Selkirk supplied over half the 6000 pairs of shoes required in 1745 by the army in Edinburgh.]

that has been allowed was made in favour of one of their most recent burgesses, Duke Leopold of Saxe-Coburg, the present King of the Belgians.[11]

From the County of Selkirk we entered the County of Roxburgh, which is an **'inland county'** and not a **'maritime county'**. The English habitually mention this in the case of every county, according as whether it is totally surrounded by land or borders the sea[12]. It is a completely hilly county. In it, in a village called Kirk Yetholm[13], lives the biggest colony of Scottish gypsies. In all there are said to be one hundred of them here. In other parts of Scotland too there are several such colonies of gypsies, but not as large. They are said to have still preserved their dark complexion, their nomadic customs and their characteristic language.

The rivers of this county, which is also simply called **Teviotdale** after its main river, the Teviot, all flow into the Tweed. The Tweed marks the boundary between Scotland and England in fact only along a stretch of not quite three German miles[14], and hence the reader will perhaps scarcely understand why it is so famous and is so often mentioned in the history of the two kingdoms as forming the boundary between these relatively large kingdoms. (I mean 'relatively large' in relation to a stretch of river, marking the boundary, of three German miles). Indeed it is so regarded to such an extent that even now the English and the Scots are still described as the people on this side and on that side of the Tweed. If one says 'this side and that side of the Rhine' for Germany and France, 'this side and that side of the Pyrenees' for Spain and France, then that is understandable for there is a comparable relationship between what is divided and what divides. But I believe that in no other instance were two such *large* countries separated by such a *short* river. The entire border between Scotland and England is fifteen miles long. The Tweed therefore is the boundary of only a fifth part of this. The Cheviot Hills run along the greater part of the border. It appears that it would have been much more natural to determine the partition according to *them*. However, the two nations have simply continued to lay stress on the above mentioned short stretch of river with extraordinary perseverance and great stubbornness.

It is almost as though all ill-will and all enmity between England and Scotland had been cast on to the district round this short stretch of river and in fact on to its entrance to the sea, the town of Berwick. This was the eternally sore spot and an incessant bone of contention between both kingdoms, and indeed so much so that, when both crowns were united, King James[15] did not dare decide to which of the two countries the town should belong. He wished to stir up neither the discontent of the Scots, who regarded Berwick as their worthy ancient legitimate property because it lay on this side of the Tweed and since ancient times had belonged to Scotland, nor that of the English, who had captured the town from the Scots and for long years had occupied it. Therefore the town of Berwick was granted a certain independence; all laws that were enacted either for England or for Scotland and did not include this town explicitly and by name, had no relevance to it. This may account for the fact that Berwick has such an exceptional appearance and resembles no other English town. There are other such examples in history where the hostilities between two great nations finally centred for a long time on only one point, as, for example on Calais in the case of France and England. Therefore, since most quarrels about the border centred on the Tweed, it

---

[11] [The custom of the new burgess dipping three or four pigs bristles in wine and then passing them through his lips was not ancient and may have been the invention of Walter Scott. It was indeed omitted in 1819 in the case of Prince Leopold of Saxe-Coburg.]

[12] [The County of Selkirk was also entirely surrounded by land.]

[13] [Yetholm was home to the Faa family, the 'royal house' of Scottish gypsies. At the time of the author's visit to Scotland, the 'King' of the Yetholm gypsies was William Faa II, who reigned from 1784 to 1847.]

[14] [A German mile was roughly 7,420 metres, a statute mile is 1,609 metres.]

[15] *Jacob* [It was earlier, in 1551, that Berwick was made a free town, 'independent of both states'. This arrangement was made by Edward VI of England and the Regent Mary of Guise on behalf of Mary, Queen of Scots (only 9 years old and in France).]

might have come about, as I have said, that this river was typically regarded as marking the border and continues to be so regarded.

On the border between Teviotdale and Eskdale, which belongs to the county of Dumfries, the road crosses the actual central ridge of the range of hills. The traveller therefore still remains in Scotland. For, after forming for some distance the border between England and Scotland, the central axis of the Cheviot Hills runs into the main part of the latter country and occupies its entire southern portion. Therefore when it is stated that the Cheviot Hills form the boundary between Scotland and England, this has to be understood with a similar qualification as in the case of the Tweed. The Tweed is eighty miles[16] long and marks the border for only a stretch of fourteen miles. The Cheviot chain is one hundred miles long and marks the boundary for a stretch of twenty-five miles.

The Cheviot Hills are entirely different in character from the mountains of the Highlands. They are conical in form, pleasantly rounded on top, and on their sides and also on their rounded summits they are covered with the most beautiful grass in the world. With regard to the regularity and the infinitely frequent repetition of the same shape, they resemble no other chain of mountains that I have ever seen, and their outward appearance is completely different from the appearance both of the Welsh and of the Irish mountains, as well as of the mountains in the Scottish Highlands. For this reason, when we had reached this chain of hills and began to cross them, I was confronted by a view that was indeed quite novel and remarkable in the extreme. It consisted of a large number of rounded grass hilltops of the type described, standing close to each other, of which the one appeared exactly like the other, and which together resembled a veritable labyrinth of conical peaks. The principal aspect can be delineated in a few lines, rather as follows:

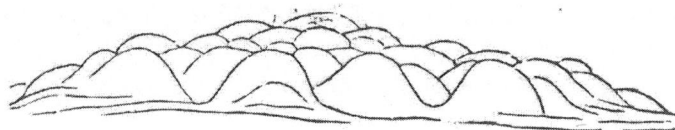

Our road wound its way through this maze of hills. The slopes of the hills were not covered with great masses of rock debris as in Wales but all was only beautiful grass. Neither were they covered with forest, but everywhere I looked they were completely treeless. Neither did rocks and spikes of stone peer out of the summits as in Ireland, but they were rounded and even. Likewise the valleys were not faced on both sides, as in the Highlands, with rocky reefs and walls of stone, but everything was smooth, rounded and grassy.

I have, of course, seen the Cheviots at only one point. However, firstly it can already be assumed **a priori** that this aspect is not purely local but is repeated several times on the same range of hills; and secondly, if you will only read, as I have, the descriptions of all the individual Scottish counties that border on this range, then you will find almost everywhere the hills of every county depicted similarly. In almost every account the form of words is repeated: '**the hills and mountains of this county are round, smooth and green to the very summits**'. I therefore believe that in the above portrayal I have given a fairly correct picture of the peculiar characteristics of this entire range of hills. In particular, the actual central line of the range appears to be constituted as I said. In the lower large valleys that extend out from it to the north and to the south, more forest is seen, and here and there also bare rock. Its appearance alters in the western parts as well, in the counties of Kirkcudbright and Ayrshire, just as the rule invariably holds throughout the whole of Great Britain that everywhere the western end is wilder and rougher than the eastern. Merely looking at the names of these hills, one finds none of those *glens*, *craigs* and *carricks*, *Trossachs*[17] and

---

[16] [The author must be referring to statute miles.]
[17] *Trosachs*

Ardcheanacrochans[18] of the Highlands. The *straths* of the Highlands are also absent. The valleys are called '**dales**', thus: Clydesdale[19], Tweedsdale, Teviotdale, Eskdale, Annandale, and the unusual thing about that is again that these names are given not only to the narrow valleys in which the river flows, but to whole counties and districts.

The great areas of heathland, the rugged moors, with their wildness and great distances are also not encountered here as they are in the Highlands, and, with the craggy rock-formations, there have vanished as well not only the '**forests and wildhanging woods**' but also the '**torrents and loudpouring floods**'. When we look at these hills, so gently fashioned by nature, we can scarcely understand how they could be inhabited by such wild tribes as the Scottish '**Borderers**' who, in barbaric and rapacious savagery, were in no wise the inferiors of the Highlanders; nor can we understand how, scarcely two hundred years ago, there could take place in these valleys events of such bloodthirstiness and incomprehensible brutality that one cannot but be revolted by them. Even as recently as half a century ago, every county in these uplands was in such a state as regards agriculture and road construction as would not have allowed anyone even to dream of their present condition.

The songs of Daphnis and Chloe and the shepherd's pipe answering them must have constantly been heard among these gentle and attractive grass hills; I declare that one cannot help but assume this from the appearance that they present. Admittedly their lush pastures have for long also been the producers of a fine and famous breed of sheep, the Cheviot sheep, universally known in Great Britain. But these peaceful animals, with which human beings were daily in contact, taught them nothing. The extraordinary thing is that now, since *human beings* have ceased to indulge in hostilities here, the *sheep* have begun a campaign against each other. This breed of Cheviots is now becoming increasingly common in Scotland and has already taken even a part of the Highlands by storm, every day displacing the old black-faced Highland breed[20], which we described above, from all glens and mountains.

The green, hilly, treeless pasture land that we have described continues almost uninterruptedly as far as the small town of Langholm, where the actual Esk valley is reached. This little town lies on the confluence of the Esk and the Ewes and, in its lonely position in the hills between forest and grassy hills, presents an interesting enough appearance. The ruins of the old castle of Langholm area are situated nearby. This place was the seat of the famous family of Armstrongs who belonged to the most celebrated '**Border depredators**'. As recently as the middle of the sixteenth century King James V had one of them, who had come to pay homage to the King, hanged on the top of The Cheviot together with all his retinue[21]. On the open squares of several of these small Scottish towns in the Border hills I saw recent monuments in honour of outstanding people. And here near Langholm there even arose an obelisk, one hundred foot high, on a hill in the neighbourhood of the town in honour of a General Malcolm[22]. In many such isolated towns in Great Britain I have seen similar magnificent monuments.

---

[18] *Ardkenkrokrans*

[19] *Clyde-dale, Tweed-dale, Teviot-dale, Esk-dale, Annan-dale*

[20] [In the early 1700s black-faced sheep were introduced from somewhere unknown in England into the Scottish Lowlands; only in 1752 were they introduced from Ayrshire into Dunbartonshire and thence on a large scale into the Highlands. The Highland Clearances (see Introduction p. xxiii) imposed an economy based on Blackfaces and Cheviots.]

[21] [The Armstrongs were notorious for being unruly and relations between them and the kings of Scotland were scarcely amicable. In 1530 James V, in violation of his own promise of safe passage, hanged John Armstrong and fifty of his followers. Another John Armstrong was hanged as a rebel in 1610.]

[22] [Sir John Malcolm (1769 – 1833), Governor of Bombay.]

It is noteworthy that here too, at the western end of the Scottish-English border, there is a piece of land, that, like Berwick and its surrounding district, was disputed between Scotland and England. This piece of land lies between the two rivers Esk and Sark[23] and has always even been called '**the debateable** [sic] **land**'. A concord has also been reached *there*, namely that, like Berwick and its surroundings, this debatable land now also belongs to England and not to Scotland. In the middle of this stretch of land lies a peat bog, called '**the Solway Moss**', which I shall mention only because I have told about the '**moving bogs**' in Ireland, and because it appears that here in Scotland similar phenomena are not uncommon. This Solway Moss in fact, distended and swollen because of continuous rain, broke loose during the night on 17 November 1771, surged over the lower-lying ground, buried four hundred acres of it under its mud, tore several houses away in its wake, like the so-called 'mud avalanches'[24] in the Tyrol, and finally flowed into the sea like that lava stream of Vesuvius.

Taking leave of Scotland was doubly depressing for me, firstly because of the bleak foggy weather that we were experiencing, and secondly because of the attractions of nature that the valley of the Esk poured out here in amazing profusion over the Scottish Border country. In spite of rain and fog I could not help but remain sitting **outside**. In fact, I rubbed my eyes, for I had not dared believe in anything so lovely and ravishing here in the untamed Scottish Borders. And in vain did I rack my memory to recollect whether I had ever seen a more impressive valley in my life. Its woodlands are the most beautiful in the world, for they mostly consist of splendid oaks and beeches. And every one of these trees seems immemorial and primitively strong and eternally young. There were so many thousands of them, yet I did not see one that I would not fain have sketched. Each one seemed to have chosen a picturesque situation and to have unfolded its branches agreeably and according to the canons of good taste. From time to time the valley broadened, and pleasant meadows spread out between and under the shady trees. Here and there stood the ruined castle tower of an old Border chieftain. Sometimes grassy hilltops gazed out above the trees and the valley floors. It is not to exaggerate one whit to call the whole of Eskdale an uninterrupted gallery of the most wonderful paintings of oak-trees, meadows and river, as beautiful as only the brush of a Hobbema[25] or a Ruisdael has ever conjured up. I understand fully that in a country, in which there are such valleys, those two artists are so cherished. However I understand it not at all that neither Hobbema nor Ruisdael visited this Eskdale, since their paintings seem to be such faithful copies of this scene.

Once more – and again once more the valley opened out, and closed. The trees became fewer – the open spaces more extensive – and finally we found ourselves on the frontier of Caledonia, and the broad fertile plain that surrounds Carlisle and Longtown, the most north-westerly corner of England, spread out before our eyes.

* * * * * * *

---

[23] *Sark*

[24] [The original reads *Dreck-Länen (Koth-Lawinen)*.]

[25] [See Chapter XXIII, fns 23 and 24.]